# Digital Images: A Practical Guide

*"Whether you've been involved with computers for many years or are a newcomer eager to gain a broader knowledge of all that's out there, you will find this book to be a great resource."*

—Lynda Kusnetz, Art Director, The Columbia House Company

# About The Authors

Adele Droblas Greenberg is a New York-based
designer, retoucher, and desktop publishing/
prepress consultant. She teaches at Pratt Institute in
Manhattan and Columbia University. She is also the
former training director at a New York City
prepress house.

Seth Greenberg is a member of the Apple Solution
Professionals Network, computer consultant,
database/multimedia programmer, and free-lance
writer. He has worked as a television producer and
script writer, and has written for several computer
magazines. He and Adele Droblas Greenberg are
the authors of the best-selling *Fundamental
Photoshop: A Complete Introduction.*

# Digital Images: A Practical Guide

Adele Droblas Greenberg
and
Seth Greenberg

Osborne **McGraw-Hill**

Berkeley   New York   St. Louis   San Francisco
Auckland   Bogotá   Hamburg   London   Madrid
Mexico City   Milan   Montreal   New Delhi   Panama City
Paris   São Paulo   Singapore   Sydney
Tokyo   Toronto

**Osborne McGraw-Hill**
2600 Tenth Street
Berkeley, California 94710
U.S.A.

For information on translations or book distributors outside the U.S.A., or to arrange bulk purchase discounts for sales promotions, premiums, or fundraisers, please contact Osborne **McGraw-Hill** at the above address.

## Digital Images: A Practical Guide

1234567890 DOC 998765

ISBN 0-07-882113-4

| | |
|---|---|
| **Publisher** | **Proofreader** |
| Lawrence Levitsky | Pat Mannion |
| **Executive Editor** | **Computer Designer** |
| Scott Rogers | Jani Beckwith |
| **Project Editor** | **Illustrator** |
| Claire Splan | Lance Ravella |
| **Copy Editor** | **Cover Designer** |
| Gary Morris | California Design International |

To our family for their love and support.

CONTENTS

## by Kai Krause

There is so much to learn, it's not even funny!

I always have people ask me, in seminars, after keynotes, online, in letters, and most of all in e-mail: "What should I buy? What system should I have? Which software?" And once they are all wrapped up in the world of Imaging it only gets worse...

Much, much worse!

Slowly it dawns on them that pixels on screen with glowing phosphor are not the same as points on paper with ink.

That continuous tone images on a dye-sub are not the same as dithered rosettas with angles and frequencies.

And some programs have no pixels at all, they play with Vectors... and then you have paths and stencils and masks.

I think if a small group of very vicious evil scientists tried very, very hard to come up with some way to mass-torture the beginning digital imagineer, they could hardly have succeeded any better than the state of affairs we ended up with.

And what is the best way for anyone to deal with these challenges? Well, I think by far the best would be that you can have an experienced teacher shrunk to about 3 inches tall glued to your left shoulder for the duration of the work.

This, of course, poses slight technical challenges and is a real problem with the union as well. Short of that, I would say the very very best way is to simply get a good book or several, close the door, take the phone off the hook for a month and JUMP RIGHT IN.

Seriously, there simply is no shortcut for experience and no book in the world can give you that. BUT, you also cannot manufacture knowledge and information out of thin air, and so it IS a very valuable piece of the growth process to learn from someone who has been there and knows.

Sometimes I hear people scoffing at the price of a new book. Or to have the sense of frugality to rest on the knowledge that they already have a book.

This is silly. It's false frugality, pound foolishness!

Really, if you just learn ONE new thing from a book, it can pay for itself in one minute. One technique, one little trick, one enlightening description or explanation of a term ... just ONE!

And anyone who does get absorbed in this insipid and torturously seductive area we call Digital Imaging will realize that the costs are many and the potential for saving the cost of a book many times over are plenty! Not only the obvious expenses such as the machine itself, or the RAM or the disk or the screen or the software—it doesn't end there either.

Getting things printed, preparing your files the right way, having the right resolution, the right color calibration and dealing with printers, service bureaus—it all can be quite a drag. Literally a drag: it will drag out amazingly as you do and redo your work, save and resave, and still lose files.

One word of encouragement: We have ALL been there. Don't let the supposed "pros" that you meet on the way pull that wool over your eyes, they all started out SOME day as bleeding novices who hardly knew the difference between pixels and pickles. There IS a light at the end of the tunnel (hint: it's in RGB) and you CAN get there.

Adele and Seth have made it their mission to be there with you and for you. They may not be 3 inches tall glued on your shoulder to see every move, but probably the next best thing might be to get a condensed, tight box full of their knowledge, and as luck would have it: this is IT. You are holding it in your hand!

The chapters weave the path of all the pitfalls to avoid, all the questions to be answered, all the solutions for problems you don't even know you have yet (but trust them, you will).

Parts of the book cover the more basic ground which is so often taken for granted and assumed as pre-requisite knowledge. True enough though, not only are there always more and more newbies entering the fray, it's also simply a fact that the facts themselves are constantly changing and need redefining!

It was almost eight years ago when the first book on Photoshop came along. But that's more like 80 dog-eared years in this world of technology. Many of the basic descriptions of current references have to be reworked on an almost annual cycle.

And what is unique about this book is that it is not about any ONE of the specific software tools, but rather tries to encompass the wide range of them all at once.

That's a very valuable addition to the individual tomes that might take any one of them apart in great detail.

Armed with information backup like this I am still convinced that each person really has to lose her or himself in the process, all alone at 2:00 in the morning sitting there naked in front of the glowing phosphor and shouting "YES! This is GOOD" as the bits flicker magnetically on the hard disks...

There is a deeply satisfying sigh that can happen when you create an image, a good kind of tired as you lose sleep over masks and stencils, textures and gradients.

Do the one thing that NO ONE can help you with really:

Find what you like to do best, because thats what you are likely to be best at.

I ALWAYS think I am quoting someone with that line, I just never saw it anywhere else. Hmm. Its just one of those things that strike you one day as being just "so true" and then it lives in one corner of your brain for a looooong time...

So, meander through the many many options you will have. Try the programs, click those buttons, swipe that mouse around. And as you get towards your 100th image, you can decide where you want to go from there. Try not to do that much sooner than that or you will regret it. No one can be smart enough to know what the smart thing will be down that road.

On that road, let this book be there, maybe with some others to the left and right of it (the authors will happily point you to earlier works) and guided with the wisdom in analog-molecules-on-paper form you can feel equipped.

Color Models and File Formats are not the type of thing you want to carry around in your brain right in the beginning. Sometimes the right thing is not to learn everything, but to learn where to find it when you need it.

As luck would have, a whole lot of that is right in here.

Enjoy...

So many pixels, so little time,
Kai

A book that encompasses the wide world of digital images could not have been written without the help of a dedicated team of talented people. We'd like to start by thanking our publisher, Osborne McGraw-Hill, who asked us to write this book. We'd especially like to thank Publisher Larry Levitsky and Executive Editor Scott Rogers for their enthusiasm, encouragement, and many suggestions throughout the project. Special thanks to Project Editor Claire Splan for her conscientiousness, help, and a job well done! We also thank all these people for their fine and hard work; Managing Editor Cindy Brown, Copy Editor Gary Morris, Proofreader Pat Mannion, Director of Manufacturing and Production Deborah Wilson, Production Supervisor Marcela Hancik, and Computer Designers Peter Hancik, Lance Ravella, Jani Beckwith, Roberta Steele, Rhys Elliott, and Kristie Reilly. We also thank technical editors Sybil and Emil Ihrig for the fine job they did, and for the suggestions they gave us while writing this book. Thanks also to Editorial Assistants Daniela Dell'Orco and Kelly Vogel.

Thanks to Kai Krause for graciously taking the time from his busy schedule to write the foreword for our book. We (and we're sure all of the users of digital imaging software) thank Kai for the tremendous contribution he has made to the world of digital imaging over the past few years.

We'd also like to thank the many digital artists whose excellent work appears in the color insert and in the black-and-white portions of this book. Thanks also to the artists and software experts who contributed to the Tips of the Trade sections of this book.

Thanks to Patricia Pane, Rich Brown, Dave Roban, Steve Cherneff, Mary Leong, Jane Tuwe, Andrew Eisner, Loren Luke, Tom Mitchell, Rich Green, Debra Vogel, Nancy Carr, Sheila Beaumont, Kerri Walker , Robin Hradesky, Bonnie McDowall, Josh Bevins, Kristin Keyes, Barbra Woolf, Wendy Bozigian, Laurie Lupo, Joe Rundi, Marilyn Kilian-Kruger, Ashley Sharp, Kelly Ryer, Chris Johnson, Charles Smith, Burt Holmes, Dave Keller, Lisa Smith, Pilar Guzman, Mike Belfie, Jeff Butterworth, Eugene Hernandez, Diane Reynolds, Catherine Greene, Sherri Melchione, Lisa Beverly, Amy Rable, Bill Lyon, Sabille Millard, Ann Burgraff, Ted Cheney, David Cian, Gary McLoughlin, Carl Ludwig, Peter Ryce, Alexandra Yessios, Stacy Hurwitz, Paul LaFain, Beatriz Bravo, Diane Reynold, Lisa Herbert, Shelly Pina, and Charles Gutierrez.

We'd also like to thank the many corporations that helped make this book possible: ABC Television, Adobe Systems, A&R Partners, Acuris Inc., ADC

**ACKNOWLEDGMENTS**

Image Vault, AGFA Corp, Alias Research Inc., Alien Skin Software, American Databankers Corp., Andromeda Software Inc., APS, Apple Computer, Arro International, ArtBeats, Autodesk Inc., autodessys Inc., Avid Technology, BeachWare Inc., Blue Sky Productions, Boxlight Corp., Byte by Byte Corp., Caligari, Canon USA, Classic PIO Partners, ColorBytes Inc., Connectix, CMCD Inc., Crystal Graphics Inc., Corel Systems Corp., D'pix Inc., Dana Publishing, DayStar Digital, D Portfolios, Digital Stock Inc., Digital Wisdom Inc., Digital Zone Inc., DuPont Crosfield, Dycam Inc., (EFI) Electronics for Imaging, Eastman Kodak, Elastic Reality, ElectricImage Inc., ElectroGIG Inc., Equalibrium Technologies, Fauve Software Inc., Fotosets, Fractal Design, Frame, FWB Inc., Graphsoft Inc., Greenstones Roberts Advertising, Gryphon Software, HSC Software, Hasselblad Inc., Human Software, IBM, Image Club Graphics Inc., ION, IRIS Graphics, JP Morgan, Killer Tracks, Linotype-Hell Co., Leaf Systems, Light Source, Linker Systems, 3M, Macromedia, Mainstay, Microsoft, MicroFrontier, Monaco Systems, Neo Custom Painted Environments, New Vision Technologies Inc., Newer Technology, Nikon, Nintendo, Optima Technology, PANTONE Inc., Periwinkle Software, Photodex, PhotoDisc Inc., PixelCraft Inc., Pixar Corp., Pixal Resources Inc., Planet Art, Polariod, Praxisoft Inc., QMS Inc., QFX, Quark Inc., Radius Inc., Raydream Inc., RasterOps Corp., Saphar & Assoc. Inc., Scitex Technology Inc., Silicon Graphics, Sony, Specular International, Stat Media, Stirling and Cohen, Storm Techology Inc., Strata Inc., SyQuest Technology, T/Maker Co., Tektronix Inc., Truvision, Valis Group, VIDI Inc., VideoLabs, Viewpoint, Visioneer, Visual Software Inc., Virtus Corp., Vivid Details, Voyager Co., WACOM Technology Inc., Wayzata Technology, The Webber Group, Weka Publishing Inc., Work for Hire, Xaos Tools Inc., and X-Rite.

We'd also like to thank the hardware and software vendors who have made creating digital images possible.

Last, but certainly not least, we'd like to thank our relatives, friends, and clients for their support. Thanks also to everyone else who helped along the way.

The digital imaging revolution is truly here. You can now create and use digital images in ways that were never before possible and in ways that few would have imagined a few years ago. Today, digital images are not only used in print media, but in multimedia productions, TV shows, and movies. Turn on your TV and you just might see a TV commercial or rock video that was assembled in a digital movie-editing program like Adobe Premiere. The individual images in the video production just might have been created in an image-editing program like Adobe Photoshop or a paint program like Fractal Design Painter. The fantastic background might have been created with Kai's Power Tools. The animation might have been created in a high-end animation program like ElectricImage Animation System.

All of this is possible because of the steady stream of newer, more powerful digital imaging hardware and software. With so many new products on the market, it's hard for the artist, business person, student, educator, or video and multimedia producer to stay abreast of all the latest developments. For newcomers, the onslaught of technology is even more of a challenge. Not only is there too much to learn, but it's difficult to know what to learn and where to find the information your need to learn. This book is designed to meet the needs of both newcomers and digital imaging professionals.

## Why This Book Is for You

We think this book is quite unique. We not only cover basic digital imaging topics such as scanning and resolution, but explore how to use painting, image editing, multimedia, 3D modeling, rendering, and animation programs. We also cover capturing video, outputting to print, video CD-ROMS, and—one of the hottest topics these days—the Web.

Why cover such an extensive range of subjects? We've found that many artists and business people need to understand and use a broad range of software and hardware. It's helpful to know how to use an image-editing program, but if you also know how to use a drawing program, 3D program, or multimedia program, you may be able to get your work done more efficiently and professionally. Knowing how to use a scanner and a digital camera—and even knowing the copyright laws—can prove valuable to anyone who uses digital images.

As you read through this book, you'll not only explore hardware and software features; you'll also learn how to create, edit, and correct digital images. You'll receive tips from industry professionals on a wide range of

INTRODUCTION

subjects. Apart from being an easy-to-understand reference manual on digital imaging, this book can serve as a buyers' guide. Save yourself time and money before you invest in new hardware and software: First read about the features you need to understand, and then go out and make your purchases.

## Macs or PCs?

This book is a cross-platform book. When reviewing software or providing instructions on how different digital images are created, we've tried to focus on cross-platform programs, particularly those that are available on both Mac and PC platforms. To keep you completely up to date about the world of digital images, we also discuss several programs only available on Silicon Graphics workstations. But, whether you use a Mac, PC, or SGI workstation, you'll find the basic concepts of digital imaging are the same. Color theory, concepts of resolution, and 3D terms are the same on all computer platforms. Even if you find yourself reading about a product that is not available on your Mac or PC, we still think you'll find the discussions about software and hardware to be valuable.

## How This Book Is Organized

Chapters 1 through 5 provide information about the fundamentals of digital imaging. You'll explore the basic concepts of digital images, such as resolution, color theory, and the difference between bitmap and vector programs.

Chapters 6 through 13 cover how to create digital images. You'll learn how to digitize images with a scanner and digital camera, and how to use images stored in Kodak's Photo CD format. You'll find out how to create two-dimensional and three-dimensional images, as well as multimedia productions. If you don't know the difference between modeling and rendering, or the difference between Phong shading and ray-tracing, you'll find the answers here.

Chapters 14 through 16 explore image editing. In these chapters you'll learn how digital images are corrected, and how amazing special effects are created with warping, morphing, and special effects plug-in filters. Chapter 16 shows how to work with multimedia programs.

Chapters 17 and 18 look at outputting digital images. Here you'll learn how to output images for print media, video, and CD-ROM. We've also included an appendix providing contact information for many of the vendors whose products are discussed in this book.

Have fun!

# Disk Offer

To help get you started using digital images, we've prepared one high-density disk filled with low-res color backgrounds and buttons that can be used in multimedia productions and database entry screens. You can also use the images to experiment in painting, image-editing, and drawing programs, or to use in multimedia programs. If you're interested, please make out a check or money order for $6.95 payable to "AD Design" and send it to:

Digital Images
PO Box 3117
Westport, CT 06880

Please specify whether you would like a Mac or PC disk.

This offer is subject to change or cancellation at any time, and is solely the offering of the authors. Osborne/McGraw-Hill takes no responsibility for the fulfillment of this order.

# 1

# The World of Digital Images

**"** The future isn't what it used to be." Although Yogi Berra, the late, great N.Y. Yankee, never used Adobe Photoshop, his well-known quote may be one of the best ways to describe the ever-changing world of digital images. A few years ago, few could have predicted the explosive growth of digital images, nor the necessity for artists, designers, film/TV producers, and businessmen and women to learn how to use digital images and understand their potential.

You don't have to look too far to see how digital images have invaded the visual landscape: Just take a look at all the images around you—in magazine covers, print advertisements, newspapers, TV commercials, movies, corporate presentations, CD-ROMs, the Internet, and of course, in this book. Chances are that many of these images—whether mundane or fantastic—were created, retouched, manipulated, enhanced, and/or color-corrected on the computer.

There are many reasons why the computer has become a digital imaging workhorse. Here are just a few: It's often more efficient and cost effective to create images on the computer than it would be to use traditional methods. It's also easier to perfect digital images and integrate them with text and other media. In addition, the computer provides new outlets for images in new media such as CD-ROM. In many instances, techniques for creating images in the new electronic media can't be replicated using traditional techniques, because there are no traditional techniques—only digital techniques. Finally, many artists simply enjoy creating images on the computer. They find it a powerful tool and an inspirational means of creating artistic magic.

If you're unfamiliar with the countless ways digital images are being used, prepare for your jaw to drop. This chapter provides you with a quick introductory tour to bring you up to date and prepare you for the future. Subsequent chapters focus on how digital images are created, and how you can work with them on your own computer.

# How Digital Images Are Created

Before getting started on this digital imaging tour, let's define exactly what a digital image is. A digital image can be an image created from scratch using a computer program. It can also be an image such as a slide or photograph that is translated into electronic data so it can be viewed, edited, and manipulated on the computer screen.

How is a digital image created? Although some of the computer programs that allow you to create digital images are quite sophisticated, others can be straightforward, emulating traditional approaches. For instance, many painting programs such as Fractal Design Painter allow the user to choose an electronic paint brush, pick a color, and paint. When you click and drag the mouse or move the stylus (an electronic pen)—voilá! Digital paint appears on the program's electronic canvas, much the same way that it would appear on a traditional painter's canvas. The results are sometimes indistinguishable from traditional art.

If you don't believe that a computer "painting" can look like it was created using traditional methods, just take a look at Figure 1-1. Artist Chelsea Sammel of Hollister, California used Fractal Design Painter to create this painting of poppies. With stylus in hand, Chelsea first created a sketch using Painter's electronic equivalent of colored pencils. Then she added color, using Painter's chalk brush, and used digital water to blend colors together. When the image was complete, Chelsea saved it to disk. (You'll learn the basics of computer color in Chapter 3, and explore the features of computer painting programs in Chapter 10.)

Poppies created in Fractal Design Painter by Chelsea Sammel

**FIGURE 1-1**

## Digitizing Images

Many digital images are not born on an artist's blank electronic canvas. They first arrive on a computer via a scanner or a digital camera. A scanner can scan a slide, chrome, or photograph and translate the image into digital data, much the same way that a copy machine reproduces an image. Many flatbed scanners even resemble copy machines. You lift the lid, place a photograph down on the glass imaging area, and close the lid. On the computer screen, you click on a Scan button with the mouse. In a minute or so the image appears on the computer screen instead of on paper. (You'll learn about different types of scanners in Chapter 2, and you'll learn how to scan in Chapter 7.)

Scanning is the primary technique that stock houses use to create their product line before outputting them to CD-ROM. (Obtaining images from stock suppliers is discussed in Chapter 12. Copyright issues concerning the use of stock and other images are covered in Chapter 13.)

The process of digitizing an image using a digital camera is even more direct than scanning. The photographer simply points the camera and presses the shutter. The image is instantly digitized, often to a tiny hard disk in the camera. You never need to buy or develop film—because there is no film. Instead of outputting the images to slides or photographic paper, they are downloaded to a computer via a cable or phone line. Once the image appears on the computer screen, it can be color-corrected, retouched, bent, twisted, or skewed to create special effects in image-editing programs such as Adobe Photoshop, HSC Live Picture, Micrografx Picture Publisher, or Fauve Xres. (For more information about image-editing software, see Chapter 15.)

**OTE:** *If you're interested in the technical and mathematical aspects of digital images, particularly scientific uses of digital imaging, you might wish to purchase the book (and accompanying CD),* Visualization of Natural Phenomena *($59.95, Telos/Springer Verlag) by Robert Wolff and Larry Yaeger. It covers digitizing issues involving astrophysics and medical imaging, as well as the formulas used to create spatial and color transformations.*

# Commercial Uses of Digital Images

The technique of scanning an image and then color-correcting or retouching it is frequently used in printed digital images, primarily in the creation of advertisements and magazine covers. No matter how beautiful a model is, a computer can whiten his or her teeth, smooth away wrinkles, and add sparkle to the eyes. In fact, the computer is used in virtually all print ads to touch up models, remove blemishes, and correct the colors. Frequently, digital artists also add special effects to photographs in magazines and advertisements just to jazz them up and attract interest. (To learn more about creating special effects on the computer, see Chapter 15.)

# Digital Images in Print

Successful digital art catches the eye, often causing the viewer to read an advertisement or an article, purchase a magazine, or maybe even take a break with some Doritos and a glass of Mountain Dew. Figure 1-2, and various versions of it, appeared in stores, as well as on billboards, key chains, and other promotional materials. To create this ad for Pepsi Corporation, Dallas artist J.W. Burkey digitized images of a basketball player, Doritos, and Mountain Dew. He used Photoshop to composite the images together, and to convert the color images to black and white. When converting to black and white, he chose Photoshop's Dither option to create

© 1994 J. W. Burkey

Promotional ad for Pepsi Corporation by J.W. Burkey

**FIGURE 1-2**

a dot effect. Then he loaded the black and white image into Fractal Design Painter. Using Painter's Airbrush tool, he colored the image, creating a glowing, neon effect.

Many ads and promotional materials are also created in computer drawing programs. Images that once would take days to create, perfect, and color by hand can be created in a fraction of the time with software such as Adobe Illustrator, Macromedia Freehand, and CorelDRAW. Figure 1-3 shows an image from a direct mail brochure created by Salt Lake City artist Rob Magiera for a Sprint ISDN network campaign. Rob used Freehand's Pen tool to create the shapes of the images, and then employed the program's extensive filling and coloring options to produce the final scene. (Chapter 10 provides a review of drawing programs and how to use them.)

Using the computer, digital artists can also blend common or unusual images together to create provocative, enticing, and sometimes humorous results. For instance, *Sports Illustrated for Kids'* Nik Kleinberg frequently turns to his Macintosh to create whimsical covers that occasionally border on the surreal. To produce the cover shown in Figure 1-4, athletes' pets were photographed, along with hockey jerseys, skates, helmets, and medals. All the photos were digitized using a scanner. The scanned clothing was then scaled down in Adobe Photoshop. Using only a few of Photoshop's many magical electronic tools, Nik outfitted several athletes' pets

Promotional
material for
Sprint Corp.
by Rob
Magiera

**FIGURE 1-3**

Cover for
*Sports
Illustrated for
Kids* by Nik
Kleinberg.
Photographs
by Jeffrey
Lowe, Philip
Salstonstall,
Kevin Horan

**FIGURE 1-4**

with their owners' clothes. Imagine trying to clothe a pet pig in a hockey jersey and skates without using the computer!

Digital tricks are also very evident in Figure 1-5. This clever image was created by J.W. Burkey to help illustrate an article for *CIO* (Corporation Information Office) magazine. It imaginatively conveys the concept of how hotels and businesses cooperate using computers. To create this image, J.W. shot photographs of hands, two buildings, and two monitors. Using Photoshop, he placed the hands in the monitors, and stretched reality to place the monitors in the buildings.

Image created
by J.W.
Burkey for
*CIO* magazine

© 1992 J. W. Burkey

**FIGURE 1-5**

Image created
by Steven
Lyons for the
*Wall Street
Journal*
**FIGURE 1-6**

Figure 1-6 shows another eye-catching and inventive example of a digital image used to help illustrate the written word. Here, the subject is the World Wide Web of computers "wired" through the Internet. The image was created entirely in Adobe Illustrator by San Francisco artist Steven Lyons for the *Wall Street Journal*'s Technology section.

A satirical juxtaposition of digital images can also attract a reader's attention. The image shown in Figure 1-7 helped illustrate a *Worth* magazine article describing the blind rush to cash in on the virtual reality craze. To create the image, artists Alejandro Arce and Mirko Ilić of the design firm of Oko & Mano, used Adobe Photoshop to blend George Washington into the 21st century. The three-dimensional effects were created on a Silicon Graphics Indigo computer using Microsoft SoftImage. (See Chapter 2 to learn more information about Silicon Graphics computers.) If you look closely at Figure 1-7, you'll spot many tiny images of George Washington floating in the background with shredded dollars. (Popular 3D modeling programs, such as SoftImage and Alias Animator Pro created for Silicon Graphics minicomputers, are covered in Chapter 11. 3D programs for Macs and PCs are also covered in that chapter.)

Image created
by Alejandro
Arce and
Mirko Ilić
for *Worth*
magazine

**FIGURE 1-7**

# Animating Digital Images

Although 3D programs such as Microsoft SoftImage and Alias Animator Pro are often used for illustration and advertising purposes, they've also become a mainstay in the world of animation. Alejandro and Mirko used SoftImage to create a corporate animation presentation on networking for Sony Electronics. Figure 1-8a shows a highway of three-dimensional trucks created from 1s and 0s. Once the models were created, Alejandro and Mirko drew a path that they wanted the trucks to move over. After creating the path, they had SoftImage animate the steps along the path. Thus, instead of arduously creating each individual frame for the animation, the artists essentially only needed to create endpoints. Figure 1-8b shows another scene in the animation sequence. Here a three-dimensional crane, cleverly disguised as a computer chip, lifts one of the trucks. After the animation was created, it was sent on an optical disc to a post-production house to be transferred to video. (Optical discs are discussed in Chapter 2.)

The use of computer-created animation extends well beyond the world of corporate presentations. Production companies such as R. Greenberg Associates and George Lucas' Industrial Light and Magic create special effects on the computer and

a)

Images
created by
Alejandro
Arce and
Mirko Ilić
for Sony
Electronics

b)

**FIGURE 1-8**

transfer them to film. Movies such as *The Mask, The Shadow*, and *Forrest Gump* all
include stunning visuals created on Silicon Graphics computers with software such

as Microsoft SoftImage and Alias Animator Pro. Fantastic, big-budget TV commercials featuring dancing cars, cola-drinking polar bears, and a gigantic Las Vegas lion are also the product of many of these high-end graphics software products. In all of these commercials, the computer was used to create images that could not be created by any other means. Figure 1-9 shows a frame from a Nestlés TV commercial featuring a cute lifelike bear animated from a cookie jar. The commercial was produced by Blue Sky Productions of Ossining, New York. To create the commercial, Blue Sky producers used their own proprietary 3D modeling and animation software which they created in the C programming language.

If you think that all of this high-end animation is beyond the scope of any computer you can afford, you'll be happy to learn that various video production companies often rely on personal computers to help create professional animation. For instance, New York City's Edgeworx Inc. has used its Mac, Adobe Photoshop, Adobe Premiere, and Adobe After Effects to create animation for MTV, Nickelodeon, PBS, and the Learning Channel, as well as a television commercial for Reebok. Examples of their work are shown in the color insert and Chapter 16.

Frame from
Nestlés TV
commercial
created by
Blue Sky
Productions

**FIGURE 1-9**

## Digital Images in Multimedia

Animated computer images not only come alive on the silver screen and TV screen, but also on the home computer screen. Turn to the color insert in this book to see a frame from Rodney Greenblat's fantastic interactive children's CD, The Dazzeloids. Published and distributed by Voyager, The Dazzeloids features a cast of funny and unforgettable cartoon characters that sing and tell stories. Rodney's New York production company, The Center for Advanced Whimsey, primarily created The Dazzeloids in Macromedia Freehand and Fractal Design Painter. (In Chapter 16, you'll learn how Rodney and other multimedia artists create interactive entertainment and education CD-ROMs using animation and authoring tools such as Macromedia Director, Adobe Premiere, and Macromedia Authorware. Chapter 16 also discusses how companies are using multimedia software to create their own corporate presentations.)

Figure 1-10 shows a screen shot from ABC Television's CD-ROM, The Stand, which was created with Macromedia Director, Adobe Photoshop, and Adobe Premiere. Sent to newspapers across the country, the CD-ROM allowed entertainment writers to quickly view different clips from each night of the mini-series, along with interviews and a synopsis of each night's chilling fare. To

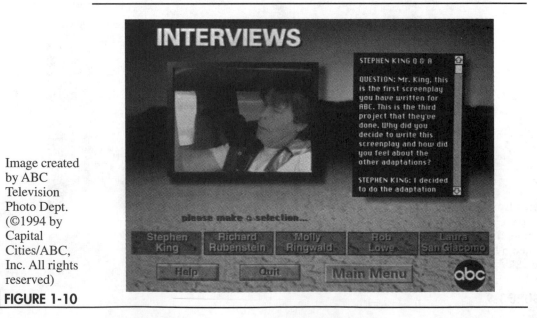

Image created by ABC Television Photo Dept. (©1994 by Capital Cities/ABC, Inc. All rights reserved)

**FIGURE 1-10**

create the digitized film clips, ABC transferred video clips of the movie to the computer to create QuickTime movie files. (QuickTime movies are described in Chapter 16.) Using Macromedia Director, the CD-ROM's creators programmed buttons that the user could click to choose different clips. Also included on the CD-ROM were digitized photos for the writers to import into their own desktop publishing programs for publication. Despite the cost of assembling and producing them, ABC feels CD-ROM productions are an extremely efficient means of conveying information to the press.

## CAD/CAM Digital Images

The last stop on this tour is to take a look at some digital images that the public seldom, if ever, sees. Many architects and designers use computers to create floor plans, blueprints, and 3D models of buildings that don't yet exist. Using programs such as AutoDesk AutoCAD, architects can design buildings and even budget construction costs.

CAD (computer-aided design) software is used to create floor plans and models. Figure 1-11 shows a Cartier jewelry boutique floor plan created by Raymond Mastrobuoni, the company's Vice President of Visual Merchandising and Store

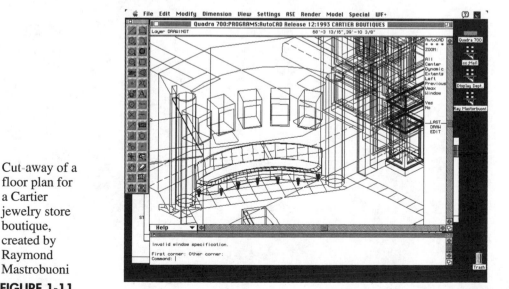

Cut-away of a floor plan for a Cartier jewelry store boutique, created by Raymond Mastrobuoni

**FIGURE 1-11**

Planning. By using AutoCAD, Ray estimates that he can re-design floor plans and displays much more efficiently than he did before he started using the computer. AutoCAD even allows him to keep track of expenses for the items in his designs. (CAD/CAM programs are discussed in Chapter 4, where you'll also learn how virtual reality programs allow users to "walk through" computer-simulated environments.)

## Other Uses for Digital Images

The many uses of digital images go on and on. 3D computer programs are being used to re-create animated versions of crimes to help illustrate prosecution and defense arguments. Corporate presentations that once took days to create and illustrate are now completed in a few hours using presentation software such as Adobe Persuasion, Macromedia Action!, and Microsoft PowerPoint (covered in Chapter 16). Artists are even creating images that appear as landmarks in online computer services accessed from a modem.

As the power of computers and software increases, the importance of digital images will undoubtedly grow. The following chapters of this book will prepare you for that future, no matter what it holds—and you can bet that the future won't be "what it used to be."

# 2

## The Digital Imaging Studio

C reating digital images on the computer is like creating magic. The tools a digital artist uses to create this magic are like a magician's bag of tricks. The better the tools, the more effective the tricks. Certainly two of the artist's primary tools are hardware and software.

Although much of this book focuses on software, computer programs can be useless without the right hardware. Only when artists and computer graphics users possess the right hardware can they effectively utilize their graphics software and apply their own creativity and skills to generating professional digital images.

This chapter focuses primarily on the hardware you need to harness the power of digital imaging software. If you're not familiar with computer graphics, you'll soon learn that more than just the right Macintosh or PC is needed to work efficiently with digital images. For instance, purchasing a "slow" video board could mean the difference between spending more time exploring design possibilities and sitting idle while your image crawls through a screen update. Using the wrong scanner could mean spending valuable time re-digitizing images because the original scans were murky and flat. Hardware should help unleash your creative vision, not restrain it.

In this chapter, you'll learn about the equipment used to input, edit, and output digital images. As you read through the chapter, you might wish to refer back to Figure 2-1, which shows the variety of approaches to the digital imaging production process.

# Choosing a Computer System

The power of digital image creation lies in the computer. In order to evaluate a computer's performance, understand its potential, and gain a better idea of how to purchase one, you should have a basic concept of what elements make a computer fast or slow. Speed is of vital concern to the digital artist. If you plan to work with complex, high-quality color images, you'll soon find that just opening and closing a large color image can be a time-consuming affair.

# The CPU

Undoubtedly, the most important element governing a computer's speed is its CPU, or *central processing unit*. The CPU is the computer's brain. Its primary task is to

The digital imaging production process

**FIGURE 2-1**

receive program instructions, process them, and send them. The CPU's sophistication and speed in managing information are crucial to the efficient use of programs like Adobe Photoshop, CorelDRAW, and QuarkXPress.

# The PowerPC CPU

On the Mac (and forthcoming IBMs and Mac clones), the most sophisticated CPU is the PowerPC chip. The PowerPC, designed by IBM, Apple, and Motorola, is a RISC (Reduced Instructions Set Computer) chip. RISC chips are particularly suited for graphics and 3D applications. They achieve their high processing speed by relying on a set of simple core programming instructions and using them to perform complex tasks. RISC chips also can simultaneously juggle multiple instructions. This makes them more efficient and less expensive than their predecessor, the CISC (Complex Instruction Set Computer) chips.

To help you understand the difference between the two types of chips, think of the RISC chip as a sleek new circus that hits town. Instead of a long extravaganza featuring hundreds of performers appearing one act a time, the RISC circus breaks down the acts so that they occur simultaneously in different rings with only a few performers, who appear again and again. Not only is the circus better performed than the old-fashioned circus, but the ticket prices are cheaper. Most importantly, it finishes more quickly.

The speed of the PowerPC chip varies and different versions of the chip provide different degrees of processing power. Chip speed, often referred to as *clock speed,* is measured in megahertz (MHz), which equals 1 million clock cycles. The greater the clock speed, the faster the chip. The slowest PowerPC runs at 60MHz, the fastest at over 100MHz. The newest family of PowerPC chips, the 604, is faster and more sophisticated than the first PowerPC chip, the 601.

If you own an older Macintosh running Motorola's 68000 CPU family, you still may be able to take advantage of RISC technology. Both Apple and DayStar, Inc. manufacture cards that upgrade many of Apple's older Quadra computers into PowerPCs. (DayStar even sells a PowerPC upgrade card for Apple's older IIci computer.) The PowerPC upgrade usually doubles the clock speed of the older computer. Thus, if you have a Quadra 650 running at 25MHz, Apple's upgrade card would boost the clock speed to 50MHz. If you are using large color files and working with programs like Photoshop, Painter, or 3D programs, the upgrade is well worth the price.

If your Mac can't be upgraded to a PowerPC, you still may be able to beef it up. DayStar and several other companies manufacture accelerator boards for many of

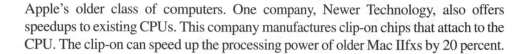

Apple's older class of computers. One company, Newer Technology, also offers speedups to existing CPUs. This company manufactures clip-on chips that attach to the CPU. The clip-on can speed up the processing power of older Mac IIfxs by 20 percent.

## The Pentium CPU

On the PC side of the fence, the most sophisticated CPU is the Pentium. Although the Pentium is not a RISC chip, its sophisticated architecture and speed make it a powerhouse for Windows applications. Like the newer PowerPCs, Pentium clock speeds generally run from 60 to over 100MHz. Two advantages of the Pentium chip over older PC chips like the 80486 are that the Pentium can process more operations per second, and it can send information over a wider data channel, known as a *bus*. The popular 486 can send data over 32 channels simultaneously, compared with the Pentium, which, like the Power PC, can send data over 64 channels at a time. This means that a 60MHz Pentium, should provide better computing power than a 100MHz 486.

If you've got an older PC and wish to upgrade its CPU, check with your dealer or computer manufacturer. Intel, as well as a variety of third-party providers, offers a variety of upgrade paths. Many newer 486 PCs have the potential to be upgraded with Pentium overdrive chips.

## Multiprocessing CPU Power

When you're dealing with digital images, even the fastest CPU may not be fast enough. In an attempt to bolster the speed of microcomputers as much as possible, hardware and software manufacturers have developed systems in which several CPUs can drive one computer. Both Windows NT and OS/2 operating systems can drive computers with multiple CPUs (Windows 3.1 and Windows 95 cannot). The speed increase for a Windows NT system with two Pentium processors has been reported to be from 60-90% faster than a one-Pentium CPU system.

On the Mac, DayStar, in conjunction with Apple computer, has developed *nPower* architecture, which allows multiple processors to run with Macs using Mac Operating System 7.5 or later. Using nPower technology, DayStar will be selling its Genesis MP (MediaPublisher) Mac clone, which can be powered by as many as four 604 PowerPC CPUs. As you can imagine, a computer with 4 CPUs can run almost 4 times as fast as a computer with one CPU.

## The PCI Bus

If you're trying to decide between a Mac and a PC or between one PC clone and another, don't base your computer purchase simply on CPU or brand name. There are a few other elements to consider. A computer's CPU doesn't work alone. It processes information flowing to and from it over a data highway called the bus. Fortunately for digital artists, the maximum speed limit on the data highway is increasing thanks to the PCI (Peripheral Component Interconnect) bus, available on both Macs and PCs.

In older computers using bus structures such as Apple's Nubus or PC-compatible Vesa, Eisa, and VL buses, data can become bottlenecked because the computer's CPU must be aware of all electronic comings and goings under the computer's hood. One reason that PCI technology speeds data flow is that the CPU can back off from overseeing data flow on the bus and concentrate on other chores. PCs running Windows 95 should be able to take full advantage of the PCI bus. Although the throughput of Macs with the new PCI bus structure will approximately be double the throughput of older Macs, they won't take full advantage of PCI technology until Apple's new operating system arrives in 1996.

Another consideration when purchasing a computer is its networking capabilities, discussed in the following section.

# Ethernet

If you will be outputting large graphic files or sending files to other computers over a network, you may wish to purchase a computer with built-in Ethernet capabilities. Ethernet is a *network* protocol. This network protocol allows data to be transferred to printers and other computers faster than Apple's standard Localtalk protocol, and much faster than data sent over a standard serial port. For instance, Apple's Localtalk, built into all Macintoshes, has a throughput of about 230KB a second. Ethernet can speed up the process from three to five times faster. Be aware that Ethernet (which is built into all high-end Macs) on Macs and PCs is only useful if you are printing to an Ethernet printer or sending data to another computer over an Ethernet network. If you already own a computer, and wish to add Ethernet, an add-on board can usually be purchased for about $200. For more information about Ethernet and different networking setups, contact your computer dealer.

# Silicon Graphics and Other Workstations

For many years, the personal computer of choice among graphics professionals has been Apple's Macintosh family of computers. Apple, along with Adobe Systems, Inc., were pioneers in proving to the world that sophisticated graphics could be created and professionally output on a desktop computer. As more and more Mac-based software has become available for Windows, and as software is rewritten for Windows 95, the PC is expected to offer stronger competition to the Mac. But despite the graphics power of PCs and Macs, some graphic artists consider both platforms too slow for the highest of high-end computing tasks.

If your computer system can't give you the high-quality output your work demands, you might wish to seek the help of a prepress house which uses Scitex or Quantel workstations. A Scitex system runs on proprietary software and consists of extremely powerful color-correcting workstations and output devices. Some prepress and production houses use the Quantel Paintbox (which costs hundreds of thousands of dollars) for high-end image editing, painting, and special effects. Other popular high-end workstations are manufactured by Sun and Silicon Graphics, Inc. (SGI).

In recent years, SGI computers have become the standard for artists creating very complex 3D images and sophisticated animation effects. As mentioned in Chapter 1, Silicon Graphics computers are used to create effects in TV commercials and many Hollywood movies. Why are SGI computers so powerful? One reason is that they use the UNIX operating system, which is more powerful and versatile than either the Mac or Windows operating system. In addition, SGI computers use a highly sophisticated RISC processor. SGI machines are lightning fast, and can be purchased with add-on boards featuring "geometry engines." A Silicon Graphics computer can transform a wire-framed model into a photo-realistic 3D object many times faster than most Macs and PCs. Although some software that runs on SGIs has been rewritten for Macs and PCs, the most powerful programs run exclusively on UNIX workstations. The downside of using an SGI system is that the computer, memory, peripherals, and software cost far more than a Mac or PC system.

# The Importance of RAM

Whether you are using a Mac, a PC, or a Silicon Graphics workstation, one fact remains: Digital images and digital imaging software can quickly gobble up all the RAM in your system.

If you're unfamiliar with the concept of *RAM,* think of it as a temporary storage area for an image when you are working with it on the computer. As you work—let's say changing colors or editing a picture—the software works fastest directly in RAM, because it doesn't have to laboriously load program instructions from your hard disk or constantly save changes to your hard disk.

In subsequent chapters of this book, you'll learn how high-quality graphic images can easily consume many megabytes of RAM. (Each character the computer uses consumes about one byte of memory. A kilobyte is a thousand bytes; a megabyte, a million bytes.) Thus, it's important to realize that without enough RAM, you may not be able to load or create a digital image at the size and with the number of colors you wish. For instance, the recommended memory requirement for Photoshop on a PowerPC Mac is 11MB. On older Macs and the PC, the minimum recommended is 8. The minimum for HSC's Live Picture (Macintosh only) is a little over 20MB. The minimum memory requirements for Micrografx Picture Publisher are 8MB.

Even if your system does meet a program's minimum standard, you may find that your work quickly bogs down. In general, the more RAM you have, the faster most graphics applications work. RAM doesn't make the computer run faster, but it allows most software to avoid constantly accessing the hard disk. Reading and writing data to RAM is much quicker than reading and writing it to a hard disk.

With many graphics programs, you'll find that the recommended minimum is scarcely enough to efficiently complete complicated jobs. Often a program needs memory not only for itself and the digital image, but also for basic imaging tasks such as painting, color correcting, and special effects. Some software vendors of digital imaging programs, such as Adobe, recommend keeping at least three to five times an image's file size free in memory. If there is not enough RAM available, the software turns to your hard disk's *virtual* memory.

Nevertheless, not all software utilizes virtual memory, so your best bet is to purchase as much RAM as you can afford. If your pockets aren't deep enough today, make sure that the system you buy provides enough RAM expansion capability to meet future needs. If you're in the market for a computer, you'll find that cheaper models do not feature as many memory expansion capabilities as their more expensive counterparts.

 **OTE:**  *To learn more about the difference between bits and bytes and about what's under the hood of your computer, you might wish to purchase Warner New Media's interactive CD-ROM, How Computers Work.*

# Storage Media

Digital images are voracious. In no time they can quickly eat up all of the space on your system's hard drive. Thus, for anyone working in the digital imaging field, having enough storage capacity is crucial. You need storage to work with the images that you are currently editing, to back them up, and to archive them.

## Hard Drives

Since many graphics software packages turn to your hard drive when there's insufficient RAM available, hard disk speed and capacity can be crucial to peak performance. One of the easiest ways to satisfy memory-hungry digital images is to provide them with high-capacity, fast hard drives.

Many graphics professionals recommend a minimum of 500MB of storage space for graphics systems. Depending upon the type of work you do, you may be able to get by on less, but it's always convenient to have more. As an added bonus, high-capacity drives are usually faster than low-capacity drives.

The speed of a hard drive is measured primarily in two ways: seek time and transfer rate. A drive's *seek time* measures how fast its read/write head can leap to the area it is seeking on one of the drive's spinning platters. The faster the hard drive, the lower the seek time speed in milliseconds (ms). If you're purchasing a computer or shopping for an external drive or a transplant for a sputtering internal drive, try to obtain one with a low seek time. A 160MB drive could have a seek time of 13 ms. An inexpensive 500MB drive might have a seek time of 11 ms. One gigabyte (a thousand megabytes, abbreviated "GB"), and 2GB drives boast seek times of less than 10 ms. For instance, FWB's 2050 PocketHammer drive features an average seek time of approximately 8 ms. Its *transfer rate,* the rate at which it transfers data to the computer, is 5.75MB a second. In contrast, a 160MB drive might have a transfer rate of 1.3MB a second.

If you truly need peak hard-drive performance, you should consider purchasing a RAID drive array (described later). If you're working in multimedia, you may wish to purchase an AV drive.

## AV Drives for Multimedia

*AV (Audio-Visual) drives* are optimized for transferring long sequences of video and audio. Standard drives generally only need to read and write data in short bursts. AV drives achieve superior performance because they are optimized to handle steady and long transfers of data.

AV drives also are more reliable than standard drives in transferring long sequences of data. This added reliability is the result of delaying a calibration cycle called *thermal calibration.* Drives need thermal calibration to ensure data integrity as the temperature of the drive rises. Non-AV drives enter into thermal calibration on a regular cycle regardless of whether the drive is reading or writing data. AV drives wait until data transfer is completed so that video frames will not be dropped during the process.

Before purchasing an AV drive, check specifications with manufacturers. Some AV drives actually don't perform as well in non-AV situations because they don't handle short data transfers as fast as some standard drives.

## RAID Drive Arrays

If you're seeking the ultimate in hard-drive performance, consider installing an array of hard disks, usually called a *RAID array.* RAID systems can easily cut read/write times

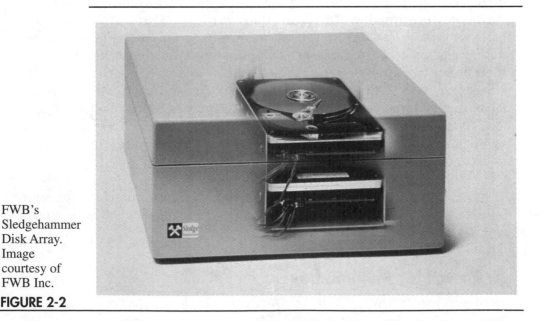

FWB's Sledgehammer Disk Array. Image courtesy of FWB Inc.

**FIGURE 2-2**

in half and double transfer rates. A RAID system typically works by splitting data up among multiple drives, usually two, as shown in Figure 2-2. Each time data is saved, it splits the data between the two drives in a process called *data striping*. By reading and writing from multiple drives, access time and transfer rates are significantly enhanced. To the user, the process is transparent. Only one drive appears on the computer screen, which the user works with as if only that drive were connected.

RAID systems are divided into different levels from 0 to 5. Level 0 provides only data striping. The setup is relatively easy because most of the process is automatically handled by software. In Level 1 RAID systems, the same data is written to both disks in a process called *mirroring*. Although write times are not as fast as in Level 0 systems, Level 1 provides data redundancy—if one drive fails, the other is immediately available to take over the load. RAID systems often include SCSI accelerator boards to speed up data throughput. RAID systems are available from many drive manufacturers and retailers, including APS, FWB, MicroNet, Optima Technology, and SPIN.

## Removable Hard Drives

Removable hard drives are the most widely used media for backing up digital images so they can be sent to service bureaus, prepress houses, clients, and other artists. Graphic artists and others who work with digital images turned to removable hard drives as they discovered that the size of their files quickly overwhelmed the capacity of floppy disks.

To many artists, removable hard disks provide a fast, convenient, and easy means of backing up and storing files. The removable hard drive cartridge slips in and out of the drive mechanism much the same way a videocassette pops in and out of a VCR. The drive appears on the Mac or Windows desktop just like its nonremovable cousins.

The most popular manufacturer of removable drives and cartridges is SyQuest. For years, the company's 44MB removable hard disk cartridges were the industry standard. Today SyQuest has expanded its product line to include 88 and 200MB 5-inch cartridges, as well as 105 and 270MB 3 1/2-inch drives. Figure 2-3 shows the latter two. An 88MB cartridge costs about $55, a 200MB cartridge, $85. A 200MB drive that reads 44, 88, and 200MB formats costs about $400. 270MB cartridges cost about $65. Drives for the 270 run about $400.

Much of the artwork for the color insert in this book was sent to us on 44MB SyQuest cartridges. We copied the images onto our 270MB cartridges as a backup.

SyQuest
105MB and
270MB
external
removable
cartridge disk
drives.
Courtesy of
SyQuest
Technology

**FIGURE 2-3**

The cartridges were then sent to a prepress house for final output. If you'd like to learn how the color images were produced, turn to the last page of the color insert.

Although SyQuest cartridges are the most popular, there are other manufacturers of removable media. SyQuest's chief competitor is the Iomega Corporation, makers of Bernoulli 90, 150, and 230MB removable cartridges. Presently, Iomega's best selling new product is its low-priced Zip drive which retails for about $200. Cartridges for the Zip drive can store up to 100MB and cost less than $20. SyQuest intends to compete with its EZ135 drive. The EZ135 is faster and stores more data than the Zip, and is comparably priced. In the coming months, expect to see even higher capacity, low-priced removable drives from both SyQuest and Iomega.

Despite the convenience of removable drives, after a few years of using them, you may find yourself crowded out of your studio by stacks of SyQuests or Bernoullis. When this happens, your best bet is to consider magneto-optical or DAT drives as a backup alternative.

## Magneto-Optical Drives

*Magneto-optical* (also called simply *optical*) *drives* are like digital oxcarts. They're very reliable and can store cartloads of data, but they won't get your data to its destination too quickly. Optical drives typically store between 500MB and 1.3GB of data. On the Mac and in Windows, they appear on the computer desktop like hard drives, so you can easily grab the file you want and copy it to the optical or from the optical back to your hard disk. Although lower-capacity opticals can't rival the speed of the fastest hard disks, some newer 1.3GB drives come close. Prices run between $1,500 and $2,000 for the magneto-optical drive; prices for 1.3GB magneto-optical cartridges run a little less than $100.

If you want to spend less money, you might consider a smaller capacity drive that stores between 128 and 230MB on 3 1/4-inch magneto-optical disks. These drives cost under $1,000. The average price of a 230MB magneto-optical disk is $50.

If you need even more storage capacity, want to save money, and don't mind slower access time, you should consider DAT drives.

## DAT Drives

A *DAT (Digital Audio Tape) drive,* shown in Figure 2-4, is not for audio only. DAT tapes are one of the most economical media for storing data. Tapes are sold in 60, 90, and 120 meter sizes. Many older DAT drives store between 1 and 2GB. Newer models costing about $1,000 store about 8GB (of compressed data) on a $25 tape. This translates into a gigabyte of storage for $3.

The downside of using DAT tape is that archiving and retrieving data is not very fast because the information is recorded and accessed sequentially on the tape. Another inconvenience is that data is usually accessed through backup software.

APS DAT drive and DAT tape. Image courtesy of APS Technologies

**FIGURE 2-4**

This means you can't just click and drag files and groups of files to copy from your hard disk to your DAT tape, or vice versa. You need to execute a series of menu commands to get the backup process rolling.

 **OTE:** *Desktape, by Optima Technology, allows Mac users to mount a DAT tape of up to 4GB on their desktops. The software lets you click and drag on icons to copy files from your hard disk to a DAT and back. A Windows version is in the works.*

## File Compression Software

If you don't have room to spare on your backup media, compressing files can be helpful. Compression programs can dramatically trim file sizes of digital images. If you are going to compress your files, be aware that certain compression formats actually remove data from your file, which can result in a loss of image quality. This form of compression is commonly called *lossy* compression. Compression schemes that do not remove data are called *non-lossy*. On the Mac, Stuffit Deluxe and Disk Doubler are two well-known non-lossy compression programs. On the PC, Stacker, PKZip, and LHARC are commonly used. If you don't own compression software, you may be able to compress files within the graphics applications you own.

# Monitors

A monitor's sharpness, size, and clarity of colors are crucial to creating professional-looking digital images.

To many digital artists, size is the prime consideration when buying a monitor. Although graphics software runs on any size monitor, most professionals recommend buying the largest monitor you can afford. If you're working on graphic images, you'll find that the more screen real estate you possess, the easier it will be to work.

Even if you will only be working on small images, a large monitor still comes in handy. Almost every major graphics application includes multiple *palettes*—windows that constantly float above an image and allow you to choose colors, switch brush strokes, or move from layer to layer. The more screen space available, the easier it is to keep track of and maintain palettes, other open images, or desktop icons. Extra screen space is also useful for zooming in to fine-tune work, or if you wish to keep multiple versions of the same image onscreen for comparison.

If you can't afford the largest monitor available, you might consider purchasing a 17-inch monitor. Many newer models allow you to switch resolution settings. This can allow a 17-inch monitor to display the same image area as a 20-inch monitor. For instance, most Mac 17-inch monitors create images out of a matrix of 832 x 624 pixels. A *pixel* is the smallest visible colored dot the monitor can display. With the proper software and video board, the 17-inch monitor can switch to display 1024 x 768 pixels. This makes the image onscreen smaller, but provides the same overall image area as that of a 20-inch monitor. On the PC, monitor resolution is broken down into three main categories: VGA (640 x 480 pixels), SuperVGA (1024 x 768 pixels), and a high resolution mode (1280 x 1024). Like the Mac, the PC allows you to switch from one resolution to another, depending on the monitor and the video card.

If you are purchasing a monitor, make sure it is *non-interlaced*. Many inexpensive PC monitors are *interlaced*. This means that the image is created by first scanning every other line onscreen. First the odd lines are scanned, then the even ones. Non-interlaced monitors scan straight down, providing sharper images and less flickering. Another consideration when purchasing a monitor is dot pitch. *Dot pitch* is the distance between each trio of red, green, and blue phosphor dots that merge to create the colored pixels onscreen. Dot pitch on most graphics monitors is 29mm or less. The lower the dot pitch value, the finer the apparent screen resolution.

When evaluating a monitor, it's best to be fussy. Remember, you could be staring at it day after day for many years. Before purchasing a monitor, make sure images are sharp, not blurry. Straight lines should be straight and not bend or waver. Color and brightness should be consistent throughout all image areas. Glare should be kept at a minimum.

# 24-Bit Color Cards

The human eye can discern countless colors. Unfortunately, the standard number of colors most PCs offer when you break open the cardboard box is 256. If you are going to create, digitize, or view photo-realistic images, you'll want to view millions of colors. In order to display millions of colors, you'll need to add either a *24-bit* video display card or VRAM (video RAM) chips to your computer.

Most older Macs and PCs require a 24-bit video card to be purchased in order to display millions of colors onscreen. When purchasing a card, you should be aware that not all cards support millions of colors on all monitor sizes. The more VRAM on a video card, the more colors you will obtain on larger monitors. If you are purchasing a PowerMac or own a high-end Apple Quadra, you'll be able to obtain millions of colors simply by installing VRAM in the computer. Herc's how the relationship between internal VRAM and monitor size breaks down on the Mac: 1MB of VRAM provides millions of colors on a 14-inch monitor, thousands on a 16-inch monitor. 2MB of VRAM provides millions of colors on a 14- or 16-inch monitor, thousands of colors on a 19- or 21-inch monitor. Only top-of-the-line Macs can accommodate 4MB of VRAM, which will provide millions of colors on all monitor sizes.

Although it's not necessary to understand the math involved in jumping from hundreds to thousands to millions of colors, it's helpful to have a basic understanding. In programs like Macromedia Director and Adobe Photoshop, you'll see references to 8-, 16-, and 24-bit color in various dialog boxes.

The term *bit* refers to an electronic signal that can have one of two states: on or off. Thus, 8-bit color (2 x 2 x 2 x 2 x 2 x 2 x 2 x 2) calculates to 256 colors, while 24-bit, $2^{24}$, produces approximately 16.7 million colors.

If you need to purchase a 24-bit video card, make sure that the card is the right one for your system. An older, low-priced Macintosh won't accept PCI cards, and some won't accept Nubus cards. On the PC, VL, ISA, and PCI are all bus standards for expansion slots. The right card must be inserted into the right slot.

If you do conclude that you need millions of colors on your screen, your next concern is how fast these colors can be displayed.

It takes quite a bit of computing power to quickly redraw the thousands of pixels that comprise a 24-bit color image on a 21-inch color. To expedite the process, most 24-bit color cards include coprocessor chips that give the CPU a break from handling its screen redraw chores. This can speed up every change that occurs on the screen.

Before purchasing a 24-bit board, you might wish to contact manufacturers or read reviews in computer magazines to see whether the video board you plan to purchase has enough acceleration for your needs. The fastest boards are the most expensive, and some allow input to and output from VCRs and video cameras.

Recognizing the necessity for improved Windows performance for graphics applications, Dell, Compaq, Gateway, and IBM have released computer systems that include 64-bit accelerators, which expedite the processing of color images. These accelerators pump data over 64 data channels and can speed up image processing by 50 percent. Some of the better-known manufacturers of accelerated video graphics boards include ATI, Radius, RasterOps, TrueVision, Matrox, and NEC.

## Graphics Tablets and Stylus Pens

If you currently create art with a traditional paintbrush, pencil, or pen, you'll definitely want to consider purchasing a *graphics tablet*. A graphics tablet is a flat piece of plastic sold with a pressure-sensitive stylus. The stylus resembles a pen with a plastic tip. Figure 2-5 shows artist C. David Pina working with a Wacom tablet and pen on a title scene from the 63rd Annual Academy Awards show.

Many artists prefer the stylus to a mouse because the stylus' fine tip is more precise when editing intricate image areas, and it can easily be used to trace over sketches placed on the tablet. In some graphics applications such as Fractal Design Painter, Adobe Photoshop, Adobe Illustrator, and Corel PhotoPaint, applying more pressure to the pen allows the user to alter color and brush strokes. Before purchasing a tablet (expect to pay between $250 and $500), investigate whether your software is compatible with it. Most major painting and image-editing software packages are compatible with graphics tablets manufactured by companies such as Wacom, CalComp, Kurta, and Summagraphics.

If you're purchasing a graphics tablet, you might want one that allows the mouse and the tablet to operate at the same time. This way, you can easily switch between the two input devices without restarting your computer or issuing a menu command.

A Wacom tablet and stylus pen. ©A.M.P.A.S.® Main Title design by C. David Pina. Courtesy of Wacom Technology Corp.

**FIGURE 2-5**

Before purchasing a tablet you might want to try out the feel of the pen at a trade show. You'll find that some pens are lighter than others (particularly those that don't need batteries), some provide more levels of pressure, and some are more precise than others.

 **OTE:** *Wacom has recently introduced electronic pens that actually write with real ink, as well as "digital ink." The new pens are intended for drawing and sketching on paper that is placed on top of Wacom's graphics tablet.*

## TIPS of the TRADE

### What to Look for When Buying a Tablet

**By Laurie Hemnes, Technical Support Manager and Shawn Grunberger, Technical Support Specialist, Fractal Design Corp.**

The most well-known tablets available for Macs and PCs are Wacom, CalComp, Kurta, CIC, Acecad, and Summagraphics—so far. Each manufacturer has so many different features, it's best to choose a tablet based on your specific needs. The following is a list of considerations and features we've compiled from our own experiences with the many tablets now available.

1.  **Pressure-Sensitivity**—Fractal's products take advantage of this feature spectacularly! Paint strokes can be wider or more saturated with the amount of pressure applied. Pressure can control brush size, opacity, texture, and color. Not all models are pressure-sensitive, so be sure you check before you purchase.

2.  **Levels of Pressure**—Levels available vary somewhere between 120 and 256. Painter can utilize the highest level of pressure that is currently available. However, whether or not a high number of levels is perceivable in actual use is debatable.

3.  **Tablet Size**—Because a tablet of any size will take advantage of your full screen area, larger tablets offer more drawing space per unit of

# TIPS of the TRADE

screen real estate. In practical terms, this means drawing a line all the way across a full-screen image might take 8 inches of hand motion on a small tablet, but might take 12 inches of motion on a larger tablet. For some users, this offers greater detail, control, and freedom of movement. For others, it just means their arms get tired sooner. When picking a tablet size, therefore, consider not only the space on your desk, but also your personal painting and drawing style. For most non-professional users, tablets with a 6 x 8 or 6 x 9-inch active area offer a convenient compromise. Professional artists may want to go for a 12 x 12-inch or larger tablet—but don't expect to hold these on your lap!

4.  **Stylus/Pen**—Variations include: pen attached to tablet with cord, cordless pens with batteries, and cordless pens with no batteries. We'd suggest that if you choose a tablet and pen combination that requires batteries, you have extra batteries on hand in case they run out. Pens that require batteries are usually "thicker" in the hand, and somewhat heavier. Also, some pens have programmable buttons on them. These can be useful, because you can set up a button to equal a double-click, for example.

5.  **Tracing Screens**—Some tablets have plastic overlays that allow you to slip something under to trace. This may not be a necessary option if you have access to a scanner, although Laurie finds hers useful for holding a list of associates' phone extensions.

6.  **Programmable Buttons on the Tablet**—These can be useful for macros (i.e., Open Paper Palette, Undo), etc. We'd like to hear some feedback from users who want to share their button "tricks."

7.  **Connectivity**—Some tablets connect through serial ports, others through Apple ADB ports. Keep in mind what ports you have available on your machine. Using a serial mouse and serial tablet requires two free serial ports.

8.  **Tablet Software**—There usually are some useful customization features within the software. For example, you can isolate a part of

# TIPS of the TRADE

your tablet as a smaller working area that allows you to get around a large screen or tablet with less effort. Or you can change the mapping to trace an image at a different size. When tablet and software arrive, call the manufacturer to ensure you have the most current software version.

9.  **Tilt and Bearing**—A couple of tablets (CalComp and Hitachi) offer these two features that Painter can use. Tilt is the angle between the stylus and the tablet surface. This is similar to the traditional manner in which an artist holds charcoal. The direction your stylus faces determines bearing. In Painter, you can base your brush size, color, grain, and other variables on tilt and bearing.

10. **Price**—You get what you pay for. Obviously, pressure-sensitive tablets cost more than the non-pressure variety.

11. **Try Before You Buy?**—Unfortunately, graphics tablets are still hard to find in many retail outlets, making a presale test difficult. However, being able to use a tablet for a while before you buy is a great way to pinpoint subtle differences and aesthetic concerns. The best place to find demo tablets is a computer convention. At events like Siggraph, MacWorld, Windows World, Seybold, and ImageWorld, you'll find demo tablets of all varieties under one roof. And, most tablet companies demonstrate their tablets with Painter.

When in doubt, call and ask the tablet manufacturers questions. Some manufacturers to try are: Acecad, CalComp, CIC, Hitachi, Kurta, Summagraphics, and Wacom. (See Appendix A for contact information.)

We hope you'll be using your tablet and Fractal products together for a long time—so buy smart! No matter what tablet you choose, you'll wonder how you got along without one.

# Digitizing Devices

Digitizing devices convert photos, artwork, and the raw materials of the real world into digital data that can be edited by graphics programs. The most common digitizing devices are scanners and digital cameras. Part Two of this book discusses the digitizing process in detail.

The following sections provide an overview of digitizing hardware.

## Scanners

Scanners are primarily used to digitize photographs, artwork, and slides. They come in all shapes and sizes, some producing sharp, high-quality images, others producing output acceptable only for positioning purposes.

If you're interested in purchasing a scanner or if you are evaluating one to use for digitizing your work, choose your equipment carefully. Don't buy a scanner merely because it's cheap. An inexpensive, low-end scanner may not capture crucial image details or display critical differences in tonal changes. Ensuring that images are digitized with the proper equipment can ensure high quality in all stages of an image-editing project.

Knowing the different types of scanners available and how they work can help you predict image quality and better plan digital imaging projects. The most widely used types are flatbed, slide, rotary drum, and handheld. For more information about scanners and scanning, see Chapter 7.

**FLATBED SCANNERS**   The most common type of scanner is the *flatbed*. As mentioned in Chapter 1, flatbed scanners resemble copy machines. You open the cover and place the image on the flatbed platen, usually a plate of glass. Unlike a copy machine, scanning does not start by pressing a button on the machine; instead, software controls when the scan begins, how it saves the image, and the image quality.

Agfa, Hewlett-Packard, Sharp, La Cie, Microtek, Nikon, and UMAX are all well-known scanner manufacturers. All produce a variety of flatbeds with different features at different prices. (For more information on scanning, see Chapter 7.)

Most flatbed scanners sold today can digitize color images. Very low-priced models only scan black-and-white images. When analyzing a scanner, one of the first factors to consider is resolution. Scanning resolution is measured in pixels per inch. Together the matrix of thousands of tiny pixels creates the digital image.

In general, the greater the number of pixels per inch, the sharper the image—and the larger you can make it without a loss in quality. If you're scanning images that need to be enlarged, you'll probably need a scanner that can output higher than 300 pixels per inch. (For more information about resolution, see Chapter 6.)

Apart from resolution, one of the most important factors governing image quality is dynamic range. *Dynamic range* is the range of tones from light to dark that a scanner can capture. The better a scanner's dynamic range, the better it will be able to capture subtle changes in tone. Dynamic range is measured on a scale from 0 to 4. Usually, the more expensive the scanner, the better the dynamic range. Some high-quality, mid-range flatbed scanners have a dynamic range of 3.0 or greater.

One factor governing dynamic range is how many bits the scanner uses to record information. An 8-bits-per-pixel scanner (also referred to as 24-bit) can theoretically reproduce millions of colors (8 red x 8 green x 8 blue bits = approximately 16.7 million). Often, 2 bits are wasted on noise that is introduced during the scanning process; thus, 8-bits-per-pixel scanners usually don't produce high-quality color scans. Mid-range scanners such as the Agfa Arcus II Plus, shown in Figure 2-6, is a 12-bits-per-pixel scanner (also referred to as 36-bit). The Arcus II Plus features an impressive 3.0 dynamic range. The Arcus StudioScan II, Epson ES1200C, and UmaxPowerLook are 10-bits-per-pixel scanners (also referred to as 30-bit). Many mid-range scanners also allow for a transparency attachment to enable you to scan slides. Generally, slides and transparencies are better handled by slide scanners or high-end drum scanners.

**SLIDE SCANNERS**    Slide scanners are specifically designed to digitize slides. Since a translucent slide has a greater dynamic range than an opaque print, scanning slides often produces better digitized images than scanning photographs. High quality is more easily obtained from slide scanners because they often have better optical systems than flatbeds. Kodak, Nikon, and Polaroid are all well-known manufacturers of slide scanners. Some slide scanners can be attached to devices that let the user quickly scan multiple slides one after another. For instance, Kodak's Professional RFS 2035 Film Scanner, shown in Figure 2-7, can be attached to a slide-stacking device which allows for the "unattended" scanning of up to 300 slides. Lower-priced slide scanners (under $2,000), such as those manufactured by Nikon and Polaroid, allow you to quickly pop a slide into a scanner very much the way you load a floppy disk into a disk drive.

**ROTARY DRUM SCANNERS**    To ensure optimum quality when digitizing images, many graphics professionals send their photographs, slides, and *chromes* (transparencies) to be scanned on a drum scanner, shown in Figure 2-8. Before an

Agfa's Arcus
II scanner.
Courtesy of
Agfa Corp.

**FIGURE 2-6**

image is digitized on a drum scanner, it is taped onto the scanner's revolving drum.
A stationary light source transmits light to the image as it rotates. The drum scanner's

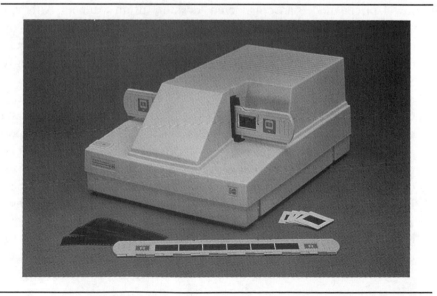

Kodak's
Professional
RFS 2035
Film Scanner.
Courtesy of
Eastman
Kodak Co.

**FIGURE 2-7**

Dupont
Crosfield
drum scanner.
Courtesy of
Dupont
Crosfield

**FIGURE 2-8**

sophisticated optical system can discern critical color transitions and minute detail usually passed over by less sophisticated scanners.

Drum scanners range from $20,000 to hundreds of thousands of dollars. Some lower-priced models are considered "desktop" drum scanners. Although the quality of a desktop drum scanner will be high, it won't match the sharpness or the true life colors output from more expensive models. If you wish to output your images on a drum scanner, contact a service bureau or prepress house. Prices usually range from $50 to over $100 per scan.

**QUICK DOCUMENT SCANNING**    If you need to quickly scan black-and-white and grayscale documents and logos into your computer, Visioneer's Paperport, shown in Figure 2-9, provides an efficient and inexpensive solution. Paperport, which retails for under $400, was developed to allow you to quickly digitize any images or text on paper that can fit through its sheetfeeder. As soon as you place a document into the sheetfeeder, Visioneer sucks it through its rollers and in a few seconds the image appears on screen. Paperport's top resolution is 400 ppi and it can be quite useful for quickly collecting images and text that you might need to digitize for different projects. Accompanying software allows you to easily fax the scanned images over a fax modem or send them to colleagues over interoffice e-mail.

Visioneer's
Paperport
scanner
**FIGURE 2-9**

## Video Capture

The advent of multimedia has created a growing demand for capturing video images on a computer. This allows moving images to be output into multimedia software, or frozen video frames to be "grabbed" for placement in image-editing software.

Apple and a handful of PC makers manufacture *AV computers.* These computers feature video jacks that let you plug video cameras and VCRs directly into the computer. If you don't have an AV computer, the most common way to capture video is to install a video digitizing board. Most video digitizing boards are sold with software that lets you capture video. More sophisticated systems, such as RasterOps MoviePak2 Pro Suite and Radius VideoVision, let you not only capture video, but also record images from your computer to videotape. Other manufacturers of video equipment boards are DiaQuest, TrueVision, and Radius. To learn how to capture video, see Chapter 8. Chapter 18 covers how to output to video.

In addition to capturing video from camcorders and VCRs, video boards can capture images from a new class of video cameras developed primarily for the computer. VideoLabs Flexcam and Flexcam Pro are tiny video cameras mounted on gooseneck wands, which make the cameras as easy to adjust as a desk lamp. The cameras can be used for video capture, video conferencing, and presentations. The

Windows version of the Flexcam sells for about $700, which includes the camera and the video board.

## Digital Cameras

If you need to photograph images that will be digitized, you might consider buying a digital camera. Digital cameras digitize an image at the click of a button, often storing the image to a tiny hard disk or a battery-powered memory chip. Images are then downloaded to a computer through a cable connected to its SCSI or serial port, or they can be sent to a computer over the phone lines.

Perhaps the best-known digital cameras are Kodak's DCS series. The Kodak DCS 420, which uses a Nikon 35mm camera body as its optical engine, is shown in Figure 2-10. Professional cameras such as Kodak's retail for over $10,000 and have proved quite popular with press photographers for sporting and news events. Leaf Systems also makes a high-end studio digital camera back that can attach to professional high-end cameras such as the Mamaya RZ67. Digital studio cameras attached to camera backs usually must remain connected to a computer.

Drastically less expensive than the Leaf or Kodak camera is Apple's QuickTake camera, which retails for less than $800 (see Figure 2-11). The QuickTake is not suitable for high-end publishing, but image quality can be suitable for newsletters and multimedia presentations. Chapter 8 covers digitizing images using both the QuickTake and Kodak's DCS 420 camera.

## CD-ROM Drives

*CD-ROM drives* have become the newest essential peripheral for the digital artist. If you wish to use a CD-ROM to view Photo CD images, you'll need a drive that supports *XA (extended architecture) format*. Most drives sold today are not only XA, but are *multisession*. This means you can add new Photo CD images on one CD-ROM until its storage capacity is full.

Since Kodak introduced its Photo CD technology, stock photography houses have raced to distribute stock images on CD-ROM. Today, CD-ROMs are the most widely used method of distributing stock images, digital background images, and clip art. Unfortunately, CD-ROM speeds lag far behind those of hard disks. Loading a digital image from a CD-ROM could take several times longer than from a hard drive.

If you're purchasing a CD-ROM drive, an important consideration is speed. Most present models are *double speed*. This means they transfer data at twice the

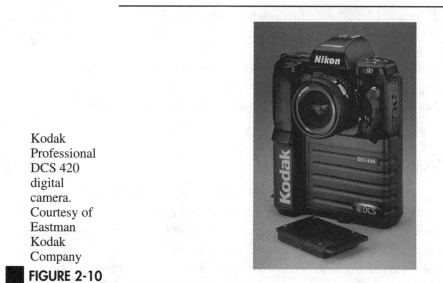

Kodak
Professional
DCS 420
digital
camera.
Courtesy of
Eastman
Kodak
Company

**FIGURE 2-10**

150KB-per-second standard. *Quad speed* drives transfer data at four times the standard rate. Despite these specifics, benchmark tests run by several reputable computer magazines indicate that performance among double-speed and quad-speed drives can vary greatly. For instance, the double-speed AppleCD 300e

Apple's
QuickTake
camera.
Courtesy of
Apple
Computer Inc.
Photographed
by John
Greenleigh

**FIGURE 2-11**

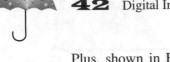 

Plus, shown in Figure 2-12, is faster than many lower-priced CD-ROM drives. Although quad-speed drives are faster than double-speed models, performance is not always twice as fast.

If you own a Macintosh, connecting a CD-ROM drive to your computer is as simple as attaching a cable and installing software. On most PCs, you'll need to install a SCSI adapter board as well as attach the cable and install the software.

# Output Devices

No matter what graphics programs you're going to be using, at some point in the creation stage you'll undoubtedly want to output your digital images to a printer or possibly to a large screen using a digital projector. Most affordable output devices are generally used to print a *proof*, a sample of the final image. If you are working in black-and-white, a standard 300 to 600 *dpi* (dots per inch) laser printer might be sufficient. For color output, the choices are broader and the price range wider. Color proofs are generally output on a color laser, ink-jet, dye sublimation, or thermal wax printer.

## Black-and-White Laser Printers

If you are working primarily with black-and-white images, a 300 or 600 dpi laser printer is essential for proofing your work and analyzing design elements. A black-and-white *laser printer* creates an image from patterns of tiny dots. In every square inch of an image, a 600 dpi printer creates 360,000 dots (600 x 600). Output from a black-and-white laser printer can be acceptable for low-end production, but if you wish to output photographic quality black-and-white images, you will probably have to pay to have your images output on an *imagesetter*, which outputs at 1,250 dpi and higher.

## Color Laser Printers

For several years, the color laser printer market was dominated by Canon's ColorLaser, which could not only output color images but also serve as a copy machine. Recently, QMS, Apple, and Hewlett-Packard have begun marketing 300 dpi color laser printers that use Cyan, Magenta, Yellow, and Black toner bottles to provide the basis of color output. These printers all retail below $7,000. QMS also sells a more expensive model that produces color output at 600 dpi. The output of

AppleCD
300e Plus.
Courtesy of
Apple
Computer Inc.
Photographed
by John
Greenleigh

**FIGURE 2-12**

color laser printers doesn't rival that of dye sublimation printers, but they are usually much faster and paper costs are lower.

## Ink-Jet Printers

Low-end *ink-jet printers* are probably the least expensive option for outputting color images. Ink-jet printers from Apple and Hewlett-Packard sell for well under $1,000. Color is created from different colored inks sprayed from tiny jets above the paper surface. The output of low-end color ink-jet printers will not adequately indicate how a digital image will print on a printing press.

High-end ink-jet printers, such as the Scitex IRIS shown in Figure 2-13, produce startling, photo-realistic images and can come close to matching final output colors on a printing press. IRIS printers are usually found at prepress houses and service bureaus. A typical IRIS system could retail for over $100,000. IRIS prints are typically used as a type of *digital proof,* meaning the image is created directly from digital data, rather than from the film negatives eventually used by a printer to create printing plates.

Many digital artists also use IRIS proofs to showcase their portfolios. They have become so popular that they are a standard offering at most service bureaus. If you wish to obtain an IRIS print, contact your local service bureau for instructions on how to save your file. Most service bureaus will ask that the image be saved in TIFF format. (File formats are covered in Chapter 5.)

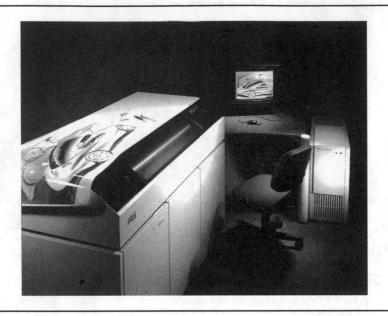

Scitex's IRIS printer. Image courtesy of Scitex America Corp./ IRIS Graphics, Inc.

**FIGURE 2-13**

## Thermal Wax Printers

*Thermal wax printers* are quite popular for evaluation of a particular graphic concept and for showing initial composed images (called *comps*) to clients. As the name implies, thermal wax printers output color images using wax. During the printing process, cyan, magenta, yellow, and black wax are melted to create thousands of dots on each square inch of thermal paper. The combination of dots produces the illusion of countless colors. The results greatly surpass those of low-end ink-jet printers, but the colors are still not reliable enough to adequately predict final output on a printing press. Manufacturers of thermal wax printers include Tektronix and Océ.

## Dye Sublimation Printers

Like IRIS printers, *dye sublimation printers* output striking photo-realistic color printouts. Although the costs of many dye sublimation printers has dropped to below $10,000, high-quality models can run over $20,000.

In the dye sublimation printing process, colors are created with dyes that *sublimate* or turn into gas when a heated print head strikes a colored cyan, magenta, or black plastic ribbon (some dye sublimation printers use red, green, and blue ribbons instead). The process fills thousands of dots with different amounts of colors, which produces smooth tonal transitions.

Manufacturers of dye sublimation printers include DuPont, Kodak, 3M, and Tektronix. Before purchasing this kind of printer, analyze the cost of all consumables. Ribbons and paper alone can raise the price per printout to several dollars. You should also compare output from printers at different price ranges. Many lower-priced models can produce very high-quality images that may suit your needs. However, if you compare low-priced to high-priced images, you'll undoubtedly see a difference in sharpness and color. If you begin investigating dye subs, you'll find that some models, such as 3M's excellent Rainbow printer, require a dedicated computer or an expensive coprocessing board. This can increase the final cost of the printer by several thousand dollars.

## Imagesetters

Imagesetters, such as the one shown in Figure 2-14, produce high-resolution printed output from 1,000 to over 2,500 dots per inch. For black-and-white publishing, imagesetters output type and graphics with a maximum of 256 shades of gray.

For color output, imagesetters produce four film negatives, each corresponding to the cyan, magenta, yellow, and black components of color images. High-quality proofs such as *Matchprints* can be output from the negatives to predict color quality on a printing press. Once the proofing process is complete, the negatives are sent to a commercial printer who creates printing plates from the negatives.

## Multimedia Output

If you will be creating business or multimedia presentations and plan to make your presentation directly from a desktop or notebook computer, you may wish to purchase an LCD panel or projector, or an external encoder which will allow you to view the production on a television screen.

*LCD panels* generally run about $5,000 and work in conjunction with an overhead projector. The panel sits on top of the projector, which projects the computer image on a screen. In recent years, the image quality of LCD panels has improved dramatically. Older panels couldn't produce the crisp, clear color images of today's models. Among the better-known makers of LCD panels are 3M, In Focus Systems, Polaroid, and Proxima.

If you are making a multimedia presentation and do not want to be tied to an overhead projector, consider an LCD projector. *LCD projectors* are self-contained

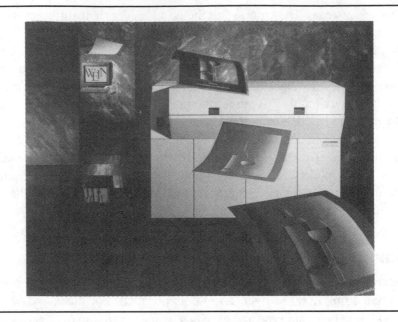

Linotronic
930
Imagesetter.
Courtesy of
Linotype-Hell
Company

**FIGURE 2-14**

units that project not only video, but often audio, from a computer. LCD projectors usually run from $5,000 to $10,000. Manufacturers of LCD projectors include Boxlight, In Focus Systems, and Proxima.

If you need to display a presentation on a color TV monitor, the price of a hookup is much less than purchasing an LCD panel or projector. A variety of manufacturers make *encoding scan converters,* which basically convert your computer signal to one that can be read by a television. Prices are generally about $300 and up. You'll often find a variety advertised in computer software catalogs.

## Modems

Graphic artists use *modems* to send and receive type and images over the phone lines. The word "modem" was created from the words "modulate" and "demodulate." When a modem modulates, it translates the computer's digital signal to analog, allowing it to be transmitted over the phone. When a modem demodulates, it reverses the process so that the telephone's analog signal is converted to a digital signal.

When dealing with graphic data, the most important factor to consider is a modem's speed. The faster a modem sends data, the faster digital images are sent. If you're paying for the time you use a modem, obviously higher speeds mean money saved.

Most modems sold today send and receive data at a minimum of 14,400 bps (bits per second) to a top speed of 28,000 bps. (It's important to understand that a bit is not a byte. A byte is comprised of 8 bits. To create a letter of the alphabet, your computer uses 8 bits.) A modem's speed is known as its *baud rate*. If you'll be connecting to online services or service bureaus, you'll probably want to buy at least a 14,400 baud modem, which will send or receive a file six times faster than a 2400 baud modem. This means that if you were downloading a 300KB file, it would only take about 5 minutes on the 14,400 modem, compared to 15 minutes on the 2400 modem. Prices of modems have dropped so dramatically in the past few years that you can pick up a 14,400 baud modem for around $100. Obviously, though, if you can connect with an online service or service bureau at 28,000 baud, all the better.

Despite the convenience of using a modem to transfer digital images, if you're working with large color images, you're likely to find that sending or receiving files over the phone just isn't worth the time. In most cases, your best bet is to copy your files to a removable hard disk and call a messenger or an overnight delivery service.

# Conclusion

Now that you've reviewed some of the hardware required to create digital images, you should have a basic idea of how to build your own digital imaging studio. Before making any purchases, though, be sure to shop around. Ask colleagues for their recommendations, and try to stay up to date with the latest technologies.

The world of digital imaging changes so quickly that it's difficult to stay abreast of the latest developments. Nonetheless, if you are a digital artist or your work requires you to use digital images, it pays to stay current. In addition to computer books, see what the major Mac and PC magazines have to offer. You should also explore magazines specifically geared to digital imaging, multimedia, and desktop publishing. Some of the better-known periodicals are *Publish, Print, How, Color Publishing,* and *Digital Imaging.*

# 3

# Understanding Color Concepts

Color enlivens dull images, grabs an audience's attention, communicates complex concepts. If you're working with digital images, using color can be vital to conveying your artistic, commercial, or administrative goals. In digital art, the right colors can heighten reality, evoke a distinct and desired mood. In a digital presentation, the right colors help make arguments more powerful and can help an audience gain a better understanding of what is being presented.

Unfortunately, using color on the computer can be confusing and frustrating. In most computer programs, you don't pick colors as you would in an art supply store. You can search high and low in a program's menus and submenus, and delve into the depths of each of its palettes, and you still probably won't find the words "burnt sienna," "cerulean blue," or "aureole yellow." You're more likely to be confronted with a dialog box where you must define colors based upon percentages of red, green, and blue, or of cyan, magenta, yellow, and black.

As an artist, you might wonder why everything on the computer needs to be broken down into numbers. Why can't you just pick nature's beautiful colors from a scrolling palette filled with tiny paint tube icons labeled with each color's name? To answer that question, assume for a moment that you don't need to create digital images on a computer. Imagine that you need to bake an apple pie that tastes just as delicious as your grandmother's. Armed with grandma's recipe explaining the precise amounts of flour, apples, butter, and sugar (and some baking skills), you'd be able to re-create the taste of the pie. Even if it wasn't a perfect re-creation, it would probably come close. But if you didn't have the recipe, your attempts to re-create the pie from memory alone would probably be doomed.

# Color Models to the Rescue

Just as human taste buds can sense a wide variety of tastes, the human eye can perceive countless numbers of colors. To describe colors so that they could be consistently re-created, scientists developed a means for describing colors called a *color model*. As you'll learn later in this chapter the most important color model for computer users is the RGB (red, green, and blue) model. Using the RGB color model, you can precisely describe colors that can be created on the computer in terms of red, green, and blue. For instance, the color brown could be described as red 147, green 72, and blue 17. Since the colors created by the computer and those created when an image is printed are not exactly the same, physicists created another color model specifically for printed colors, known as the CMYK color model. In this model, colors can be created with percentages of cyan, magenta, yellow, and black (K). For instance, the color brown in the CMYK color model could be described as cyan 27%, magenta 77%, yellow 100%, and black 18%.

To successfully use color on the computer, you should understand the concepts behind color models. This chapter will take you on a colorful tour describing how to define color on the computer using these models. Along the way, you'll have a chance to sample how various software packages handle the vital task of creating colors. At the end of this chapter, you'll take a look at Pantone's ColorDrive software created to help artists manage color. You'll also learn about one of the most revolutionary products in the color industry, Light Source's Colortron. Colortron is a device that measures colors in the real world. This product can take a "snapshot" of a color and transfer it to the computer for analysis and creation.

Before you look at the different color models and how various software packages use them, it's important to understand how we perceive color.

# How We Perceive Color

The human eye perceives colors based upon various wavelengths of light that are absorbed and reflected by objects. The actual color of an object is based upon the light, the object being viewed, and the viewer. For instance, assume that you've got an apple on top of your computer monitor and a digitized image of an apple on the monitor. In order for you to see the real apple, light waves are reflected off the apple's surface, some waves are absorbed into the apple, and other waves—particularly red ones—are reflected back to your eye.

How red is the apple? This primarily depends upon the apple itself. The more red light waves reflected back to your eye, the redder it will appear. But, if the ambient or surrounding light is low, the red apple may appear duller than it would if it were on a picnic table on a sunny day. Another factor determining how red the apple appears is you, the viewer. If you're very hungry, the apple may appear even redder. If you just ate a sandwich, you may not even notice that the apple is red.

If you turned out the lights in your room, you wouldn't see the real apple, but you'd still see the computer screen version. This is because your monitor emits light. Dealing with the difference between colors created by emitted or reflective light is

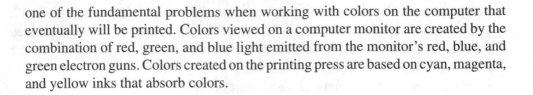

one of the fundamental problems when working with colors on the computer that eventually will be printed. Colors viewed on a computer monitor are created by the combination of red, green, and blue light emitted from the monitor's red, blue, and green electron guns. Colors created on the printing press are based on cyan, magenta, and yellow inks that absorb colors.

## Additive and Subtractive colors

Although light is comprised of different wavelengths, our eyes primarily react to red, green, and blue light wavelengths. Red, green, and blue are called the *additive primaries* (see Figure 3-1) because countless colors can be created by adding different intensities of red, green, and blue light. By adding each of the additive primaries to one another, three more colors are created: cyan, yellow, and magenta. If you add red, green, and blue, white is created. Here's how red, green, and blue can be added together to create white, cyan, magenta, and yellow.

red + green + blue = white
green + blue = cyan
blue + red = magenta
red + green = yellow

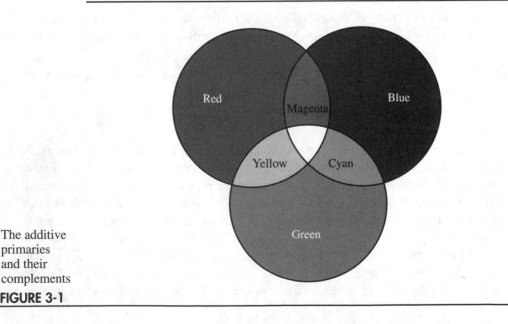

The additive primaries and their complements

**FIGURE 3-1**

From cyan, magenta, and yellow, countless other colors can be created. For instance, here's how these three colors can be used to create black, red, green, and blue.

$$cyan + magenta + yellow = black$$
$$cyan + magenta = blue$$
$$yellow + magenta = red$$
$$yellow + cyan = green$$

Cyan, magenta, and yellow create colors by subtracting or absorbing colors. That is why they are sometimes called the *subtractive primaries* (see Figure 3-2). This is the basis of much of color printing. For instance, when specific-size yellow ink dots overlap specific-size magenta ink dots, red is created. When the two inks combine, they absorb green and blue wavelengths of light and reflect red back to you.

## The RGB Color Model

Colors created by the computer are based upon the fundamentals of how our eye and mind break down red, green, and blue wavelengths of light in nature. The colors you see on a computer screen are created from glowing red, green, and blue

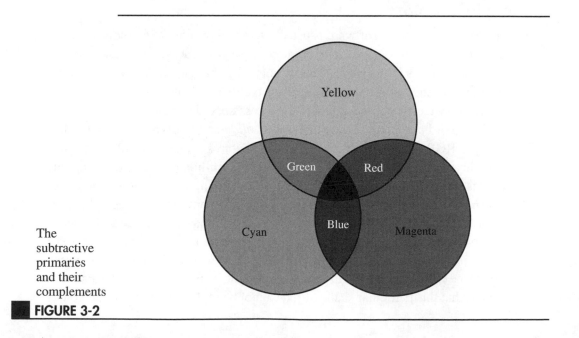

The subtractive primaries and their complements

**FIGURE 3-2**

phosphors emitted from your monitor. By combining red, green, and blue phosphors, your monitor can create millions of colors. This is the basis of the RGB color model.

Although the human eye can discern even more colors than your monitor can produce, the RGB model is sufficient to create the colors and gradations needed to produce photo-realistic images on your computer screen.

Most computer software used to create colors for print and multimedia allows you to pick colors using red, green, and blue color components. Many paint, drawing, and image-editing programs can choose from over 16 million combinations of RGB colors.

When you're dealing with such a wealth of possibilities, colors are generally picked numerically. Most software allows you to pick any one of 256 shades of red, 256 shades of blue, 256 shades of green. 256*256*256=16.7 million colors.

**OTE:** *A computer allows you to pick 256 shades of red, green, and blue because it uses 8 bits of memory ($2^8$) for each color component. The combination of the three color components provides $2^{24}$ colors (approximately 16.7 million)—hence, the term 24-bit color. Unless your computer has a 24-bit color card, or sufficient video RAM, you will not be able to see millions of colors on your screen. See Chapter 2 for more details on 24-bit video boards.*

## Using RGB Colors

Picking colors in graphics software is usually handled through a dialog box, often called a *color picker* or *color palette.* Figure 3-3 shows HSC Live Picture's RGB Color Picker. In this palette, you can choose colors by changing red, green, and blue values or by clicking in the color wheel. The Live Picture Color Picker allows you to store color swatches so you can quickly access specific colors when you need them. The three bars in the palette are called *sliders.* Figure 3-4 shows Adobe Photoshop's RGB Picker palette, which also features sliders. By clicking and dragging the sliders, you can define any one of 16.7 million colors. Each point on the slider is assigned a number from 0 to 255. When all three sliders are set to zero, black is created. Dragging any slider to the right adds a component of red, green, or blue light. If you look closely at Figure 3-4, you'll see that the red slider has been dragged to the far right, all the way to 255. The green and blue sliders are set to 0. As you can probably guess, this combination of red, green, and blue creates the color red. Notice the exclamation mark in the tiny triangle at the bottom right of the palette. This means that this particular shade of red cannot be replicated when printed on a

Color Wheel

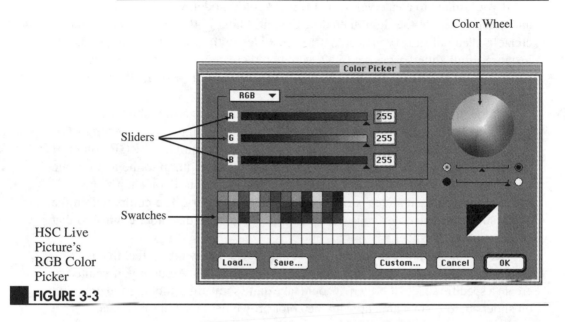

Sliders

Swatches

HSC Live
Picture's
RGB Color
Picker

**FIGURE 3-3**

printing press. The red created in the palette is beyond the gamut or color range of printable colors. You'll learn more about the printable range of colors later in this chapter.

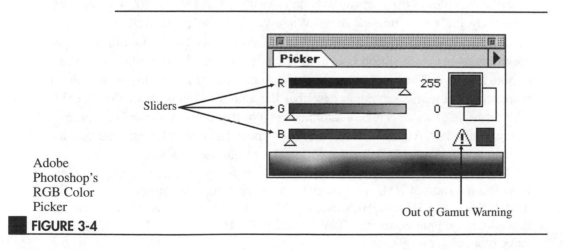

Sliders

Out of Gamut Warning

Adobe
Photoshop's
RGB Color
Picker

**FIGURE 3-4**

If you wanted to create yellow in the RGB color model, you would drag the red and green sliders to the right, then drag the blue slider to the left. If you wanted to create a shade of gray, you would set each slider to the same numeric point. For instance, if all sliders were set to 32, you would create a dark shade of gray. If all sliders are set to 200, you would create a light shade of gray. When all three sliders are set to 255, white is created.

Although not apparent from the black-and-white screenshot shown in Figure 3-4, Photoshop's RGB Picker includes several very helpful tools for creating RGB colors. The bottom of the palette features a color spectrum bar of RGB colors. If you click on a blue shade in the spectrum bar, the sliders jump to the appropriate RGB values to create the color. Another handy feature is Photoshop's *dynamic sliders* in which each slider is filled with a range of colors. The colors within the slider show you the color you will create when you drag the slider control to that color point on the slider.

Despite the help of Photoshop's dynamic sliders, many artists feel that picking colors based upon RGB components is not very intuitive. Assume you wanted to create a specific shade of brown. It could take quite some time clicking and dragging on sliders before you came up with the color brown, let alone burnt sienna.

## The HSB, HSV, and HSL Color Models

The HSB (hue, saturation, brightness) color model was created to provide an intuitive means of picking colors. HSB is helpful because most people don't think of colors based upon their red, green, and blue components. For instance, when you describe the color of the sun, you wouldn't say it's 100% red and 100% green. You would say the sun is bright yellow. When you use the word "yellow," you are describing a color in terms of its *hue,* or in terms of its color name in the color spectrum, or on a color wheel. *Saturation* is a term often used to describe how intense or pure a color is. The purer or more intense a color is, the greater the saturation. In more technical terms, saturation describes the amount of gray in a color. A color with no grays or white is highly saturated, a color that is less saturated has more of a gray component. A color's *brightness* is how much light the color contains. A color with no brightness is black; a color with 100% brightness is white.

Most computer programs that allow the user to create more than 256 colors feature some form of HSB color palette. Some programs use variations of the HSB model. Some use HSL or HLS, where "L" stands for lightness. Others, such as Fractal Design Painter, use the HSV model. In the HSV model, "V" stands for the value of a color's brightness.

## Using HSB Colors

To understand how the HSB and HSV color model variants work, it's best to take a look at a specific color picker. One of the easiest to use is Fractal Design Painter's HSV Colors palette, shown in Figure 3-5.

In Painter's HSV Colors palette, the hues are chosen by clicking on a color wheel. Around the major points of the wheel are the primary colors and their complements. This makes picking colors for harmony and contrast easier. Similar colors are closer on the wheel, while colors exhibiting the most contrast are opposite each other.

To select a blue color, you need only find blue on the circle and click on it. As soon as you click, the triangle within the circle changes to show all possible brightness and saturation levels of blue. If you click and drag to the right in the triangle, the blue becomes more saturated. Click and drag to the left, and you add more gray to the color, as it becomes less saturated. If you want to add brightness to the color, you click and drag up in the triangle. By clicking and dragging down, you make a color darker. Once you've chosen the color you want, you can then paint with it using a brush tool or select an area and fill it with that color

Fractal
Design
Painter's
HSV Colors
palette

**FIGURE 3-5**

# The CMYK Color Model

When you see a color created on the computer screen, it is based on light emitted from your monitor. Since the printed page doesn't emit light, the RGB color model shouldn't be used to create colors for the printed page. Instead, the CMYK model is used to describe colors for printing.

In the CMYK color model, different percentages of cyan, magenta, yellow, and black combine to produce countless colors. In theory, high percentages of cyan, magenta, and yellow create black. But because of the impurities of ink pigments, the colors often produce a muddy brown. Thus, printers add black ink to create a clean black and sharpen the shadows and gray areas of images.

## Using CMYK Colors

When a page is printed using CMYK colors, different size colored ink dots combine to create the illusion of colors. The size of each ink dot is measured in percentages from 0 to 100%. Software packages that allow you to create and/or edit CMYK colors often feature four adjustable sliders for each of the CMYK color components.

Figure 3-6 shows Adobe Illustrator's four CMYK color sliders in its Paint Style palette. This palette features a set of tiny color boxes called swatches. If you wish to reuse the CMYK color you create, you can drag the color from the "fill" or "stroke" box to the swatch area. Macromedia Freehand has CMYK color sliders in

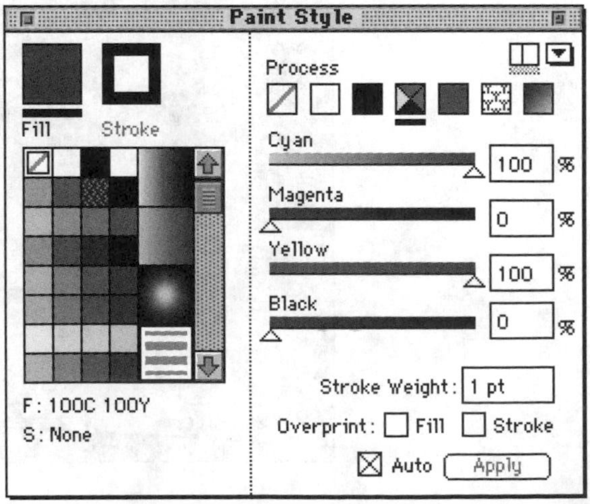

Adobe
Illustrator's
Paint Style
palette

**FIGURE 3-6**

its Color Mixer palette. Once a CMYK color is created, it can be added to the program's Color List palette so it is readily accessible. CorelDRAW's CMYK color dialog box allows you to choose CMYK colors by changing percentages or by clicking in a color box representing the CMYK color model.

To the beginner, choosing colors using the CMYK color model can be quite difficult. Fortunately, there are several techniques you can use to make your job easier. Working with a color wheel (shown in Figure 3-7) nearby can help you create colors more efficiently because each color is situated between the two colors that create it.

Thus, to add more red to a color onscreen, you could increase the percentages of yellow and magenta. To create blue, add magenta and cyan. To create green, add yellow and cyan. To make a color more intense, you can subtract its complement. For example, to make a color redder, you can remove cyan from it.

A program's color palette can also ease the task of choosing CMYK colors. Like its RGB picker, Photoshop's CMYK picker utilizes dynamic sliders. A CMYK color spectrum can also be added to the bottom of the palette. By clicking on the spectrum, you can quickly choose different CMYK colors. Figure 3 8 shows FrameMaker's color palette. FrameMaker is a sophisticated desktop publishing program available on Macs, PCs, and most UNIX workstations. It's often used to create long documents, such as user manuals and books. In FrameMaker's Color Definitions

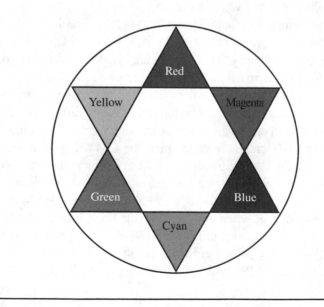

The Color
Wheel

**FIGURE 3-7**

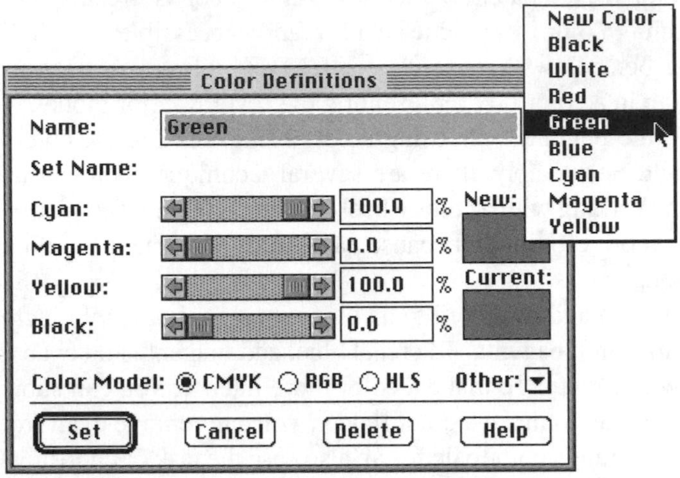

**Color Definitions**

| | |
|---|---|
| Name: | Green |
| Set Name: | |

| | | | |
|---|---|---|---|
| Cyan: | ◄□▶ | 100.0 | % |
| Magenta: | ◄□▶ | 0.0 | % |
| Yellow: | ◄□▶ | 100.0 | % |
| Black: | ◄□▶ | 0.0 | % |

New Color
Black
White
Red
**Green**
Blue
Cyan
Magenta
Yellow

New:

Current:

Color Model: ● CMYK ○ RGB ○ HLS    Other: ▼

[ Set ]    [ Cancel ]    [ Delete ]    [ Help ]

FrameMaker's Color Definitions dialog box

**FIGURE 3-8**

dialog box, you can choose any of the primary or secondary colors by name, and the sliders will jump to the appropriate percentage.

As a further aid in picking CMYK colors, many painting and image-editing applications feature eyedropper tools. When you click on a color in an image with the eyedropper tool, the sliders in the colors palette automatically are adjusted to re-create the color that was clicked on.

Another helpful tool for picking colors is a process color *swatchbook*. Swatchbooks show a printed sample of a color and provide the exact CMYK percentages needed to replicate the color when printed. You simply find the color that you want, then adjust the CMYK colors to match the percentages in the swatch book.

As you work with CMYK colors, it's important to realize that the number of colors the printed page can reproduce is far fewer than the number produced by a video monitor. As mentioned earlier, the spectrum of colors provided by a color model is called its *gamut*. The RGB gamut is larger than the CMYK gamut. Figure 3-9 shows the relationship of the CMYK gamut to the RGB gamut and visible spectrum.

Essentially, this means that you can create colors onscreen that can't be printed by a printing press. Programs such as Photoshop and QuarkXPress provide gamut warnings that appear when you overstep the bounds of the CMYK gamut.

If you take a look back at Figure 3-4, you'll see Photoshop's gamut warning in its RGB Color Picker. The warning is the tiny exclamation mark in a triangle, which can appear in any of Photoshop's color palettes, including its CMYK color palette.

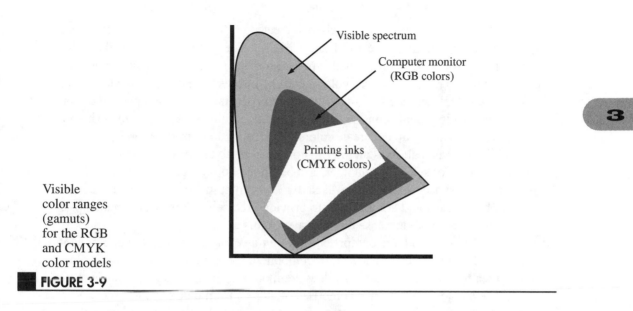

Visible spectrum

Computer monitor
(RGB colors)

Printing inks
(CMYK colors)

Visible
color ranges
(gamuts)
for the RGB
and CMYK
color models

**FIGURE 3-9**

When the warning appears, you can click on it, causing Photoshop to change the color to its closest CMYK equivalent.

The differences between CMYK and RGB color gamuts open up a Pandora's box of problems. Perhaps the main problem for artists is color matching. Your monitor creates colors by emitting light, and CMYK colors are viewed because of reflective light. This means that onscreen CMYK colors often do not match their printed equivalent. Usually, a CMYK color onscreen will be brighter than the same color when it's printed.

The problem of converting between color spaces prompted Adobe Systems and other companies to begin using a device-independent color space. A *device-independent* color space is one not affected by the idiosyncrasies of any piece of hardware.

## The CIE and Lab Color Models

In the early 1900s, a group of scientist formed the "Commission Internationale de l'Eclairage" (often referred to as the CIE). Their goal was to create a color system that would allow the manufacturers of inks, dyes, and fabrics to consistently specify color. They wanted to create a color system based on how the human eye sees color, not on how any one specific device produces it. The result of their labors is the *CIE color space.*

In 1976, this color model was revised to create L*a*b or Lab color. *Lab* is a color space that comprises both the RGB and CMYK color gamuts. Lab provides color scientists and software engineers with a precise method of determining how close one color is to another. Using the Lab color model, physicists have created standard color reference charts. Using these charts, they can compare the gamuts of input and output devices in order to provide consistent colors among monitors, scanners, and printers.

Most digital artists do not create colors using Lab. Lab is used by some programs such as Adobe Photoshop as an interim color space. To aid in the exact translation between one color space and another, Adobe Photoshop images are first translated to Lab color space. Lab is also used by color measuring equipment such as spectrophotometers and colorimeters to provide precise readings of the makeup of colors. You'll learn about these devices later in this chapter.

The Lab color model is comprised of a *lightness* or *luminance (L)* component and two color components. The *a* color component is comprised of an axis of colors from green to magenta. Positive *a* values are more magenta, negative *a* values more green. The *b* color component is comprised of an axis from blue to yellow. Positive *b* values are more yellow, negative b values more blue. The Lab color model is particularly useful if you wish to change the lightness or luminance values in an image.

Lab is often recommended as the color space to use when editing Photo CD images, which use YCC color space, a variant of Lab created by Kodak. In the YCC color space, the Y component controls luminance and the CC axes are the color components. Theoretically, if you use Lab instead of RGB or CMYK when editing Photo CD, you will be working with the full range of colors provided by a Photo CD image.

# Indexed Color

This chapter has focused primarily on color gamuts involving millions of colors. Some color work does not require the use of countless colors. For instance, if you are designing a multimedia production that will be viewed on many different computers, you may need to restrict your color palette to 256 colors, the minimum number on most computer systems.

When a computer uses only 256 colors, it often looks them up in a *color table,* sometimes called a *color lookup table (CLUT).* The lookup table serves as a type of index of colors for the computer system. Thus, you may hear the term *indexed color* in reference to color palettes that utilize 256 or less colors.

If a multimedia producer needs to reduce the number of colors from millions or thousands to hundreds, his or her software can come to the rescue. For instance, Adobe Photoshop includes an indexed color mode, which allows you to restrict an image's color to 256 colors or less. Both Photoshop and Macromedia Director also allow you to edit, create, and name different color palettes as well as choose from different preset palettes.

Figure 3-10 shows the Macromedia Director NTSC color palette. This palette is chosen to ensure that the colors in an image do not fall beyond the range of colors acceptable by television.

Director and other multimedia software also allow the user to switch from one 256-color palette to another. Figure 3-11 shows the Macromedia Director dialog box used to choose different palettes. The dialog box allows the user to specify the duration of the palette change in frames per second. Additionally, you can fade to white or black before a palette transition. This can help prevent a flash that occurs when one palette switches to another.

Not all digital images require countless colors. Some digital images only require two or three colors. When outputting two or three colors, the CMYK process colors often do not need to be used; *spot colors* can be used instead.

## Using Spot Colors

In spot color printing, inks are mixed together to produce a specific color. Spot colors are often used to produce certain metallic colors that are beyond the CMYK color gamut. Some graphics publishing requires the use of the four CMYK colors and an extra "fifth" color that can only be printed through the use of spot colors.

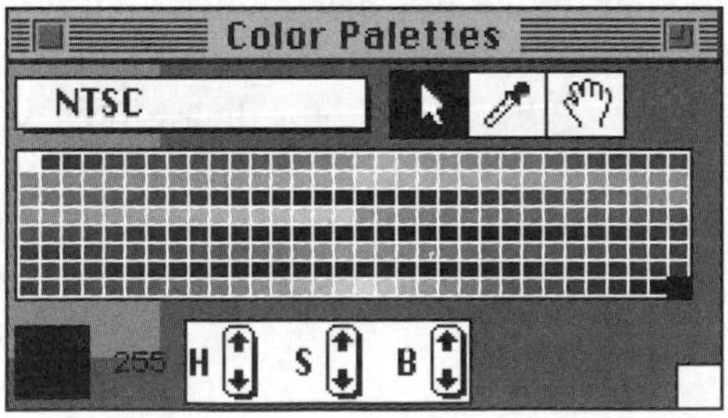

Macromedia Director's 256-color NTSC color palette

**FIGURE 3-10**

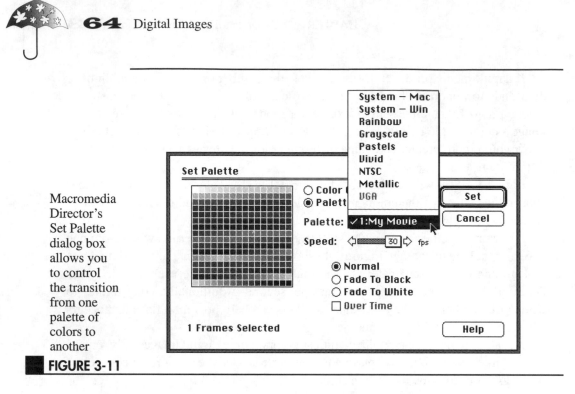

Macromedia
Director's
Set Palette
dialog box
allows you
to control
the transition
from one
palette of
colors to
another

**FIGURE 3-11**

Most artists who work with spot colors don't use a color picker to create them. Instead they use a color-matching system. In the United States, Pantone and TruMatch are the best known.

Picking spot colors removes much of the guesswork from computer color matching. Spot colors are generally picked from a swatchbook. For instance, assume you wanted to print a blue border at the top of a page. Your first step would be to hunt for the blue you want in the Pantone swatchbook. Once you found it, you could then use your software's color palette to locate the color in a library of stored spot colors.

Most graphic software geared to the publishing industry allows you to at least pick Pantone colors. Figure 3-12 shows QuarkXPress's color palette. Notice that the program's Edit Color dialog box also allows you to utilize several color-matching systems including Pantone, Toyo, TruMatch, and Focoltone.

Using the QuarkXPress Edit Color dialog box, you can quickly find Pantone colors by typing a swatchbook color's number at the bottom of the screen. Even though the color onscreen won't exactly match the swatchbook, the swatchbook allows you to predict how the color will look when printed.

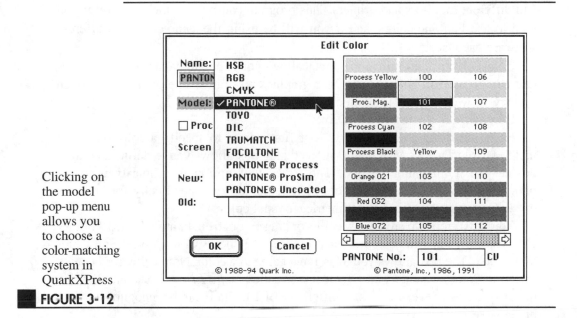

Clicking on the model pop-up menu allows you to choose a color-matching system in QuarkXPress

**FIGURE 3-12**

# Color Management

If you've been working with digital images, you might have noticed that the same color often looks different on different monitors, even when the same graphics application is viewed on different computers. When a color image is printed or output to slides, it doesn't look exactly the same way it did onscreen. One solution to this problem is to *calibrate* the various devices in your printing system so that digital colors are consistent as possible throughout all steps of the production process.

Although calibration techniques are discussed in detail in Chapter 17, calibration topics related to choosing color are worth considering now.

## Using Pantone ColorDrive

Pantone ColorDrive is a software package specifically designed to help you pick colors and ensure that colors are consistent when using different software packages and different monitors and printers. This program can be extremely helpful if you plan to use Pantone colors, and if you will be using the same colors in different software packages.

ColorDrive's main attraction is that it allows you to create standard color palettes that can be used in both PC and Mac graphics programs. The program can even preview how colors will print on different output devices.

Here is a quick tour of ColorDrive:

Before creating a color library, your first step is to specify a color-matching method. ColorDrive's Matching Options dialog box allows you to define an output device and a matching method. The Perceptual option is primarily used for photographic images. Other choices include Saturation (specifically for business presentation graphics) and Colorimetric (for spot colors).

Your next step is to create new colors or drag colors from Pantone's preset library choices into your own custom library. Figure 3-13 shows ColorDrive's Edit Color dialog box. The box allows you to assign a name to a color. Notice the Δ E beneath the New Color swatch. *Delta E* (sometimes called *Delta Error*) is used to describe the differences between colors. A difference of 1 Delta E can be recognized by the human eye.

Once you've created a library, ColorDrive allows you to convert from one color model to another. For instance, you could have your colors created for a print job, but need to show your images in a presentation program that only accepts RGB images. Figure 3-14 shows ColorDrive's menu command that allows you to switch from one color model, such as RGB, to another, such as CMYK

---

```
┌──────────────────── Edit Color ─────────────────────┐
│                                          Old: ▓▓▓▓▓  │
│      C:  [ 43.0 ] %  ⬍                                │
│                                          New: ▓▓▓▓▓  │
│      M:  [ 47.0 ] %  ⬍                    ΔE = 105.24 │
│      Y:  [  0.0 ] %  ⬍          Space: [ CMYK  ▼ ]  │
│      K:  [  9.0 ] %  ⬍                [ Picker... ]  │
│                                       [  Revert   ]  │
│               Name                                   │
│              [ Violet          ]                     │
│              ..............................          │
│                              [ Cancel ] [  OK  ]     │
└──────────────────────────────────────────────────────┘
```

Pantone
ColorDrive's
Edit Color
dialog box

**FIGURE 3-13**

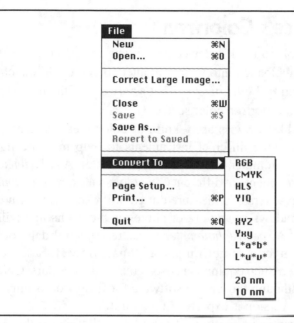

Pantone's
Convert To
submenu
allows you
to convert
from one
color space
to another

**FIGURE 3-14**

Once you've gathered your colors together, you can export them to other software packages. ColorDrive can export to CorelDRAW, Adobe Photoshop, Adobe Illustrator, Adobe PageMaker, QuarkXPress, Claris MacDraw Pro, and Micrografx Designer.

Pantone ColorDrive can also load or create colors based upon the readings of color measuring devices. In the next section, you'll learn about a color-measuring device that hooks up to a desktop computer.

*n* **OTE:** *Pantone also makes Cross-Reference, a software package for both Mac and Windows that helps users find the closest color match across all Pantone color systems. For instance, you can specify a Pantone color using Pantone's Textile color system, and Cross-Reference will find the nearest match in Pantone matching systems for coated and uncoated papers, metallic colors, process colors, pastel colors, and plastics.*

*n* **OTE:** *Praxisoft Color Compass allows you to transfer color palettes from one application to another. It also includes a utility that automatically looks up the Pantone color that is the closest match to a color that you've created.*

# Light Source's Colortron

Imagine being able to hook a device up to your computer, point it at a color, and have the color data loaded into your computer so you could match the color when creating or correcting digital images. That's only one of the many features provided by Light Source's Colortron color sensor.

Colortron is like a Swiss army knife of color measurement. Normally, color professionals use three different instruments to help measure light and color: a colorimeter, a densitometer, and a spectrophotometer. A *colorimeter* breaks colors down into the components of different CIE color spaces. A *densitometer* can be used to calibrate imagesetters and measure dot gain. It can also measure the highlights, midtones, and shadows of artwork or photographic prints that will be reproduced on the computer. A *spectrophotometer* measures spectral data, or wavelengths of light. Colortron can function as a densitometer, a colorimeter, or a spectrophotometer. Such equipment costs thousands of dollars. Colortron retails for about $1,000. Although the current software for Colortron is only available on the Mac, a Windows version is expected in the future.

Before you can use Colortron, it must be hooked up to the ADB (Macintosh mouse port) of a computer. Using Colortron is simple and straightforward: You simply position its lens above the color you want to sample and click a small button. The key to Colortron's ease of use is its excellent manual that discusses the basic concepts of color measurement and its software.

The command center for Colortron's software is its Toolbox, a palette of digital color tools accessed by clicking the mouse. The Toolbox includes utilities which find the RGB and CMYK colors closest to a sampled color. Colortron's other tools include a Compare tool that can be used to compare a printed color to one that you wish to re-create on the computer. It can also be used to compare fabrics, swatches, or paint chips. The bottom of the Compare tool palette, shown in Figure 3-15, shows the difference between the two measured colors. As mentioned earlier, color difference is measured in Delta E's.

Colortron also helps you find attractive color combinations. The Color Harmony palette, shown in Figure 3-16, allows you to find colors that complement a sample color.

One of Colortron's most useful tools for choosing colors that will be printed is its Colorimeter. The Colorimeter tool, shown in Figure 3-17, shows a sampled color broken down into CIE color space components.

Colortron's Color Tweener tool can even create blends by showing you the color between two different colors. Colortron's Match tool allows you to find the match of a sampled color in a Pantone color library. Colortron's Lighting tool allows you

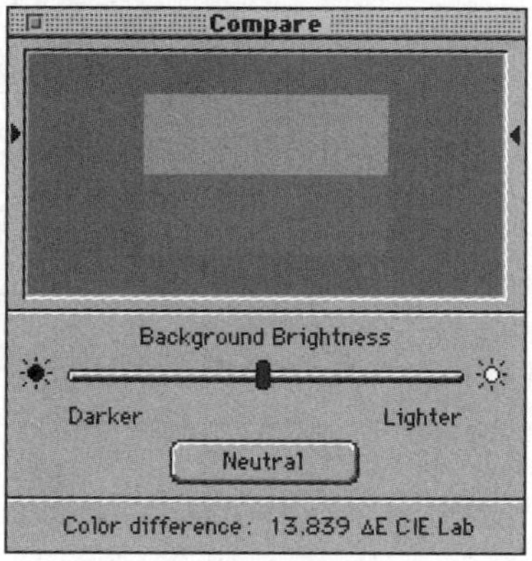

Colortron's
Compare
tool
measures the
difference
between two
colors

**FIGURE 3-15**

to predict how colors will appear under different light sources—including those you would use when evaluating color proofs (sample printouts).

**OTE:** *X-Rite's Digital Swatchbook is a color-capturing device that connects to a Macintosh through its serial port. Digital Swatchbook is also sold with software that matches Pantone colors, finds RGB and CMYK equivalents, and allows you to compare colors under different lighting conditions.*

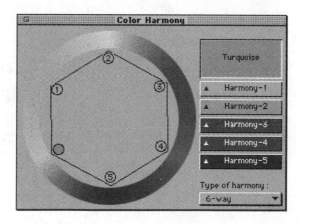

Colortron's
Color
Harmony
palette

**FIGURE 3-16**

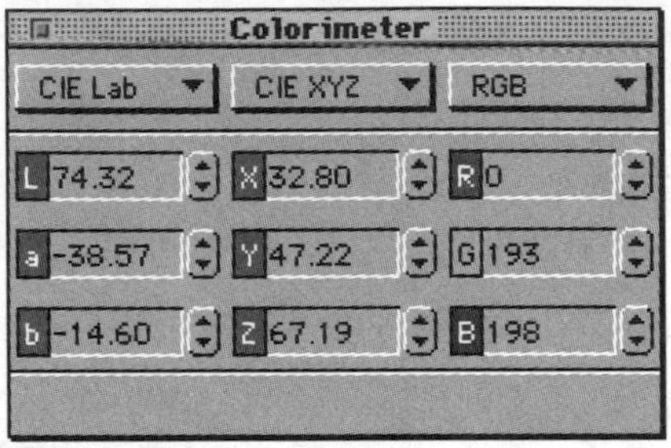

Colortron's
Colorimeter
tool displays
colors in
CIE color
space
components

**FIGURE 3-17**

# Conclusion

Now that you've learned the basics of creating color on the computer, you're ready to proceed to the next chapter to begin exploring the many different features graphics software has to offer.

# 4

# Digital Imaging Software Overview

The tools that digital artists and graphics users need to create images are many and diverse. Like a painter or sculptor, the digital artist needs the right tools to do a good job. These tools are computer graphics programs. Some graphics programs are specifically designed to emulate the effects of traditional media such as paintbrushes and airbrushes. Other programs are like digital Swiss Army knives, allowing you to do everything from painting to color-correcting images to creating animation.

If you will be creating, outputting, or supervising the production of digital images, it's important to know exactly what software is right for the job. For instance, you may try unsuccessfully to improve the quality of a scanned image in a page layout program, only to discover it easily could have been corrected in an image-editing program. You may spend hours trying to create a 3D effect in a painting or image-editing program, when it could have been created in minutes in a 3D modeling program. You may also try to use a scanned logo, but find that the scanned image looks ragged and unusable. The solution is to trace over the scanned logo and re-create it using a drawing program's Pen tool so that the logo looks sharp and can be resized without adversely affecting output quality.

Knowing what software packages are right for a specific job is not always easy. But if you plan to work with digital images, it's important to stay abreast of the latest developments in the software industry. Often the easiest way of staying up to date is to subscribe to computer magazines that focus on or frequently review graphics software. It's also important to gain a basic understanding of how different types of programs do their job. That's our goal in this chapter—to provide you with a concise overview of digital imaging software.

# Bitmap (Raster) vs. Vector Programs

Computer graphics programs are generally divided into two categories: *bitmap*, or *raster,* programs; and *vector,* or *draw,* programs. It's important to understand the distinction between the two types because each has its strengths and drawbacks.

## Bitmap (Raster) Programs

Most painting programs, such as Fractal Design Painter, and image-editing programs, such as Adobe Photoshop, are bitmap programs. In these programs, an image is created from a grid of tiny squares called *pixels*. The pixels are mapped to a specific location on a computer screen that is scanned from top to bottom. Since each pixel on the computer screen is mapped to a specific area of the screen, programs that create images this way are called bitmap or bitmapped programs. This grid of pixels is scanned from top to bottom in a procedure called *raster* scanning. Thus, bitmap programs are also referred to as raster programs.

*n* **OTE:** *The first bitmap programs only allowed for a one-bit pixel depth. This meant that each pixel in the image could either be on or off—black or white. Some programs, such as Photoshop, use the term "bitmap mode" to refer to black-and-white images only.*

Perhaps the easiest way to conceptualize how a bitmap image is created is to imagine a picture that is created by coloring the tiny squares on a sheet of graph paper. Each square has an exact location and can be addressed according to its row and column coordinates. Bitmap programs work in much the same way—they allow you to create and edit images according to the coordinates of each square pixel in the image.

In an image created by a bitmap program, the size of the pixels that compose the image are tiny, usually smaller than 1/72 inch. The pixels are so small that an image can appear as sharp as or sharper than a photograph. One of the reasons images look so realistic is that powerful bitmap programs can change any one of the hundreds of thousands of pixels in an image to any one of over 16 million colors.

But bitmap programs also have their drawbacks. When an image is created in a bitmap program, it's quite similar to an artist painting with real paint on a canvas. Once the paint is stroked onto the canvas, it begins to dry. Once the pixels in a bitmapped image are assigned a color, it's as if they also dry into place, into the rows and columns in the electronic canvas. This means that you can't easily alter parts of a bitmap image.

For instance, assume you paint a still life of fruit onscreen. After you're done, you decide to move one of the pieces of fruit an inch or two to the right. Unfortunately, the fruit is locked down on the same bed of pixels as the image background and all other elements. You can't just click on part of the image and move it. If you do attempt to move part of the image, you run the risk of destroying the entire picture. (Fortunately, software developers have designed solutions such as *layers* to help avoid this problem. When an image is in a layer, it's as if it's in a plane floating above the underlying pixels.)

Text in a bitmap program also presents problems. In most bitmap programs, you can usually edit text as you create it; but once you click someplace else on the screen, the type locks down as if it were painted on a canvas. If you wish to edit the text, you can't simply slip a cursor between two letters, delete one, and start typing again. Figure 4-1 shows a magnified view of text created in a bitmap program. Notice that you can see the jagged edges of the pixels composing the text. Since each pixel is locked down to the same image plane, individual letters cannot easily be deleted and retyped.

If you will be using bitmap programs, you also must take special care when outputting images, because image quality is tied to *resolution*, the number of pixels per inch in an image.

This means that the resolution of the image must be properly set before the image is output or before it is resized. If an image is created at too low a resolution, output quality can suffer, even if the output resolution—the number of dots per inch used for printing—is high. (To learn how resizing an image affects resolution and how to create images at the correct resolution for outputting, see Chapter 6.)

You might think the solution to this problem is to always create high-resolution images. Unfortunately, the higher the resolution of an image, the greater its file size. This can create a problem if you need to typeset a page of high-resolution text. In a bitmap program the file size would be gigantic. This is one reason why bitmap programs are not used for typesetting. When you do see type that is created in a bitmap program, it's often used for artistic effect, as shown in Figure 4-2.

## Vector Programs

Images created in vector, or drawing, programs are based upon mathematical formulas, not on pixel coordinates. The curves and lines that are created

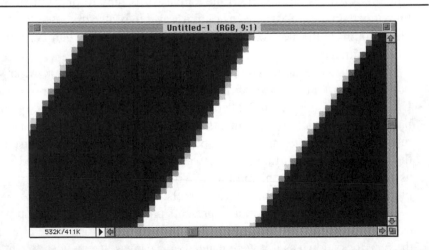

Individual
pixels from
type created
in a bitmap
program

**FIGURE 4-1**

Text effect created in Adobe Photoshop. Stock image courtesy of ColorBytes. Photograph by Joe Lange

**FIGURE 4-2**

mathematically are called *vectors*. Since mathematical formulas are used to define objects onscreen, image elements created in programs such as Adobe Illustrator, CorelDRAW, and Macromedia Freehand can easily be moved and resized. Often, all you need to do to move an object is to click on it and drag. The computer recalculates its position. As you resize an object, the computer recalculates its size. Since the image is created mathematically, drawing programs are usually used for work that requires crisp sharp lines. They're also often used for logos and visual symbols that need to be output at many different sizes.

When you output an image created in a vector program, quality is based not on image resolution but on the resolution of the output device—the number of dots per inch printed. This means that an image output on an imagesetter at 2,540 dots per inch will look much better than if it were output on a 300 or 600 dpi laser printer. Since image quality is not based on resolution, images created in vector programs typically have smaller file sizes than those created in bitmap programs.

If you want to output high-resolution type in a drawing program, you need only create the file, type the text, and output it on a high-resolution device. As mentioned earlier, if you were using a bitmap program, you might need to boost the resolution so high that the file size would be enormous. This is one reason why typographical effects such as those seen in Figure 4-3 are often created in drawing programs.

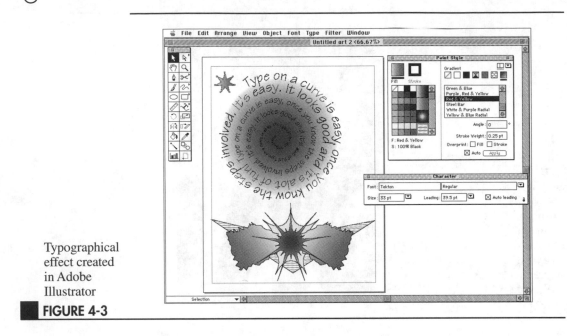

Typographical
effect created
in Adobe
Illustrator

**FIGURE 4-3**

# Painting Programs

In 1984, Apple Computer began the computer graphics revolution when it introduced the Macintosh. Along with each Macintosh sold, Apple gave away a simple painting program called MacPaint. Although MacPaint would be considered crude by today's standards, it proved that a desktop computer could be used to create sophisticated graphics. It also proved that the software to create graphics need not be difficult to learn.

Today, computer paint programs are like digital art supply stores. They're packed with features that emulate not only the paintbrush, paint, and paper textures, but virtually all other artistic media. Programs like Fauve Matisse, Fractal Design Painter, and Pixel Resource's PixelPaint allow you to create images with digital versions of airbrushes, pencils, pens, and paintbrushes. Fractal Design Painter even provides an Image Hose brush that can paint using pieces of digital images.

Most high-end paint programs allow you to create custom brushes, patterns, and paper grains for image backgrounds. Many paint programs also allow you to access third-party plug-ins primarily created for Adobe Photoshop. *Plug-ins* (often called filters) are programs that can be accessed without exiting the painting programs. Most plug-ins allow you to create special effects (plug-ins are covered later in this chapter).

Many paint programs also allow you to perform image-editing tasks. Painter, PixelPaint, and Fauve Matisse all allow you to scan an image directly into the program. They also provide a sprinkling of color-correcting and retouching controls, some similar to those found in Adobe Photoshop, HSC Live Picture, and Micrografx Picture Publisher.

Despite these features, painting programs should not be seen as replacements for image-editing programs because image-editing programs generally feature more sophisticated commands for color correcting and image manipulation. Most users who work in image-editing programs often use painting programs to add special brush effects to their images. None of the major image-editing programs provide as many different brush and media styles as the leading paint programs.

# Drawing Programs

The first drawing programs on the market, such as MacDraw and Micrografx Draw, were often used to create simple floor plans, drawings, and organization charts. Simplicity gave way to sophistication with the arrival of Adobe Illustrator and Aldus Freehand (now Macromedia Freehand). These new programs were the first crop of *PostScript* drawing programs. PostScript is a *page description language* first developed for the Macintosh by John Warnock and Charles Geschke of Adobe Systems. A page description language is essentially a computer programming language specifically designed for creating and manipulating type and graphics. PostScript provides a means of creating sophisticated curves and type effects and outputting them at high resolutions.

PostScript allowed drawing programs to offer a *Pen tool* that could create *Bézier curves* (named after the French mathematician Pierre Bézier who showed how curves could be controlled mathematically). Using a Bézier curve, the digital artist could finally create perfect, smooth curves, essential to producing beautiful and intricate artwork. Pen tools also allowed artists to trace over scanned black-and-white logos to create clean logos without jagged edges.

 **OTE:**   *Adobe Streamline is a software package specifically designed to trace over scanned images and create digital drawings out of them.*

Today's high-end drawing programs are so packed with features that they're used in the creation of all types of illustrations, including advertisements, book covers, and magazine illustrations, to name a few.

One reason high-end drawing programs are so widely used is that you can do much more than draw in them. All of the major drawing programs allow you to create custom *gradients* in which one color gradually blends into another. Gradients can be used as backgrounds and to create lighting effects. High-end drawing programs also allow type to bend around curves, and individual pieces of letters to be stretched and twisted. Figure 4-4 shows an image created in CorelDRAW in which the text of the product label follows the curvature of the bottle. Adobe Illustrator and Macromedia Freehand also provide *filters* that allow you to create drop shadows at the click of a button.

Illustrator, Freehand, and CorelDRAW also allow the importing of scanned images. This makes it possible, to some extent, for such drawing programs to be used as page layout programs that integrate text and graphics on one page. But if you want to produce long documents that combine text and graphics, you're better off using page layout programs, which are designed to handle documents with many pages.

# Page Layout Programs

*Page layout programs* allow you to integrate text and graphics to create newsletters, magazines, brochures, and advertisements. Among the most popular programs are Adobe PageMaker, Corel Ventura, FrameMaker, and QuarkXPress.

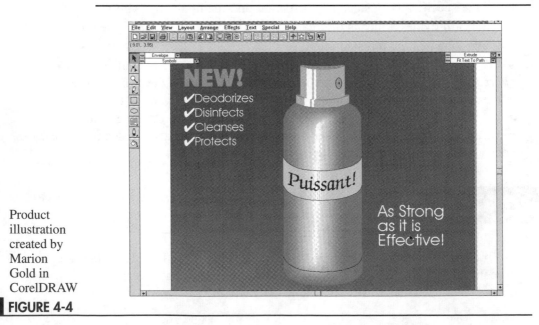

Product illustration created by Marion Gold in CorelDRAW

**FIGURE 4-4**

Most page layout programs are used to assemble elements on a page rather than create text and graphics from scratch. Text for long documents is typically written in word processors and then imported into the program. Although most page layout programs include basic drawing tools, these tools are primarily used for drawing lines and creating borders. Graphics are often created in drawing and image-editing software, then imported into the page layout program. Figure 4-5 shows text and graphics integrated into a QuarkXPress page. The globe image was imported into the layout from an Image Club Graphics CD-ROM.

Although the features of all major page layout software overlaps, different products have gained popularity for different reasons. For instance, PageMaker is generally considered the easiest to use of the high-end page layout programs, primarily because it uses a pasteboard metaphor familiar to most artists and designers. Although PageMaker was largely responsible for helping spark the desktop publishing revolution, it was gradually overtaken in sales by QuarkXPress on the Mac. As more and more advertising agencies and magazines switched production to the computer, they began to choose QuarkXPress for its sophisticated typographic features. As more and more computer users began working in color, QuarkXPress retained its lead because it was one of the first page layout programs to allow four-color separations to be created from the desktop. Today, QuarkXPress is still the most popular page layout program, although it does lack a few features, such as indexing, that PageMaker and FrameMaker offer.

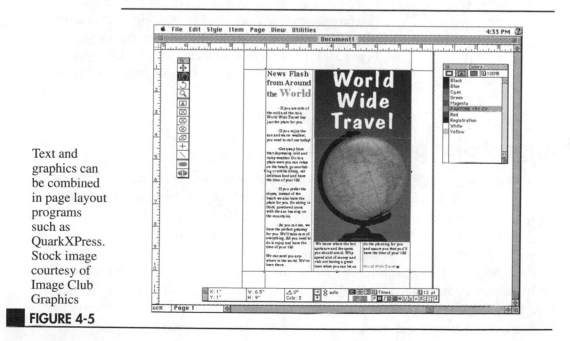

Text and graphics can be combined in page layout programs such as QuarkXPress. Stock image courtesy of Image Club Graphics

**FIGURE 4-5**

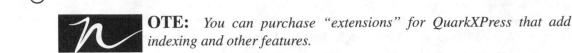

**OTE:** *You can purchase "extensions" for QuarkXPress that add indexing and other features.*

Of all the major page layout programs, Corel Ventura is the only program that is not available on the Macintosh platform. The program was created by the Xerox Corporation and later sold to Corel Corporation. It became popular because of its ability to publish long documents such as books. Many of the major computer book publishing companies use Corel Ventura.

Although not the most popular in terms of sales, FrameMaker is certainly one of the most feature-packed. FrameMaker began its life on the UNIX computer platform and later migrated to Mac and PC desktops. Many companies, particularly those with UNIX workstations, use FrameMaker to create technical manuals. FrameMaker is primarily used for long documents requiring indexes, tables of contents, and multiple chapters. FrameMaker not only allows you to assign style names to text paragraphs as other page layout programs do, but also allows you to assign style names to individual characters as well. One of its most helpful features is its ability to easily create complex mathematical equations and an assortment of different tabular formats. It also features a *conditional document* format which allows you to create multiple versions of a document that are based upon one

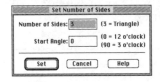

document. When a conditional document is output, specific words and graphics replace words and graphics in the text based upon pre-set conditions. FrameMaker also provides a few more graphic capabilities than most other page layout programs. For instance, shown here is the FrameMaker Set Sides command, which allows you to quickly create triangles or polygons out of other graphics.

# Image-Editing Programs

Image-editing programs let you color-correct, retouch, and create dazzling effects from digital images. Using digital imaging software such as Adobe Photoshop, HSC Live Picture, Micrografx Picture Publisher, Fauve Xres, or Corel PhotoPaint, you can create collages, vignettes, photo montages, and prepare digital images for color printing. Today, image-editing programs are used in virtually every printed image that requires a photograph. They're used to remove wrinkles from models' faces, brighten up dark and cloudy days, and change moods with special lighting effects. They are also commonly used by multimedia producers to create type and background effects, and change the number of colors in an image.

# TIPS of the TRADE

It's a bird. It's a plane. It's New York City's Flat Iron Building!

Robert Bowen, an artist and principle of Robert Bowen Studios, a high-end facility in New York City for creating computer visual effects, photo-design, and retouching for print media, created this intriguing image using Adobe Photoshop on a Macintosh and Barco Creator on a Silicon Graphics workstation. Robert believes that playing with symmetry can create very interesting effects.

"Anything is symmetrical unto itself," says Robert. "A lot of artists work with symmetry, but there is something visually cacophonous about perfect symmetry, and so it helps the design process to throw symmetry off balance or edit it and make slight changes to it."

Robert rotated the Flat Iron building in one file using Barco Creator, and rebuilt the sky in another. Then he composited the building with the sky in Adobe Photoshop, and added motion using the Motion Blur filter. He used two layers in Photoshop—one for the sky and the other for the building. By using two layers, Robert could move the building in different positions until he was satisfied with the results. Finally, he placed the composited image in Barco Creator and added the birds as flying companions for the building.

Programs likc Adobe Photoshop and HSC Live Picture feature many tools and options that help seamlessly blend one image into another. The many features provided by image-editing programs also allow you to work in layers. Using layers, you can work as if image elements were created on different sheets of clear acetate. This allows you to edit images in one layer independently of the images in other layers.

Figure 4-6 shows an image created using Photoshop layers. First the background was created in Fractal Design Painter, then loaded into Photoshop. Photographs were scanned and placed into layers. The 3D brush holder in the lower-left corner and the sphere in the lower-right corner below the painter's palette were created in Strata VisionPro, and then loaded into the final image.

Apart from creating special effects (see Chapter 15, for more information about creating special effects), most image-editing software allows you to digitize an image directly into the software. Once an image is digitized or is opened into an image-editing program, it can be color-corrected, resized, or retouched. Afterwards, the image can be placed in a page layout or drawing program before being printed or placed in multimedia programs such as Macromedia Director.

# Special Effects Programs

*Special effects programs* have had an enormous impact on computer graphics over the past few years. Some special effects programs can take a flat 2D image and bend

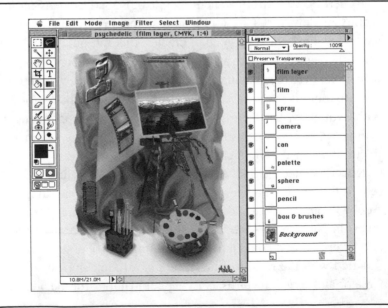

A collage created using layers in Adobe Photoshop by Adele Droblas Greenberg

**FIGURE 4-6**

it, spherize it, or transform it into a 3D cube. Others can take a real life image and transform it to look like it was created in water or oil paints. The speed and ease with which some of these effects can be created has convinced more and more artists to enter the world of computer graphics.

Most special effects software is designed to enhance the capabilities of editing and painting programs. Such software programs are often called *plug-ins* because they can operate within other software programs such as Adobe Photoshop, Micrografx Picture Publisher, Fractal Design Painter, and Corel PhotoPaint. Plug-ins are also called filters because many produce effects similar to those created by photographic filters. The variety of effects created by plug-ins is enormous. In fact, an entire industry has grown up around creating plug-ins for programs like Photoshop and Painter.

The best-known special effects plug-in is Kai's Power Tools (KPT). Using KPT, you can make a menu choice or click on an onscreen button and transform an image into a beautiful marble texture. Other amazing KPT effects include folding part of an image over itself to create a page turn, or making the image look as if it were seen through a fish-eye lens.

Another popular set of software plug-ins provides 3D effects. Using Andromeda Software plug-ins, you can quickly transform an image so that it is floating in a 3D cube or sphere. Other well-known plug-ins include Adobe Gallery Effects and Xaos Tools Paint Alchemy; both can add painterly effects to digital images.

If you're interested in learning more about special effects software, see Chapter 15. You'll see a variety of examples of how plug-ins such as Knoll Software's CyberMesh, and Alien Skin's Black Box. These and other stand-alone special effects programs such as KPT Bryce, Adobe TextureMaker, Specular TextureScape, and Alien Skin Textureshop by Virtus (both a stand-alone product and a plug-in) can produce startling effects. Chapter 15 also covers how morphing software such as Elastic Reality, Gryphon Morph, and HSC Morph can take one image and magically transform it into a completely new one.

# 3D Modeling and Rendering Programs

Stunningly realistic effects can be created by 3D modeling and rendering programs, everything from simple models of everyday objects to space stations hurtling through space.

Many 3D programs are used as temporary stops for images that eventually find their way into image-editing software or multimedia programs. For instance, the creators of the best-selling CD-ROM Myst (see color insert for a sample image) created their fantastic 3D world in Strata StudioPro, a Macintosh 3D modeling program. Later the images were placed into the multimedia software program Claris HyperCard, which does not provide for 3D imaging. (It allows for navigational programming.)

If you're interested in entering the third dimension of image editing, prepare to spend some learning time before your first spaceship rolls off the digital assembly line. To use 3D modeling programs, the user must work and think in 3D space governed by X, Y, and Z axes.

Although most 3D modeling programs are vector-based, the programs work quite differently than standard draw programs. In most 3D modeling programs, you start by creating wire-frame models of shapes. Most programs include primitives—basic shapes such as cubes and polyhedrons that you can load onscreen and use in their own form or easily convert into other shapes. The process of turning the wire-frame shapes (as shown in Figure 4-7a) into 3D object with lighting and texture (as shown in Figure 4-7b) is called *rendering*. Rendering a 3D image can take as little as a few minutes or as long as hours or even days, depending on the computer and the software as well as the image complexity and rendering option used.

*n* **OTE:** *Most rendering software takes a vector-based image and renders it into a bitmap image. Adobe Dimensions, however, is a 3D vector-based program that does not create a bitmap image when it renders. 3D images in Dimensions are always vector-based. Figure 4-8b shows a 3D image created in Adobe Dimensions from the wire frame shown in Figure 4-8a.*

Choosing a 3D modeling program can be quite difficult because using the software requires a knowledge of terms unfamiliar to most computer users. Once you start analyzing 3D software, you'll encounter words such as *spline modeling*, *Boolean operations,* and *NURBS*. If you find these terms confusing, you'll be happy to know that the mystery of such features as NURBS and spline modeling is unraveled in Chapter 11.

# Virtual Reality Walkthrough Software

3D software also allows the user to walk through images. Most walkthrough programs are helpful in visualizing architectural and construction work. They are also being used by film production companies to plan shooting sequences. Programs like Virtus Walkthrough allow you to create a 2D model in one window, while a

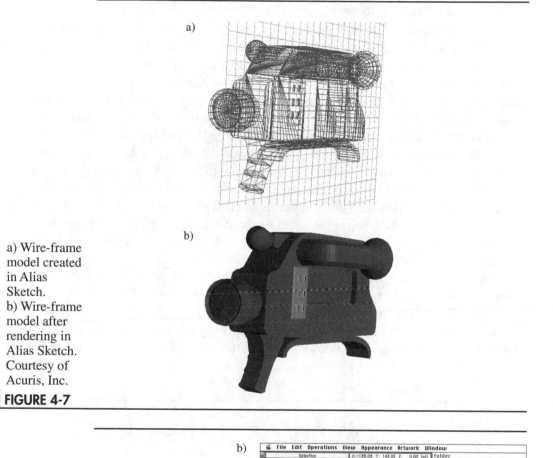

a) Wire-frame
model created
in Alias
Sketch.
b) Wire-frame
model after
rendering in
Alias Sketch.
Courtesy of
Acuris, Inc.

**FIGURE 4-7**

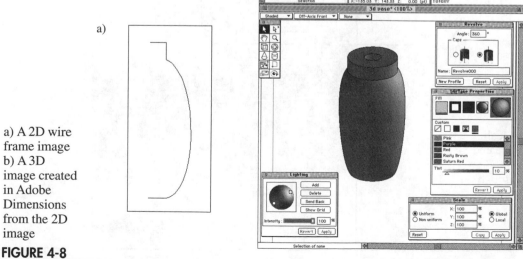

a) A 2D wire
frame image
b) A 3D
image created
in Adobe
Dimensions
from the 2D
image

**FIGURE 4-8**

"live" walkthrough 3D model is created in another window. After you set the entry point, the program animates the scenery as if you were walking through the building.

Virtus Walkthrough Pro is a complete 3D dimensional walkthrough program that allows you to create your own 3D walkthrough environment, then animate the process of walking through the environment. The program features drawing tools and basic 3D objects that allow you to create a 3D environment. One of its more unusual tools is its Slice tool which can slice a three-dimensional object, and thereby provide it with another surface. Rendering is handled by flat and smooth shaders—with the smooth shader providing the most realistic effects. Once you've created your environment, you can walk through it and record each step of your walk. Figure 4-9 shows a walkthrough scene created in Virtus Walkthrough Pro. The cube in the figure shows the orientation of the observer in the walkthrough world. The slider in the image allows you to adjust the zoom factor of the observing "lens." If you look carefully at the floor plan, you'll see a circle with a line from its center. This circle indicates the position of the observer in 2D space.

Virtus Walkthrough Pro is packaged with a step-by-step tutorial which leads you through the process of creating a model that includes a few rooms, a roof, and a steeple. The Mac version of the program can save in QuickTime format; the Windows version can save in AVI format. The program ships with Virtus player which provides anyone who does not have Virtus Walkthrough with the ability to walk through your 3D world.

You are here

Virtual reality image created in Virtus Walkthrough Pro. Image courtesy of Virtus

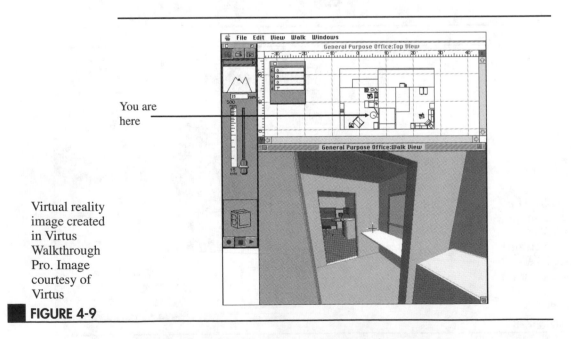

**FIGURE 4-9**

Virtus VR is an inexpensive entry-level virtual reality program. Walkthrough environments are created by dragging and dropping pre-constructed objects from galleries. Thus, no object needs to be constructed from scratch. The program allows you to resize and reshape objects as well as add textures, such as clouds, grass, carpets, wood, tile, etc. As you create and combine objects together, Virtus VR renders them into 3D objects in a "cyberspace" window through which you can roam using your mouse.

*n* **OTE:**  *Virtus also sells Virtus VR Galleries, a series of preconstructed 3D objects that can help speed creation of walkthrough projects. VR galleries includes office, home, and ancient ruin models, as well as spaceships and space stations. Objects are compatible with both Virtus VR and Virtus Walkthough Pro.*

Strata Virtual 3D allows users of StrataVision 3D and Strata StudioPro (Strata's modeling, rendering, and animation packages) to enter the world of virtual reality. Essentially, Strata Virtual 3D takes models created in Vision 3D and StudioPro and renders them to create virtual walkthrough environments. Once the models are rendered, you can use Strata Virtual navigational tools to walk through the 3D environment. The program's manual likens its navigational tools to an automobile's, controlled by the mouse. When you click and drag on the mouse, you can steer, accelerate, and brake as you move through the 3D environment. Figure 4-10 shows a walkthrough image created in Strata Virtual 3D.

# CAD/CAM Programs

CAD/CAM programs are vector-based software that allows architects and artists to create blueprints and floor plans. Some even allow 2D images to be rendered into 3D models.

Undoubtedly, the best-known CAD/CAM program is Autodesk's AutoCAD, which costs several thousand dollars. AutoCAD not only creates floor plans, but also provides multiple 3D views of images created. It can even help you budget a large architectural or engineering project.

As you might expect, high-end CAD/CAM programs can be quite complicated to use. If you're a newcomer to CAD/CAM, you might wish to start with Autodesk AutoCAD LT for Windows. Mac and Windows users who want a very powerful, yet user-friendly CAD program should investigate Graphsoft's award-winning MiniCAD.

Walkthrough image created in Strata Virtual 3D. Image courtesy of Strata

**FIGURE 4-10**

MiniCAD features 2D drafting, interactive 3D modeling, and database and spreadsheet reporting. For advanced users, it includes a macro programming language. MiniCAD also provides 3D walkthrough and "flyover" capabilities, and automatic roof, wall, and floor tools. It automatically shows dimensions of objects onscreen and allows for the creation of unlimited layers. Figure 4-11 shows a 3D model of a house created in MiniCAD. By clicking in the Set Up window, you switch views to see the foundation, or the first or second floor plan.

If you need drafting capabilities but don't require 3D features, you might wish to investigate Graphsoft Blueprint, which can often be purchased for under $200. Blueprint can be used to create floorplans, technical illustrations, and landscapes, as shown in Figure 4-12. Blueprint features numerous drawing tools as well as tools that trim, butt, and join walls. It also features a "Duplicate Along Path" command, which allows you to quickly duplicate and space multiple objects along a straight or curved line. If desired, images created in Blueprint can be exported into MiniCAD to create 3D models.

# Multimedia

Multimedia programs allow you to combine digital images and sound to create animated or interactive presentations. Productions created from multimedia software are used for training, business presentations, and CD-ROM productions.

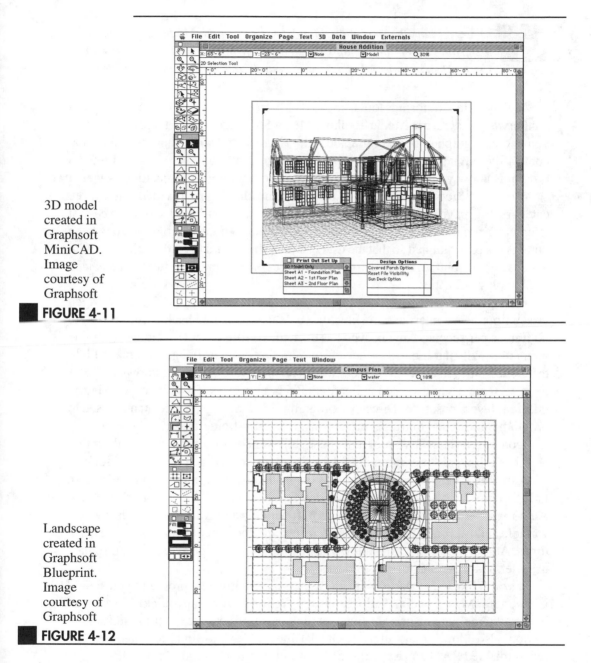

3D model created in Graphsoft MiniCAD. Image courtesy of Graphsoft

**FIGURE 4-11**

Landscape created in Graphsoft Blueprint. Image courtesy of Graphsoft

**FIGURE 4-12**

Multimedia programs generally fall into two categories: interactive authoring tools and video-editing programs. Both groups of programs can also be used to create animation from digital images.

**OTE:** *Linker Animation Stand is a high-end Macintosh animation program that emulates sophisticated cell-frame animation. It allows you to create many special effects, add sound, and work in multiple layers.*

Multimedia authoring tools such as Macromedia Director, Macromedia Authorware, Asymetric Media Toolbox, Media Shop, and Claris HyperCard allow you to create graphics or place graphics onto a screen and write short programs that control the navigation of those graphics through a production. Most multimedia programs allow you to play digital video clips from within a presentation as well.

Most interactive multimedia authoring products are divided into three categories: 1) page- or card-based, 2) time-based, or 3) icon-based. Often the easiest interactive programs to learn and use are card-based. In these programs, onscreen buttons are programmed so that the user can jump from card to card by clicking with a mouse on the button. Cards can contain images or scrolling text fields, and can be used to play animation.

Perhaps the best-known multimedia program is Macromedia Director, which uses a time-based interface. In Director, you can set the playback speed from 1 to 30 frames per second. Anyone who has ever edited film or created frame-by-frame animation will find himself or herself on familiar ground. Images are placed into different frames in different tracks, called channels. This interface allows Director to easily create sophisticated animation effects almost as if you were working in different layers onscreen. Director's programming language, Lingo, can be used to program buttons and to trigger effects on a frame-by-frame-basis.

Icon-based interactive programs make allowances for users who would rather not hear the word "programming." In an icon-based interactive software such as Macromedia Authorware, navigation is controlled by assembling icons, as shown in Figure 4-13. To access images, you double-click on one of the icons. If needed, Authorware allows for the scripting of functions and variables. Authorware's variables allow you to count and store correct and incorrect responses and elapsed times. Authorware's functions allow you to jump from one file to another, and create user-defined functions for custom tasks.

If you'd like to get started with an easy-to-use multimedia program, you should investigate Macromedia Action!. Using Action!, you can quickly create an interactive multimedia presentation that includes user-activated buttons and sound. Action! also allows you to integrate QuickTime movies into your presentations. The recommended RAM for Action! is 5MB; minimum RAM required is 4MB.

Digital video-editing programs such as Adobe Premiere and Adobe After Effects (formerly Cosa After Effects) are also quite popular among multimedia producers.

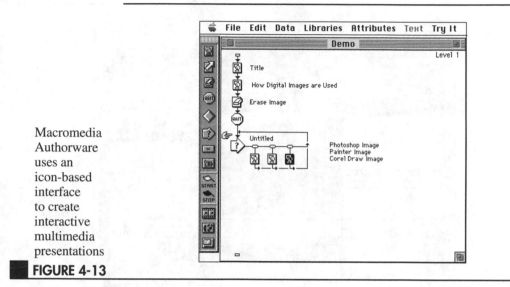

Macromedia
Authorware
uses an
icon-based
interface
to create
interactive
multimedia
presentations

**FIGURE 4-13**

Premiere allows you to create digital movies on the Mac and on the PC. Movies can be created by assembling stills, text, and digitized video. The digital image format used by the Mac is called QuickTime, created by Apple Computer. Microsoft's digital movie format is called AVI—Audio Video Interleave. Premiere creates QuickTime movies on the Mac and AVI movies on the PC. Figure 4-14 shows Premiere's digital movie-editing set-up. In this image, two QuickTime stock movie clips from CD-ROMs were loaded into Premiere's A and B video tracks. Track A includes a video clip from Wayzata's World of Motion stock clips. Track B includes a video clip and soundtrack from BeachWare's MultiWare Multi-Media Collection.

Both Adobe Premiere and Adobe After Effects allow you to not only assemble movies but also to create effects commonly seen on television. These effects include dissolves and mattes in which one image is superimposed over another. For professional video users, one of Premiere's most helpful features is its edit decision list (often referred to as EDL) feature. This feature allows you to do a pre-edit on your Mac or PC, then have the edit replicated on high-end equipment.

Macromedia's Mediamaker is another program that allows users to assemble video, sound, and still frames on the desktop. Mediamaker can also be used to control videotape and videodisc players—if you have a videoboard connected to your computer. Using Mediamaker, you can click an onscreen button that resembles the controls of a videotape recorder to play a sequence from a VCR or camcorder that can be used in your multimedia production.

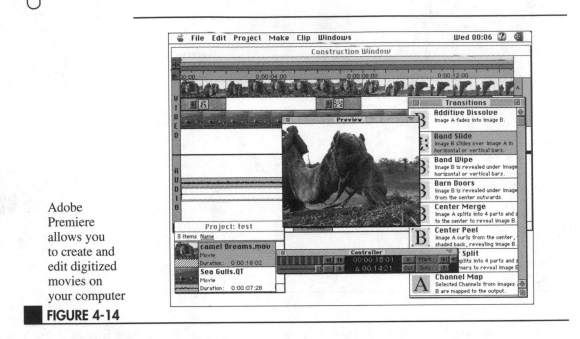

Adobe
Premiere
allows you
to create and
edit digitized
movies on
your computer

**FIGURE 4-14**

*𝓃* **OTE:**   *To learn how to use multimedia software, see Chapter 16.*

# Presentation Programs

Not too long ago, creating a sales or business presentation meant you had to spend endless hours writing the text, waiting for the art department to create charts and other graphics, and waiting for the images to be returned from a slide outputting service. On the dreaded day of the presentation, you had to spend time nervously juggling the slides into a slide projector to ensure that they were in the right order and were not placed into the slide trays upside down.

Computer presentation programs such as Adobe Persuasion, Gold Disk Astound, Macromedia Action!, and Microsoft PowerPoint make creating a presentation a breeze. Most programs allow you to start a presentation in an outline view where you can write your presentation and collect your thoughts, unhindered by worries about what the actual slides or overhead presentation images look like. In the outline view, you type the title of the slide and text. When you later move to slide view, the text automatically appears on the slide.

Most presentation programs also feature many preset slide or background templates. *Templates* usually feature preset background textures and colors, with typeface and size already in place. If you want to edit or create text on the sliders, presentation programs allow you to change fonts, styles, and colors and to format the text with bullets or hanging indents. Most also include mini-drawing programs that allow you to create shapes and simple drawings. If you don't want to create your own art with the presentation program's drawing tools, you can import art created in other programs, or load clip art that is supplied with the program. Figure 4-15 shows a slide being created from a template in Adobe Persuasion along with clip art that is included with the program.

Many presentation programs usually include graphing modules so that you don't need to leave the program to create graphs. Perhaps the most impressive feature of presentation programs is that they can create an animated slide show. This allows you to specify transitional effects such as screen and Venetian blind dissolves. You can also make bulleted text dissolve on the screen, fly, or drop down into view one bullet point at a time.

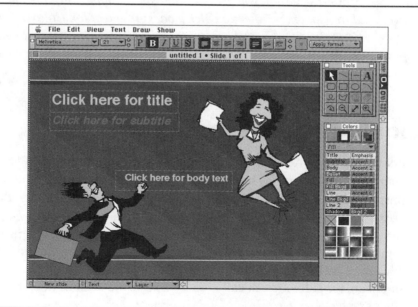

Template
with Clipart
in Adobe
Persuasion

**FIGURE 4-15**

# Screen Capture Programs

Screen capture programs are used to take snapshots of your computer screen. Frequently, the captured images are saved in TIFF or PICT format and placed in page layout or multimedia programs. Computer training manuals, books, and instructional CD-ROMs make use of screen capture programs. On the PC, one of the most popular screenshot programs is Inset Systems Highjack Pro, which allows you to capture DOS and Windows screens and save them in different file formats such as TIFF, BMP, and PICT. For years, Mainstays Capture has been one of the most popular Macintosh screenshot programs. Mainstay recently released a new screenshot program called Captivate, which not only allows you to capture and save screenshots in TIFF, PICT, or GIF format, but also provides a module that allows you to play sounds and movies and to quickly view TIFF and PICT images. The program also includes Captivate View, a module that provides utilities for cropping, rotating, and scaling images.

**OTE:** *Pantone ColorUP is a program designed to help you choose matching colors for business presentations. You start by choosing the type of presentation you are creating: slides, paper, onscreen presentation, or overhead transparency. After you pick a background color, ColorUP builds a series of color palettes filled with harmonious colors that can be exported to different programs. ColorUP even assigns the colors that should be used for text, text shadows, outlines, highlighted words, graphs, and bullets.*

# Image Database Programs

Image database programs provide an electronic file card system to keep track of your images. Some of the better-known image database programs are Adobe Fetch, Imspace Kudo Image Browser, Kodak Shoebox, and ULead Image Pals.

Most of these programs provide thumbnail versions of the images on disk so you can quickly browse through images without loading the actual image file. Image database software also includes data entry screens in which you can enter a title and other relevant information about each image in the database. When you need to find an image, the software can call it up by a keyword such as title, date, category, or photographer.

One of the most important features offered by image database programs is that they keep track of the images in a small catalog file, meaning that your images don't need to be on the same hard disk as the image database software. Prices for image database software usually run from one hundred to several hundred dollars. Adobe Fetch even offers a multiuser version of Fetch, so that users on a network can all use the same image database at the same time.

# Conclusion

You should now have a good idea of the different types of software used to create digital images. In later chapters, you'll learn specifics about how to create digital images. In the next chapter, you'll learn about digital imaging file formats. Once you understand these, you'll be able to export or import images from one program to another, or to export them for specific types of printing output.

# 5

## Using Digital File Formats

A digital image often visits several graphics software packages before it is finally printed or appears in a multimedia or business presentation. Typically, the image may be shuttled from program to program for corrections, enhancements, or the addition of special effects. Using this approach, artists and other digital image users can take advantage of the power of many different software packages. For instance, a digital image may be scanned directly into Adobe Photoshop where it is sharpened and color-corrected. The image may then be exported to a painting program such as Fractal Design Painter to add painterly effects. While in Photoshop or Painter, textures can be created that will later be applied in 3D graphics software. If the image is being created for a book or magazine article, the next stop might be a page layout program such as QuarkXPress or Adobe PageMaker. If it's intended for a multimedia production, it might be exported to Macromedia Director or Macromedia Authorware.

Transferring an image from one program or computer platform to another is extremely common in the digital imaging world because each graphics program has specific strengths and weaknesses. To take advantage of the strengths, images must be imported and exported quickly and efficiently. To smooth this process, software developers have created a set of computer file formats that most software programs can read. In many respects these file formats are like a common language. When computer software can read and save files in a common language, even digital images created in a proprietary software package can take advantage of what other packages have to offer.

This chapter focuses on some of the most common file formats used to create digital images. As a computer graphics user, you should understand the differences between graphics file formats in order to take an image created in one program and export it to another. You also may be asked by a prepress house or service bureau to save your file in a format such as TIFF or EPS so the file can be output by that company's equipment. Although it may sound technical, the subject of file formats is really quite simple. For the most part, you just need to know what formats are available, and how to save a file in a particular format. In most software, saving in a different file format other than the one used to create an image is usually handled by choosing a file format in a dialog box, and occasionally by specifying a few saving options.

# Native File Formats

Normally, when you save a file in a graphics application, you save it in its own *native* file format. A program's native file format is usually a proprietary format created specifically for the software you are using. In most software this format is the most efficient means of saving a file. Typically, the steps are simple—you choose Save from the File menu, then enter a name for the file, then click the Save or OK button. Figure 5-1 shows the Save dialog box used by Fractal Design Painter. Although you could save the file in a number of different formats, Fractal Design's native format RIFF is generally used. Files saved in the RIFF format have the advantage of being quickly loaded and opened in Painter whether they are saved on the Mac or PC version of the program.

If you are creating a file that will be exported to other programs or sent to a service bureau, you will probably need to save it in a different file format other than the one in which it was created. The two most commonly used graphics formats for print media are EPS and TIFF.

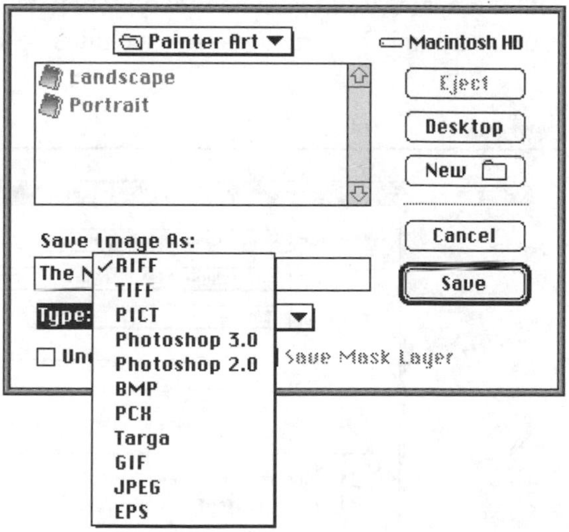

Fractal
Design
Painter's
Save dialog
box

**FIGURE 5-1**

# EPS File Format

EPS (Encapsulated PostScript) is one of the most widely used graphics file formats. Images created in both drawing and painting programs can often be saved in EPS format. Most page layout programs, such as QuarkXPress, Corel Ventura, Adobe PageMaker, and Frame Technology's FrameMaker all read files saved in EPS format.

When you save an image in EPS format, you usually must do more than just name a file and click the Save button. Most programs that save in EPS format provide a variety of choices. Figure 5-2, which shows Adobe Photoshop's EPS Save dialog box, illustrates some of these choices.

## Common EPS Saving Options

When you save a file in EPS format, the following options are provided:

▶ Preview—EPS files are often placed in page layout programs that provide a low-resolution image preview which can quickly be resized and manipulated in the page layout program. You can choose whether you want a preview file, and whether you want the preview file to be in black and white or color.

▶ ASCII/Binary—An EPS file can be saved in ASCII (often called text format) or binary format. Text files are often twice as large as binary files. Since binary files are smaller, they are more efficient to use. However, since not all graphics files can read binary EPS files, most packages that allow you to save in EPS format provide a choice between ASCII and Binary.

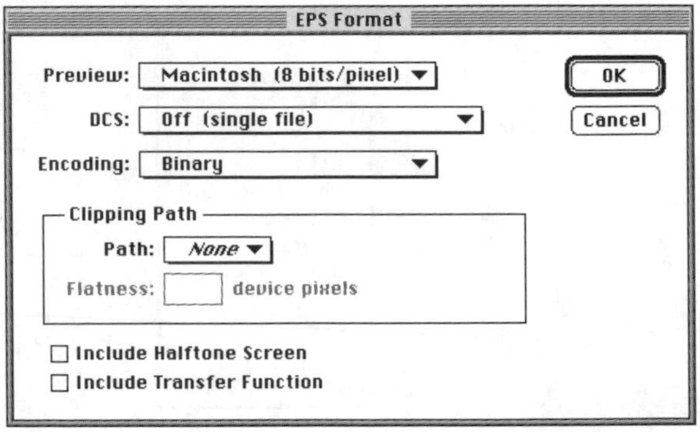

Adobe
Photoshop's
EPS Save
dialog box

**FIGURE 5-2**

## DCS

Many programs that allow you to save in EPS format include a DCS (document color separation) option. DCS is used for exporting CMYK files into page layout programs. The file format is used to help reduce the image data size of CMYK files that are loaded into page layout programs.

The DCS file format (occasionally referred to as EPS 5) is composed of five files. Four of the files contain CMYK color data information. The fifth file is used as a low-resolution composite that appears as a preview image in the page layout program.

 **OTE:**  *Some new versions of software support DCS 2.0, which can save color data for more than just the four CMYK components. Thus, saving a file in DCS 2.0 could result in more than five files.*

# TIFF

The TIFF file format is frequently used to save both Mac and PC bitmap files. Most image-editing and painting and scanning software packages allow you to save in TIFF format. Drawing programs usually do not provide a TIFF format (CorelDRAW is a notable exception). Virtually all page layout programs allow TIFF files to be imported.

Many file utility programs such as Equilibrium DeBabelizer and some image-editing programs such as Photoshop allow the TIFF file to be saved in either Mac or PC TIFF format. They often allow the TIFF format to be compressed using LZW compression. LZW is

| TIFF Options |
|:---|
| ┌─ Byte Order ─┐   ┌──── OK ────┐ |
| ○ IBM PC |
| ● Macintosh    ┌── Cancel ──┐ |
| ⊠ LZW Compression |

a *non-lossy* compression format. This means that when the file is compressed, data is not subtracted; therefore, no loss of quality should occur. Photoshop's TIFF Options dialog box, shown here, allows you to save a file in either Mac or PC TIFF format.

# JPEG

The JPEG file format is a popular format used to compress files. JPEG (Joint Photographic Experts Group) is a *lossy* file format. This means that image data is subtracted when the file is compressed, possibly causing loss of image quality. Most programs that provide for JPEG compression allow the user to choose the quality of the final image. If the user picks high quality, less compression occurs. When the low-quality setting is used, the file size is smaller but the image quality suffers more.

# PICT

PICT is a Macintosh file format created by Apple Computer as a graphics standard for Macintosh software. PICT is widely available in most Macintosh painting and drawing programs, and even PC programs such as CorelDRAW. An added benefit of saving color files in PICT format is that file size is often smaller than in many other formats. If you will be creating images to be loaded into the Macintosh version of Macromedia Director, Macromedia Authorware, Adobe Premiere, or Adobe After Effects, you should save your images as PICT files.

 **OTE:** *Adobe Premiere and Fractal Design Painter allow you to load and save an animated or digital video sequence as a Numbered PICT file. This format outputs frames as individual, consecutively numbered PICT files for use in multimedia software.*

# Photoshop

Photoshop is unquestionably the most popular image-editing software in the world. It is widely used in design studios and prepress houses, and it comes bundled free with a variety of different scanners. The popularity of Photoshop has prompted file utility programs such as Equilibrium DeBabelizer, and graphics programs such as Fractal Design Painter to support the Photoshop format so that artists can export and import files into Photoshop without the need to first convert to a generic file format such as TIFF.

# Scitex CT

Scitex computers are high-end workstations often used in prepress houses for color correcting and image processing. The Scitex CT (Continuous Tone) format is the proprietary system used by Scitex workstations. High-end image-editing software packages such as Adobe Photoshop and HSC Live Picture allow you to save files in the Scitex CT format.

# IVUE

The IVUE file is used by HSC's Live Picture. The file format is quite unique because whether the file is 3 or 300MB, it loads almost instantly on screen. The IVUE format accomplishes this by not loading the entire high-resolution file into the computer's memory, but only the data it needs to provide a high-quality visual image onscreen.

# CompuServe GIF

GIF was developed by CompuServe to provide a means of compressing bitmap files downloaded over the telephone. This file format is commonly used to save graphics files before uploading them to the Internet. If you wish to use the GIF format, be aware that this format does not support more than 256 (8-bit color) colors. GIF files can be imported into many graphics PC programs, including the PC version of QuarkXPress. On the Mac, many painting and image-editing packages allow files to be saved and imported in the GIF format.

# PCX

PCX is a file format that has been used for many years in PC graphics programs. It was created for use in the PC Paintbrush painting application by Zsoft. To a large degree, PCX has been abandoned by users in favor of TIFF because older versions of the format do not support thousands (16-bit color ) or millions (24-bit color) of colors. Thus, if you are saving images with more than 256 colors, check with your software's user guide before saving in PCX format. On the PC, PCX files may have either a PCX or PCS extension.

# TGA

The TGA (Targa) format is widely supported among MS-DOS computer software packages. The format was originally designed for PC compatibles using TrueVision video boards.

# BMP

BMP (Windows Bitmap) is a widely used DOS and Windows graphics file format. It is popular because it is the default for the Windows Paintbrush program.

# CGM

The CGM (Computer Graphics Metafile) graphics format is used by a wide variety of PC object-oriented graphics programs including Harvard Graphics, Lotus FreeLance Plus, and Arts & Letters. Since CGM is not one file format, but really several different variants, consult your software instructions to ensure file compatibility between applications.

# DXF

DXF (Drawing Interchange) is an ASCII text format developed by Autodesk for importing and exporting AutoCAD files. The file saves geometric data. No shading or lighting information is included in the file. The format is supported by CAD/CAM and many 3D software packages. Figure 5-3 shows how the DXF file format is chosen in Macromedia Swivel 3D Pro, a 3D modeling program.

# RIB (RenderMan)

Many 3D modeling programs do not include high-end rendering features. When an image is rendered, lighting, texture, and color are applied to it. The RIB (RenderMan Interface Bytestream protocol) format is provided by modeling software so that users can export their files into Pixar's acclaimed rendering program, RenderMan.

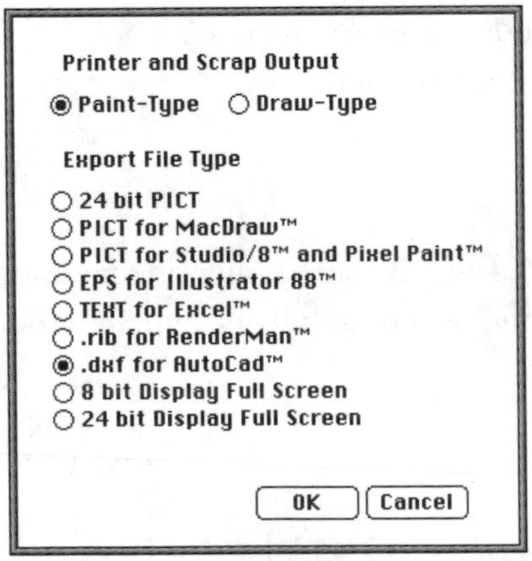

Macromedia Swivel Pro's Export Options command allows you to save in DXF format

**Printer and Scrap Output**

⦿ Paint-Type     ○ Draw-Type

**Export File Type**

○ 24 bit PICT
○ PICT for MacDraw™
○ PICT for Studio/8™ and Pixel Paint™
○ EPS for Illustrator 88™
○ TEXT for Excel™
○ .rib for RenderMan™
⦿ .dxf for AutoCad™
○ 8 bit Display Full Screen
○ 24 bit Display Full Screen

[ OK ]  [ Cancel ]

**FIGURE 5-3**

Programs that support the RIB format include Macromedia MacroModel, Macromedia Swivel 3D, Pixar ShowPlace, and the Vallis Group's Pixel Putty.

# 3DMF

3DMF (3D Metafile) is Apple's new cross-platform 3D file format. 3DMF provides a standard file format that allows users to share 3D images across different applications. For instance, 3DMF allows you to drag and drop a 3D image from a 3D modeling program into other graphics programs.

# IGES

The IGES file format was created by a committee hired by the U.S. Department of Commerce's National Bureau of Standards. IGES was an attempt to standardize digital representation of geometric, topological data. The format is supported by 3D programs such as StrataVision and Alias Sketch. Figure 5-4 shows how Alias Sketch's Save As dialog box allows you to save a file in IGES format.

# Filmstrip

The Filmstrip file format is the native file format used by Adobe Premiere, a digital video-editing and multimedia program. It can be imported into Adobe Photoshop where a video movie can be edited one frame at a time.

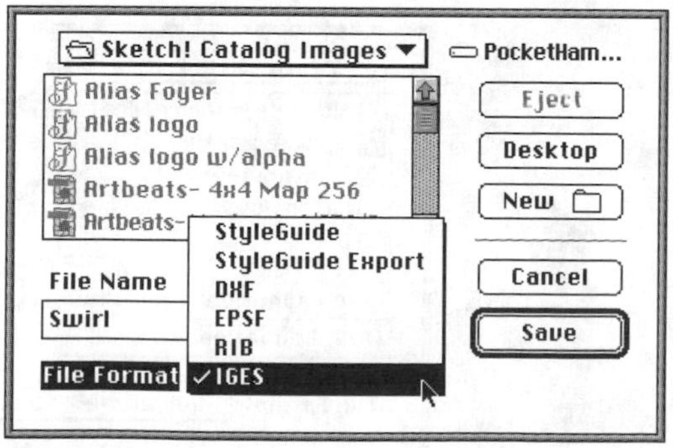

Alias Sketch's Save As dialog box

**FIGURE 5-4**

# QuickTime Movie

QuickTime, developed by Apple Computer, allows computers to play digital movies and sound. It was developed as a system-level extension to seamlessly integrate multimedia with Macintosh software. On the Mac, QuickTime is copied to your hard disk automatically when system software is installed. For the PC, Apple created QuickTime for Windows to allow digital video movies to be used across the Mac and PC platforms.

Software products such as Fractal Design Painter, multimedia programs such as Adobe Premiere, and 3D modeling and animation software such as Strata StudioPro, Strata Vision, Specular Infini-D and Electric Image, all can save files in the QuickTime movie format. In Strata StudioPro you can use the Save As dialog box, shown in Figure 5-5, to save a 3D animation sequence in QuickTime format. After you name the file, the QuickTime file format allows you to choose a compression setting and specify how many colors you want in the QuickTime movie, as shown in Figure 5-6. On the Macintosh, many programs—even spreadsheets, word processors, and databases—can play movies created in the QuickTime format. For more information about QuickTime, see Chapter 16.

# Microsoft Video for Windows

Microsoft Video for Windows (also called AVI, Audio Video Interleaved) is a multimedia file format created by Microsoft Corporation. When animation is saved in this format, both sound and picture are integrated so that they always remain in

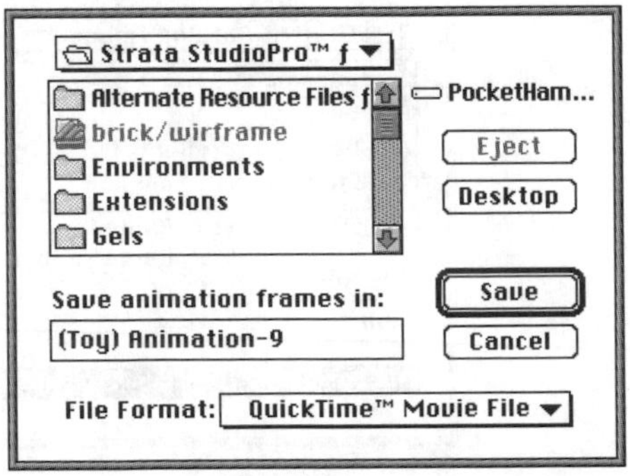

Strata
StudioPro
allows 3D
animations
to be
saved as
QuickTime
movies

**FIGURE 5-5**

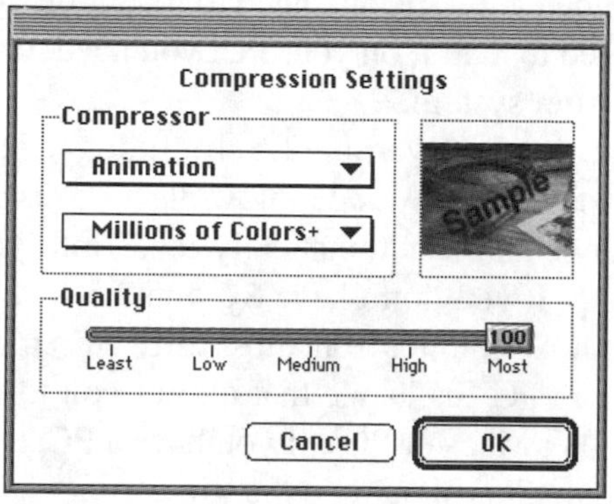

Strata
StudioPro's
QuickTime
compression
settings

**Compression Settings**

Compressor

Animation ▼

Millions of Colors+ ▼

Sample

Quality

Least    Low    Medium    High    Most    100

Cancel    OK

**FIGURE 5-6**

5

sync. Movies created in Video for Windows can be played back from a hard disk or CD-ROM. Like QuickTime, Video for Windows can compress movies to save disk space. Many Windows programs that create movies and animation support the Video for Windows format.

# File Transferring Utilities

What do you do if your software doesn't support a specific file format or can't read a file created on another computer platform? To prevent your being trapped by one file format, several software companies have created transfer utilities. Some file transfer programs are specifically designed to convert graphics file formats; others allow you to share files between computer platforms.

## Mac to PC and Back

If you have a Macintosh and need to read PC graphics files (or vice versa), the task of transferring from one platform to another is often quite simple. Before the file can be translated, you need to copy it from one computer to another. If your computers are on a network, you can simply send the file to the other computer on the network. If you have a modem, you can send the file to the other computer over the phone.

 **AUTION:** *If you are sending a Macintosh file to a PC via the telephone, do not use MacBinary format.*

If you are handed a PC file and need to load it on your Mac, or if you are given a Mac file and need to load it on your PC, you need to use software to "mount" the foreign file onto your system.

On the Macintosh, System 7.5 includes file-mounting software that automatically loads PC floppy and removable hard disks. The mounting software is called PC Exchange and it automatically loads into your system's memory when your Mac boots up. If you don't have System 7.5, you can purchase it or purchase PC Exchange or DOS Mounter from most software supply houses. Figure 5-7 shows the pop-up menu in PC Exchange that allows you to format floppy or removable hard drives for either Macs or PCs. If you have a PC, and need to mount Mac disks, DataViz' ConversionPlus should do the trick.

 **OTE:** *Some file utility software includes cables that hook up to a computer's serial port. Files are then sent from one computer to another over the cable.*

Once the foreign file appears on your desktop, you may be able to load it directly into the software you are using, particularly if that software is available on both Mac and PC. For instance, the Mac versions of Adobe Photoshop and Fractal Design Painter automatically read files created in the PC versions of the same software. The PC versions of Photoshop and Painter automatically read files created on Mac versions of Photoshop and Painter. To load the file, all you need to do is choose File/Open, and open the file as if it were created on your own computer. The translation is handled internally by the software.

## Converting File Formats with Equilibrium DeBabelizer

If your software cannot read a file format, you may need to purchase graphics file conversion software such as Equilibrium's DeBabelizer on the Macintosh,

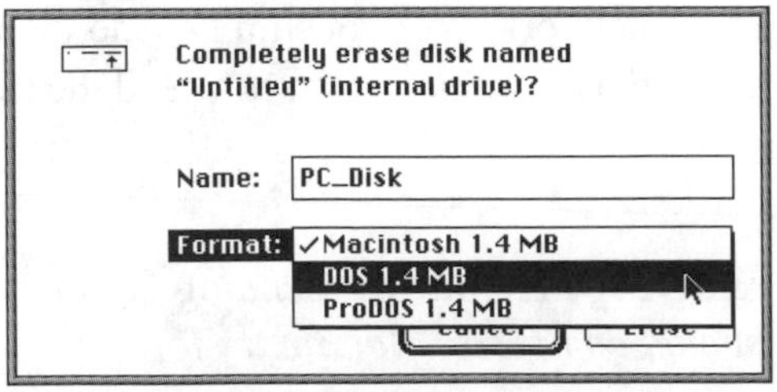

PC
Exchange
allows you
to format PC
disks on the
Mac

**FIGURE 5-7**

Completely erase disk named
"Untitled" (internal drive)?

Name: PC_Disk

Format: ✓Macintosh 1.4 MB
DOS 1.4 MB
ProDOS 1.4 MB

considered to be one of the most powerful translating utilities. On the PC, HiJackPro and ULead Systems Image Pals provide file translation between one graphics format and another.

Usually, converting files via file translation programs is quite easy. Figure 5-8 shows DeBabelizer's Save As dialog box. Notice that the different TIFF formats allow the file onscreen to be saved as either a Mac or PC TIFF, with LZW compression or not. Most conversions in DeBabelizer only require you to load a file, then choose Save As from the File menu. The Save As pop-up menu provides numerous choices for industry standard file formats. DeBabelizer will also batch convert graphics images, automatically converting one file after another. DeBabelizer can also convert Photo CD files, QuickTime movies, and UNIX graphics formats (SGI, Sun, SoftImage, WaveFront) to and from PC and Mac formats. The program also can utilize Photoshop-compatible plug-ins, convert images to black and white, reduce the number of colors in an image, and run programmed scripts. Figure 5-9 shows a list of preprogrammed scripts that can be run by choosing DeBabelizer's Scripts/Execute command.

 **OTE:** *Equilibrium also sells DeBabelizer Lite, an easy-to-use graphics file converter that can translate 55 bitmapped graphics formats.*

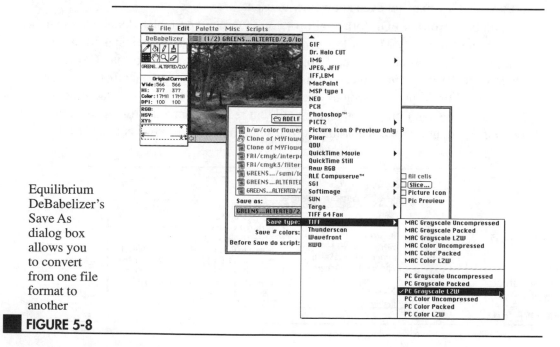

Equilibrium
DeBabelizer's
Save As
dialog box
allows you
to convert
from one file
format to
another

**FIGURE 5-8**

# Using Adobe ScreenReady to Create PICT Files

Adobe ScreenReady is a Macintosh graphics utility package that converts files from graphics applications into a format used by multimedia packages. Using ScreenReady, you can take a layout created in Adobe PageMaker, Illustrator, Macromedia Freehand, or QuarkXPress and quickly convert it into PICT format. Once in PICT format the image can be easily imported into multimedia applications such as Adobe Premiere, Adobe After Effects, Macromedia Director, and Macromedia Authorware.

ScreenReady allows the user to select the bit depth (number of colors) needed in the exported file and allows batch processing so that many files can be converted at one time. The program features a "Chooser" extension, which means that users can simply choose the Print command to export the PICT file.

# Using Acrobat to Create Portable Documents

In many offices, graphic files need to be sent to non-graphics computer users for their approval before images can be output. Often it is most convenient to send the files over a computer network or on disk. Unfortunately, those who need to approve graphic images may not have graphics software installed on their computers. And if they do, they may not even know how to use it.

Adobe Acrobat's PDF format allows you to create "portable" documents that can be viewed on any Mac or PC, even if no graphics software is installed on the computer. With Adobe Acrobat, you save your file in PDF format (Portable Document Format). Then you can copy it to disk or send it electronically to another computer. For instance, assume you created an advertisement in Macromedia Freehand. You can't output the image until you receive approval from a colleague in your Account Services department. You send the file over your network to that

DeBabelizer's
Execute
can run
programmed
scripts

**FIGURE 5-9**

| Scripts | |
|---|---|
| Execute ▶ | NOTHING |
| New... | Dither to Stashed Palette |
| Edit... ▶ | Dither to Super Palette |
| Delete ▶ | Drag&Drop To PICT |
| | Mask Original with Alpha Channel |
| Execute AppleScript... | Print Best on 300 DPI B&W Printer |
| Export AppleScript... ▶ | Print Best on 300 DPI Color Printer |
| | Print Best on Color Imagewriter |
| Watch Me | Trim to Solid Edges |
| Stop Recording... | |

department. In order to view the file, your colleague does not need a copy of Freehand, or even the fonts you used to create the advertisement. He or she only needs a copy of Adobe Acrobat Reader.

The Adobe Acrobat Pro Package includes several modules, each helping to provide—as Adobe puts it—"All the benefits of paper, without the chase." Included in the package are:

▶ Acrobat Exchange, which allows users not only to view and print, but also to annotate PDF files.

▶ The PDF Writer printer driver, which allows a "common" Mac or Windows word processing or spreadsheet file to be converted into a PDF file.

▶ Acrobat Distiller, which can turn a complex graphics document into PDF format.

▶ Acrobat Reader, which allows others to view and print PDF files. This file can be distributed free to all in your workgroup who might need to view PDF files.

Once Acrobat is installed in your office, you can create a reviewing system that allows colleagues and clients to review and annotate graphics files. The system might work as follows.

1. You create a project that includes digital images for a client.

2. You save the file in PostScript format, then use Acrobat Distiller to compress the file, and save it as a PDF file. Figure 5-10 show Distiller's

```
                        Job Options
        ┌─General──────────────────────────┐
        │ ☒ Compress (LZW) text and graphics│
        │ ☐ Generate Thumbnails             │      ┌────────┐
        │ ☐ ASCII Format                    │      │   OK   │
        │ ☒ Make Font Subsets               │      └────────┘
        └───────────────────────────────────┘
        ┌─Color Images─────────────────────┐      ┌────────┐
        │ ☒ Downsample to [72  ] dpi        │      │ Cancel │
        │ ☒ Compression: [ JPEG Medium ]    │      └────────┘
        └───────────────────────────────────┘
        ┌─Grayscale Images─────────────────┐
        │ ☒ Downsample to [72  ] dpi        │      ┌────────┐
        │ ☒ Compression: [ JPEG Medium ]    │      │Defaults│
        └───────────────────────────────────┘      └────────┘
        ┌─Monochrome Images────────────────┐
        │ ☒ Downsample to [300 ] dpi        │
        │ ☒ Compression: [ CCITT Group 4 ]  │
        └───────────────────────────────────┘
```

Acrobat
Distiller's
Job Options
dialog box

**FIGURE 5-10**

Job Options dialog box, which allows you to compress your PostScript file. Figure 5-11 shows Distiller in action, creating a PDF file.

3. You distribute PDF files electronically over a network or phone lines to colleagues and clients.

4. Clients and colleagues view the image using Acrobat Reader.

5. Some clients and colleagues use Acrobat Exchange to annotate the PDF file with suggestions and comments.

6. Using Acrobat Exchange, you collate and summarize notes into one PDF file.

7. Based on comments and notes, you make the appropriate changes in the original digital images.

# Conclusion

This chapter has provided you with an overview of the various file formats used to create digital images. With this introduction under your belt, you may now wish to explore importing and exporting options provided by your software. If you've created an image in one program, and it's not quite perfect, maybe the answer is to export the file into another software package and continue to enhance it.

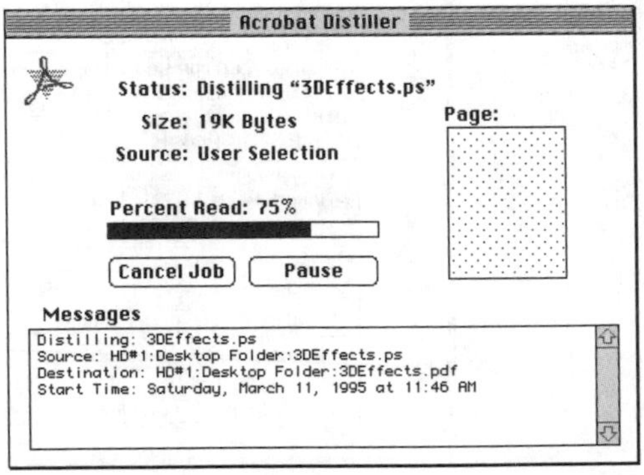

Creating a
PDF file
with Acrobat
Distiller

**FIGURE 5-11**

# 6

## All About Resolution

On your computer screen, digital images are modern-day optical illusions. The images you see are actually composed of tiny black, white, gray, or colored squares. These squares are packed so closely together that your mind blends them into continuous tones to form realistic looking images. In many respects, viewing a digital image onscreen is like looking at a painting by Georges Seurat: both use small dots rather than large strokes to create wondrous images.

When you work with a digital image, the quality of the image—whether saved on disk, viewed on a monitor, or printed—is based upon the tiny elements that make up the image. As you learned in previous chapters, the tiny squares that create a digital image are called *pixels*. The term for the number of pixels in an image is *resolution*. Resolution also describes the number of image elements—pixels, or dots—used to output an image on a printer. Understanding basic concepts of resolution is extremely important to anyone working with digital images because the output quality of an image often depends upon its resolution. However, for many computer graphics users, the subject is confusing because resolution can refer to either the pixels that comprise a digital image, the pixels that appear on a video monitor, or the dots that make up a printed image. Further confusion arises because the number of pixels per inch in an image can change when you enlarge or reduce it.

This chapter is designed to help reduce confusion by providing an overview of the basic concepts of resolution. As you read through the chapter, you'll also learn how to choose the correct resolution for outputting images for commercial printing, video, business and multimedia presentations, and slides.

## Image Resolution

In order to fully understand image resolution, you must remember that images created in raster or bitmap programs or digitized by scanners are composed of a rectangular grid of tiny squares called pixels. An image's resolution can be described by the number of pixels per linear inch in the image, or its dimensions in pixels. Thus, you might see an image's resolution described as 72 pixels per inch, or as 640 x 480 pixels (640 columns of pixels by 480 rows).

**IP:** *If you wish to calculate an image's size in inches based upon its pixel dimensions, divide the pixel dimensions by the pixels per inch in the image. Thus, a 640 x 480, 72 ppi image's dimensions can be calculated: 640/72 = 8.89 inches; 480/72 = 6.67 inches.*

How does an image get to be a specific resolution? Often, image resolution is designated when an image is digitized using a scanner or digital camera, or when it is created in a painting or image-editing program. When you take a picture with a digital camera, the image resolution is determined by the camera's resolution. When digitizing an image with a scanner, or creating an image in a painting or image-editing program, resolution is usually specified in pixels per inch. See Chapter 7 for more information on using scanners, and Chapter 8 for more information on using digital cameras and capturing video clips.

**OTE:** *If you are working in a vector (or drawing) program, you don't change or set image resolution. As mentioned in Chapter 3, the quality of a vector image is not based on image resolution but on the resolution of the output device.*

Figure 6-1 shows the scanning dialog box used by Agfa scanners. Note that the scanning dialog box allows you to choose a resolution from 20 to 2,400 pixels per inch.

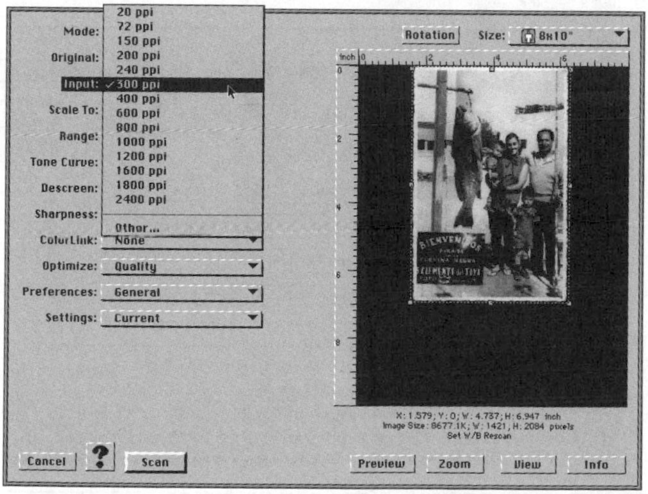

Agfa FotoLook Scanning software allows you to choose a scanning resolution

**FIGURE 6-1**

When you create an image in most image-editing software and most high-end painting programs, you can specify the number of pixels per linear inch that make up the image. Figure 6-2 shows Photoshop's New dialog box, which automatically calculates image file size when the values in the Width, Height, and Resolution fields and Mode pop-up menu are changed. Notice that the dialog box includes a pop-up menu for the Width and Height fields. This enables you to enter the image dimensions in pixels as well as inches or centimeters.

Whether you digitize an image with a scanner or create it in a painting or image-editing program, the resolution you set determines how many pixels are in the image. If you set the resolution at 72 ppi, each square inch of the image is composed of over 5,000 pixels (72 x 72). If you set the resolution at 300 ppi, each square inch is composed of 90,000 pixels (300 x 300).

 **OTE:** *Resolution is sometimes measured in pixels per millimeter. When using millimeters, a resolution of 12 millimeters per inch (approximately 300 ppi) is commonly written "res 12."*

As you work with digital images, the number of pixels in an image becomes extremely important. File size in a bitmap image is based upon the number of pixels in the image. The greater the number of pixels, the larger an image's file size. In order to work efficiently with bitmap images, you won't want to use large images packed with many pixels per inch. Even with a powerful computer system, working with large, high-resolution images can be quite cumbersome.

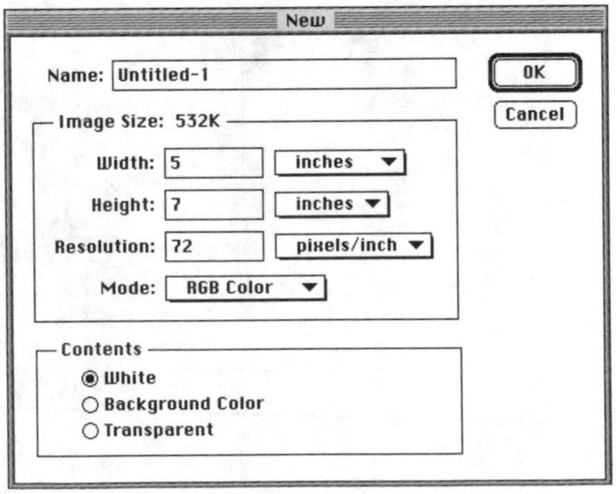

Photoshop's
New dialog
box

**FIGURE 6-2**

**IP:** *To estimate a digital image's file size, first multiply its dimensions in pixels, then multiply by 32 for a CMYK color image, 24 for a 24-bit RGB image, 8 for an 8-bit grayscale image, or 1 for a black-and-white image. This provides the number of bits in the image. Divide this number by 8 to calculate the number of bytes in the image. Thus, the file size of a 640 x 480 pixel, 24-bit RGB image is approximately 920KB (640 x 480 x 24)/8. The file size of a 640 x 480 pixel, greyscale image is approximately 307KB (640 x 480 x 8)/8.*

## Avoiding Memory Problems with High-Resolution Images

Color images that will be printed on a printing press often require high resolution. If your computer can't handle the high memory requirements (often several megabytes for one image), one solution is to use low-resolution versions of your images as working copies, then substitute high-resolution versions as you complete your project. Another solution used by many digital artists is to create their own low- and high-res versions of each image. By working on a low-res version, you can complete all of your design work and experimentation faster than if you work on high-res files because low-res images use less memory than high-res ones.

Some software packages are designed to help you streamline work on high-resolution images. For instance, Photoshop provides a Quick Edit utility that lets you load only part of an image at a time. Fractal Design's Painter allows you to record a painting "session" at a low resolution. You can then create a high-resolution file and have Painter automatically play back the session at a higher resolution.

Other solutions include macro programs such as Tempo II on the Mac and Daystar's Photomatic. Tempo will record and play back keystrokes in any program, while Photomatic is designed to do so only in the Macintosh version of Photoshop.

If you are dealing with very large high-resolution files, you might wish to investigate HSC Live Picture, Fauve Xres, and Specular Collage. When you work in these programs, you don't actually change the high-res file. Since the onscreen image is independent of the image resolution on disk, you can work very quickly with extremely large files. In Live Picture, as you edit an image, the program saves a mathematical description of your work in a file. The final image is created after you have completed your image editing. At this point you set the resolution and other image specifications in the Build dialog box, shown in Figure 6-3. When using Fauve Xres, the Tiff Options dialog box is used to create a high-resolution version of the image for editing purposes. By choosing 1:1 rendering, the image is created at the

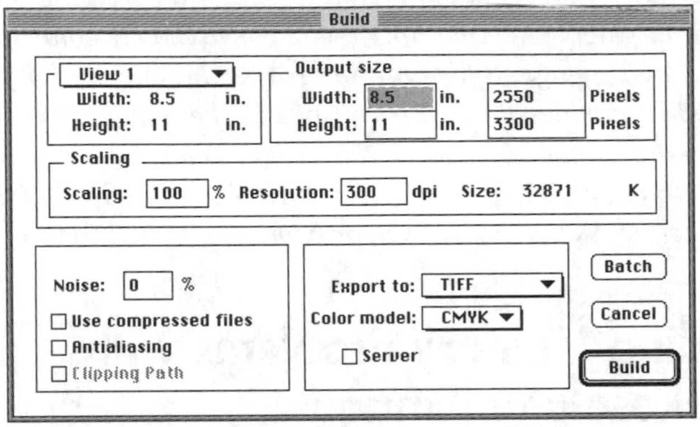

HSC Live
Picture's
Build dialog
box

**FIGURE 6-3**

high-output resolution previously specified in the program. Choosing a rendering ratio of 1:2 or lower creates a lower-resolution version of the file.

# Monitor Resolution

A monitor's resolution determines how many pixels or picture elements are displayed onscreen. For instance, the standard resolution of a Macintosh 14-inch monitor is 640 columns by 480 rows of pixels. This translates to about 72 pixels per inch. On a PC, the standard resolution of Super VGA displays is 800 x 600, 96 pixels per inch. When working with raster-based images, it's important to understand that a monitor's resolution is not tied to that of the image.

If a monitor's resolution is the same as your image's resolution, the onscreen image appears as its actual size. However, if the image resolution is higher than the monitor's resolution, the image appears larger than its actual size. For instance, assume you're viewing an image on a monitor with a resolution of 72 pixels per inch. Since the resolution of the monitor and the image is the same, the image appears onscreen as a 1-inch square. However, if you view an image that is 1 x 1 inch created at 300 ppi, the onscreen version consumes about 4 inches of screen space. The image appears larger than actual size because one inch in the 300 ppi image cannot fit in an inch of 72 ppi screen space. Although this can be confusing at first, you get used to it. Since most image-editing programs provide onscreen rulers, you can orient yourself to the true size of your image. Also, most digital artists use a program's "zoom" command to view and work with images at the most convenient size.

# Printer and Imagesetter Resolution

When you print an image on a laser printer or imagesetter, output resolution is measured in dots per inch (dpi). The greater the number of dots per inch, the higher the quality of the printout. Black-and-white and color laser printers often output images at 300 to 600 dpi. Some newer desktop laser printers can output at 1,200 dpi. Imagesetters, most often found at service bureaus and prepress houses, output images from 1,200 to over 5,000 dpi.

## Halftones and Screen Frequency

When an image is printed on a printing press, color and black-and-white images are created from tiny dots called halftones. In black-and-white printing, the combination of the different halftone dots creates shades of gray. In the color printing process, cyan, magenta, yellow, and black halftones overprinting each other create the countless colors in an image.

In the digital print production process, halftones are created by the tiny pixels or dots output by an imagesetter. The different dot patterns create different size halftones. The number of lines per inch in a halftone is called the *line screen* or *screen frequency,* and is measured in lines per inch (lpi). The relationship between imagesetter dots, halftones, and line screen is depicted in Figure 6-4.

The precise screen frequency used when an image is output is usually determined by the paper and the printing press used. The higher the screen frequency, the smoother the output. Newspapers and black-and-white catalogs are often printed at screen frequencies from 80 to 90 lpi. Magazines are typically printed at a 133 to 150 line screen. High-quality color publishing often uses a screen frequency greater than 150.

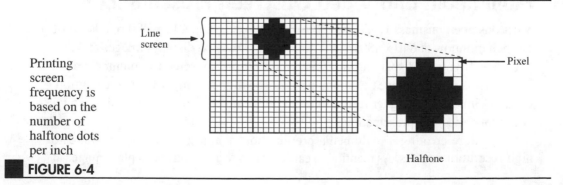

Printing screen frequency is based on the number of halftone dots per inch

**FIGURE 6-4**

If the concept of screen frequency seems confusing, don't worry; the subject will be discussed in greater detail in Chapter 17. At this point, it is only necessary to understand screen frequency as the basis for calculating resolution for images that will be printed on a press.

# Calculating Image Resolution

Now that you know the basics of image resolution, you're probably wondering how you decide exactly what resolution to use when creating or digitizing an image, or working with images created or digitized by others.

Consider the following problem faced by many artists using digital images. Assume you're working on an annual report for your company. On one page you need a 4 x 4-inch graphic to place into an advertisement. One artist sends you an image at 300 ppi, another sends one at 72 ppi. A photographer sends you an image taken on a digital camera. The 300 ppi image is 2 x 2 inches; the 72 ppi image is 6 x 6 inches. The photographer tells you that the camera captures images at 640 x 480 pixels. Which image should you use? To compound the problem, your company has decided to produce two versions of its annual report, one printed and one on CD-ROM. Should you use the same images at the same resolution in your printed and CD-ROM versions of the report?

To answer these questions, you must understand that image resolution is often determined by how it will be output. For instance, if you are creating an image for output on a commercial printing press, the image resolution must be higher than if the image were to appear on a computer screen as part of a multimedia presentation. The following sections explore how to determine image resolution for different output needs.

## Multimedia and Video Onscreen Presentations

Most onscreen business LCD projectors display images at 640 x 480 pixels, most 14-inch monitors at 640 x 480 pixels. American television displays images at 525 x 480 lines. If you are displaying your images on a projector screen, computer screen, or television screen, image resolution need not be higher than the screen resolution. Creating images at a higher resolution will only consume memory and slow down your work and your presentation.

If you are creating a multimedia presentation, you also do not need to create high-resolution images. As mentioned earlier, most Mac monitors display images at about 72 ppi, most PC monitors at 96 ppi. There's no reason to create your files at resolutions larger than the screen resolution of the monitor you will be using.

If your presentation requires scanned and colored images to look extremely realistic, raising the resolution beyond your monitor's resolution will produce no increase in image quality. Instead, consider creating and displaying your presentation on a computer with a video card that can output at least thousands of colors. Be aware, though, that the greater the number of colors in an image, the greater the file size. For more information about the number of colors that can be displayed on a video monitor, see Chapter 2.

 **EMEMBER:** *The number of colors displayed on a monitor is based on video RAM or the video board in the computer. It is not based on image resolution.*

## Calculating Image Resolution For Slide Output

6

A film recorder outputs slides and chromes from digital images. Different film recorders output at different resolutions. For instance, a film recorder at one prepress house may output slides at 2,048 x 1,366 pixels, another at 4,096 x 2,732 pixels. Thus, it's best to discuss resolution requirements with your service bureau. In general, when you output to a film recorder, the number of pixels in your image should be able to fit within the matrix of the film recorder's pixels. Also, if you are outputting an image to a slide, remember that your screen dimensions must have the same aspect ratio as a slide.

If you are outputting an image that needs to be enlarged, it's very important that you discuss exactly what resolution to use when you create your file so that your service bureau can enlarge your digital image without a loss in quality. If you use the wrong resolution, the transparency may exhibit jagged edges and color transitions may be coarse.

## Calculating Image Resolution for Line Art

Black-and-white images such as logos, technical drawings, and illustrations are usually scanned for placement in advertisements and for illustrating text. In the computer graphics world, black-and-white images are often referred to as "line art" (Photoshop uses the term "bitmap"). Since there is no color in line art, many users mistakenly assume they don't need to digitize it at a high resolution. In fact, line art must be scanned at high resolutions *because* it has no color or tones.

In a digitized color image, different shades of gray and color tones help bestow the illusion of smoothness. Since black-and-white line art possesses no shades of gray, the eye is quick to spot jagged edges and imperfections. Thus, the general rule for line art is to scan at your output resolution. If you are only outputting an image on a 600 dpi laser printer, you can scan at 600 dpi. If you are outputting to an imagesetter that will print your image at 1,200 dpi, you should scan your black-and-white line art at that resolution. Figure 6-5 shows a line art image from Periwinkle Software's Past-Tints CD-ROM stock image collection at 300 ppi and the same image at 1,200 ppi.

As mentioned earlier; the higher the resolution, the larger the file size of an image. If you do need to scan at high resolutions, try to keep your images as small as possible. Fortunately, though, black-and-white images consume much less memory than their color counterparts. For instance, a 5 x 5-inch black-and-white image with a resolution of 1,200 ppi consumes about 4MB of memory, while the same size color image at 1,200 ppi would consume about 100MB.

## Calculating Image Resolution for Print Output

The resolution for images that will be printed is based upon an image's output resolution. As mentioned earlier, output resolution is measured in lines per inch. As

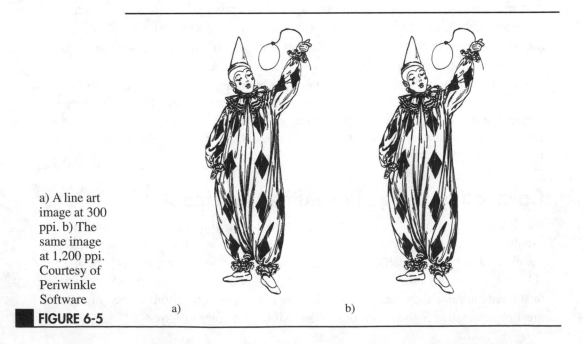

a) A line art image at 300 ppi. b) The same image at 1,200 ppi. Courtesy of Periwinkle Software

a)　　　　　　　　　　b)

**FIGURE 6-5**

a general rule, resolution for images that will be printed should be 1.5 to 2 times the screen frequency used for printing. This means that if you are printing an image at 150 lpi, an image should be scanned or created from 225 to 300 ppi—as long as you will not be resizing it (calculating resolution for an image that will be resized is covered in the next section). This relationship ensures that there is enough color data in the image when it is printed. Figure 6-6 shows you different output quality when images are scanned at three different resolutions.

If you don't know the screen frequency of your final output, you might be tempted to digitize an image at a very high resolution. Unfortunately, this presents two problems. First, the higher the resolution, the larger an image. Second, too high a resolution crams so many pixels together that the image may lack depth and look flat. Remember, always consult your prepress house and commercial printer if you have questions.

## Calculating Resolution for Images That Need Resizing

Often an image that is digitized needs to be enlarged or reduced for use in an image-editing or page layout program. When a scanned image or an image created in a bitmap program is enlarged, by default its resolution drops. For instance, if you take a 2 x 2-inch image scanned at 300 ppi and enlarge it to 4 x 4 inches, the resolution in pixels per inch drops to 150 ppi. The resolution drops because the software must enlarge the pixels of an image in order to increase its dimensions. If the pixels are enlarged, fewer pixels can fit into each inch of the image. This can create a problem: If you enlarge an image, its resolution may drop so low that it is unsuitable for output. The solution is to use a formula that tells you how high you need to scan an image to compensate for the enlargement you do later.

If you will be enlarging a scanned image, use this formula to calculate scanning resolution.

$$\frac{longest\ dimension\ in\ final\ image \times screen\ frequency \times pixel\ to\ line\ screen\ ratio}{longest\ dimension\ of\ original\ image}$$

Here's how you would use this formula:

Assume you need to enlarge an image that is 1 x 3 inches to 2 x 6 inches. Assume the screen frequency that will be used to output the image is 150 lpi.

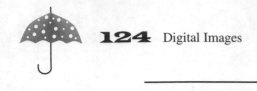 

a)

b)

c)

a) Image with resolution of 72 ppi.
b) Image with resolution of 150 ppi.
c) Image with resolution of 300 ppi.
Courtesy of ColorBytes, Inc.
Photograph by Joe Lange

**FIGURE 6-6**

1. Multiply the longest dimension of the final image by the screen frequency—in other words, multiply 6 x 150. This yields the total number of pixels necessary to output the longest dimension in the final image: 6 x 150 = 900.

2. As discussed in the previous section, the most common formula for calculating scanning resolution is to double an image's screen frequency. This means that you use 2 pixels for every line screen. Thus, your next step is to multiply 900 x 2, which yields 1,800. This number is the optimum number of pixels necessary to create the longest dimension of the final image.

3. Your last step is to divide the optimum number of pixels necessary to create the longest dimension of the final image by the longest dimension of the original image. 1,800 divided by 3 produces a scanning resolution of 600 ppi.

This formula is especially helpful when you need to enlarge scanned slides. For instance, if you need to enlarge a slide to about 5 inches in length, the necessary scanning is approximately 1,100 ppi. Since a slide's longest dimension is about 1.375, you could calculate the resolution as follows: 5 x 150 x 2/1.375.

## Resizing for Onscreen Presentations

If you will be digitizing an image that will be resized for use in an onscreen presentation, calculate digitizing resolution by multiplying the scaling factor by the monitor's resolution. Thus, if you will be doubling the size of an image that will appear on a 72 ppi monitor, you should scan at 144 ppi (2 x 72). You can calculate the scaling factor using this formula: longest dimension of the final image divided by the longest dimension of the original image.

## Resizing and Resampling Images

Understanding how resolution changes when an image is resized can help ensure that you are working with an image that can be output at the highest possible quality.

If you enlarge an image in most image-editing or painting programs, the software has one of two choices: it can enlarge the image by enlarging the pixels, or it can enlarge the image by adding pixels and creating new colors for the pixels it adds. By default, most image-editing software chooses to enlarge pixels. This prevents the file size from growing, but most importantly, it ensures that the image quality stays high (provided you don't go overboard and enlarge an image too much). But when your software increases the size of the pixels to enlarge the image, it must drop the number of pixels per square inch in the image.

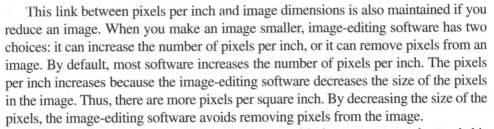

This link between pixels per inch and image dimensions is also maintained if you reduce an image. When you make an image smaller, image-editing software has two choices: it can increase the number of pixels per inch, or it can remove pixels from an image. By default, most software increases the number of pixels per inch. The pixels per inch increases because the image-editing software decreases the size of the pixels in the image. Thus, there are more pixels per square inch. By decreasing the size of the pixels, the image-editing software avoids removing pixels from the image.

When you are working with bitmap images, it's important to understand this relationship between image size and resolution. Obviously, if you aren't careful when resizing an image, you could change its resolution to an undesirable setting. Many image-editing and painting programs include dialog boxes that allow you to easily resize images, and clearly show the link between image dimension and resolution.

For instance, Figure 6-7 shows Adobe Photoshop's Image Size dialog box in which a 2 x 2-inch, 300 ppi image is being resized to a 4 x 4-inch, 150 ppi image. Note that the dialog box shows both the new and old dimensions and resolutions. Also notice the link icon indicating that there is a link between dimension and resolution. The link exists because both the Constrain Proportions and File Size checkboxes are selected. When the Proportions checkbox is selected, a change in width or height automatically changes the other dimension. This ensures that the image is not distorted when it is resized.

When the File Size checkbox is selected, the file size won't grow or shrink when dimensions are changed. By keeping the file size tied to a file's dimensions, the program never adds or subtracts pixels from an image. As mentioned earlier, graphics software simply makes pixels larger if the image is enlarged (thereby reducing the pixels per inch), or makes the pixels smaller if the image is reduced (thereby increasing the number of pixels per inch). If you turn off the File Size checkbox, Photoshop needs to add or subtract pixels from an image. This process of adding or subtracting pixels is called *resampling*.

Resampling is sometimes unavoidable. For instance, you may need to reduce the size of an image but don't want the resolution to be too high. Or you may need to enlarge an image and also keep its resolution high. The downside of doing this, however, is that you can lower the quality of a digital image—particularly if you are enlarging it. When an image is enlarged through resampling, image-editing software must add pixels and color them so they look like they belong in the image. The process of adding new pixels and filling them with color is called *interpolation*. Although many painting and image-editing programs use sophisticated interpolation algorithms to ensure the highest quality images, it is best to avoid interpolation whenever possible. Too much interpolation can lead to blurry images.

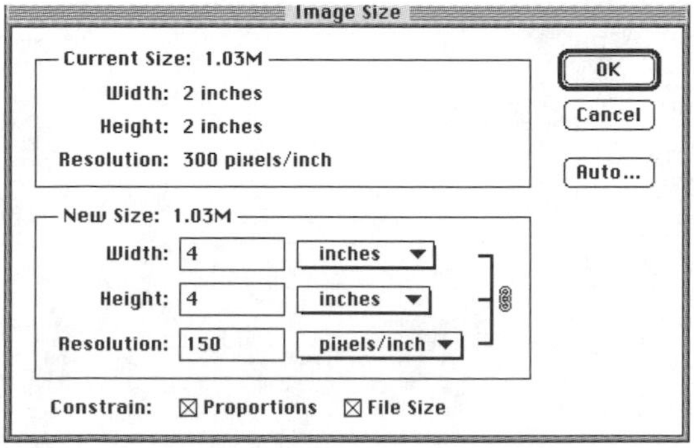

Adobe
Photoshop's
Image Size
dialog box

**FIGURE 6-7**

$\mathcal{N}$**OTE:**   *Some software packages such as Adobe Photoshop allow you to choose an interpolation method. If you choose a slower method, image quality is high. If you choose a faster method, image quality is lower.*

6

# Conclusion

Now that you know the basics of choosing the correct resolution for digital images, you're ready to start digitizing images. In the next chapter, you'll learn how to digitize photographs, line art, and transparencies using a scanner.

# 7

## Using a Scanner

Before you can integrate images from photographs, slides, and traditional artwork into your computer graphics projects, the images must be digitized. Undoubtedly, the most common device used to digitize images is a *scanner*. As discussed in Chapter 2, a scanner converts visual information into digital information. Once an image is digitized, you can then edit it in an image-editing or painting program. You can trace over it in a drawing program, or you can place it alongside text in a page layout program.

If you are going to use a scanner to digitize artwork and photos, you'll want to ensure that the scanning process produces crisp images and rich, consistent color. To achieve this goal you should acquire an understanding of how the scanner, the image being scanned, and the scanning software all affect image quality. This chapter provides an overview of scanning techniques and terminology. As you read, you'll learn the difference between high-end, mid-range, and low-end scanners. You'll also learn how to prepare for a scanning session and how to work with scanning software.

# Obtaining a Quality Scan

Whether you will be outputting your images on a printing press, a computer screen, or a projected screen, the quality of your final images depends in part on the quality of the original image. You might have heard the saying "garbage in, garbage out." This certainly applies to digital images. If you start with a poor quality digital image, there may be no way to improve it. Undoubtedly, image-editing programs like Adobe Photoshop, HSC Live Picture, Fauve Xres, and Micrografx Picture Publisher can boost the quality of digital images. However, if the image isn't properly digitized, you may have little to work with, and enhancing it might be quite time consuming—even impossible.

If the tones and details are missing from the original scan, don't expect that all problems can be fixed by an image-editing program. If the image isn't properly scanned, it may become blurry or *posterized* (lacking in gray levels, blotchy) when it is enlarged. Even with the latest software and hardware, you'll have a hard time making a poorly digitized image look enticing. You'll feel like a master chef in a four-star restaurant with only leftovers in the refrigerator.

How do you ensure the best quality scan? Start with the highest quality scanner possible.

## Choosing a Scanner

In many respects, you should choose a scanner as you would a camera. An inexpensive camera might take an acceptable picture, but a more expensive camera with a sophisticated optical system is going to produce a sharper image. Just as there are different levels of cameras, there are different levels of scanners. Apart from a scanner's optics, another crucial element is its CCD (charge-coupled device) array, which converts reflected light to digital data. Figure 7-1 shows how a CCD and a light source digitize images. When an image is scanned on a flatbed scanner, a light source moves across the image, much as a bright light in a photocopier crawls over an image being copied. In a scanner, the light is reflected back to a linear array of

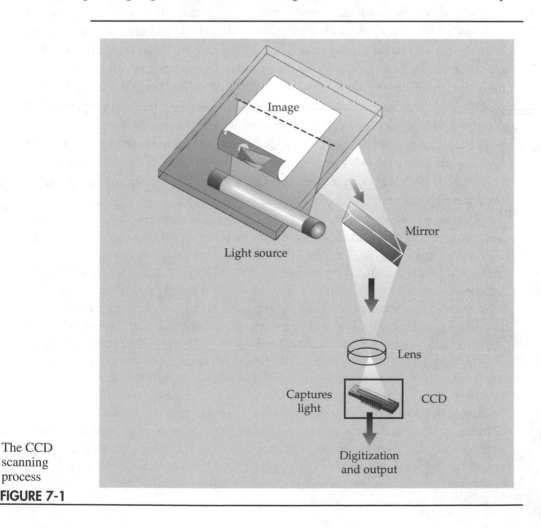

Image

Mirror

Light source

Lens

Captures light

CCD

Digitization and output

The CCD scanning process

**FIGURE 7-1**

thousands of CCDs. The number of CCDs in the array is directly related to the scanner's *optical resolution,* which determines how much information (in pixels per inch) the scanner can capture. The more CCDs there are, the higher the scanner's optical resolution. When evaluating scanners, you don't need to worry about how many thousands of CCDs are built into a scanner; look instead for high optical resolution. For instance, a low-end scanner might have an optical resolution of 300 x 600 pixels; a mid-range scanner, an optical resolution of 600 x 1200 pixels; a high-end flatbed, an optical resolution of 1200 x 1800 or better.

## Low End Scanners

Low-end scanners are usually flatbed scanners; typically, they are used for catalog and newspaper output, and for in-house newsletters. Low-end scanners may also be suitable for multimedia productions that don't require high-resolution images. Low-end scanners are not used for high-quality commercial printing because the digitized images they produce often lack the fine detail and smooth color transitions produced by mid- and high-end scanners. Many design studios and graphic artists use low-end scanners for FPO (For Position Only). This means that the scans are used only in a sample design, or *comp*, to allow the designer to experiment with layout ideas and to provide clients with a taste of the final product. Once the design is finalized, the images can be rescanned on a high-end scanner and placed in the final work by the design studio or a prepress house.

Low-end scanners usually cost $1,000 or less. Most are 24-bit scanners (8 bits per red, green, and blue pixel), which means they're supposed to capture and record millions of colors ($2^8 \times 2^8 \times 2^8$ = 16.7 million). Unfortunately, low-end scanners often don't record a full 24 bits of perfect color. Often, 2 of the 8 bits are used to handle *noise*—something similar to the static that mars the reception on your TV. Many mid-range scanners produced higher quality images by scanning 10 or 12 bits per pixel. Additionally, low-end scanners often have less sophisticated optical systems than more expensive scanners. Also the CCD array (that converts picture data to digital data) has fewer elements. This means that the low-end range scanner can't create images at the same resolution as a mid- or high-range scanner. In order to output images at a high resolution, many low-end scanners must *interpolate*. As discussed in Chapter 6, interpolation is a process that increases resolution by adding colored or black-and-white pixels to an image. When pixels are added, scanning software usually takes the average color value of surrounding pixels to create the colors for the pixels it adds. Thus, interpolated images aren't as sharp, nor will their colors be as precise as images scanned without interpolation.

*n* **OTE:** *Windows users who seek a low-cost home scanner might wish to investigate Storm Technology's EasyPhoto Reader, which sells for about $250. The scanner digitizes photos up to 4 inches wide at 133ppi. Unlike most scanners for PCs, EasyPhoto Reader does not require an inteface board; instead, it connects directly to the PC's printer port.*

## Mid-Range Scanners

Mid-range scanners can cost as little as $2,500 and are used for black-and-white publications and color catalogs. In recent years, the quality of mid-range scanners has improved so much that you'll be seeing images scanned by these devices in more and more magazines and other color publications. A major reason why mid-range scanners can output such high-quality images is that they now provide a bit depth higher than 8 bits per pixel.

Recently, Agfa, UMAX, and Microtek have increased the bit depth of their mid-range scanners. The extra bits help boost the scanner's dynamic range—the range of colors that the scanner can capture from the lightest to darkest colors in an image. Better mid-range scanners boast a bit depth of 10 to 12 bits per pixel. When the actual 24-bit color image is created, software picks the best 8 bits to produce the best possible color. (You often see 10-bits-per-pixel scanners advertised as 30-bit scanners, or 12-bits-per-pixel scanners advertised as 36-bit scanners.)

Many mid-range flatbed scanners allow transparency attachments to be connected to them so that slides and 4 x 5- and 8 x 10-inch transparencies can be scanned. Although the quality of the scanned transparencies is good, if you are going to be scanning many slides, you should consider using a slide scanner. Slide scanners usually scan at higher resolutions than flatbed scanners. High resolutions are needed because slides must be enlarged by the scanner or by image-editing software. (To learn more about resolution, see Chapter 6.) Many mid-range flatbed scanners need to interpolate when scanning at resolutions higher than 600 ppi. Slide scanners should be able to scan at a resolution of at least 1,000 ppi without interpolating. In fact, many have an optical resolution of 2,000 ppi or better.

## High-End Scanners

High-end scanners can cost anywhere from $10,000 to hundreds of thousands of dollars. These devices, usually found at prepress houses and service bureaus, feature advanced optics and focusing controls that ensure images are created as sharply as possible. Most high-end scanners can also produce a color-separated CMYK file when used in conjunction with scanning software. This means that the image is broken down into cyan, magenta, yellow, and black color components when the scan is saved to disk. High-end scanners usually are 36-bit scanners or greater and feature a dynamic range many times greater than low- and mid-range scanners.

Companies such as Scitex and Agfa produce high-end flatbed scanners that produce extremely high-quality scans. These scanners are starting to provide competition for high-end *drum scanners,* traditionally the choice of prepress professionals. As discussed in Chapter 2, in the drum scanning process, an intense beam of light and one or several PMT (photomultiplier) tubes digitize an image placed on a spinning cylinder. PMTs are extremely sensitive to light and highly efficient at preventing noise from being introduced during the scanning process. Figure 7-2 shows how a PMT tube is used to digitize an image. The process enables images to be scanned at very high resolutions. For instance, the optical resolution for drum scanners costing over $35,000 is often over 5,000 ppi, which enables images be to enlarged by several thousand percent.

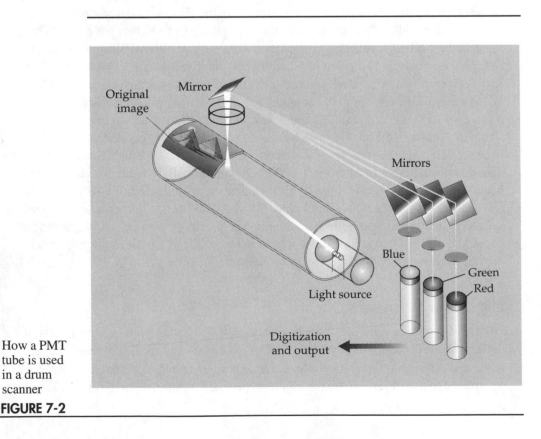

How a PMT
tube is used
in a drum
scanner

**FIGURE 7-2**

Drum scanners produce exquisitely sharp images with fine details and smooth color transitions. In fact, drum scanners can record data in an image that the human eye doesn't even notice. That is why most images that appear in slick ads, fashion magazines, and catalogs are scanned on drum scanners.

If you do pay to have a service bureau produce a high-end scan for you, you may wish to request a low-resolution version "for position only" work and to experiment with design ideas. As discussed in Chapter 6, the file size of a low-res image is lower than that of a high-res image. This allows for faster manipulation on your computer.

# Evaluating Images to Be Scanned

No matter what quality scanner you use to digitize your images, the better the image that is digitized, the better the final output will be. Even when a high-quality image is scanned, its dynamic range is usually compressed, meaning that the color range from light to dark is not as great as that of the original. Thus, it's always best to choose images that exhibit a full range of tones: highlights, very light areas; shadows, dark areas; and midtones, mid-range tones between dark and light. If your image is overly dark or light, you'll probably need to carefully set the light and darkness options provided in your scanning software or correct the problem in image-editing software. You'll learn the basics of tone and color correcting, and image sharpening in Chapter 14.

When analyzing a color image to be scanned make sure that the colors don't look washed out and that the image doesn't exhibit *color cast*—a color shift causing a single tint to overlay the entire image. Although image-editing software can color-correct images, this can sometimes be a time-consuming process.

When choosing originals to scan, keep in mind how the image will be output. If you will be outputting to a printing press, the spreading of ink on paper (known as *dot gain*) will darken the image. Thus, you may wish to avoid images with many shadow areas. Also, remember that colors generally print darker than they appear on a computer screen. As discussed in Chapter 3, your monitor *emits* light, while the printed page *reflects* light. This is why printed images often appear darker than their onscreen versions.

You also should try to avoid images that are grainy or have dust marks or scratches. Enlarging such flawed images will magnify their imperfections. Fortunately, as you'll learn in Chapter 14, dust and scratches can often be eliminated in image-editing programs. But why make extra work for yourself if you can start with a good original?

**OTE:** *Dust marks and spots may also appear in scanned images due to dust in the scanner. Removing dust spots using image-editing software is covered in Chapter 14.*

In addition to considerations of clarity and color quality, it is best to know beforehand whether the final size of your image will be larger or smaller than the image you are scanning. Pictures scanned on low-end scanners may exhibit noise and become blurry when enlarged. Scanned images should be as close as possible to the size of your final output. If you plan to enlarge the images, make sure you properly calculate the resolution before scanning. Calculating scanning resolution is reviewed in this chapter, but Chapter 6 contains a full discussion.

# Preparing to Scan

Before you begin to scan an image, you should know what resolution you will be using. Here's a brief review of calculating scanning resolution.

1. If you will be outputting on a printing press, scan at 1.5 to 2 times the screen frequency used to print the image. Thus, if the image will be output at 150 ppi, you should scan at 225 to 300 ppi.

2. If you will be enlarging your image for print output, calculate scanning resolution using the following formula discussed in Chapter 6:

$$\frac{\text{longest dimension in final image x screen frequency x pixel to line screen ratio}}{\text{longest dimension of original image}}$$

 **OTE:** *In the above formula screen frequency is your output in lpi; the pixel to line screen ratio is either 1.5 or 2. See Chapter 6 for more details.*

3. If you will be outputting on video or on a computer screen, you need not scan at a resolution higher than that of your monitor, provided you won't be enlarging your images. If you will be enlarging, you will need to scan at a proportionally higher resolution. For instance, assume your monitor's resolution is 72 ppi—the standard on most 14-inch Mac monitors. (On

PCs, the SVGA standard is usually 96 ppi.) If you will be scanning an image and then enlarging it to twice its original size, you should scan at 144 ppi.

4. If you will be outputting to slides on a film recorder, the width and height of the pixels in your digital image should fit within the film recorder's pixel map. Consult your service bureau if you have questions.

## Test Scans

Before you start using a scanner, you should scan several test images, and, if possible, print proofs or test images to evaluate the color and clarity. To ensure that your scanner is properly calibrated, you might wish to scan a gray bar, load it into an image-editing program such as Photoshop, and analyze whether the gray bar exhibits color casts. If you know that a color cast exists, you can use your image-editing software to correct it. For more information about color calibration, see Chapter 17.

## Using a Scanner

In recent years, most scanning software has been programmed so that it can be controlled directly from image-editing and painting software. Scanning programs that can be accessed through image-editing and painting programs are called *plug-ins*. To install a plug-in, you usually need to copy your scanning manufacturer's plug-in file to a specific folder or directory on your hard disk. In most image-editing programs, you need to choose a "preference" menu command to direct the software to the folder on the hard disk that contains your scanning plug-in. After you reset the preferences, you usually must restart your software in order to access the plug-in.

toLook PS 2.05   The Plug-in icon for Agfa's FotoLook scanning software is shown here.

Once your software is installed, be sure to turn on your scanner. Most scanning software will not operate unless the scanner is on and connected to your computer. To operate scanning software in many programs, you often access it by choosing Acquire from the File menu. Figure 7-3 shows Photoshop's Acquire submenu with plug-ins for Agfa's Arcus II scanner (FotoLook) and for Kodak's RFS 2035 Plus slide scanner.

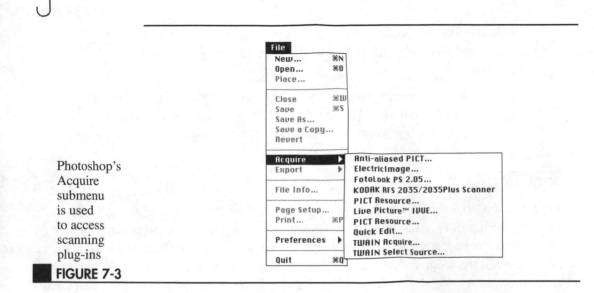

Photoshop's
Acquire
submenu
is used
to access
scanning
plug-ins

**FIGURE 7-3**

# Using a Flatbed Scanner

In order to obtain the highest quality scans, you should familiarize yourself with the software that controls your scanner. Scanning software allows you to choose resolution and often allows you to lighten, darken, and balance colors. To help familiarize you with scanning software, this section reviews some of the options provided by FotoLook, which is packaged with Agfa desktop scanners. Figure 7-4 shows the FotoLook dialog box that opens when the FotoLook scanning plug-in is chosen from Photoshop's Acquire submenu. The features in the dialog box are available when using Agfa's Arcus II, a 36-bit scanner which consistently receives high marks for consistent color reproduction and sharpness. The following sections review several dialog box options.

## Mode

Most scanning software allows you to choose a color, a grayscale, or a black-and-white mode. Some scanners, such as the Arcus II, allow you to separate an image into CMYK color components. You can place a CMYK file into page layout programs such as QuarkXPress. Image-editing software such as Adobe Photoshop, Fauve Xres, and HSC Live Picture allow you to edit CMYK files.

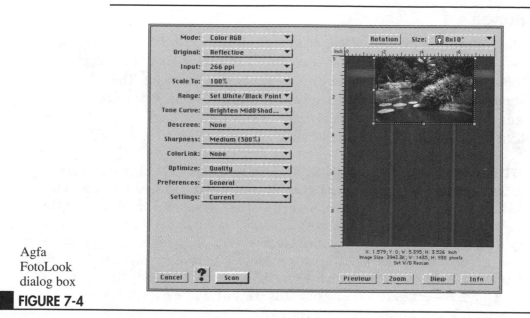

Agfa
FotoLook
dialog box

**FIGURE 7-4**

## Original

FotoLook's Original pop-up menu allows you to choose whether you are scanning reflective images (such as photographs and art) or transparencies (such as slides). FotoLook also provides a menu choice for scanning a negative transparency, such as a film strip.

## Input (Resolution)

The Input pop-up menu allows you to choose your scanning resolution. In many scanning software modules, this pop-up menu is named Resolution. FotoLook's Input pop-up menu, shown here, allows you to choose a range from 20 to over 2,000 ppi. FotoLook also allows you to change the Input pop-up menu to an Output pop-up menu. When the menu changes to Output, resolution is chosen in lines per inch (lpi).

| 20 ppi |
| 72 ppi |
| 150 ppi |
| 200 ppi |
| 240 ppi |
| 300 ppi |
| 400 ppi |
| 600 ppi |
| 800 ppi |
| 1000 ppi |
| 1200 ppi |
| 1600 ppi |
| 1800 ppi |
| 2400 ppi |
| ✓266 ppi |
| Other... |

## Range

Most scanning software automatically sets the dynamic range of an image. When the user chooses Automatic, the scanner picks the lightest portion of an image as its *white point*, and the darkest part of an image as its *black point*. This allows the scanner to try to reproduce the greatest color range possible. If you don't choose Automatic, FotoLook allows you to manually set white and black points which can help you fine-tune the quality of the image to be printed.

**SETTING WHITE AND BLACK POINTS**   By picking white and black points, you can ensure that the tonal balance in an image is correct and that details appear in the darkest and lightest portions of an image. If you let software automatically pick the white and black points, it may choose a *specular* highlight for the white point. A specular highlight is an image area that is a pure white pixel that might be produced from a sparkle or a reflection. Often, the solution is to specify grayscale, RGB, or CMYK percentages that you wish to set for the lightest and darkest portions of your image. The percentages chosen are often based upon the screen frequency and paper used for printing. After the percentages have been entered, you then click with the mouse in image areas that you wish to set as your white and black points.

When setting the white and black points manually, you often want to choose an image area that is not entirely white, one that exhibits tone. When choosing a black point, you often want to choose an image area that is not entirely black. This will help ensure that dark areas show detail. Figure 7-5 shows the FotoLook window that allows you to manually select white and black points in a preview scan. Icons on the left side of the screen allow you to choose whether you wish to set the white point or black point. For more information about choosing white and black points, see Chapter 14.

## Tone Curve

Some scanning software can utilize a *tone curve* when scanning. Choices in FotoLook's Tone pop-up menu include: Brighten Shadows, and Brighten Midtones and Shadows.

White
Point
tool ⟶

Black
Point ⟶
tool

FotoLook's
Set White/
Black Point
dialog box

**FIGURE 7-5**

## Descreening

*Descreening* is a blurring process that can help reduce *moiré patterns,* unwanted

patterns that appear when a previously printed image is scanned. FotoLook allows you to descreen based upon the screen frequency of newspapers and magazines, as shown here.

## Sharpness

Many scanners feature sharpening options. Sharpening often increases the contrast

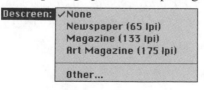

range from None to High, and allows you customize sharpening by entering a sharpening percentage.

## Batch

FotoLook's Batch button allows you to place several images on the scanner flatbed, adjust the settings for the images, and then scan all of the images in one "batch."

## Preview

Before scanning, most scanning software allows you to execute a preview, or test scan. By previewing the scan, you can see exactly what image areas you may wish to digitize. You can also see whether you've placed the image crookedly or upside down on the scanner's flatbed.

In order to avoid scanning a larger area than necessary, most programs will let you click and drag the mouse over the preview scan to set the specific image area to be scanned. When you click and drag to set the preview area, FotoLook calculates the image area in pixels and the file size, as shown earlier in Figure 7-4. In this process, it's often a good idea to scan a bit more than necessary—just in case you later need more of the image area in your final project.

## Scan

When you click the Scan button, the image is digitized at the specified number of pixels per inch. If you are scanning from within an image-editing, page layout, or painting program, the digitized image opens up into a window in that program. Figure 7-6 shows the final image scanned at 225 ppi.

 **OTE:** *If your scanning software doesn't provide all of the features you need, you might consider purchasing third-party scanning software such as PixelCraft ColorAccess, Light Source Ofoto, and Flamenco Bay ScanPrep Pro (a Macintosh Photoshop plug-in). Before purchasing any third-party scanning software, check to see that it is compatible with your scanner.*

Singapore
Botanical
Garden image
scanned at
225 ppi using
Agfa Arcus II
scanner and
FotoLook
software

**FIGURE 7-6**

## Using a Slide Scanner

Slide scanner software is quite similar to desktop scanner software. Figure 7-7 shows the scanning dialog box for the Kodak Professional RFS 2035 Plus Film scanner, a 36-bit device. The RFS 2035, which retails for over $8,000, not only produces excellent quality images, but is one of the fastest scanners in its class. When resolution is set to 1,000 ppi, the RFS 2035 can scan a slide in just 11 seconds. It takes about 40 seconds for the RFS 2035 to scan a slide at 2,000 ppi.

## Scanning Resolution

Since slides invariably need to be enlarged for output, the resolution of a slide scanner must be very high. The top scanning resolution for the RFS 2035 is 2,000 ppi.

## Film Type

Kodak's scanning software also allows you to choose the film type used for the slide, as shown in Figure 7-8. When you choose a film type, such as Kodachrome, the

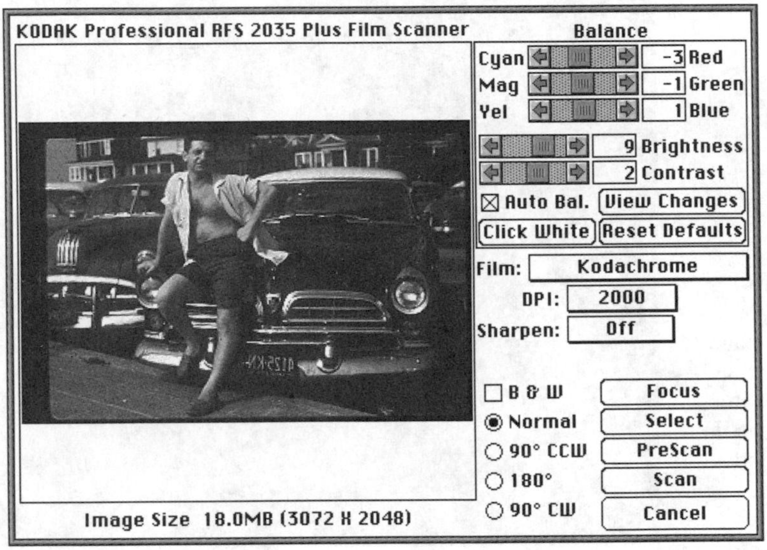

KODAK Professional RFS 2035 Plus Film Scanner

Balance

Cyan ◄ ▶ -3 Red
Mag ◄ ▶ -1 Green
Yel ◄ ▶ 1 Blue

◄ ▶ 9 Brightness
◄ ▶ 2 Contrast

☒ Auto Bal. | View Changes
Click White | Reset Defaults

Film: Kodachrome
DPI: 2000
Sharpen: Off

☐ B & W | Focus
◉ Normal | Select
○ 90° CCW | PreScan
○ 180° | Scan
○ 90° CW | Cancel

Image Size 18.0MB (3072 × 2048)

Scanning
dialog box
for the Kodak
Professional
RFS 2035
Plus Film
scanner

**FIGURE 7-7**

Positive
Negative
Ektachrome
Ektach... Elite
Ektach... Lumiere
Ektach... Panther
Ektach... Select
Ektach... Tungsten
Ektach... Underwater
Kodachrome
Kodach... Tungsten
Ektacolor 160  GPF
Ektacolor 160  GPH
Ektacolor 400  GPV
Ektapress 100 PJA
Ektapress 100 PPA
Ektapress 200 PJZ
Ektapress 400 PJB
Ektapr. 400 PJB-2
Ektapress 400 PPB
Ektapress 1600 PJC
Ektapress 1600 PPC
old Ektap. 1600 PPC
Ektapress Multi PJM
Ektar 25  PHR
Ektar 100
Ektar 125
Ektar 1000
Gold 100
Gold Plus 100-3
Gold Plus 100-4
Gold 200
Gold Super 200-3
Gold Super 200-4
Gold 400
Gold Ultra 400-4
Gold Ultra 400-5
Gold 1600
Kodacolor VRG 200
Pro 400 MC PMC
Pro 400 PPF
Royal Gold 25 RZ
Royal Gold 100 RA
Royal Gold 400 RC
Royal Gold 1000 RF

KODAK Professional RFS 2035 Plus Film Scanner

Cyan
Mag
Yel

☒ Au
Click

Film:

Sharp

☐ B
◉ N
○ 90
○ 18
○ 90

Image Size 18.0MB (3072 × 2048)

Kodak RFS
2035's Film
Type pop-up
menu

**FIGURE 7-8**

scanner makes tonal adjustments to compensate for the film's characteristics and ensure the highest quality output.

# Post-Scanning Procedures

After scanning an image, you will often wish to execute some quick image-editing commands to ensure the scanned image is not crooked and to remove extraneous areas. The following is a review of some of the commands you might find useful after scanning an image. Sharpening and color-correcting are discussed in Chapter 14.

## Cropping

It's probably a good rule of thumb to scan a bit more of the image than you need—just to ensure you don't inadvertently omit needed image areas. If you've scanned too much of an image, you can crop it in a page layout or image-editing program. When you crop an image, it's like cutting a photograph with a pair of scissors: you reduce the size of the image but don't scale it.

If you crop an image using page layout software, the program merely hides image areas you want cropped out. For instance, in QuarkXPress, you can reduce the size of a picture frame to hide image areas. If you later need to use more of the image, you simply enlarge the picture box.

Image-editing programs can also be used to digitally crop an image. When you crop in an image-editing program, you actually are cutting the image's size. This can be helpful because the image's file size is also reduced. Some programs such as Photoshop allow you to crop using a cropping tool, shown here. In Photoshop, you also can change the image's resolution setting when you crop.

| **Cropping Tool Options** | |
|---|---|
| ☒ Fixed Target Size | Front Image |
| Width: 3.5 | inches ▼ |
| Height: 3.5 | inches ▼ |
| Resolution: 72 | pixels/inch ▼ |

**OTE:**   *If your software doesn't allow you to crop an image, select an area with the program's rectangular selection tool, then copy and paste it into a new file.*

## Rotating an Image

In order to scan some images, you may need to place them sideways on the scanner flatbed. In order to later view the scanned image at its proper orientation, you'll need to rotate it. (Some scanning software, such as Agfa's FotoLook, can rotate an image in 90-degree increments.) The ability to rotate an image can also be essential if you've scanned an image crookedly and need to straighten it. Most image-editing, painting, and page-layout programs allow you to rotate an image. Often, you will need to first select the entire image, then choose the Rotate command. This will allow you to use the mouse to click and drag and rotate the image, or you can set the rotational degrees in a dialog box. Adobe Photoshop's Rotate dialog box, shown here, also lets you rotate an image clockwise or counterclockwise.

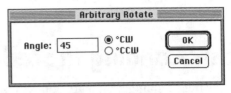

## Flipping an Image

Flipping an image can be necessary when you want it to face a different direction. In most software, the Flip command allows you to flip horizontally and vertically.

# Conclusion

Although scanning is undoubtedly the most popular method of digitizing images, your needs may require you to quickly digitize large 3D images or outdoor scenes rather than photographs or slides of these images. In the next chapter, you'll learn how to use the latest technology—the digital camera—to digitize the world that won't fit under a scanner's flatbed cover.

# Using a Digital Camera and Capturing Video

Instant feedback, fast turnaround times, financial savings, and environmental benefits—these are some of the reasons why interest in digital cameras is booming. If you've ever gone through the process of photographing an image, waiting for the photos to be developed, setting up the photos in your scanner, and then cooling your heels while your scanner digitizes the images, you can appreciate the value of a device that instantly digitizes an image and stores it for later use. The digital camera uses no film; therefore there's no waiting time for processing and no chemicals are used to output the image. If you're shooting in the field, and realize that a picture you've taken is poor, you just press a delete button. Most digital cameras used for studio work can even preview a shot directly onto a computer screen. This allows you to change lighting and rearrange compositional elements until they're perfect.

As you'll see in this chapter, digital cameras provide many advantages over scanners. With prices from $700 to as high as $50,000, there may be a model in your price range. But are digital cameras really suited for the type of work you do? This chapter will answer that question. You'll learn about the features, the advantages, and the disadvantages of various digital cameras. You'll see how the cameras interface with computers and image-editing software. You'll also learn about an alternative to digital cameras—capturing images from video.

## How Digital Cameras Work

In many respects a digital camera is like a portable scanner, except that the digital camera doesn't emit light (unless a flash is attached) when capturing images. As in flatbed and slide scanners, the heart of a digital camera is a CCD, a charge-coupled device. A CCD is an array of light-capturing components that produces a range of electrical charges depending upon different intensities of light. An analog-to-digital converter transforms the electrical charges into digital information. Unlike the CCD in a flatbed scanner, those in digital cameras capture an entire image at once. The CCD can do this so quickly (with exposure times as fast as 1/10,000th of a second) that some digital cameras can capture a brief smile, blink, or the wagging of a dog's tail.

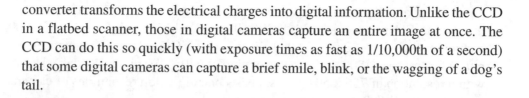

**OTE:** *Some high-end digital studio cameras can only capture still images because of slow exposure times.*

# Analyzing Digital Camera Features

For many photographers and graphics users, the easiest way to evaluate a digital camera is to analyze its optical system, because many digital cameras utilize professional 35mm cameras as their optical engines. The confusing aspect of digital cameras is how digital specifications such as bit depth and resolution relate to image quality.

## Understanding Digital Camera Bit Depth

As in a flatbed scanner, a digital camera's *dynamic range*—the range of tones captured from the lightest to darkest elements—is primarily determined by bit depth. Low-cost digital cameras such as Apple's QuickTake 150, Kodak's DC 40, and Dycam's Model 4 can capture 24 bits of color (8 bits of information for each RGB color). Higher end cameras, such as Kodak's DCS 460, capture 36 bits, which provide a more detailed picture with less noise. At the very high end of the scale is the Leaf Digital Camera Back, which captures 14 bits per each RGB color.

## Understanding Digital Camera Resolution

A digital camera's resolution is based upon the number of horizontal and vertical image elements it can capture. As in a scanner, these image elements are called pixels. The greater the number of horizontal and vertical pixels, the higher the camera's resolution and thus the sharper the image and the smoother the transitions between colors.

As you might expect, the more expensive cameras usually offer the best resolutions. For instance, Kodak's DCS 460 model, which retails for about $30,000, features a resolution of 2,000 x 3,000 pixels. Apple's QuickTake 150 camera, which retails for less than $800, has a top resolution of 640 x 480 pixels. Kodak's DC 40, with a resolution of 756 x 504 pixels, boasts one of the top resolutions of cameras costing under $1,000.

Unfortunately, many people—even those familiar with digital imaging—find it difficult to understand how pixel dimensions translate into image quality. To understand this, you first must realize that pixel dimensions are normally based on a resolution of 72 pixels per inch. You also must understand that reducing the size of a digital image increases the number of pixels per inch (see Chapter 6 for more information about resolution and resizing images). Thus, the resolution issue usually boils down to: What is the largest size to which you can safely reduce an image and still produce high-quality output?

To achieve the best results for print output, resolution should be about 1.5 to 2 times the screen frequency (measured in lines per inch) used to output the image. As discussed in Chapter 6, many magazines are output at a screen frequency of 150 lpi. Assume you are using Kodak's DCS 460 and need to send a 7 x 7-inch, 225 ppi image to a magazine. To determine whether you can shoot an image that meets these requirements, simply divide the required pixels per inch into the camera's horizontal and vertical resolution. The results tell you that the maximum image size possible at 225 ppi is approximately 13 x 9 inches (3,000/225 = 13.33 inches and 2,000/225 = 8.89 inches). Thus, you'll have no problem delivering the 7 x 7-inch, 225 ppi image. However, if you were using a camera that has a top resolution of 640 x 480 pixels for print work, you'd have a problem. The optimum image size at 225 ppi is 2.84 x 2.13 (640/225 = 2.84, 480/225 = 2.13) for output at a screen frequency of 150 lpi.

If you don't like math and you own an image-editing program, you'll probably be able to let your software perform the calculations for you. For instance, if you are using Photoshop, you can use either the New File or Resize dialog box to calculate maximum image size for a given resolution. If you are using the New File dialog box, switch the measurement units to pixels. Enter the camera's horizontal and vertical dimensions into the width and height fields with the resolution set to 72 ppi. Next, change measurement units to inches, and then switch the resolution to 225 ppi. Photoshop will automatically compute the image, as shown here. Most image-editing and some painting programs work similarly to Photoshop.

# Using Digital Cameras

Once you understand how a digital camera's bit depth and resolution affect its output quality, you'll have a better idea whether you need one. Before you start using a digital camera, you should also be aware that not all models (not even some expensive ones) capture every nuance of color in an image, particularly if lighting conditions are bad. This doesn't mean that digital cameras produce low-quality images that often can't be used; rather that you may need to use an image-editing program such as Adobe Photoshop, HSC Live Picture, Fauve Xres, Micrografx Picture Publisher, or Corel PhotoPaint, or correction software sold with your camera, to expand the dynamic range of an image, sharpen, and color-correct it. Using an image-editing program to enhance digital images is discussed in Chapter 14.

## Using Kodak's DCS 420 and 460 Cameras

Kodak's DCS 420 (seen in Chapter 2) and 460 digital cameras are perfect for catalog, news, and business photography, as well as scientific and multimedia applications. Some companies, such as ABC-TV, have used them to take pictures of the Super Bowl and the Academy Awards before posting them on America Online.

Each DCS camera features a Nikon N90 SLR camera body attached to a digital back manufactured by Kodak. The digital back translates the image captured by the Nikon's optics into digital information and stores it. One of the chief advantages of the DCS series is that each model uses virtually all of the features of the Nikon camera. Auto-focus, metering modes, flash, and self-timer controls operate exactly as they would if the camera were not attached to the Kodak digital back. (Note that the camera cannot be used without the digital back.)

Both DCS cameras hold up to 300 images in memory per battery charge. For storage, both cameras can utilize PCMCIA-ATA cards—the same type of cards used in portable computers. A 170MB card can store 100 images in the 420 and 30 images in the 460. (Since the resolution of the 460 is greater than the 420, the file size of its images is greater than those of the 420. Thus, a 170MB card can store only 30 images inside the 460.)

Both cameras capture images using 36-bit color (12 bits per each RGB color), which means they provide fine detail from highlight to shadow areas. The DCS 420, which retails for under $10,000, captures 1,524 x 1,012 pixels, while the 460, which retails for about $30,000, features a 2,000 x 3,000-pixel resolution. At 300 ppi, the DCS 460 provides a maximum image size of 8 x 13.4 inches; the DCS 420, 4.5 x 6.7.

Using the DCS camera is as simple as operating a 35mm camera. Since the N90 is fully automatic, you can allow it to set exposure and focus. If you are taking pictures in a studio, you can attach the camera directly to a Mac or PC via its SCSI port (PC users must purchase a SCSI board to make the connection; a SCSI interface is built into all Macintoshes). When connected to the computer, you can preview images as you shoot them.

If you take pictures in the field, images can later be downloaded to your computer over a SCSI cable. The software that allows you to preview and load images into your computer is an Adobe Photoshop-compatible plug-in. This plug-in allows images to be loaded directly into most image-editing software. Figure 8-1 shows the Kodak DCS's plug-in dialog box after the plug-in was loaded from Adobe Photoshop's Acquire menu command. Notice that the Source pop-up menu is set to Camera. This setting allows the images to be downloaded directly from the DCS camera. When the Source is set to Folder, you can use the Kodak plug-in to preview and load images that have already been saved to your hard drive. Notice that the plug-in allows some color-balancing and color-correcting features; nevertheless, most color-correcting is best handled in image-editing software.

Once you've decided which image you want to load into your image-editing software, you can click on the image, and then click on the Preview button. The preview screen, shown in Figure 8-2, allows you to see an enlarged version of the image. When you move the mouse over the image, readouts of the red, green, and blue color values appear. The preview box can also show statistical information about how the image was taken.

Figure 8-3 shows the final image after it was reduced and corrected in Photoshop. In order to correct the tonal range of the image, white and black points were reset in Photoshop (setting white and black points is discussed in Chapter 14).

## The Kodak DC 40 Digital Camera

Kodak's newest entry into the digital camera field is the DC 40, a low-priced model designed for people who need to add photographs to presentations, newsletters, and

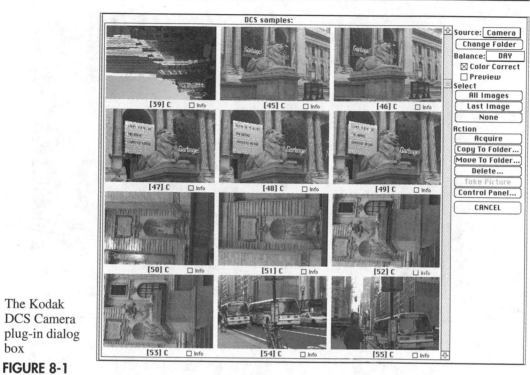

The Kodak
DCS Camera
plug-in dialog
box

**FIGURE 8-1**

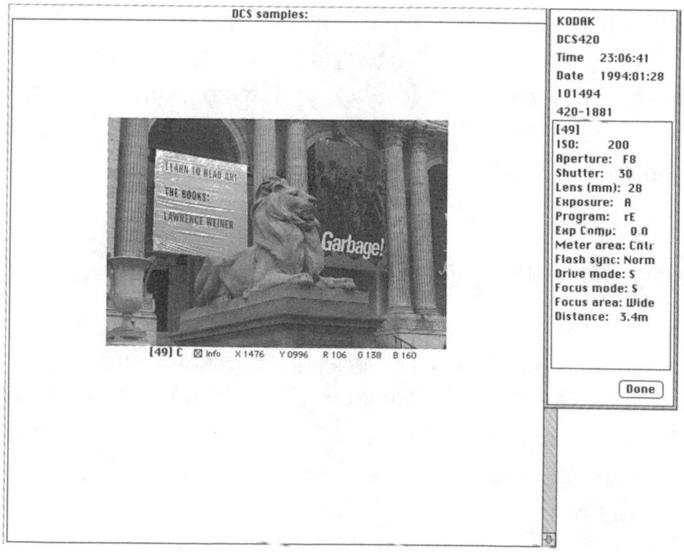

The DCS
plug-in
provides
statistical
information
about an
image

**FIGURE 8-2**

Image taken
by Kodak's
DCS 420
camera

**FIGURE 8-3**

multimedia productions. The DC 40, shown in Figure 8-4, retails for under $1,000 and captures 8 bits per pixel at a resolution of 758 x 504 pixels. At this resolution, the camera can store up to 48 images; in low-resolution mode (378 x 256), it can store 99 images. The DC 40 features a built-in flash and automatic exposure control with an adjustable lighten/darken switch for fine-tuning shots. The focal length of the DC 40's standard lens is nearly the same as that provided by a 42mm lens on a standard 35mm camera. Close-up, wide-angle, and telephoto lenses also can be attached to the camera. Images can later be downloaded to a Mac or PC using a serial port cable.

## Using the Apple QuickTake 150 Camera

If you don't need high-resolution images but still wish to take advantage of many of the features that digital cameras offer, you might wish to investigate Apple's QuickTake 150 (seen in Chapter 2), available for both Macs and PCs. The QuickTake retails for under $800, with a street price of under $700. QuickTake images can be used for newsletters, in-house publications, presentations, and multimedia productions.

Kodak's DC
40 digital
camera
**FIGURE 8-4**

Although the QuickTake cannot rival pictures taken with a Kodak DCS digital camera, it utilizes some of the same technology. In fact, the QuickTake's CCD system was designed and manufactured by Kodak.

The QuickTake can save 16 24-bit color images at a resolution of 640 x 480 pixels. Since this is the same resolution used by many computer monitors, the QuickTake images are appropriate for multimedia and onscreen presentations. Although the QuickTake is not recommended for high-end publishing, its 640 x 480 resolution can produce to a 4 x 3-inch image at 160 ppi. Thus, if you were outputting a publication at 80 lpi (a common screen frequency for newspapers), the quality and size of QuickTake images may be sufficient for your needs. Remember, though, that a digital camera in the QuickTake's price range does not have the dynamic range of more expensive digital cameras, nor can its optical system and automatic exposure controls rival those of a Nikon N90.

The QuickTake includes a built-in flash and a fixed-focus lens with a focal length equivalent to a 35mm camera with a 50mm lens. Exposure and focusing are entirely automatic, so using the camera requires little more than pointing and clicking a "shutter" button. As mentioned earlier, the QuickTake can take only 16 shots in its high-resolution mode. However, its standard mode resolution (320 x 240 pixels) allows 32 pictures to be taken.

QuickTake's software provides a thumbnail view of images taken with the camera

**FIGURE 8-5**

After you've taken your pictures, the QuickTake's proprietary software allows images to be downloaded to a computer through the serial port. Figure 8-5 shows the filmstrip of thumbnail previews that the QuickTake software provides. The QuickTake's Camera Controls dialog box, shown here, duplicates the functionality of buttons on the camera itself. By clicking on the icons in this dialog box, you can take a picture from the QuickTake when it is connected to your computer, change resolution modes, and delete images from the camera's memory. In order to save an image, you simply double-click on its thumbnail, then choose Save in the File menu. The QuickTake's Save dialog box allows you to save an image in PICT or TIFF file format. This lets you import QuickTake images into different applications. It also allows you to save a 24-bit image or reduce the number of colors in an image to keep file sizes low. Figure 8-6 shows an image taken by the QuickTake camera and reduced to 3.2 x 2.4. Reducing the image to this size yields a resolution of 200 ppi.

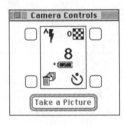

# The Leaf Digital Camera Back

The Leaf Digital Camera Back is a high-end digital camera back that can be fitted to Hasselblad, Sinar, Cambo, and Mamima RZ67 studio cameras. It can be used for catalog work, magazines, newspapers, and technical photography.

The Leaf Digital Camera Back captures 14 bits of information for each red, green, and blue color, ensuring an image with fine details over a broad range of colors. In order to deliver an image with a high-dynamic range, the Leaf must capture color images in three separate exposures; it does this with an automatic filter wheel.

Image taken
with Apple's
QuickTake
100 camera

**FIGURE 8-6**

Since three exposures are needed for each image, the Leaf can only be used for shooting inanimate objects. It also must remain attached to your computer. The high quality of the images the Leaf Camera Back produces is reflected in its retail price, about $30,000.

The Leaf Camera Back captures images at 2,048 x 2,048 pixels. If you needed to output an image at 225 ppi, the Leaf could produce an image at a maximum size of 9 x 9 inches. At a resolution of 300 ppi, the maximum image size would be 6.8 x 6.8.

**OTE:** *Leaf also manufactures the Catchlight Digital Camera Back. This high-end studio camera back allows you to capture color and black-and-white images of live models and moving subjects.*

## The Nikon E2 Digital Camera

One of the newest entries in the growing field of digital cameras is the Nikon E2 series, which retails from about $14,000 to $17,000. These cameras can be used for news, sporting events, and catalogs. They can use any of Nikon's SLR interchangeable lenses without loss of view (some digital cameras do not let you use the entire area in the viewfinder).

The E2 cameras feature a resolution of 1,280 x 1,000 pixels and a high-speed, 15MB storage card that can store 84 compressed images. Using the E2, you can shoot one frame per second; the E2s allow three frames per second with up to seven continuous pictures.

## Dycam Inc. Digital Cameras

The Dycam Corporation manufactures several grayscale and color digital cameras which retail for under $1,000. All of these cameras create images with a resolution of 496 x 365 pixels. This makes them inappropriate for high-end publishing but suitable for in-house newsletters and some catalog work. Dycam's cameras are available for both Macs and PCs.

If needed, you can purchase wide- and super-wide-angle lenses with your Dycam camera, along with telephoto and super-telephoto lenses. Dycam's top-of-the-line color camera can save 36 images at 496 x 365 pixels. After the images are taken, they can be downloaded to Macs or PCs using a cable connected to the computer's serial port. Pictures for downloading are chosen using a Photoshop-compatible plug-in. The plug-in also can be accessed through Color-It image-correction software included with the camera. The Dycam's Acquire dialog box, shown here, allows you to choose the picture that you want downloaded using the plug-in. To see an image taken with the Dycam camera, see Chapter 14.

If you wish to take quick digital photographs from your laptop, Dycam's Gator Digital Camera for Mobile Computer clamps directly to it. When using the Gator, each image must be downloaded before the next shot is taken.

# Digitizing Video

If you are working in a multimedia production, you may need to integrate video clips into your project. If you're creating an image in a page layout or image-editing program, you may need to place a freeze frame from video in your work. If you are using a multimedia program, you may wish to integrate a video clip into it. In order to digitize video, you'll need the right hardware to convert the analog signal of a video image into a digital signal that can be read by your computer. Before you get started transferring and digitizing video images, you should have a basic idea of how a video signal is created. This will help you understand some of the important issues involving quality and compression when you start to use your video clips on your computer.

# How Video Images Are Created

A video sequence is actually composed of many indvidual still frames. Motion is created on American and Japanese TV systems because 30 frames are displayed each second (29.7, to be precise). In European and Australian systems, 25 frames are displayed each second.

In the United States and Japan, a video frame is created from 525 horizontal scan lines of information—a standard set by the National Television Standards Committee (NTSC) in the early '50s. In the NTSC standard, a video frame is created from two passes of the monitor's screen. First the odd lines are scanned, then the even. The two passes combined consume 1/30th of a second. The PAL (Phase Alternate Lines) system used in much of Europe, Australia, and South Africa creates images from 625 lines. The SECAM (Sequential Couleur avec Memoire) standard used in France also uses 625 lines.

If you start to do a little math, you'll see that video storage requirements can become staggering. Each 24-bit full frame (640 x 480) can consume over 900KB of storage space. Since there are 30 frames in one second of video, a one-second, full-frame video clip without sound could consume over 27MB of memory. This translates to over 1.5GB per minute. Thus, to save memory while working with video, multimedia producers often work at a frame size smaller than full frame, compress the video, and don't always record every consecutive frame.

# Video Digitizing Boards

In order to convert the video signal to a computer signal, you need a board that converts the video's analog signal to a digital one. Manufacturers of video digitizing boards (sometimes called video capture boards) include Matrox, Intel, TrueVision, RasterOps, and Radius. Most digitizing boards used on personal computers can handle two types of video signals: *composite* and *S-video*. Consumer-grade video equipment delivers a composite signal. In a composite signal the video's brightness and color information are input and output in one signal. Better grade video devices such as Hi-8 camcorders utilize S-video. The S-video signal is superior to the composite signal because the color and luminance (brightness) are separated into two different signals. Although S-video quality is good, professional video equipment requires a higher standard: *component video*. In a component video system (also called YUV), the video signal is broken down into two separate colors and one luminance component.

**n OTE:** *You'll only find component video input and output available on higher-end professional systems such as Radius Telecast. The Telecast system can output component Betacam SP images and offers CD-quality multi-track audio. Telecast reads and writes time code and can generate a frame-accurate edit decision list (EDL).*

Here are some features to consider when evaluating a video digitizing board:

► Will the board capture a full frame of video at 30 frames per second?

RasterOps MoviePak2 Pro Suite, Radius VideoVision, Radius Telecast, and TrueVision Targa 2000 all allow you to capture a 640 x 480 image at 30 frames per second.

► What digitizing software is included with the board?

Many video boards include software called *plug-ins* that allows you to grab a frame from image-editing or paint programs, such as Adobe Photoshop and Fractal Design Painter. Figure 8-7 shows the Image Capture dialog box from a Photoshop plug-in included with RasterOps MoviePak2 Pro Suite. The image was captured from a camcorder connected to a Macintosh computer with a RasterOps 24XLTV video board included with MoviePak2 Pro Suite. Notice that the dialog box allows you to pick the size for the image capture, choose a television standard (NTSC or PAL), and increase or reduce contrast. If you choose the Grab button, the frame is automatically loaded into a new window in Adobe Photoshop. Also included in the MoviePak2 package is a full working version of Adobe Premiere which allows you to capture frames and clips. Premiere is also bundled with Radius' VideoVision system which includes VideoFusion, a digital special effects program.

► Does the digitizing board provide 24-bit color?

RasterOps 24XLTV, packaged with its MoviePak2 Pro Suite, is not only a 24-bit color card, but also provides 24-bit color for monitors as large as 21 inches.

► Does the digitizing board support international standards?

Boards and software created by vendors such as RasterOps and Radius provide support for NTSC, PAL, and SECAM.

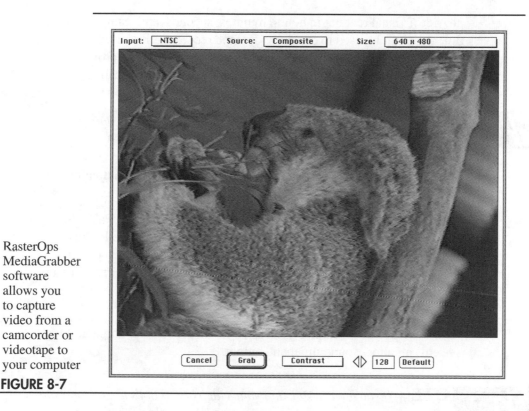

RasterOps MediaGrabber software allows you to capture video from a camcorder or videotape to your computer

**FIGURE 8-7**

► Does the digitizing board offer hardware compression?

Hardware compression is necessary to play back full-frame, full-motion video at a normal speed. Look for boards that include JPEG compression and decompression. Radius VideoVision, Radius Telecast, and RasterOps MoviePak2 Pro Suite all include boards providing JPEG compression. Radius VideoVision also includes an advanced compression feature called *Adaptive Compression,* which helps prevent individual frames from being lost during a recording session.

► Does the digitizing board include utilities that allow you to start and stop video devices?

Both RasterOps MoviePak2 Pro Suite and Radius VideoVision include Adobe Premiere plug-ins that allow you to control videotape machines from within Premiere. The plug-ins also allow you to time-stamp your digital movies with onscreen SMPTE time code. (SMPTE time code can provide a visual readout in hours, minutes, seconds, and frames. SMPTE time code can be used to control videotape recorders. It is used by video producers when editing videotape productions.) Cables are provided for videotape machines that can be controlled through a serial cable.

 **OTE:** *If you wish to execute frame-accurate playback and recording, you will need a frame-accurate videotape deck.*

▶ Does the board allow you to output to video, and view the output on a TV monitor?

Radius VideoVision, Radius Telecast, and RasterOps MoviePak2 Pro Suite all include encoder boxes that allow video output. The Radius VideoVision also allows for two video input sources and includes an expansion port for SMPTE time code input through third-party software.

▶ Does the board allow sound input?

Radius VideoVision, Radius Telecast, and the TrueVision Targa 2000 systems all allow sound input and output.

 **OTE:** *If you have a Mac and your video board does not include sound input, you can input the sound in many Macs through the computer's built-in sound input jack.*

## Capturing Video Clips

Once you have a video digitizing board installed in your computer, recording a video frame or clip is quite simple. First, connect a video cable from the video board to either your VCR or your camcorder. Typically, for composite video, you will connect a cable from your video board or encoder box to the video output jack of your VCR or camcorder. If your software provides color-correcting and calibration control, you should make these adjustments before you start your video capture session. Often, you can set Hue, Saturation, Brightness, Contrast, Sharpness, Black Level, and White Level. Figure 8-8 shows Premiere's Waveform dialog box, which also allows you to use Premiere's Waveform monitor and Vector scope to match reference color bars to color bars on the videotape. If you are working with Premiere, you can use its Recording Settings dialog box to change the size of the recording window and

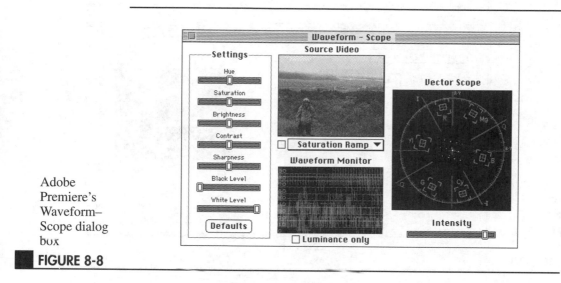

Adobe
Premiere's
Waveform–
Scope dialog
box

**FIGURE 8-8**

report if any frames were dropped during the recording process, as shown in Figure 8-9. The Post Compress video option in the dialog box is used if your hardware board does not provide compression. If you choose this option, the clip is compressed after the video has been captured.

Often, the next step in the recording process is to select a frame rate and compression options. Figure 8-10 shows Radius VideoFusion's Video dialog box with the Radius Studio setting chosen. This compression setting was chosen to ensure that Radius VideoVision's hardware compression was used when capturing

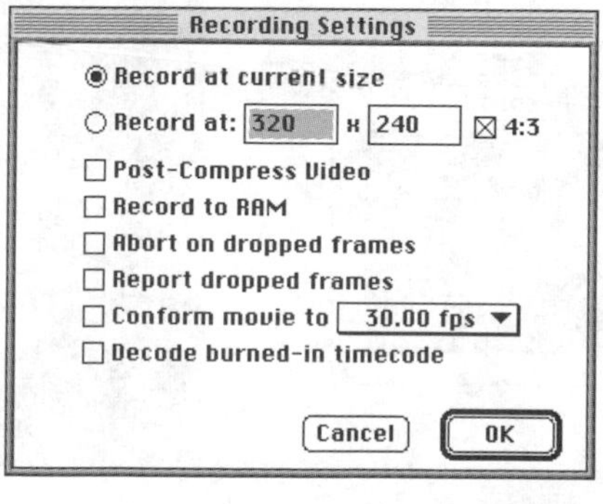

Adobe
Premiere's
Recording
Settings
dialog box

**FIGURE 8-9**

Radius
VideoFusion
Video dialog
box

**FIGURE 8-10**

the video. In the dialog box, notice that frame rates up to 30 frames per second are possible. In this session, we connected the video and audio output jacks from our camcorder to the audio and video input jacks of VideoVision's encoder panel to capture both video and sound simultaneously.

Next, simply start your videotape deck, and click a record button onscreen. Premiere's Record button in the Movie Capture dialog box is shown here. After a clip is captured, it opens into a clip window as shown below. If your video digitizing board includes software to control a tape deck, you can often click a button onscreen to start the tape deck.

## Using the Connectix QuickCam

If you'd like to begin experimenting with computer video recording but don't wish to spend a lot of money, your best bet is Connectix QuickCam, which retails for less

than $150. QuickCam is a tiny, round video camera, smaller than a tennis ball. It records black-and-white video images and sound directly into your computer without the need of a video digitizing board. QuickCam records 150 x 120-pixel movies (about 2 x 2 inches) at 15 frames per second (twice as slow as normal video). The camera can record a 320 x 240 image at 4 frames per second. QuickCam can record video movies, as shown here, in Apple's QuickTime digital movie format, and it can grab still frames.

Clicking the record button starts the recording process. Brightness can be adjusted by clicking and dragging on the horizontal slider below the image.

Although QuickCam cannot be used for professional video, it can be handy for video conferencing or for multimedia producers who need to quickly prototype a production. It also can be used to create simple training videos.

# Conclusion

This chapter provided an introduction to the basics of digitizing images using a digital camera and capturing video clips using video capture boards. In Chapter 14, you'll learn how to enhance images captured by a digital camera. In Chapter 16, you'll learn how to integrate video clips into multimedia productions. In Chapter 18, you'll learn how to output to video.

# 9

# Using Photo CDs

If you need to digitize photographic prints, negatives, transparencies, or slides but don't wish to purchase a scanner or pay a service bureau to scan your images, Kodak's Photo CD digital imaging process may be your best bet. It's one of the easiest and cheapest methods of obtaining high-quality digital images. In fact, the quality is so high that several stock image houses have chosen to distribute their images in Photo CD format.

If you wish to digitize your images on Photo CD, all you need to do is deliver a roll of film, slides, or previously developed negatives to a photofinisher or service bureau equipped with a Photo CD authoring system. The service bureau scans your images and stores them on a CD-ROM. You can then load the images from the CD-ROM onto your computer. Figure 9-1 shows the entire Photo CD production process, which includes a printout or index of the images on the CD. The entire process appears very easy and enticing. Unfortunately, once your images are digitized on a Photo CD, you may find yourself a bit bewildered: How do you load the pictures into your image-editing or page layout software? How do you pick the correct resolution for printing or for multimedia applications?

This chapter provides the answers to those questions. You'll learn about the different Photo CD formats and the various ways you can load Photo CD images into your software programs. You'll also learn how to use Kodak's *precision device profiles,* which enable you to better control Photo CD color quality for printing.

# Master Photo CD and Pro Photo CD

Before you drop off your first roll of film or package of slides at a Photo CD photofinisher, you should understand exactly what types of film formats you can use and how your images will be saved on a CD-ROM disc.

Kodak provides two main Photo CD formats, Photo CD (also called Photo CD Master) and Pro Photo CD (also called Pro Photo CD Master). The Photo CD format can digitize only 35mm film and slides onto a CD-ROM disc. The cost is about $20 for 24 Photo CD images. If you have a *multisession* CD-ROM drive (most newer drives are multisession, sometimes called *extended architecture*), you can add images to a CD-ROM until it is full. If you don't have a multisession CD-ROM, you can still use Photo CDs; you just can't keep accumulating images on the CD disc.

About 100 images fit on one Photo CD disc. Thus, Photo CDs are an excellent medium for image archiving.

Kodak's Pro Photo CD system can digitize images shot on 35, 70, or 120mm, as well as 4 x 5 film. Since the Pro Photo CD images can be larger than Master CD images, fewer images fit on a CD-ROM. Depending upon the image size, you may be able to fit 100, 25, or 6 images on a CD disc.

 **OTE:** *Kodak also offers Photo CD Catalog and Portfolio formats. Photo CD Catalog allows you to store over 4,000 low-res images on a CD. Photo CD Portfolio is used for creating interactive presentations from Photo CD images. Both formats are created from Master Photo CD or Pro Photo CD files*

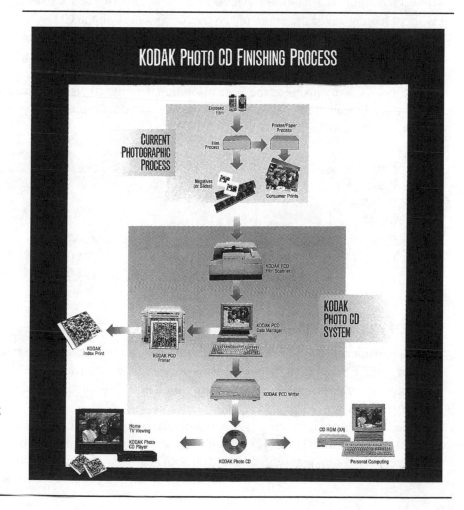

The Photo CD finishing process. Courtesy of Eastman Kodak

**FIGURE 9-1**

# Photo CD Image Size and Resolution

When a Photo CD image is digitized, it is stored on disc in Kodak's *proprietary YCC* format. YCC is also the name of the Photo CD color space. Like the Lab Color space (described in Chapter 4), YCC format separates a color image into one luminance (brightness) component and two chroma (color) components. This allows files to be compressed so that the same image can be stored at five different resolutions (six for Pro Photo CD) on a CD-ROM disc. The separate files are called an *Image Pac*. When an Image Pac is created, disk space is saved because the color data for the image is saved only once at a *Base* resolution, but the luminance data is saved once for each resolution.This means that the user can access five or six sizes of an image without having saved the entire image five or six times on the CD.

The following table shows the resolution and approximate file sizes of Photo CD images. In the table, notice that Kodak defines the resolution of each image in terms of its relationship to its Base image. For instance, a Base 4 image contains four times as many pixels as the Base resolution, and the file is four times as large. As you read through the chart, note that the file size quadruples as the dimensions of the image double.

| Resolution Type | Resolution | File Size |
| --- | --- | --- |
| Base/16 | 126 x 192 | 72KB |
| Base/4 | 256 x 384 | 288KB |
| Base | 512 x 768 | 1.12MB |
| Base 4 | 1024 x 1536 | 4.5MB |
| Base 16 | 2048 x 3072 | 18MB |
| Base 64 (Pro only) | 4096 x 61444 | 72MB |

## Analyzing Photo CD Resolution

When considering the suitability of digital images for publication and multimedia output, image resolution is crucial. Image resolution determines the maximum output size (when printed or viewed in multimedia presentations) before image quality is degraded.

Kodak's Base/4 resolution (128 x 192 pixels) translates to 1.8 x 2.5 inches at 72 ppi. At this size, Base/16 images are suitable primarily for viewing thumbnail images onscreen. Base/4 images (256 x 384 pixels) can be used in multimedia presentations at a maximum size of approximately 3.5 x 5 inches onscreen. Kodak's Base resolution (512 x 768 pixels) is highly suited for full screen images in multimedia presentations and publishing at smaller sizes. Base 4 (1024 x 1536) files can provide a full screen image for output on high-definition television.

The larger image formats, Base 16 and Base 64 (Pro Photo CD only), may be used for color publishing depending on the size of the image being output. The chart below lists the maximum size for each image if the resolution were 225 ppi. This resolution was chosen as a benchmark because it is the resolution commonly chosen when outputting at a screen frequency of 150 lpi. The subject of screen frequency is introduced in Chapter 5, and is covered in more detail in Chapter 17.

| Dimensions in Pixels | Maximum Dimensions in Inches at 225 ppi |
|---|---|
| 1024 x 1536 | 4.5 x 6.8 inches |
| 2048 x 3072 | 9 x 13.6 inches |
| 4096 x 6144 | 18 x 27.3 inches |

*n* **OTE:** *You can calculate maximum dimension in inches by dividing an image's dimensions in pixels by its pixels per inch. For instance, 1024/225 = 4.5 and 1536/225 = 6.8. Also note that when you load a Photo CD image into an image-editing program, the image's resolution in pixels per inch will be set to 72. If you resize by increasing the number of pixels per inch in the image, its dimensions in inches are reduced. To learn more about resolution and resizing images, see Chapter 6.*

Once you've ascertained that you can utilize at least one size in a Photo CD Image Pac, your next concern is whether the color and exposure of your photographs will be replicated in the Photo CD images.

# Ensuring Photo CD Color and Exposure Match Your Expectations

During the Photo CD scanning process, the photofinisher can use either a *Scene Space* or *Universal Film Term* option to set how closely the Photo CD images match the color of your original photographs. If the photofinisher chooses Scene Space, an overall color correction is made. This is done to remove color casts and enhance exposure based on standardizing memory colors (memory colors are those you recognize from memory). If you are a photographer, though, you may have chosen specific exposure settings or film for a certain color or tonal effect. Thus, you may wish to direct your photofinisher to use Universal Film Term to ensure that the Photo CD images you view on your computer capture the mood you intended when you took your pictures.

# Opening Photo CD Images on Your Computer

Because Photo CD images are stored on CD-ROMs in Kodak's proprietary YCC format, you can't simply load any software package, choose File/Open, and expect a Photo CD image to load. Fortunately, some page layout and most image-editing software allow you to import Photo CD images as you would any other graphics file. Before loading a Photo CD image, though, you might wish to investigate all options because some are more efficient or provide better color fidelity than others.

**OTE:** *Viewing the directory of a Photo CD disc can be confusing. Depending upon the computer system and software you are using, you may see numerous folders onscreen. For instance, on the Mac you often see a folder for every Photo CD image size. Don't try to load files directly from these folders. To ensure the best color quality, always load Photo CD images according to the instructions specified by the software you are using.*

## Using Kodak's Access Plus Software

If your graphics software cannot import Photo CD images, you may wish to purchase Kodak's Access Plus software. Using Access Plus, you can view and crop Photo CD images. Most importantly, you can save Photo CD files in different formats so that they can be imported into other software.

After loading Access Plus, you'll probably want to take a quick look at all of the images on the Photo CD disc. The easiest way to do this is to use the Load Contact Sheet command, which simulates a photographer's contact sheet, providing a miniature view of all the images on disc, as shown in Figure 9-2. If you wish to view the image at a larger size, you can either double-click on it, or choose the Load Image Pac command to load the image onscreen. When you choose Load Image Pac, a list of Photo CD files appears onscreen, as shown in Figure 9-3. Notice that the Photo

CD files listed in Figure 9-3 all have numbers as filenames. This is a standard naming convention for Photo CD files. In order to know exactly what file to load, you'll need to look at onscreen contact sheets, preview boxes, or catalog listings that accompany stock Photo CD collections. Before loading a file in Access Plus, your next step is to choose the image size in the pop-up menu and the number of colors you wish the image to have. The choices in the pop-up menu also include an option for converting the color image into grayscale.

Once the image is onscreen, you can crop or save it using Access Plus' Export command. When you export, you can save files in TIFF, PICT, or EPS format. The Export dialog box also allows you to reduce the number of colors in the image, change a color image to grayscale when exporting, and change the image resolution.

Access Plus also allows you to export an image as a CMYK file. However, this function can be used only if you purchase Kodak *device color profiles,* which control the conversion from YCC to CMYK color space. Using device profiles and converting Photo CD images to CMYK are covered later in this chapter.

Access Plus
Contact Sheet
from Kodak
Photo CD
Sampler

**FIGURE 9-2**

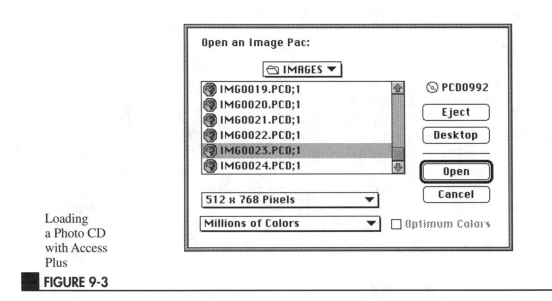

Loading
a Photo CD
with Access
Plus

**FIGURE 9-3**

# Using Kodak's Photo CD Acquire Plug-in Module

In order to enhance the colors and tonal range of Photo CD images during the file-loading process, Kodak created a Photoshop-compatible plug-in module. This module works with most image-editing and painting programs that support Photoshop-compatible plug-ins.

To use Kodak's Photo CD Acquire plug-in module, it first must be installed in your software's Plug-in folder (directory). When you wish to load a Photo CD, you access the plug-in by choosing Kodak Photo CD from Photoshop's Acquire submenu. The dialog box that opens provides a preview of each CD image when you click on it in the directory listing, as shown in Figure 9-4. The image in the preview box is from Digital Stock Corporation's Active Lifestyles disc. In the dialog box, you choose your image and resolution. To make color adjustments, click on the Edit Image button. In the Edit Image dialog box, shown in Figure 9-5, you can click and drag over the preview area to crop the image; you can sharpen the image, and you can make color adjustments using the sliders. In the Metric pop-up menu, you can load the Photo CD image as a grayscale image or you can choose a monitor *gamma* setting. A monitor's gamma setting is a numerical representation of its contrast. The recommended gamma setting for most monitors displaying images that will be printed is 1.8.

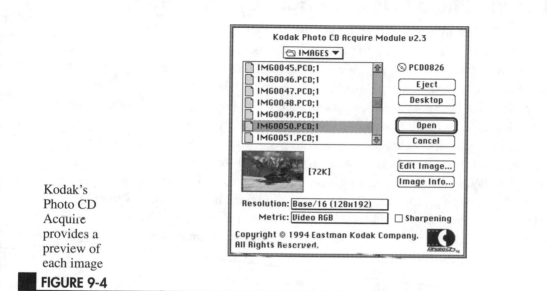

Kodak's
Photo CD
Acquire
provides a
preview of
each image

**FIGURE 9-4**

When you are ready to load the Photo CD image, you exit the Edit Image dialog box by clicking either OK or Cancel. This returns you to the original dialog box where you must click Open to load the image.

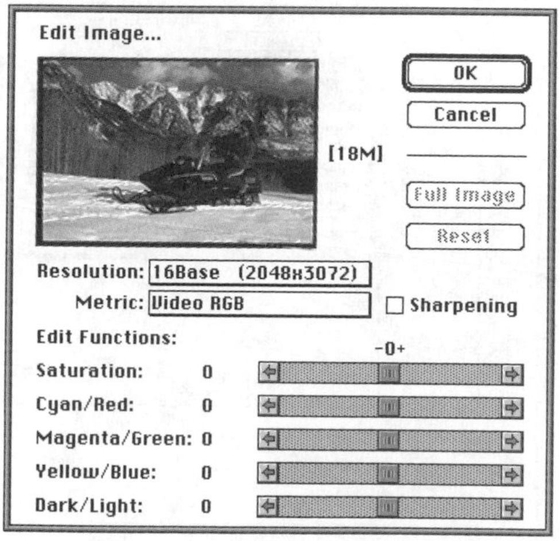

Kodak Photo
CD Acquire's
Edit Image
dialog box

**FIGURE 9-5**

## Placing Photo CDs into Page Layout Programs

Photo CD files are supported by a long list of graphics software. Although many software packages allow you to preview and choose the resolution of the image being loaded, some do not. For instance, QuarkXPress only provides a preview of the Photo CD image being loaded. Adobe PageMaker allows you to choose resolution, but does not provide a preview. Figure 9-6 shows a Photo CD image from ADC ImageVault being loaded into QuarkXPress. When loading a Photo CD into Adobe PageMaker, a dialog box appears, allowing you to choose the resolution for the image you will be loading. If you wish to place high-resolution Photo CD images in a page layout program, you may want to load it into an image-editing program first. Image-editing programs allow you to crop your Photo CD images to reduce file size. (When you crop an image in a page layout program, the image's file size is not reduced.) You also can sharpen and color-correct an image before importing it into your page layout program.

## Using Photo CDs with Image-Editing Software

Certainly one of the reasons for the growing popularity of Photo CDs is the sharpness, color fidelity, and detail of the images they hold. Over the past years,

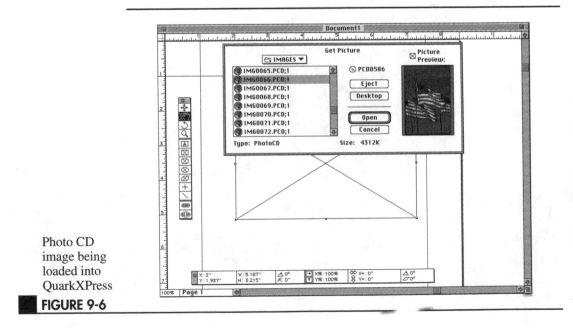

Photo CD image being loaded into QuarkXPress

**FIGURE 9-6**

experiments have shown that the quality of Photo CD images can often rival that of high-end drum scans. As mentioned earlier, the quality is so high that stock image houses such as ADC ImageVault, CMCD Library, Corel Professional Photos, Digital Stock Corporation, Planet Art, and Photodex all use the Photo CD format for distributing their stock images. Despite the high reputation of Photo CD quality, some users have been disappointed with the final printed output because color fidelity did not match their expectations. To help alleviate this problem, Kodak has integrated its Color Management System (CMS) into graphics software packages.

In order to ensure that colors match those of original photographs as closely as possible, and that highlight and shadow image areas have sufficient detail, Kodak created a plug-in for image-editing programs that use their Color Management System. The plug-in provides input and output device profiles to ensure the best quality color output for the printing industry. The device profiles are created to take into account the color characteristics of printers and other output devices. Profiles that can be purchased separately can also provide an accurate means of converting a Photo CD image to CMYK.

At least one digital stock house, Digital Stock Corporation, recommends using Kodak's CMS plug-in as the best means of attaining high-quality Photo CD output for color publishing. In fact, the company provides its own device profile to help ensure that its stock photography does not need color correcting. Digital Stock Corporation also intends to provide free device profiles to its customers so they can convert Photo CD files to CMYK color files when they are loaded into image-editing software. (As discussed in Chapter 4, CMYK is the color space used for printing continuous-tone color images. Before the color image can be printed, it must be converted to a CMYK color file.)

## Using Kodak's CMS Plug-in with Photoshop

When Adobe Photoshop is installed, Kodak's CMS plug-in system files are automatically saved to your hard disk (when you install all components that come with Photoshop). The plug-in is automatically activated when you try to load a Photo CD file. Thus, all you need to do to load a Photo CD image is choose File/Open. Select the Photo CD image you wish to open. After you click Open or OK, the KCMS dialog box appears with a preview of the Photo CD image, as shown in Figure 9-7. The Panda image you see is from the Digital Stock Corporation stock image Animals collection. After you choose the image resolution, your next step is to click the Source button.

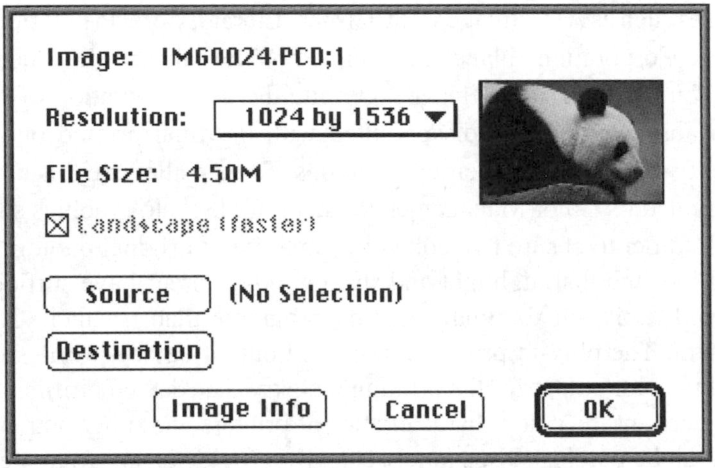

**Image:** IM60024.PCD;1

**Resolution:** [ 1024 by 1536 ▼ ]

**File Size:** 4.50M

☒ Landscape (faster)

[ **Source** ] (No Selection)

[ **Destination** ]

[ **Image Info** ]   [ **Cancel** ]   [ **OK** ]

Kodak's CMS
plug-in dialog
box

**FIGURE 9-7**

**OTE:**   *If Kodak's CMS plug-in does not load, make sure it is installed in your Plug-ins folder. If you need to reset the folder that Photoshop looks in for plug-ins, choose File/Preferences/Plug-ins.*

The Source button allows you to choose the film *term,* which refers to the emulsion used for processing. The choices include Ektachrome, Kodachrome, and Photo CD color negative, as shown in Figure 9-8. If you have any additional Source device profiles installed, they will appear in the Device pop-up menu. For instance, if you purchase stock images form Digital Stock Professional, you can choose a device profile created by Kodak specifically for Digital Stock images. Choosing the profile helps ensure that the image will appear as the photographer intended.

**IP:**   *If you don't know which film term was used to process your Photo CDs, you can exit the Source dialog box by choosing Cancel. The film term used can be found by clicking on the Image Info button in the plug-in's main dialog box screen.*

After you click OK, you then must click on the Destination button to choose whether you want to open the image in Photoshop's RGB or Lab format. If you want the Lab format, choose CIELAB in the Device pop-up menu. Kodak recommends

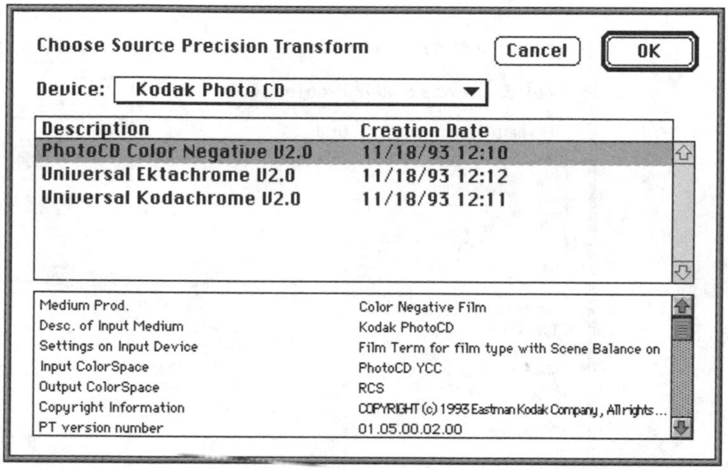

| Choose Source Precision Transform | | Cancel | OK |
|---|---|---|---|

**Device:** Kodak Photo CD ▼

| Description | Creation Date |
|---|---|
| **PhotoCD Color Negative V2.0** | **11/18/93 12:10** |
| Universal Ektachrome V2.0 | 11/18/93 12:12 |
| Universal Kodachrome V2.0 | 11/18/93 12:11 |

| | |
|---|---|
| Medium Prod. | Color Negative Film |
| Desc. of Input Medium | Kodak PhotoCD |
| Settings on Input Device | Film Term for film type with Scene Balance on |
| Input ColorSpace | PhotoCD YCC |
| Output ColorSpace | RCS |
| Copyright Information | COPYRIGHT (c) 1993 Eastman Kodak Company, All rights… |
| PT version number | 01.05.00.02.00 |

The Source dialog box with Photo CD chosen as the device profile

**FIGURE 9-8**

that images that later will be converted to CMYK be opened in this mode because Kodak's YCC color space is based on the Lab color space. If you want to open an image in Photoshop's RGB color mode, select Adobe Photoshop RGB. Don't be confused when you see the words "RCS to Adobe Photoshop"; RCS stands for Reference Color Space. This is an interim color space used when converting from one color space to another. Close the Destination dialog box by clicking OK.

If you have purchased additional device profiles, they will appear in the Destination dialog box's device pop-up menu. Figure 9-9 shows a device profile that automatically converts the Photo CD image to CMYK color. By using Kodak's own device profile, you help ensure that screen colors are matched as closely as possible when the image is output. After you have specified an option in the Destination dialog box, click OK. This closes the Destination dialog box and reopens the CMS dialog box. Click OK to load your Photo CD image.

# Other Image-Editing Software

If you don't own Photoshop or if you're looking for an easy way to convert Photo CD files to CMYK, you might wish to investigate Human Software's CD-Q plug-in.

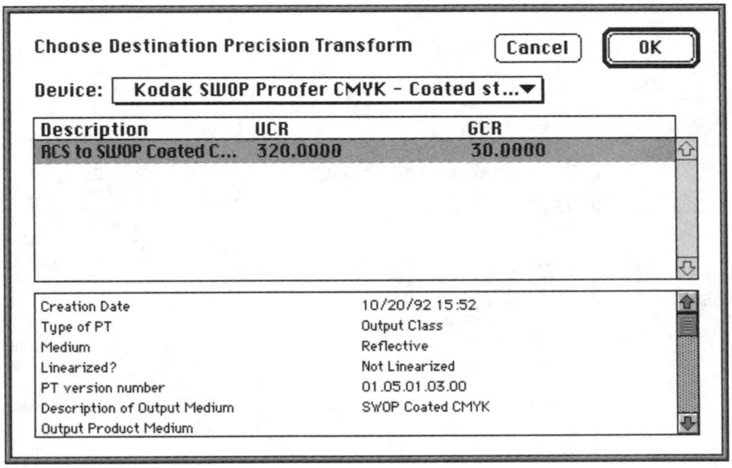

| Choose Destination Precision Transform | Cancel | OK |
|---|---|---|

**Device:** Kodak SWOP Proofer CMYK – Coated st...▼

| Description | UCR | GCR |
|---|---|---|
| RCS to SWOP Coated C... | 320.0000 | 30.0000 |

| | |
|---|---|
| Creation Date | 10/20/92 15:52 |
| Type of PT | Output Class |
| Medium | Reflective |
| Linearized? | Not Linearized |
| PT version number | 01.05.01.03.00 |
| Description of Output Medium | SWOP Coated CMYK |
| Output Product Medium | |

Kodak device profiles allow a Photo CD image to be converted to CMYK

**FIGURE 9-9**

CD-Q is a Photoshop-compatible plug-in that allows you to convert Kodak Photo CDs to grayscale, RGB, and CMYK as you load them into your image-editing software. The program requires a math coprocessor and a minimum of 12MB of RAM for your image-editing software.

CD-Q allows you to scroll through thumbnail versions of your Photo CD. Once you select an image, a dialog box opens that allows you to specify conversion options to grayscale, RGB, or CMYK. If necessary, you can use CD-Q to crop or rotate the image before it is loaded. The program includes sharpening and color-correcting features with an instant preview, allowing you to see the results before you convert the image. CD-Q also features an onscreen *densitometer* (similar to Photoshop's Eyedropper), which provides readouts of the before and after CMYK percentages as you make adjustments.

If you are doing high-volume Photo CD output and have a large production budget, your best choice for Photo CD image editing may be Purup PhotoImpress, which retails for over $2,000. PhotoImpress allows you to batch-convert an entire disc full of CD images to CMYK at one time. It also allows you to load multiple Photo CD files into a batch window. As you load the files, PhotoImpress creates a thumbnail of each image and lists the conversion information onscreen.

To set the CMYK conversion options or to correct or crop the image, double-click on a thumbnail. From the dialog box that opens, shown in Figure 9-10, with a Photo CD stock image from Photo Sets' Art Textures and Backgrounds collection, you can sharpen, crop, or rotate the image. You also can choose whether you wish the conversion to be for coated or uncoated paper or newsprint. The program also includes sophisticated color-correction controls to fine-tune the Photo CD images before they are converted to CMYK.

# Photo CD Stock Images

To give you an idea of the quality and variety of images available from stock houses in Photo CD format, we've assembled a sampling of images. Figures 9-11 through 9-15 should give you a good idea of the variety of images available. To learn more about using stock images and how they can save you money, see Chapter 12. To learn more about important copyright issues regarding digital images, see Chapter 13. See the Appendix for information about contacting stock image vendors.

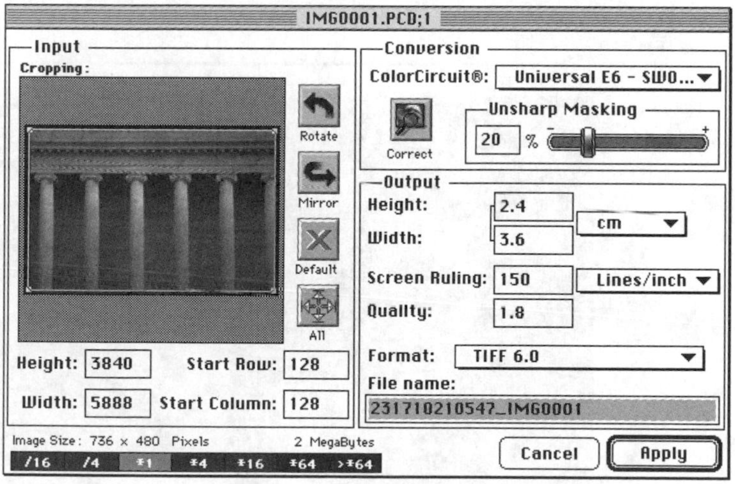

Purup PhotoImpress allows you to edit images before converting them to CMYK

**FIGURE 9-10**

Three images from the CMCD Visual Symbols CD-ROM collection, which includes 100 royalty-free photographs selected by Clement Mok. Images courtesy of CMCD, Inc.

**FIGURE 9-11**

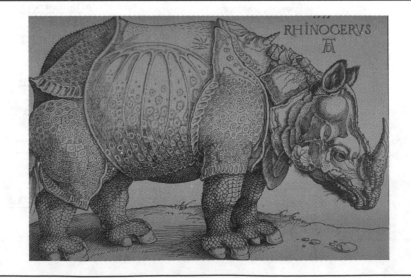

Image from the Planet Art Classic Graphics Sampler, which includes 100 royalty-free images of art from around the world

**FIGURE 9-12**

Three images from ADC's (American Databankers Corp.) ImageVault Pro Volume 1, which includes four CD-ROM discs with over 380 royalty-free images

**FIGURE 9-13**

a)

b)

Three images from Digital Stock Corporation's Photo CD collections. Figure 9-14a is from the Food collection; Figure 9-14b is from the Oceans and Coasts collection; and Figure 9-14c is from the Animals collection

c)

**FIGURE 9-14**

Three images from Corel's Professional Photos CD-ROM collection. Figure 9-15a is from the Arctic collection; Figure 9-15b is from the Italy collection; and Figure 9-15c is from the San Francisco collection

**FIGURE 9-15**

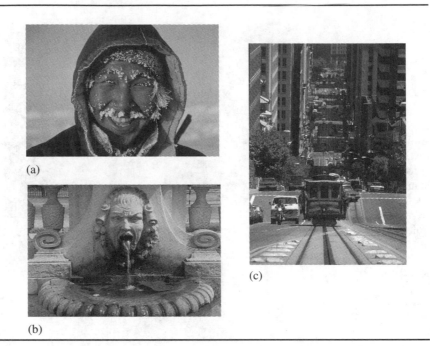

(a)

(b)

(c)

# Conclusion

Next time you need to use digital images, consider obtaining them in Photo CD format. It may save you time and money. As Kodak's Photo CD format grows in popularity it will undoubtedly be utilized by more and more software developers and photo suppliers. In the future, you'll be seeing Photo CD services offered by your neighborhood photocopy shop. Also, don't be surprised when you see home entertainment systems that not only play video games, but allow you to access Photo CD images as well.

# 10

# Creating Two-Dimensional Digital Images

Today's sophisticated painting, drawing, and image-editing software packages have sparked an artistic revolution. Images that once might have seemed too time consuming or even impossible to create can now be completed in hours, or even minutes with painting, image-editing, and drawing programs. This chapter provides a detailed look at how to use the tools and features found in these programs. To demonstrate the process of creating two-dimensional digital images, we've provided step-by-step design projects using five major programs: Fractal Design Painter, Adobe Photoshop, Specular Collage, HSC Live Picture, and Adobe Illustrator.

Even if you've never used any of these programs, the demonstrations will show you how to create digital images using these powerful tools. If you're unfamiliar with the digital art process, you will be amazed at how quickly exquisite and functional digital art can be created.

## Using Fractal Design Painter

Fractal Design Painter is the only software program sold in a paint can. This is not just clever packaging, but an indication of Fractal Design's dedication to electronically emulating natural media. In fact, the company's California headquarters rents a "wet room" where its main programmer and art director analyze the brush, pastel, charcoal, and felt pen strokes found in the real world. Their work has led to the creation of one of the most sophisticated painting programs available on both Mac and Windows platforms.

Painter gives the digital artist countless possibilities by providing electronic versions of brushes, pencils, felt markers, and crayons. Its Brushes palette contains 18 different brushes, most of which paint with at least half a dozen different *variants*. For instance, after you select Water Color from Painter's Brushes palette, you can then choose from a list of variants that includes Simple Water, Water Brush Stroke, Pure Water Brush, Spatter Water, Broad Water Brush, Large Water, Large Simple Water, and Diffuse Water. The program even allows you to emulate the strokes of

Seurat, Van Gogh, and the Flemish masters. Figure 10-1 shows how Painter artwork can easily pass for traditional art.

Painter's popularity is not based simply on its ability to emulate the brushes, pens, pencils, pastels, and chalks of the real world. Painter has expanded the definition of a painting program; it offers not only painting capabilities, but also image editing, special effects, and animation.

One of Painter's most eye-catching features is its Image Hose brush, which allows you to paint the screen with brush strokes composed of digital images. Figure 10-2 shows a sample of the fascinating effects possible with this unique feature. Image Hose brush strokes are created from different digital images saved in a *nozzle* file. This particular nozzle file was created from images found on several stock image CD-ROM collections: Specular Replicas (the little girl and boy, modeled by Tracy Bezesky), CMCD Everyday Objects (the bear and balloons), and StrataClip3D (the rabbit and dinosaur). The StrataClip3D and Specular Replicas CD-ROMs contain 3D images.

To encourage experimentation with the Image Hose brush, Painter's creators package the program with nozzle files that allow you to spray the screen with shamrocks, quarters, dimes, nickels, and pennies, and a variety of colored "splats." Although the effects of the Image Hose brush are quite sophisticated, creating a nozzle file is very simple.

In this section, you'll learn how a nozzle file is created and how to paint with Painter's Image Hose brush. If you follow the steps described on the next page, you'll learn how Painter's Image Hose paints, and you'll gain an understanding of the many tools and features that Painter offers.

Image created by Adele Droblas Greenberg in Fractal Design Painter

**FIGURE 10-1**

Image painted
with Fractal
Design's
Image Hose
brush using
CD-ROM 2D
and 3D Stock
images

**FIGURE 10-2**

1. Painter allows you to import files created in a variety of different file formats including EPS, TIFF, BMP, and Photoshop, GIF, and JPEG. Since Specular's and Strata's 3D stock images had to be modeled in their 3D programs, we loaded the stock images into Strata StudioPro and Specular Inifini-D. We rendered (added lighting and texture) the images in these programs and saved them in TIFF format. Then we loaded the TIFF files into Painter simply by choosing File/Open. The stock images from CMCD were in Photo CD format, so we loaded them into Photoshop, converted them to TIFF format, and then opened them in Painter.

2. All of the stock images that we used included white backgrounds. Since we did not want a white background as part of every image, we removed it. To do so, we needed to select the essential image areas (described in the next step), thus creating a digital mask around each image. (Some CD-ROM stock images already include masks. Since the ones we wanted to use didn't, we needed to create them.)

In Painter, we created a mask around each object by first activating Painter's Outline Selection tool. When this tool is selected, you can access Painter's Controls :Outline Selection palette, shown here, which

allows you to create Straight Lines, Freehand, or Bézier Curves. To
create a mask around the object, we used the Bézier Curve tool
option, which allows you to create a wire frame outline around the
object called a *path*. Painter's Bézier tool option works very much
the way Bézier Pen tools do in image-editing programs such as Adobe
Photoshop and HSC Live Picture and in drawing programs such as Adobe
Illustrator,
Macromedia
Freehand, and
CorelDRAW.

3. Once the path was created, it was converted to a selection by clicking on
   the oval selection icon in Painter's Objects: Paths List palette.

4. With the selection marquee around the object, it was copied and then
   pasted into a new Painter file. In order to create Figure 10-2 for
   publication in the black-and-white section of this book, we opened a new
   file 600 x 400 pixels and set the number of pixels per inch to 200.

5. Next, we placed a grid onscreen in order to help position the images that
   we would place in the file. To fit six images in the 600 x 400-pixel file,
   we set the width and height of the grid to 200 pixels in Painter's Grid
   Options dialog box.

6. Next, we copied and pasted each masked image into the Painter file that
   contained the grid and positioned each object into a cell in the grid. When
   you paste an image in Painter, it is automatically turned into a *floater*,
   which is an image or portion of an image that floats in another layer
   above the background pixels. Once an image is a floater, it can be moved
   around without affecting the background pixels. Floaters can also be
   selected and deselected simply by clicking on them. Thus, even though
   Painter is a bitmap or raster program, it provides some features that once
   could only be found in vector programs.

7. After all of the images were assembled onscreen, we decided to apply a
   drop shadow to each image. In Painter, you can easily apply a drop
   shadow to a floater by choosing Effects/Objects/Create Drop Shadow. In
   the Drop Shadow dialog box we checked Collapse to one layer so that the
   object and the floater would be one floater rather than two grouped
   floaters. Figure 10-3 shows the nozzle file images and their drop shadows.

10

8. Next, we needed to group the floaters before we could convert the document to a nozzle file. To do so, we selected all the floaters in the Floaters List palette with the Floating Selection tool, and then clicked on the Group button.

9. To turn the images into a nozzle file, we executed the Make Nozzle from Group command from Painter's Tools/Image Hose submenu.

10. Next, we saved the file in Painter's native file format, RIFF, and closed it.

11. To use the Image Hose brush with our nozzle file, we opened Painter's Brush Controls palette, then clicked on the Nozzle icon (shown here) which opens up the Nozzle palette. Next, we clicked on the Load button and loaded our nozzle file from disk.

12. Once the nozzle file was loaded, we selected the Image Hose brush in the Brushes palette and began to paint. As the brush stroked the electronic canvas, the digital images from the nozzle file flowed onto the screen.

13. Once we were sure that our nozzle file was working properly, we tried painting with several different Image Hose brush variants. The Variant pop-up menu in the Brushes palette, shown on the next page, allows you

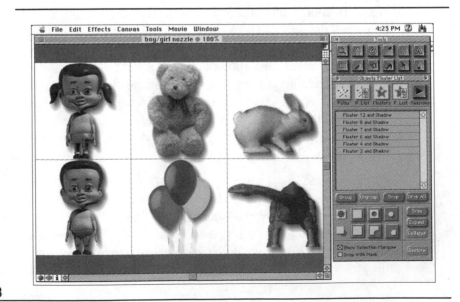

Digital images grouped together

**FIGURE 10-3**

to choose from a variety of options. For instance, you can make the Image Hose paint randomly or sequentially.

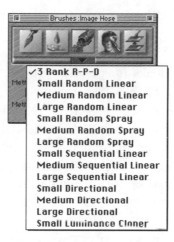

To experiment more with the Image Hose, we again returned to the Nozzle palette. Here we experimented with the Nozzle sliders. With this feature we changed settings so that speed, direction, or velocity of the brush stroke altered the Image Hose brush stroke. The Nozzle palette also contains an Add to Mask checkbox. When selected, the Image Hose paints masks onscreen in the shape of the Image Hose objects. These masks can be converted to selections so that you can fill, paint, and create many more special effects.

# Using Pixel Paint Pro and Fauve Matisse

**10**

If you need a painting program with lots of power but require fewer bells and whistles than Fractal Design Painter, you have several alternatives. On the Mac, Pixel Paint Pro features many customizable brushes, a pen tool, multiple layers, and scripts. It also provides a CMY color palette, and several quick techniques for blending different images, some quite similar to those found in Adobe Photoshop. The program provides multiple selection tools and masking controls. Like Painter, Pixel Paint Pro gives the artist sophisticated tools to create sophisticated images.

PC users looking for an inexpensive painting program with artistic potential should consider Fauve Matisse. Although it does not provide as many brush variations as Fractal Design Painter, its brushes and tools allow you to emulate pencil, crayon, pastel, calligraphy, felt tip, charcoal, watercolor, and oil paint strokes.

Fauve Matisse lets you clone images and apply *filters* that change colors and provide special effects.

# Using Adobe Photoshop

Photoshop is the most popular image-editing program in the world. The program provides enormous flexibility in editing, manipulating, and blending digital images. It is used for special effects (see Chapter 15), retouching and color-correcting (see Chapter 14), and for separating images created as RGB color files into CMYK color files so that they can be output on a commercial printing press.

At one time, Photoshop was packaged with almost every Macintosh-compatible scanner. Once digital artists saw that it could be used for more than just digitizing and color-correcting images, the program's popularity soared. Today, Photoshop is often used to create collages in which various digital images are blended to create interesting and unusual effects.

To give you some idea of how digital images can be composited together in Adobe Photoshop, we'll take you through the steps of creating the collage shown in Figure 10-4.

Although you can digitize images directly into Photoshop, to create our collage we used stock images collected from Digital Stock's New York City CD-ROM stock images, photographed by Bud Freund. One of Photoshop's strengths is its ability to read a variety of different graphics formats. We used Photoshop's File/Open command to load stock images saved in Kodak's Photo CD format, then proceeded as follows:

1. We started by opening the city skyline image that we wanted to use as the background. After loading that image, we cropped the black border around it with Photoshop's Cropping tool. Figure 10-5 shows the original city skyline image after we cropped the surrounding border.

2. Next, we slightly increased the work area on the right of the image to avoid covering the Empire State Building when pasting in the American flag and Statue of Liberty. To increase the work area on the right side of the image, we used Photoshop's Canvas Size command. This added a blank colored area to the image.

3. We filled the blank area with buildings and sky. To accomplish this, we first selected the last two buildings on the right and part of the sky. Next, we copied and flipped them and placed them in the extra canvas area.

Collage created in Adobe Photoshop from Digital Stock's New York City CD-ROM stock images, photographed by Bud Freund

**FIGURE 10-4**

Original city sky image used in the background of the collage

**FIGURE 10-5**

10

4. Before pasting in the American flag and Statue of Liberty, we decided to replace the existing sky with a more interesting one from another image. We loaded this image into Photoshop, selected the sky area, then copied and pasted it into our background image. We then scaled it disproportionately so that it would cover the old sky. Finally, we placed the new sky in a layer.

5. The new sky covered not only the old sky but also the top of the city buildings. We now had to remove the new sky from the top of the city buildings. The easiest way to do this was to use Photoshop's Composite Controls. This allowed us to specify exactly which pixels from different layers would appear in the image. Notice in Figure 10-4 the effect of applying Composite Controls to the Sky and Background Layer to create the new sky. To access Photoshop's Composite Controls, we double-clicked on the New Sky layer in the Layers palette. Shown here is the Layers palette with both the Background and the New Sky layers. Shown below is the Layer Options dialog box after adjusting the Composite Controls sliders. The settings in the dialog box were used to achieve the effect in Figure 10-4.

6. After fine-tuning the sky, we set the background color to black and increased the bottom of the electronic canvas to make room for more images.

**7.** Next, we started loading more images into Photoshop. After loading an image, we selected specific areas with Photoshop's Lasso tool. We *feathered* (placed a soft edge around) each selection so that each element would gradually fade into another. After an element was selected, we used Photoshop's drag-and-drop feature, which allowed us to simply grab an image in one file and drag it into another. Once the image landed in the final file, we placed it into a layer by double-clicking on the words "floating selection" in the Layers palette. Doing so gave us the freedom to change the design at any time by moving an image independently of the other images in the other layers—as if they were on separate sheets of acetate. Each element was in a separate layer, except the Deli and Wall Street signs. To conserve disk space, we placed the Deli and Wall Street signs in one layer.

In Photoshop, each layer adds to the file size of an image. With layers, our 5 x 5-inch, 266 ppi file was 15.4MB; without layers, the same file would have been 5.21MB. When you are satisfied with a design and know you will not make any changes, it's a good idea to merge layers to conserve disk space. For example, since we knew that the American flag and the Statue of Liberty would not change, we could have merged the two layers into one layer, thereby reducing the number of layers and the file size. Since we have a 2GB hard drive with lots of free space, we decided to keep every layer, just in case we decided to make a change at a future date.

**OTE:** *Adobe recommends that you have at least three to five times your image file size free in either RAM or on your hard disk when working with Photoshop.*

**8.** Next, we experimented with changing the opacity in the Runners layer. By doing this, we could create a blend between the Runners and the

Background layer. We also enhanced the effect by using Photoshop's Composite Controls options. We then experimented with Photoshop's different layer modes, which hide or show different parts of an image depending upon the pixel values of the image. For instance, the Lighter mode compares the pixel values of the images in two layers and only shows the lighter of the values.

**9.** For the final touch, we used Photoshop's *Layer Mask* option to blend some of the images with a fade-out effect.

**OTE:** *When you add a Layer Mask to an image, its file size increases.*

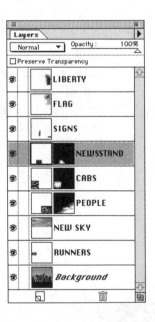

In order to create a fade-out effect, we created Layer Masks in several layers in the Layers palette. This allowed us to hide or show areas from two different layers based on the gray levels in the mask layer. For instance we created a Layer Mask in the Newsstand layer in order to gradually fade a portion of the Newsstand layer into the Cab layer. Shown here are the Layer Masks represented in Photoshop's Layers palette.

Using Photoshop's Gradient tool, we created gradients from white to black in different areas in the layer masks. By default, dark areas in the layer mask reveal the underlying layer. Light areas in the layer mask hide the underlying layer. Gray areas in the mask create a superimposition effect between layers. We fine-tuned the layer mask effect by painting with black, white, and gray in the masks.

Once we completed our design, we saved the image in Photoshop's native format. If we saved the image in another file format, our layers would have been "flattened." Once a file is flattened, images from all layers are placed into one background layer. Thus, you lose the ability to work with the layers as independent entities.

# TIPS of the TRADE

## Global Layer Adjustment in Photoshop

**by Russell Brown**

Currently, it's not possible to make overall image adjustments to a layered document in Photoshop. Adjustments affect only the layer that is selected. This super technique shows a simple solution that lets you control all layers in a document. In this example, we want to give an overall warmer appearance to the image.

1. First create a new layer that will sit on top of all other layers by clicking the New Layer icon in the Layers palette.

2. In the New Layer dialog box, select the Overlay mode, and select Fill with Overlay-neutral color (50% gray). This makes the background of the new overlay layer neutral—that is, transparent.

3. Select this new layer in the Layers palette, and press CTRL-Y (COMMAND-Y on the Mac) to bring up the Color Balance dialog box. Adjust the color balance for the layer. Because this layer is in Overlay mode, it affects the appearance of all layers below it. It doesn't change the layers; it merely tints them. Amazing, but true.

4. To apply color changes to only the highlights of the image, undo step 3 by pressing CTRL-Z (COMMAND-Z on the Mac), and then press CTRL-ALT-0 (COMMAND-OPTION-0 on the Mac) to load the luminosity values for the entire image. Loading the luminosity values as a selection lets you easily adjust just the highlights in an image.

5. Press CTRL-Y (COMMAND-Y on the Mac) to display the Color Balance dialog box, and adjust the sliders as desired.

 **IP:**   *To reload the settings last used in Color Balance, press CTRL-ALT-Y (COMMAND-OPTION-Y on the Mac). Using the ALT key (OPTION key on the Mac) to open a dialog box reloads the last used settings for many other controls in Photoshop, such as Hue/Saturation, Replace Color, and Levels.*

## Using HSC Live Picture

When HSC's image-editing program Live Picture was released in 1994, it was hailed as a revolution in the field of image editing. Unlike Adobe Photoshop and other similar programs, Live Picture allows you to work with low-resolution screen versions of your images while the program creates a mathematical representation of your work. Only after you have completed your work and executed Live Picture's Build command does the program turn to the actual pixels on your disk and create the final image at a high resolution. This dramatically increases the speed with which you can work. According to Live Picture's user manual, you can "work on 5 megabyte images at the same speed as 500 megabyte images without sacrificing on quality."

   Figure 10-6a shows an image created in Live Picture by Adele Droblas Greenberg. Adele created the image by placing a flower (shown in Figure 10-6b) and background texture (shown in Figure 10-6c) of a stone in two different layers. Both the flower and background texture are stock CD-ROM images from HSC KPT Power Photos. She then used Live Picture's Paintbrush and Eraser tools to gradually erase image areas from the flower layer so that the background would show through. When she completed her image editing, Adele used Live Picture's Build dialog box to create the image at 266 ppi.

1
Nintendo
*Donkey Kong Country*

 1

These fantastic 3D images are two scenes from Nintendo's acclaimed video game, *Donkey Kong Country*, the world's first completely computer-rendered 16-bit video game.

All of the 3D characters were created by Rare Ltd. in England (founded by Tim and Chris Stamper) with Silicon Graphics workstations using PowerAnimator™ software. Nintendo's legendary game creator, Shigeru Miyamoto (who created the original Donkey Kong and Mario Bros. games) designed the modern-day Donkey Kong figure, and the designers at Rare Ltd. brought it to life on an SGI workstation.

To create the 3D characters, skeletons of the figures were first created in PowerAnimator™. This high-end animation program allowed the artists and programmers to design by first creating wire-framed skeletons, and then rendering the images to add lighting and shading. To produce movement, the programmers moved a cursor on screen. The image of the character overlaying the skeleton would then move along the screen coordinates, generating an extremely smooth animation sequence. Head programmer on the project was C. Sutherland.

**1b**

# Digital Images Tech Notes

**2** Chuck Carter, a St. George, Utah multimedia artist and illustrator, created this image for "Manhole," a children's CD-ROM game produced by Cyan Inc. Chuck created the 3D models in Strata StudioPro using lathing and extrusion techniques (see Chapter 11 to learn more about using 3D programs). The leaves on the trees were modeled by first creating a 2D wireframe in Adobe Illustrator. The wireframe was then loaded into StudioPro and extruded to create a 3D model. Next, texture and lights were applied to the model. Spot lights rather than point lights were used because spot lights are less memory-intensive.

Chuck used Adobe Illustrator to create the basic shapes for the textures. Next, the shapes were brought into Photoshop where texture was added. To help create some of the textures, the KPT Noise filter was used. The textures were saved as PICT files and then imported into StudioPro. The entire image was then rendered using StudioPro's raytracing option.

**3** This intriguing image was created by R/GA Print and Ryszard Horowitz for a 3M advertisement. Ryszard Horowitz photographed and oversaw the computer composition.

Ryszard started by creating pencil sketches. After taking photographs, he created a collage by cutting and pasting photocopies of these images. In order to create the whirl of objects that flow from the baby's head, Joe Francis of R/GA wrote a custom 3D program in the company's proprietary software environment, Imrender, running on Silicon Graphics workstations. Frank Lantz of R/GA Print composited the elements and added 2D effects using Adobe Photoshop on a Macintosh. CME-KHBB was the advertising agency; Kalman Apple art directed for 3M on the project.

**4** This image is the official poster for the 48th Annual Cannes Film Festival. It was created by photographer/artist Ryszard Horowitz and computer artist Robert Bowen, both of New York City. Ryszard says that the concept for the poster "came to my mind when I was searching for a metaphor representing the light of the motion picture projector. The sun rays breaking from behind the clouds symbolize a universal light source projecting on the waters of the Cote d'Azur." The image is built around the famous "steps" scene in Eisenstein's *Potemkin* in which a baby carriage rolls down the steps of a building. The baby crawling courageously towards the shore symbolizes the future of cinema.

The final image is based upon a sketch presented to the board members of the Festival. The landscape and the baby were photographed by Ryszard. The image projected on the water is based upon over a dozen movie stills supplied to Ryszard and Robert by the Festival. All of the photographs were scanned and then composited using Barco Creator on a Silicon Graphics workstation and Adobe Photoshop on a Macintosh computer.

**2**
Chuck Carter
Cyan Inc. "Manhole"

**3**
R/GA Print–Ryszard Horowitz
3M

**4**
Ryszard Horowitz and Robert Bowen
48th International Film Festival, Cannes 1995

© R/GA Print—Ryszard Horowitz

# Digital Images Tech Notes

**5**    C. David Piña, a Burbank, California artist, created this image as the main design for ABC-TV's *America's Funniest People*. David designed the image on a Macintosh using Photoshop and Illustrator to layer the image and create the image montage. He used Freehand and Fontographer to manipulate the type. David designed the image to reflect the wide geographic flavor of the program. During the title sequence, icons representing different parts of America move across the screen: a San Francisco silhouette is transformed into a midwest farm and a New York skyline becomes a palm tree-lined street.

**6**    The "Sirrus" room was created for the internationally acclaimed CD-ROM game, "Myst," by Cyan Inc. of Spokane, Washington. The "Sirrus" room was modeled and rendered completely in Strata StudioPro. The apparent complexity of the model was not created from the models themselves, but from the textures that the designers created using Photoshop. Some of the textures were hand drawn, while others were scanned photographs that were later edited. When the textures were applied in StudioPro, they transformed the simple models into objects that looked quite sophisticated. Completing the entire "Sirrus" room (design, textures, and models) consumed two weeks of designing time. For more information about the making of "Myst," see the interview with its creators in Chapter 16.

**7**    Tim Landry, a Simi Valley, California artist, created "Brother's Home" as a promotional piece for a screenplay he is writing called "JO-JO's Kingdom," an Alice in Wonderland-type live action, computer-animated picture.

The trees in the image were models that were included with Macromedia Swivel 3D. The models were imported into Specular Infini-D and rendered. The leaves were first created in Adobe Illustrator and then extruded in Infini-D. The mountains were created in a shareware program called Fractal. All the textures were created using Adobe Photoshop. After all of the images were created, they were composited and retouched in Photoshop.

**8**    The dancing cars are from "Pickin' and Kickin'," one of the commericals in a ground-breaking Shell Oil campaign in which cars rock 'n' roll, square dance, and tango with gasoline pumps. The campaign was produced by R/Greenberg Associates, New York, using innovative 3D computer-animation techniques. It was created by Ogilvy & Mather (Houston, Texas) and directed by David Lane of Savoy Commercials, New York.

Using R/GA's Ascension Flock of Birds motion capture system, and the SoftImage 3D environment (on Silicon Graphics Indigo$^2$ Extreme workstations), choreographed motion of professional dancers was captured and applied to computer-generated cars and gasoline pumps to allow them to move with naturalistic motion. With computer graphics supervision by R/GA's Mark Voelpel and animation led by Sylvain Moreau and Samir Hoon, the campaign was constructed of six principal computer graphics layers—for the cars, spotlight, shadows, headlights, etc. The elements, including computer models from Viewpoint DataLabs (Orem, Utah) and R/GA's computer-generated and practically built set, were composited in R/GA's D-1 digital video environment. John Canemaker, an acclaimed cel animation director, consulted on the project to help achieve the hand-drawn look of the computer animation.

**5**

**6**

**5**
C. David Piña
*America's Funniest People*

**6**
Cyan, Inc.
"Myst"

**7**
Tim Landry
"Brother's Home"

**8**
R/Greenberg Associates
Shell Oil

**7**

**8**

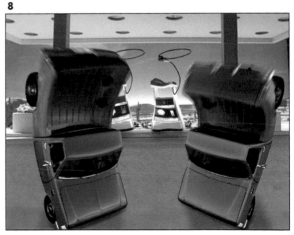

# Digital Images Tech Notes

**9**

This humorous 3D image was commissioned by *Desktop Video* magazine as an illustration to accompany an article on non-linear video editing. The image is a composite of three primary images: the background, cubes, and computer character. Rob Magiera, a Salt Lake City, Utah artist, started this image by building the computer character. The outline for the computer monitor was drawn in Adobe Illustrator. This file was then imported into Alias Sketch! where the Bézier curve information was converted to a NURBS shape. To create the 3D monitor housing, the shape was then extruded and consequently modified utilizing the various tools available in Sketch!

Rob hired photographer Erik Ostling to shoot the photos which were to be mapped onto the cube surfaces. These were scanned, cropped, resized, and saved as PICT files in Photoshop. Since Sketch! generates a mask in the alpha channel, compositing in Photoshop was a snap. To accurately position the character model, Rob imported the rendered cubes into the computer character file. The computer character was then raytraced (for the surface reflections) at high-res with an alpha channel mask and saved as a PICT file to disk. Next, all the elements were composited in Photoshop and the glows around the selected cubes were added. The masks were used to easily isolate different parts of the image.

**10**

Rob Magiera created this sleek 3D image for *New Media* Magazine as a cover illustration. The 3D wireframe of the car was originally created by D. Krumweide on an SGI workstation running Alias PowerAnimator, provided for use in the project courtesy of Alias Research. The geometry file of the car was saved in IGES format (8.5MB worth of data) and imported into Alias Sketch! IGES was ideal for Rob since it retains all of the NURBS data. In order for him to apply textures correctly to the surfaces, a spline model was essential. Next, Rob experimented with different view angles and lens settings to get just the right image distortion and feeling of speed. Much of the time on this project was devoted to setting up a dynamic view of the model, then arranging the five different light sources for proper drama. Rob opted to use Phong shading for rendering rather than raytracing, since reflections and cast shadows were not necessary to the overall impact of the image, and would actually have worked against him because of the overall complexity of the surface textures. Once the high-res rendering was complete, the image was saved and imported into Photoshop where Rob added the motion streaks and the blue glow around the nose of the car. The wavy lights in the background were created utilizing Kai's Power Tools.

**11**

Steven Lyons, a Fairfax, California artist, began this image for Marcam Inc. (a software company) by creating a sketch of the final image on paper. Next, he scanned the sketch and imported it into Adobe Illustrator. To create the digital image, Steven used Illustrator's Pen tool to trace over his scanned pencil sketches. Next, he stroked the outline of the man, and filled the image with colors from his own custom color palette. Steven's color palette consists of colors that he regularly uses. The palette allows him to quickly tint image elements and create a consistent look in his work. To create the blue and red dashed lines that taper into the background, Steven first created a long red tapered shape. He then created one blue rectangle, skewed it to the correct perspective, and copied this rectangle over the red tapered areas. He then cropped the blue rectangles, using the Cropping filter. To create the exploding area emanating from the computer, he used Illustrator's Transparency filter and added a gradient over it.

**9**

**9**
Rob Magiera
*Desktop Video* magazine

**10**
Rob Magiera
*New Media* magazine

**11**
Steven Lyons
Marcam, Inc.

**10**

**11**

# Digital Images Tech Notes

**12** Rodney Alan Greenblat created this image using Macromedia Freehand, Fractal Design Painter, Adobe Photoshop, and Byte by Byte Sculpt 3D (a Macintosh 3D modeling and rendering program). Rodney began the image on the left side of the screen by first creating sketches in Freehand. After saving the image in PICT format, he loaded the image into Painter where he used Painter's Paintbrush and Charcoal brushes to color in the different areas and texture. The robot was modeled and rendered in Sculpt 3D.

In Photoshop, Rodney created the patterns that eventually would be mapped to the surface of the robot. To help ensure that the pattern would fit in just the right place on the robot's face, Rodney took a screenshot of the Robot, then loaded the screenshot into Photoshop. Using the screenshot of the robot as a guide, Rodney shifted and shaved edges off the pattern. Once he was convinced that the pattern would be mapped to exactly the right place on the robot, he returned to Sculpt 3D where he used the Photoshop pattern as a texture map when rendering the robot.

**13** Adele Droblas Greenberg, a New York City artist, created this image using Adobe Illustrator, Adobe Dimensions, and Adobe Photoshop. She started by creating the 3D characters and balloons in Dimensions. Adele created the 3D shapes by breaking the image down into separate parts (the eyes, the mouths, the noses, etc). When creating the parts, she used primitives and revolved and extruded shapes. After each 3D shape was created, lighting was added. To create the stripes on one of the balloons, different colored stripes were created (using the Pen tool) in the Map Artwork dialog box and applied to the balloon. The flowers on the hat and body of the woman were created using the Pen and Oval tool in the Map Artwork dialog box and then applied to the image. Then Adele composited each part together using both Dimensions and Illustrator.

After the 3D shapes were created and composited in Illustrator, she imported them into Photoshop. When the Illustrator file was opened in Photoshop, it appeared over a new transparent Photoshop layer. Adele created another layer to experiment with different background ideas without affecting the 3D images. The final background was created using Xaos Tools Paint Alchemy in Photoshop.

**14** This playful image is the main screen from "Dazzeloids" (published by Voyager), a clever and whimsical CD-ROM musical storybook created by artist/writer Rodney Alan Greenblat.

The adventure starts when you click one of three storybook screen buttons. Click on "Banker Spare that Petshop" and the Dazzeloids rush off to rescue the Probe and Poke Petshop from the Mediogre's Transglumifier. Adding to the fun is the fact that the story line changes depending upon which character you send to the rescue.

To create the main screen and many of the other "Dazzeloids" scenes, Rodney first sketched out black-and-white images on paper and then scanned them. Next, he traced the scanned images using the Pen tool in Macromedia Freehand. Once the images were sketched, he saved them as EPS files and loaded them into Fractal Design Painter. To color the black-and-white sketches, Rodney filled the image outlines using the Paint Bucket tool. Afterwards, he applied Painter's Pencil and Charcoal brushes to enhance details. Once he was happy with a scene, Rodney saved it in PICT format and imported it into Macromedia Director where the final animation was programmed.

**12**

**12**
Rodney Alan Greenblat
"Pan Am Robot"

**13**
Adele Droblas Greenberg
"Balloons"

**14**
Rodney Alan Greenblat
"Dazzeloids"

**13**

**14**

# *Digital Images Tech Notes*

**15** JW Burkey, a Dallas, Texas artist/photographer, created this image for *Corporate Information Officer* (*CIO*) magazine (Kim Morneau, art director). Dave Obar built the mountain cliff and funnel as props for the image. The mountain cliff was created from styrofoam which was painted and sprayed with sand and dirt to provide texture. The funnel was also painted. The rig was created from odds and ends purchased at a hardware store and from the studio's workshop.

After JW photographed the props, he digitized, selected, copied, and pasted them into the final image. The man with the wheelbarrow is Dave Obar. JW photographed Dave with a cement wheelbarrow in two different positions, one tilting the barrow and the other standing over it. The icons on the barrows were created in a paint program. The rainbow emanating out of the funnel was created using the Airbrush tool in Fractal Design Painter. Bands of primary colors were painted. For the transitions between colors, a color was created from the color above and below. Then a thin bar was painted in between the two colors. After all of the colors were painted, they were blurred with Painter's Blur command. Some of the colors needed to be reapplied after blurring to bring some of the color back. All the images were composited together in Adobe Photoshop.

**16** This image was created for *Corporate Information Officer* (*CIO*). JW Burkey, a Dallas artist/photographer started by scanning several images that he photographed and then compositing them together with Adobe Photoshop.

JW first loaded the sky image, then silhouetted the mountain image,and then copied and pasted it into the sky image. The mountain image is a photograph taken at Monument Valley, in the Southwest United States. Later, JW photographed a model posing with her hands up in the air. He again silhouetted this image, and copied and pasted it into the sky image (final image). The magnifying lens that the woman is holding was photographed and digitized. It was then enlarged, selected, copied, and pasted into the final image. The rainbow effect was created using KPT's Gradient Designer and an alpha channel. To create the effect, JW selected an area for the rainbow using Photoshop's Lasso tool. The selection was saved to an alpha channel, then the Blur filter was applied so that the rainbow would have soft rather than hard edges. Finally, KPT's Gradient Designer was used to add color.

**17** This clever image was created to illustrate a *Worth* magazine article about frequent flyer programs. Alejandro Arce and Mirko Ilic' of Oko and Mano Inc., a New York City design studio, began the project by scanning real frequent flyer cards belonging to employees from *Worth* magazine. After scanning the cards, Alejandro and Mirko modified them using Adobe Photoshop's Cloning tool so that the names and numbers couldn't be distinguished. The airplane, motor, pilot, and suitcases were all built piece by piece using SoftImage's modeling tools (on a Silicon Graphics workstation). The card textures were applied to the wings and body. After rendering the image with an alpha channel, it was composited over a CD-ROM stock photo. Photoshop was used to paint in some additional exhaust from the engine, add a slightly foggy texture, and perform some minor color correction (pumping up the contrast and saturation in the sky).

**15**

 **Digital Images**

 **15**
JW Burkey
*Corporate Information Officer (CIO)*

 **16**
JW Burkey
*Corporate Information Officer (CIO)*

**17**
Alejandro Arce and Mirko Ilic'
*Worth* magazine

**16**

© 1994 J. W. Burkey

**17**

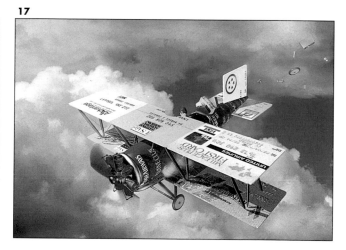

# Digital Images Tech Notes

**18**
David Teich, a Roosevelt, New Jersey artist, started this image by creating a landscape in HSC KPT Bryce. The robots were modeled in Autodessys form•Z. The body of the robot started out as a simple cube, which first had all its edges rounded, then the entire rounded cube was meshed—all of the faces were subdivided into smaller faces using the Mesh tool. The next several steps involved deformations: The shape was tapered along its Z axis (head to tail) and also on the Y axis (straight up and down) to create the streamlining. Using a Bézier deformation, Dave curved the whole body in an S-like shape, from front to back. The ridge along the top of the robot's back and the two airfoils along the bottom were created with Move Mesh deformation, a tool which draws out a series of faces and pushes them into a user-specified profile shape along a path drawn on the model. Most of the other parts of these robots were either simple primitives or lathed shapes. They were rendered in ElectricImage Animation System where the lighting was adjusted to simulate the natural light effects generated in Bryce. The individual images were composited in Photoshop.

**19**
David Teich created this image to illustrate an article on presentation software for *Computer Shopper* magazine. David modeled the 3D objects in Autodessys form•Z. These were rendered in ElectricImage Animation System with transparency and a color map applied to the slide window, and a bump or "noise" image applied to the slides themselves. This created the characteristic plastic slide mount texture. A color image was applied to the monitor screen as well.

When these elements were rendered, an alpha channel was automatically generated, making it easy to composite them with the background in Photoshop. Next, David composited and painted the background in Photoshop. For the background texture, an assortment of screen shots was taken from presentation software packages. These were converted to high-contrast grayscale images, then were filtered using High Pass, Gaussian Blur, and Emboss in Photoshop. High Pass maintains areas of the image which are already high in contrast, but fades other parts of the image to a neutral gray. An emboss applied to an image treated this way gives more depth and interest than the stock emboss texture. Before embossing, David applied a little blur to the image. Words and phrases were composited using various color and opacity settings, and the light streaks were painted using a feathered Lasso selection and the Airbrush tool.

**20**
Steven Lyons, a Fairfax, California artist, created this image for Motorola to depict the power of the Motorola PowerPC chip used by Apple computers. Steven started the image by carefully sketching the complete scene in pencil. After he was satisfied with the design, he scanned it and saved it as a PICT file. Next, he loaded the scanned image into Adobe Illustrator. Using Illustrator's Pen tool, Steven traced over the scanned images, added color, and a yellow stroked outline to the image. When creating the yellow stroke, he used Illustrator's Outline Path filter to make the stroke into a united object that could be filled with different triangles—thus, the colors could be edited on the fly. To create the background pattern of circles and network lines, he lined up the elements in a rectangle so that he could create a pattern with Illustrator's Pattern command. Starbursts were created in the image using Illustrator's Starburst command. Steven produced the triangular serrated edges by creating triangles, and duplicating as he dragged each one with the Mac's OPTION key pressed.

**18**

 **18**
David Teich
"Robots at Sunset"

**19**
David Teich
*Computer Shopper* magazine

 **20**
Steven Lyons
Motorola, Inc.

**19**

**20**

# Digital Images Tech Notes

**21** Ben Barbante, a San Francisco artist and art director of *InfoWorld* magazine, created his RoboDog illustration for an article about network protocol analyzers. He started by roughing it out using tracing paper and a pencil, then scanned it on a flatbed scanner, and saved it as a 72 ppi PICT file. He used the PICT file as a template in Adobe Illustrator and defined flat "local" colors for the main shapes in the picture and saved it as an EPS file. The EPS file was then rasterized into Photoshop at the size it would be printed with a resolution of 240 ppi. (*InfoWorld* is printed at a 120-line screen). In Photoshop, he set the Magic Wand tool's Tolerance to 1. He then selected the shapes by clicking on each of the shapes that had a slightly different flat color. He saved all of the selections to alpha channels and selectively masked out areas while primarily using the Airbrush tool to paint and the Dodge and Burn tools to model the different color shapes.

**22** Alejandro Arce and Mirko Ilic' created this image for *Worth* magazine. After the initial sketches were approved by *Worth's* art director Ina Saltz, they started building the components on their Macintosh. Dollar bill textures were scanned and retouched with Photoshop. Adobe Illustrator was used to create the outlines for the man in the desert. Next, they used SoftImage (on their Silicon Graphics workstation) to create a series of overlapping extrusions for the man. The other models were created directly in SoftImage using the patch, spline, and polygon modeling tools. The materials (gold, sand, clothing, etc.) were created and the pyramid texture was applied. The image was rendered with *depth fog* to create the haze in the background, and brought back into the Photoshop for any retouching and color correction needed.

**23** Gary Clark is an artist and assistant professor of art at Bloomsburg University in Bloomsburg, Pennsylvania. He created this image, "Postcards from the Digital Highway/Idol," as part of an ongoing series of computer images dealing with the relationship between nature and technology— a way to make tangible the notion of the "Information Highway."

To create the image, Gary used HSC KPT Bryce, HSC Kai's Power Tools, and Fractal Design Painter. The land forms were created in Bryce as wireframe pieces and then rendered. See Chapter 15 for more details.

In Painter, the top of the telescope and the sky were created as separate files. The head of the telescope was taken from a still video capture using a Canon RC570 digital video camera. It was then colored using a gradient fill in KPT. Gary then colored the landscape using Painter and made adjustments using the program's Brightness and Contrast controls. Lighting effects, such as the shaft of light extending from the telescope towards the sky, were also created in Painter.

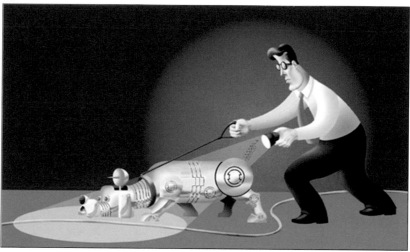

**21**

**21**
Ben Barbante
*InfoWorld* magazine

**22**
Alejandro Arce & Mirko Ilic'
*Worth* magazine

**23**
Gary Clark
"Postcards from the Digital Highway/Idol"

**22**

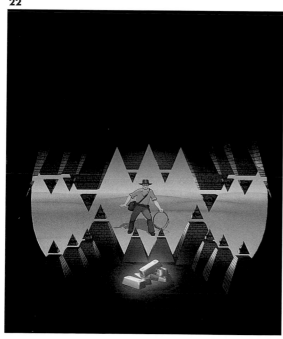

**23**

# Digital Images Tech Notes

We (the authors) began working on the color insert by asking a variety of artists to send us digital images. We contacted some by phone, others through America Online (AOL). Some artists uploaded low-resolution images to us on America Online so that we could preview them; others sent us images on 44MB SyQuest removable cartridges. Once we decided which images to use, we asked the artists to send us high-resolution versions of the images over AOL or on SyQuest cartridges.

We then laid out the text and color pages in QuarkXPress. We created the 3D ovals with the numbers using Adobe Illustrator and Adobe Dimensions. The paint roller was loaded into Illustrator from an Image Club ArtRoom CD-ROM clip art image that was then altered and colored using a custom gradient created in Illustrator. The 3D type was created in Dimensions, then imported into the Illustrator paint roller file. The files were saved in EPS file format and imported into QuarkXPress.

After the QuarkXPress layout was completed, the high-resolution color images were placed into graphic boxes. The color pages were first output on a Tektronix Phaser IISDX dye-sublimation color printer and sent to Osborne/McGraw-Hill as digital proofs.

When all of the color pages were finalized, we sent the prepress house, Alpha Systems (a division of Phoenix Color Corp.), the images and QuarkXPress layout on one 270MB SyQuest cartridge.

Since many of the high-resolution color images were RGB color files, the prepress house needed to convert them to CMYK color. The images were converted to CMYK color on a Linotype-Hell DaVinci workstation. Those images that were sent in slide, 4 x 5-inch, and 8 x 10-inch chrome format were digitized on a Linotype-Hell drum scanner 3900.

Once all of the images were digitized and the RGB color files converted to CMYK color, separations were output on a Linotype-Hell Hercules imagesetter at 175 lpi and 2,540 dpi. Laminated proofs were output using the Fuji Color Arts system. After the proofs were analyzed, several images were color-corrected. Final separations were created and sent to the commercial printer, Phoenix Color Corp., so that printing plates could be made for the printing press.

a)

b)

a) Image created in HSC Live Picture by Adele Droblas Greenberg
b) HSC KPT Power Photos Flower used to create image in a)
c) HSC KPT Power Photos Background Texture used to create image in a)

c)

**FIGURE 10-6**

10

# TIPS of the TRADE

## Resolution-Independent Effects in HSC Live Picture

**by Sydney Stein**

Live Picture's silhouetting feature can be used to calculate resolution-independent masks from any image that has interresting color or texture properties. The following project will illustrate how you might use this effect to customize a text headline.

1. Begin by selecting an image with an interesting pattern such as the one shown here. Select the Auto option from the Brush pullout menu to specify colors in the image that you want to retain. In the Multiplex bar, select the Outside option and a tolerance setting of 100%. Continue to use the Auto Brush option to specify areas of the image that will be discarded when the mask is calculated.

2. After inside and outside areas are defined, you are ready to calculate the resolution-independent silhouette mask. Click the Calculate button on the Multiplex bar. Select the Standard Compute option in the dialog box that appears and click OK to finish computing the mask.

# TIPS of the TRADE

3. Create an Artwork layer and select a color. Use the Marquee Fill option to fill a rectangular area larger than the area of the silhouetted image. With the OPTION key down, click the layer toggle to open the layer bars in the Layer stack. Select the Mask icon in the Silhouette layer and drag it to the Stencil icon of the Artwork layer while holding down the OPTION key. Use the Stencil icon toggle to invert the stencil. An interesting effect should be generated such as the pattern shown here. You may vary this effect by selecting various artwork patterns which can be found in the pulldown menu. In the Multiplex bar, use the Visibility icon in the Silhouette layer to turn off the image you used to generate the texture.

4. In order to confine the texture within the area of the text headline, you can copy the stencil from the text layer. First, select the stencil in the artwork layer, hold the OPTION key down and drag to copy the stencil into the Mask icon in the same layer. Then, copy the Stencil icon from the text layer into the Stencil icon of the Artwork layer. Your texture should now be constrained similar to the illustration above.

5. You may now use Live Picture's positioning tools or a monocolor or layer to create the perspective and drop shadow effects illustrated.

*Sydney Stein is a Group Product Manager at HSC.*

10

# Using Specular Collage

Specular Collage is a Macintosh image-editing program specifically designed to create collages with Adobe Photoshop, TIFF, and PICT files. You may wonder why you would create collages in Collage when you can create them in Photoshop or other programs. The answer is that Collage can help you create your collages quickly, especially if your system does not have enough memory to handle Photoshop's layers. Instead of loading high-resolution images onscreen, Collage loads low-res proxies. Only when the image is finally rendered does Collage generate the high-resolution elements required for final output. In this respect, Collage is similar to HSC Live Picture.

Figure 10-7 shows an image we created using Corel's The Arctic and Skiing in Switzerland Photo CD-ROM stock image collections. Since Collage does not read Photo CD files, we first loaded the images into Photoshop, then saved them in TIFF format. Once the images were in Photoshop, we adjusted the colors and silhouetted the primary image areas, using Photoshop's Magic Wand and Lasso tools. The selections were saved into *alpha channels,* which allowed us to save and reuse selections. These

Image
assembled in
Specular
Collage using
Corel Photo
CD stock
images

**FIGURE 10-7**

selections can be used to mask or hide image areas in Photoshop and other programs. For more information about masking and enhancing images, see Chapter 14.

| Layer | | Element |
|---|---|---|
| ▷ | 1 | 14035.PCD/BEARS |
| ▷ | 2 | 14016.PCD |
| ▷ | 3 | 14019.PCD/WOLF |
| ▷ | 4 | 60001.PCD/SKIER |
| ▷ | 5 | 14012.PCD/GRIZZLY |
| ▷ | 6 | 14003.PCD |
| ▷ | 7 | 14018.PCD |
| ▷ | 8 | 60003.PCD/SNOW |

To produce the collage shown in Figure 10-7, we first created a new file, then imported the TIFF files. When we imported files into Collage, they were placed in the Element palette, as shown here. To place the image onto the digital canvas, we dragged it from the Element palette into the document window. To reorder the images, we simply clicked and dragged one layer over the other in the Element palette.

If an element has a mask, you can automatically make the image appear through the mask. For instance, the background area surrounding the large polar bear in the original stock image was hidden by creating a mask in Photoshop, which was read by Specular Collage. We didn't use Photoshop to mask the birds in the upper-left corner of the collage and the skier in the lower-right corner. Instead, we used Collage's Element dialog box, which allows you to adjust which pixels appear from the overlying and underlying layers. The Element dialog box is quite similar to Photoshop's Composite Controls options.

After we finished creating the collage, we needed to render the image to the proper size and resolution. In the Render dialog box, shown in Figure 10-8, we set the image size to approximately 4 x 6 inches with a resolution of 266 pixels per inch.

# Using Adobe Illustrator

Adobe Illustrator is one of the most powerful drawing programs available for both Macs and PCs. Since its release, Illustrator has been praised for both its versatility and its precision. Illustrator was one of the first drawing programs that incorporated a Pen tool that allowed the user to create smooth curves—often called Bézier curves. Using a Pen tool (similar tools are available in CorelDRAW and Macromedia Freehand), you can create and control curves by clicking and dragging on anchor points and direction lines. Figure 10-9 shows a curve with anchor points and direction lines in Adobe Illustrator. You can change the shape of the curve by clicking and dragging on either direction line. You can make the curve larger or smaller by clicking on and dragging either of the control points. Before programs like Illustrator,

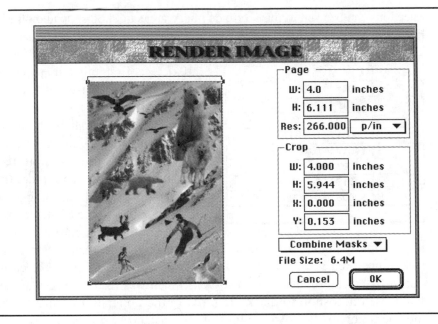

Specular
Collage's
Render dialog
box

**FIGURE 10-8**

CorelDRAW, and Macromedia Freehand provided the ability to create and edit curves, producing intricate drawing with a mouse was frustrating and sometimes impossible. Figure 10-9 was created primarily using Illustrator's Pen tool.

As discussed in Chapter 3, drawing programs such as Illustrator provide numerous features. They not only allow you to create precise illustrations but also

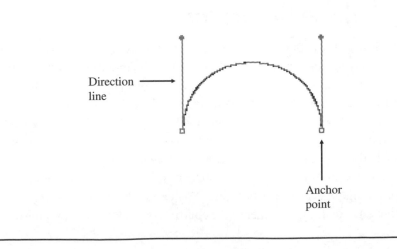

Curve created
in Adobe
Illustrator

**FIGURE 10-9**

graphs, text effects, and multicolumn page layouts. Add-on programs called filters allow many of these programs to quickly create special type, gradient, and 3D effects.

In Illustrator, you can create an object and a shape, and mask the two together. The result of this effect is shown in Figure 10-10c. In this image, we created a mask out of a turtle. In Illustrator, a mask is an object that hides parts of an underlying image. By turning the turtle into a mask, we created the effect of the landscape showing through the turtle's body. To create Figure 10-10c, images of a turtle (shown in Figure 10-10a) and a landscape (shown in Figure 10-10b) were used. The images were loaded from Image Club's ArtRoom CD-ROM clip art collection.

Here's an overview of how the image in Figure 10-10c was created.

1. First, we opened the turtle image from the Image Club CD-ROM ArtRoom collection. The turtle is one of many images in the collection created with Illustrator's Pen tool.

2. Next, we loaded the landscape scene from the same clip-art collection. This image was also created with Illustrator's Pen tool.

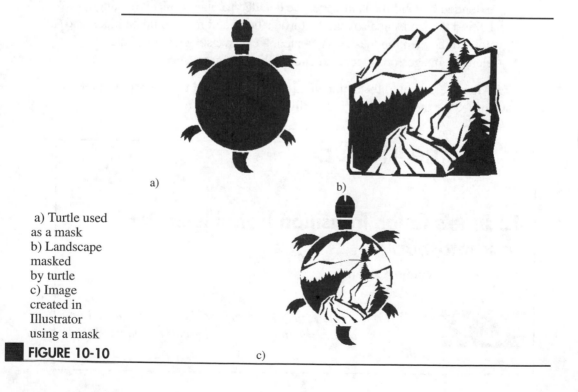

a)

b)

a) Turtle used
as a mask
b) Landscape
masked
by turtle
c) Image
created in
Illustrator
using a mask

**FIGURE 10-10**

c)

3. Once the turtle image was loaded onscreen, we selected and then copied it. Next, we opened the landscape image and pasted the turtle image into it. When the image appeared onscreen, we made the separate parts a *compound* path by choosing Make from the Object/Compound Paths submenu. A compound path is a path composed of two or more separate paths. We needed to make the turtle a compound path in order to create the mask effect.

4. With the entire turtle still selected, we pasted it into the landscape file. When the turtle image was on top of the landscape, we changed the black fill of the turtle to transparent so that we could see the landscape through it.

5. We then moved the turtle so that the turtle shell was over the more interesting areas of the landscape. We decided to reduce the turtle by 90% so that the landscape would fit better inside the shell after it was masked. To make this reduction, we double-clicked on Illustrator's Scale Tool in the Tools palette. In the Scale Tool dialog box, we entered 90%, then clicked OK.

6. Although we reduced the turtle, the head and feet of the turtle still extended beyond the landscape. We decided to place a black rectangle behind the landscape so that the turtle's head and feet would be black and not white when the mask was created. Next, we selected all of the element images on screen and chose Object/Masks/Make.

7. After we executed the command, Illustrator created the mask out of the turtle. We then saved the file in Illustrator's native format.

## TIPS of the TRADE

## Luanne's Color Transition from Illustrator to Photoshop

**by Luanne Seymour Cohen**

**AUTION:** *This is only for graphics that will be viewed on a monitor, not for graphics that will be color-separated and printed!*

# TIPS of the TRADE

Have you ever noticed that when you create a graphic in Illustrator and then open that file in Photoshop, the colors appear differently? Well, here is how to prevent that from happening. The vibrant colors you see on the screen in Illustrator will appear in Photoshop when you open the same file. Be careful though and follow these instructions precisely! If you have the printing inks setup file already then use the first set of instructions. If you don't have a custom printing inks setup file use the second set of instructions to create one and then use the first set of instructions.

**To keep colors from changing when opening an Illustrator file in Photoshop:**

1.  Create your Illustrator file and paint the artwork with the colors you want to see in the final multimedia/Acrobat/Internet/ WWWeb file.

2.  Start up Photoshop. (Don't open the Illustrator file yet!)

3.  Choose File/Preferences/Printing Inks Setup in Photoshop.

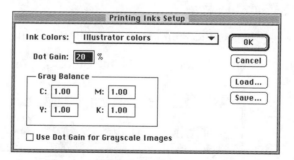

4.  Click the Load button and load the file named "Illustrator colors." Click OK.

5.  Choose File/Open and select the Illustrator file. Change the mode to RGB. Click OK.

6.  The file should now look the same as it did in Illustrator. *Before you do any CMYK work, change your Printing Inks Setup back to the original setting. If you don't do this, you will get distorted color for CMYK files.*

**10**

## TIPS of the TRADE

**To create a custom Printing Inks Setup file to match Illustrator screen colors in Photoshop:**

1. Create an Illustrator file with 7 boxes. Fill the boxes with the following color mixes:

| | | | |
|---|---|---|---|
| Box 1: | 100% Cyan | | |
| Box 2: | 100% Magenta | | |
| Box 3: | 100% Yellow | | |
| Box 4: | 100% Magenta | 100% Yellow | |
| Box 5: | 100% Cyan | 100% Yellow | |
| Box 6: | 100% Cyan | 100% Magenta | |
| Box 7: | 100% Cyan | 100% Magenta | 100% Yellow |

2. Leave this window open and start up Photoshop. Don't open any files yet.

3. Choose File/Preferences/Printing Inks Setup in Photoshop.

4. Choose Custom from the Ink Colors pop-up menu.

| | Y | x | y | | |
|---|---|---|---|---|---|
| **Ink Colors** | | | | | |
| C: | 37.00 | 0.2095 | 0.2851 | | OK |
| M: | 23.58 | 0.4706 | 0.2483 | | Cancel |
| Y: | 76.22 | 0.4112 | 0.4958 | | |
| MY: | 22.27 | 0.6132 | 0.3402 | | |
| CY: | 27.19 | 0.2620 | 0.4963 | | |
| CM: | 3.67 | 0.1698 | 0.0893 | | |
| CMY: | 0.82 | 0.3202 | 0.3241 | | |
| W: | 83.02 | 0.3149 | 0.3321 | | |
| K: | 0.82 | 0.3202 | 0.3241 | | |

## TIPS of the TRADE

5. Align this dialog box as close as possible to the Illustrator window so you can compare colors. Click on the Cyan box in the Photoshop dialog box and you will get the color picker. Adjust the color until it matches the Illustrator window that contains Box 1. Click OK.

6. Repeat step 5 for each of the 7 color boxes. All of them should match the colors you see in the Illustrator window. Click OK.

7. Now you are back to the Printing Inks Setup dialog box. Click the Save button and name your custom ink setup file "Illustrator colors." Click OK.

# Using Macromedia Freehand

Macromedia Freehand is the only Macintosh drawing program that can claim to rival Adobe Illustrator in features. In fact, every time a new version of Freehand or Illustrator is released, a debate begins as to which is the most powerful, the easiest to use, and the most feature-packed. Figure 10-11 shows an image of an Etonic running shoe with its technology pieces (the separate pieces that go into the shoe's construction). The image was created in Macromedia Freehand by Michael Scaramozzino of DreamLight in Stoneham, Massachusetts. DreamLight also created the design for the Macromedia Freehand 5.0 package.

DreamLight art director and lead illustrator Michael Scaramozzino and supporting illustrator Adam Smith created this image for the introduction of an Etonic running shoe product line. The image also appears on the back of the Macromedia Freehand 5.0 package. To help DreamLight create the running shoe, Etonic supplied its designers with a few prototype shoes as well as all the separate pieces that comprise a running shoe. The shoes and separate pieces were digitized into a Mac using a digitizer attached to a video camera on a tripod. After the shoes and separate pieces were digitized, they were imported into Freehand as templates. Next, each element was roughed using the Pen tool. Afterwards, shading and fine details such as stitching were added. To create the shading, blends were used. To

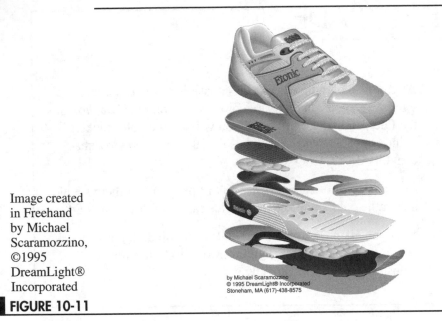

by Michael Scaramozzino
© 1995 DreamLight® Incorporated
Stoneham, MA (617)-438-8575

Image created
in Freehand
by Michael
Scaramozzino,
©1995
DreamLight®
Incorporated

**FIGURE 10-11**

control the transitions from light areas to midtone areas to dark areas in the Nylon patch, separate blends were used. To Michael, one of Freehand's most valuable features is its ability to reshape blends. In Freehand, you can reshape path outlines of a blend. When you do, the program automatically reblends the shapes.

Since the color of a running shoe is important, a custom Color palette was created. In the Color palette, custom Suede and Lace colors were created. Michael also made extensive use of Freehand's powerful Style palette, which allows the creation of multilevel styles. In a multilevel style, one style can be based upon other styles. If you need to change one of the styles, all image elements based upon that style are updated automatically. The Layers palette was also used. Different elements were placed in separate layers to help organize the illustration.

# Using CorelDRAW

On the PC, CorelDRAW is the undisputed king of drawing programs. Shown here is an image created in CorelDRAW by Homewood, Illinois artist Barry Meyer. To create the image, Barry used CorelDRAW's Ellipse and Bézier Pencil tools. CorelDRAW's Powerclip feature was used extensively to create the transparent

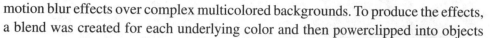

motion blur effects over complex multicolored backgrounds. To produce the effects, a blend was created for each underlying color and then powerclipped into objects of that color. For instance, to create the effect of a pinball in motion, he converted a circle to a curve, then stretched the curve into an oblong shape with a circular end. Then he used blending effects to create the motion blur. To create the effect of a rotating dial in the Turbo Boost control, Barry created a blend in a triangle and then clipped it into a circle by first selecting the blend, then choosing Effects/Power Clip/Place Inside Container.

# Conclusion

As you've seen in this chapter, painting, image-editing, and illustration programs provide emormous versatility and potential. In the next chapter, you'll learn how two-dimensional images can be transformed and rendered into three-dimensional ones.

# 11

# Creating 3D Digital Images

**T**hree-dimensional graphics programs create stunning photo-realistic images and dazzling special effects. Undoubtedly, you've already seen some of the most fantastic computer-generated 3D art ever created in movies such as *Alien II, The Terminator,* and *The Mask.* On television you can see the amazing handiwork of 3D computer software every week in programs like *Earth2* and *Star Trek: The Next Generation.* Although most of the special effects in Hollywood movies are created on Silicon Graphics workstations, Macs and PCs often chip in to help.

Three-dimensional software packages are needed for much more than creating special effects in movies and TV shows. They're used to create technical illustrations and to design new products, buildings, and of course video games. Computer manufacturers, toy makers, and electronics companies all save thousands of dollars by prototyping products using 3D software. Interior design and interactive multimedia productions also rely on 3D programs. On a simpler level, 3D software can be used to add depth, perspective, and photo-realistic lighting to shapes, text, and logos.

Not long ago, creating sophisticated 3D images was beyond the power of many personal computers and beyond the budgets of their owners. Today, Apple's new RISC-based PowerMacs and the latest Pentium chips have brought the world of 3D imaging to the desktop. In the coming years, 3D programs will undoubtedly take their place alongside page layout, drawing, and painting and image-editing software as essential tools in many design studios.

## Learning 3D Software

For designers and multimedia producers, learning a 3D software package presents quite a different challenge from learning a 2D package. In 2D software, the tools and techniques often emulate those of the real world: Painting programs utilize paintbrushes; drawing programs feature Pen tools; image-editing programs use masks. One reason that learning 3D software is more difficult is that many of the tools used have no real-world counterparts. For instance, if you wish to create a

3D-rendered shape without a computer, you can't pick up a brush called a *ray tracer* or *Phong shader* and apply it to a canvas; nor can you open up a jar of *texture maps* and paint texture on your images. When you begin using 3D software, you need to learn not only a new set of design tools but also a whole new vocabulary.

The following sections will introduce you to 3D software, its vocabulary and features. You'll start by taking a look at the basics of 3D programs, then you'll explore the different types of 3D software available and take a look at some of the wondrous images created from these programs.

## Entering the World of Three Dimensions

Initially, one of the hardest aspects of learning 3D software is to simply get yourself acclimated to working in 3D space. An object created in a 2D program has a height and a width: the width is often described by an *x-axis coordinate,* the height by a *y-axis coordinate.* A 3D object has another axis, a depth axis—which is designated as the *z-axis coordinate.* The x, y, and z coordinates are shown below. The coordinate systems of most 3D programs are based on a standard *Cartesian* space model in which the three axes share an origin and are positioned at right angles to each other. Along the x axis, distances are usually measured positively from the zero point to the right and negatively from the zero point to the left. Along the y axis, distances increase positively from the zero point upward and negatively from the zero point downward. Along the z axis, distances increase from the zero point outward and negatively from the zero point inward. When images are moved, they are rotated along x, y, and z axes using the software's rotating tools. Pixar Showplace's rotating tools, which allow you to rotate images along the x, y, or z axis, are shown here.

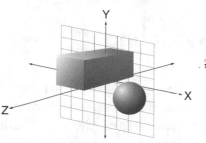

To make the process of viewing 3D space easier to conceptualize, most software packages provide viewing windows for each axis. Views can display an object's front, back, top, or bottom, as shown in Figure 11-1. Many software packages also provide a camera view, which is the point of view of the observer.

Once you become acclimated to the x, y, z coordinate system, your next step is to understand the difference between the three main features provided by 3D software packages: modeling, rendering, and animation. Before continuing, it's

11

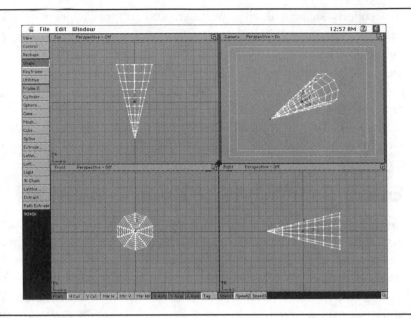

The Valis
Group Pixel
Putty's
viewing
windows

**FIGURE 11-1**

important to understand that all programs do not provide all these features. Some, such as Alias Sketch, provide modeling and rendering capabilities but no animation. Programs such as Macromedia MacroModel are primarily modeling programs.

# Modeling

Modeling is the process of creating 3D objects. Most 3D software allows you to produce models from primitives or from drawing tools. Primitives are basic shapes such as cubes, spheres, cones, and cylinders. In many 3D programs, you can simply click on a primitive tool and drag it to the center of the screen where the shape often appears as a wire-frame representation. After the primitives have been created, you then use other tools to combine the shapes to create more sophisticated objects. Specular Infini-D's tools, which allow you to quickly create 3D objects from primitives, are shown here.

Another very simple way to create a model is to first draw a flat 2D shape with the program's 2D shape tools. Macromedia MacroModel's 2D drawing tools are shown on the next page. After the 2D objects are created, they can quickly be converted to 3D objects using extrusion and lathing techniques (described later in the Modeling Features section). Once the 2D image is converted to 3D, it usually appears onscreen as a wire-frame image or a mesh created out of polygons. Some programs such as Byte by Byte's Sculpt 3D help the visualization process by providing a window in which a shaded solid object is created from the wire-frame model.

## Modeling Features

Three-dimensional modeling software programs allow you not only to create 3D models from 2D objects but also to edit the 3D models you create. Here's a glossary to help you understand these features.

**LATHING AND REVOLVING**   *Lathing* and *revolving* create 3D shapes by revolving 2D objects along an axis. Lathing and revolving are often used to convert 2D objects to symmetrical 3D objects such as vases, glasses, and the like. Figure 11-2a shows a simple 2D drawing created with Alias Sketch's Pen tool. The figure also shows Alias Sketch's Putty tool being used to adjust the curve's handles. Figure 11-2b shows the complex 3D model created after the 2D object was revolved.

**EXTRUSION**   When an object is *extruded,* it is lifted up from a 2D surface to create a 3D object. Figure 11-3a shows curves created in Alias Sketch. Figure 11-3b shows a 3D wire-frame model created after the 2D curves were extruded.

**SPLINE-BASED EDITING**   *Splines* are curves used to create and edit objects. Many 3D modeling tools allow you to edit curves by clicking and dragging control points on the splines. In many respects, using a spline is similar to working with a Pen tool in drawing programs. (The term spline is based on a tool used by shipbuilders when creating hulls.)

**NURBS**   *Non-uniform rational B-Splines (NURBS)* are splines that can have weight and tension assigned to their control points. This means that a new curve can be generated at any place along any other curve. The new curve includes a new set of control points that can be altered to create fluid curves. A program that features NURBS-based editing allows for extremely sophisticated curve creation and editing, as shown in Figures 11-4a and 11-4b. Using a NURBS, you can create perfect arcs or curves with multiple bumps within the main curve. NURBS-based editing is generally found in more sophisticated 3D modeling programs such as Alias Sketch and Autodessys form•Z.

**11**

a) 2D object created in Alias Sketch with Pen tool.
b) Image after being revolved with the Revolve tool

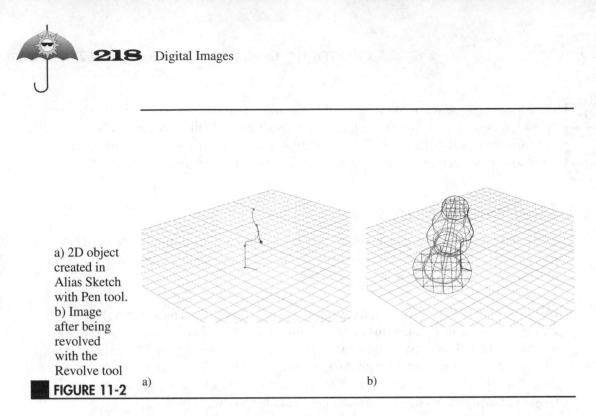

a)

b)

**FIGURE 11-2**

**VERTEX-LEVEL EDITING**   Three-dimensional models often create a mesh frame around objects. Most mid- to high-end 3D software packages allow you to click and drag to edit at the *vertex level* (where the polygons meet) of the polygons on a mesh.

a) 2D curve created in Alias Sketch.
b) 3D object created by extruding the curve

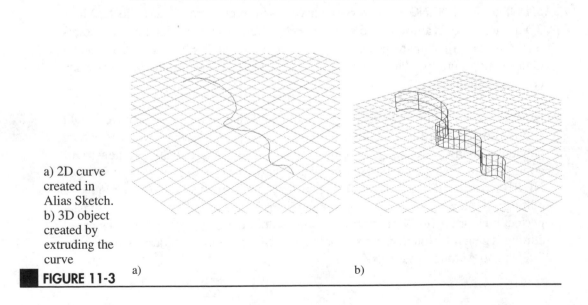

a)

b)

**FIGURE 11-3**

a) Alias Sketch's NURBS-based editing allows sophisticated control of curves.
b) After the curve is edited, the 3D model automatically adjusts

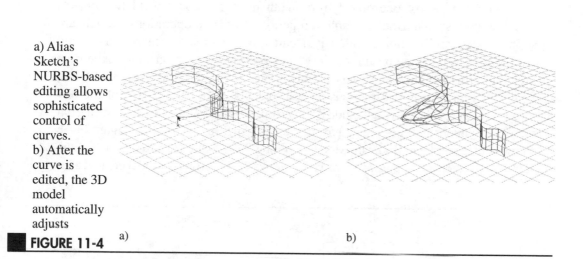

**FIGURE 11-4**    a)                                                              b)

Figure 11-5a shows a 3D image created in Strata StudioPro before vertex-level editing. Figure 11-5b shows the same image after several of the vertices at one end of the cone were dragged out using the program's 3D Sculptor option.

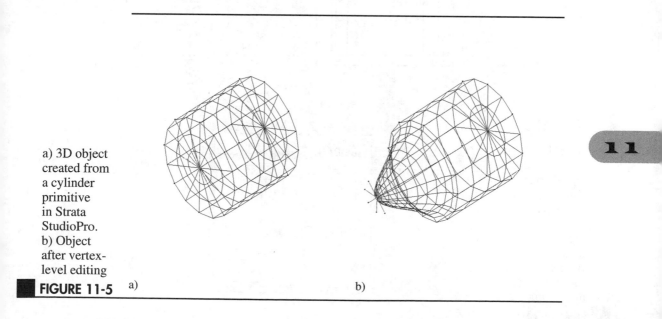

a) 3D object created from a cylinder primitive in Strata StudioPro.
b) Object after vertex-level editing

**FIGURE 11-5**    a)                                                              b)

11

**BOOLEAN OPERATIONS**   *Boolean operations* allow you to edit models by adding, subtracting, and intersecting surfaces. For instance, you can create a hole in an object by subtracting part of one object from another, or you could weld two objects together by using a Boolean union function. Boolean operations, which are sophisticated and computer-intensive, can quickly create effects that would normally be very time consuming. They are generally found on more expensive high-end programs such as Strata StudioPro, ElectricImage, AutoDesk 3D Studio, Sculpt 3D, and form•Z. Strata Vision and Specular Infini-D are two of the few mid-priced 3D packages that include Boolean operations. Figure 11-6a shows a front view of a cylinder and cube created from primitives in Strata StudioPro. Figure 11-6b shows the program's Boolean Modeler dialog box, which allows you to add, subtract, or intersect images. Figure 11-6c shows the wire-frame model created after

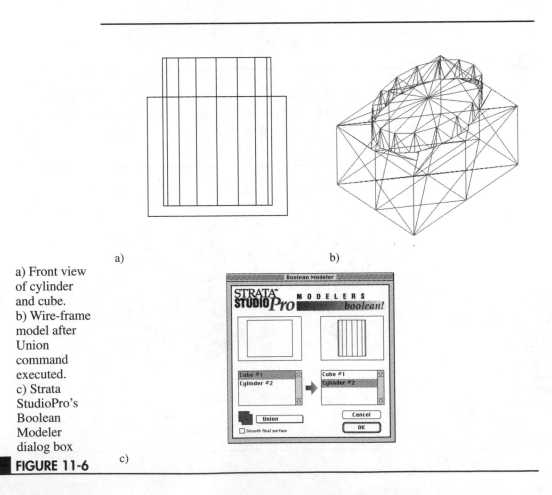

a)                                           b)

a) Front view
of cylinder
and cube.
b) Wire-frame
model after
Union
command
executed.
c) Strata
StudioPro's
Boolean
Modeler
dialog box

**FIGURE 11-6**        c)

the Union command was executed. Figure 11-7a shows the final image after it was rendered (i.e., after lighting and texture were applied). Figure 11-7b shows the image after the Subtract command was executed. Figure 11-7c shows the image after the Intersect command was executed.

**LOFT**   *Loft* creates a 3D object from a series of splines. For instance, lofting could be used to create a hull for a boat shape from a series of splines used as cross-sections.

**SWEEP**   *Sweep* is a modeling technique that combines lathing and extruding. When two objects are swept together, one is used as a template and swept around the axis of another. Sweeping can be used to create corkscrew-type effects or to spherize a flat object. Figure 11-8a shows two simple 2D objects created in Macromedia MacroModel. Figure 11-8b shows the 3D wire-frame model after the frame image was swept. Figure 11-8c shows the image after it was shaded in MacroModel.

**TWIST**   *Twist* is a "deformation" tool used in many programs to twist an object around a specified axis. Figure 11-8d shows the results of twisting Figure 11-8c on its x axis in Macromedia MacroModel.

**METABALLS**   *Metaballs* is a modeling special effect that allows you to join spheres. This effect, which can create the illusion of mercury drops merging, is often found on high-end graphics workstations. One of the few Mac/PC programs to offer this feature is Strata StudioPro. Figure 11-9a shows a wire frame of four spheres. Figure 11-9b shows Strata StudioPro's Metaballs dialog box. Figure 11-9c shows the Metaballs after the spheres were joined.

Rendered
image after
execution of
a) Union
command,
b) Subtract
command,
c) Intersect
command

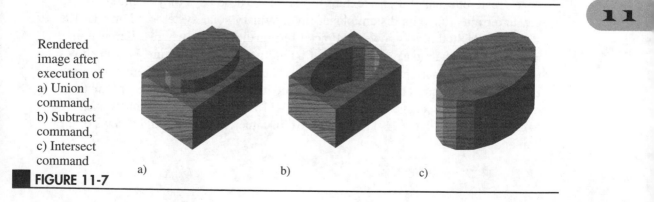

a)                              b)                              c)

**FIGURE 11-7**

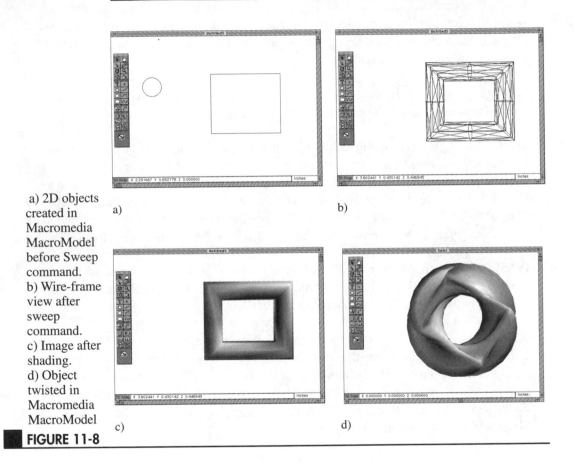

a) 2D objects created in Macromedia MacroModel before Sweep command.
b) Wire-frame view after sweep command.
c) Image after shading.
d) Object twisted in Macromedia MacroModel

**FIGURE 11-8**

**TERRAIN TOOLS**  *Terrain tools* allow you to generate landscapes that bend and flow or to create unusual cliff and texture formations. These days they're often used to create terrains found on distant planets in imaginary solar systems. Figure 11-10a shows Strata StudioPro's powerful Fractal Terrain dialog box, where different points are clicked by the mouse as a means of building the terrain. Figure 11-10b shows the preview of the terrain (Strata's terrain module must be purchased separately from the company). Figure 11-11a shows a rendered image of a cup and a "Star Function" terrain created in Specular Infini-D. Figure 11-11b shows the 2D path that was lathed to create the cup. Figure 11-11c shows the top, camera, front, and right views of the cup and terrain.

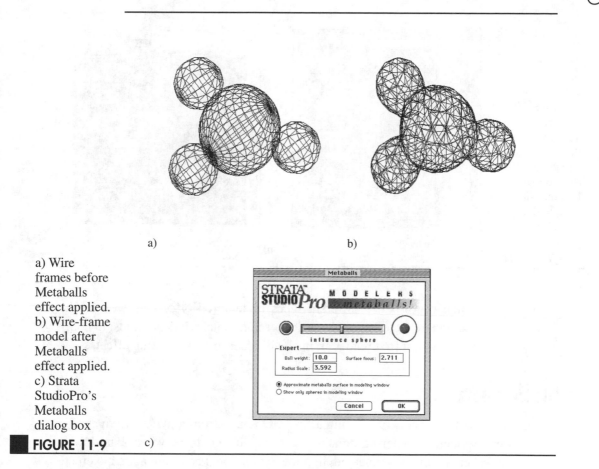

a)                                                    b)

a) Wire
frames before
Metaballs
effect applied.
b) Wire-frame
model after
Metaballs
effect applied.
c) Strata
StudioPro's
Metaballs
dialog box

 **FIGURE 11-9**       c)

**OTE:** *HSC KPT Bryce is a stand-alone program specifically designed to create 3D terrains. KPT Bryce is discussed in Chapter 15.*

# Lighting

In order for a 3D image to be seen, it must lit. Most 3D programs allow you to create multiple lighting sources, place them in 3D space, and control the intensity of lighting. Many programs divide their lights into different categories, such as spotlights, point lights (omni-directional), and ambient lights (light emanating from the object rather than from a scene). Several programs allow you to create, edit, and

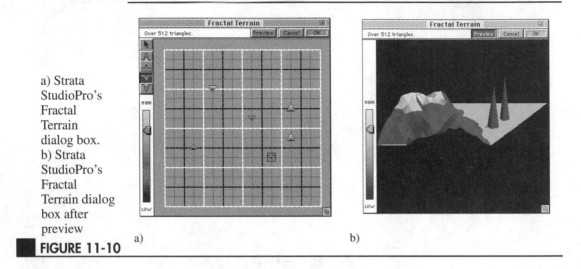

a) Strata
StudioPro's
Fractal
Terrain
dialog box.
b) Strata
StudioPro's
Fractal
Terrain dialog
box after
preview

a)          b)

**FIGURE 11-10**

use *gels,* which can produce different types of textured effects as well as the appearance of light reflected through vertical or horizontal window blinds. In many 3D programs, you must first render an image in order to view lighting effects.

# Rendering

Rendering is the process of creating a final 3D image from a model. In many 3D software packages, rendering creates a bit-map image from vector-based wire frames. When an image is rendered, lighting, texture, and color are added to create the final product. The quality of the image is often based upon the rendering algorithm used. The most widely used rendering algorithms are *Gouraud Shading*, *Phong shading,* and *ray-tracing.* When evaluating 3D software packages, it's important to understand that not all 3D programs include sophisticated rendering capabilities. Some programs, such as Macromedia MacroModel, provide basic shading; to achieve a sophisticated final image, models created in such programs must be exported to rendering software, such as Pixar's RenderMan.

 **OTE:** *In order to move a model created in one program into another to render it, you may need to save your model in DXF or RIB format. Apple is designing QuickDraw 3D to create a standard file format for Mac and Windows 3D programs. In the future, you should be able to copy and paste between QuickDraw 3D-compatible programs.*

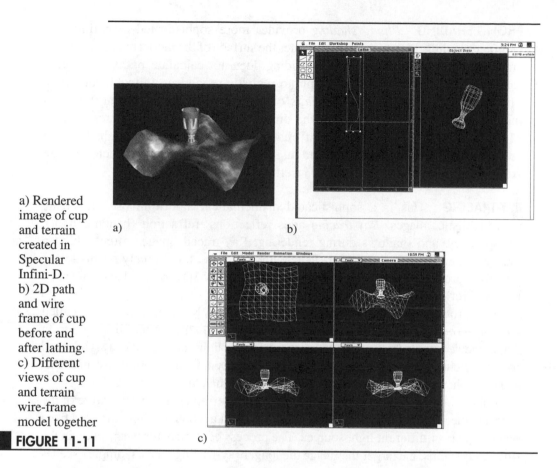

a) Rendered image of cup and terrain created in Specular Infini-D.
b) 2D path and wire frame of cup before and after lathing.
c) Different views of cup and terrain wire-frame model together

**FIGURE 11-11**

**GOURAUD SHADING**  *Gouraud shading* is a fast rendering process that shades model vertices to simulate a smooth surface. Shown here are several images rendered in Macromedia MacroModel using Gouraud shading.

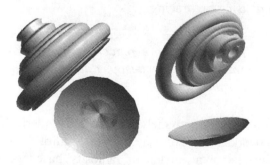

**PHONG SHADING**  *Phong shading* provides more sophisticated rendering than Gouraud shading. Phong shading evaluates the surface of the model to create surface and lighting textures. Since Phong shading does not calculate paths of light, it cannot provide the highest quality photo-realistic rendering. In technical terms, Phong shading evaluates the *normals* of the model surface. The normal is a mathematical value that indicates the direction of the surface. Figures 11-17a, 11-18, and 11-19 show examples of images rendered using Phong shading. To see examples of images rendered using Phong shading in ElectricImage Animation System, turn to the color insert.

**RAY-TRACING**  This is a sophisticated mathematical algorithm used to create photo-realistic images. *Ray-tracing* adds reflections, refraction (bending light), transparency, and shadows during rendering. Ray-traced images often exhibit a glossy or plastic looking surface. Thus, although it is an extremely sophisticated rendering process, ray-tracing is not necessary for many 3D projects that do not need mirrored reflections or shiny surfaces.

The process is called ray-tracing (for accuracy's sake, sometimes called *backward ray-tracing*) because it is based on rays of light that bounce back and forth from a viewer or camera to an image and then back to a light source. If the ray is bounced back to a light source without striking an object, the ray-tracing algorithm assumes that a ray of light must have come from a direction other than the viewer or camera.

If a ray bounces off an object, the algorithm determines the exact texture of the object at the ray reflection point. The algorithm must account for light directed from other objects or different light sources. The process continues for every pixel in the final image; thus, the larger the image the longer ray-tracing takes. Complex scenes could take many hours to render.

Three-dimensional programs that include ray-tracing include StrataVision, Strata StudioPro, PassPort Producer Pro, Crystal Topas, Specular Infini-D, Alias Sketch, Real 3D, and Caligari truespace2. Figure 11-17b shows an image rendered in Strata StudioPro using ray-tracing.

 **OTE:**  *If you need more rendering power, YARC Systems creates add-in boards specifically designed to speed up rendering in Mac and PC 3D programs.*

**RADIOSITY**  *Radiosity* is an extremely complicated rendering algorithm found only in high-end 3D workstation software. Strata StudioPro is one microcomputer product that offers its own version of radiosity based on its own proprietary algorithm. Strata's "Raydiosity" produces better rendering than ray-tracing because it increases the number of ray samples taken. While ray-tracing does an excellent job of rendering highly reflective objects, radiosity is better at rendering light reflected from many surfaces. Due to the slow speed required for radiosity rendering, Strata StudioPro's manuals caution that it should not be used on a day-to-day basis. The manual notes that it is offered as a "semi-experimental" rendering method.

**TEXTURE MAPPING**   *Texture mapping* applies a 2D image, often a pattern, to a 3D object. Many artists create designs in programs such as Fractal Design Painter or Adobe Photoshop, then wrap the image around an object using a 3D software package. Figure 11-12 shows an image rendered using a texture map created in Adobe Photoshop using a few filters: Clouds, Add Noise, Texture Fill, and Lighting Effects. The texture was saved as PICT format, and then imported into Strata StudioPro where it was mapped to a 3D shape when the image was rendered.

 **OTE:**   *Many companies sell CD-ROM collections of background textures and patterns that can be used as texture maps. For more information about using stock images on CD-ROM, see Chapters 9 and 12.*

## Animation

Animation programs allow you to add movement to 3D images. If you want to create 3D animation, you should be aware that not all 3D packages include animation

Image
rendered in
Strata
StudioPro
with a texture
map created
in Adobe
Photoshop

**FIGURE 11-12**

features. For instance, programs designed primarily for modeling may not have animation capabilities. Some of the better-known 3D programs that include animation modules are ElectricImage Animation System, StrataVision, Strata StudioPro, Infini-D, Macromedia Swivel 3D Professional, Crystal Topas, AutoDesk 3D Studio, and Caligari truespace2.

## Key Frame and Event-Driven Animation

Most 3D animation programs are considered primarily *key frame* or *event-driven*. In key-frame animation, you move the 3D objects to various points called key frames and set these as animation markers. When you run the animation, the 3D software interpolates by filling in the positions between the key frames.

Although a key-frame approach sounds very attractive, powerful 3D animation packages use a *time-based* or event-driven approach instead. In a time-based system, such as those utilized by ElectricImage and Strata StudioPro, you can animate multiple objects, using multiple views. In these programs, each change of any object on screen becomes an "event" and is set by an "event marker." The software not only fills in the events between each marker but it tracks each event in a time line for each object on screen. Shown here is a time line created in ElectricImage Animation System. Using the event time, you can easily analyze or edit any event for any object in your animation. For instance, when using ElectricImage, you can click on the camera on the time line and set a position for the camera at one point in the animation. Then you can move to another point in the animation and set another camera position. When the animation takes place, not only do the animated objects you've created move, but also the camera moves.

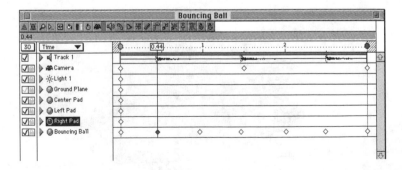

When you create animations using high-end software, you can set the animation to occur following a curve that you can draw and edit. You can add lights and multiple cameras. The most sophisticated packages, such as ElectricImage, allow you to animate *shears* (slant images), twists, and bends. Most also provide a system of hierarchical links. This allows you to have one object move based upon the movement of another object.

Almost all animation packages now provide output in QuickTime or Video for Windows (AVI) format. Many packages, such as AutoDesk Studio 3D, can control videotape players. ElectricImage allows files to be exported to 8mm tape in Abekas format for transfer to an Abekas DDR (Digital Disk Recorder), which is used by professional videotape studios to create animation and record special effects. (For more information about outputting to video tape, see Chapter 18.)

# 3D Software

The following section provides brief overviews of some of the more popular 3D programs available on the Mac and PC. As you read through the description of each program, remember that most 3D programs are so packed with features, a short review can only give you a general sense of how each program operates. If you are interested in purchasing 3D software, don't rely solely on software reviews; contact manufacturers. Many will send you a feature list of their products. Also, ask if you can obtain a demo disk or demo videotape. This is the best way to try out features and see if you feel comfortable with the program's interface.

*n* **OTE:**   *Most 3D programs require a math co-processor (FPU chip) in computers other than PowerMacs.*

## Ray Dream Designer

Ray Dream Designer is considered one of the friendliest 3D packages available. The program includes numerous features that help make the entry into the world of 3D easier for beginners. For instance, Ray Dream Designer features Wizard dialog boxes that explain and show extruding and lathing before you carry out commands. Figure 11-13a shows Ray Dream Designers Modeling Wizard dialog box. If you select Lathe Object, then click the Next button, Ray Dream's next screen explains the Lathe choices, which are Create your own object, Vase profile, Light bulb profile, and Champagne Glass profile, as seen in Figure 11-13b.

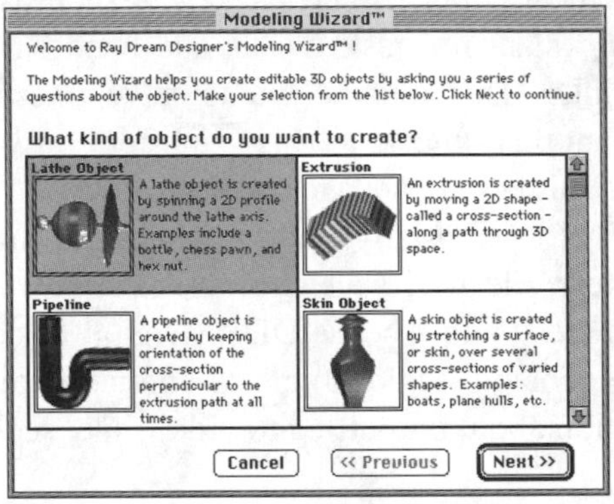

a)

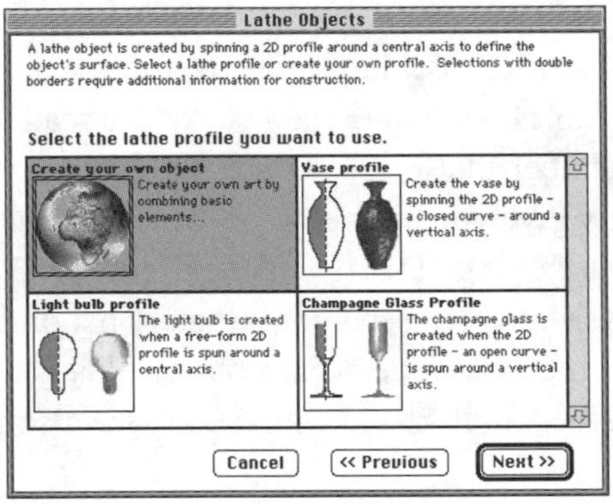

a) Ray Dream
Designer's
Modeling
Wizard
dialog box.
b) Ray Dream
Designer's
Lathe choices

**FIGURE 11-13**

b)

Ray Dream Designer also includes Bézier curve, line, circle, and polygon tools, and provides shaded previews rather than wire frames as you create objects. To create final output, Ray Dream renders using ray-traced shadows, reflections, and transparencies.

# Macromedia Swivel 3D Professional

Macromedia Swivel 3D Professional is another excellent choice for entry-level users who wish to create 3D models and animations. Models are primarily created by lathing or extruding 2D objects that can be drawn or imported into the program. Figure 11-14 shows a 3D object created in Swivel 3D from a 2D object. As the 2D object is edited, the 3D wire frames update automatically.

One of the program's most powerful features is its ability to link objects. Links allow you to create one object from smaller ones. They also help you control how one part of an object moves in relation to other parts. For instance, you can use Swivel 3D's Free Link tool to link a model of a computer monitor to a model of a computer. When you move the monitor, the computer comes with it. Swivel 3D's rendering capabilities allow you to render using Phong Shading, which smoothes tonal gradations among polygons and provides reflected highlights. If you need higher quality rendering, Swivel 3D files can be saved in *RIB* format so that they can be exported for rendering into Pixar's acclaimed RenderMan rendering program. (Swivel 3D can also be purchased as a package along with RenderMan.)

Swivel 3D uses a key-frame approach to animation. The program allows up to 16 key frames with 1,000 frames in between. If you need more key frames, you can link different animation files.

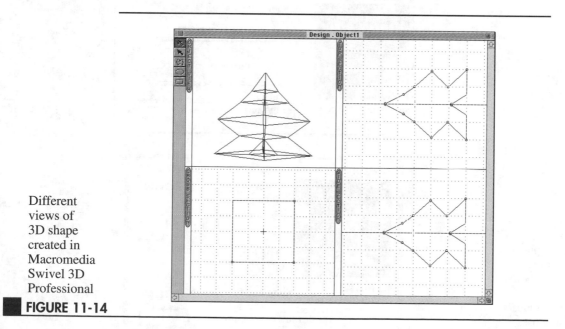

Different
views of
3D shape
created in
Macromedia
Swivel 3D
Professional

**FIGURE 11-14**

# Pixar Showplace

Pixar's Showplace is one of the most unusual and certainly one of the most entertaining 3D software packages. Showplace allows you to import 2D objects or build from its storehouse of 3D objects such as telephones, bookcases, and lamps. Once the objects are loaded, they can be lit and viewed from any vantage point and provided with a variety of realistic surfaces. As you build your scene, Showplace allows you to add to it using plug-ins that can create staircases, terrains, curtains, and fireworks. Figure 11-15a shows Showplace's Curtains dialog box, which is used to create 3D curtains in a scene. Figure 11-15b shows Showplace's Fireworks dialog box, which is used to add 3D fireworks to a scene. After you've completed the scene, the image can be rendered to produce a photo-realistic look using Pixar's RenderMan rendering software.

a)

a)
Showplace's
Curtains
dialog box.
b)
Showplace's
Fireworks
dialog box

**FIGURE 11-15**    b)

# The Valis Group's Pixel Putty Solo

Pixel Putty Solo is a 3D modeling program that packs quite a bit of power at a low price—under $400. Although Pixel Putty does not contain all of the features found in some higher-priced products, its feature set is impressive. Models are created primarily from a set of primitives whose size and shapes are created from dialog boxes. The program provides lathing and lofting tools and even allows you to collide images together to create bumps and indents. It also has a Disrupt tool that randomly displaces an image's vertex. Such a feature can be used to create the effect of rumpled pillows and sheets. Pixel Putty allows images to be edited using NURBS and rendered using Gouraud or Phong shading. For more sophisticated rendering, Pixel Putty images can be rendered using RenderMan (not included with Pixel Putty) from a Pixel Putty menu—provided RenderMan is installed.

# Specular Infini-D

Specular Infini-D is a popular modeling, animation, and rendering program. Its low price and easy-to-use interface have made it a popular choice among Macintosh 3D artists. Infini-D's modeling controls allow you to create 2D objects and extrude or lathe them to create 3D wire-frame models. For those who need 3D type effects, Infini-D allows you to convert TrueType and PostScript fonts into 3D images. Its animation controls are event-driven, and it allows morphing capabilities to blend one 3D object into another. As a renderer, Infini-D provides Gouraud shading, Phong shading, and ray-tracing.

# Strata Vision and Strata StudioPro

Strata StudioPro is a complete 3D package featuring modeling, rendering, and animation. This program, which has become known as a well-rounded package with an excellent user interface, has gained quite a bit of publicity because the creators of Myst used it in creating the fantastic effects that appear in the best-selling CD-ROM. See Chapter 16 for an interview with the creators of Myst.

Strata StudioPro allows 3D models to be created from 2D objects and provides spline-based and vertex-level editing. As a renderer, the program provides ray-tracing and its own proprietary version of radiosity. When rendering, you can actually stop the process and complete it later. Figures 11-17a and 11-17b show images created in Strata StudioPro by San Francisco artist George Krauter. To create

Image created
and rendered
in Specular
Infini-D by
Chuck Carter

**FIGURE 11-16**

the terrain in Figure 11-17b, George used KPT Bryce. Strata StudioPro retails for about $1500. Strata also sells a less expensive and less powerful version of the

a) Image
created in
Strata
StudioPro by
George
Krauter.
b) Image
created in
Strata
StudioPro by
George
Krauter

a)

b)

**FIGURE 11-17**

program, StrataVision. This program, which retails for about $700, also includes ray-tracing and can output animations in QuickTime format.

## ElectricImage Animation System

ElectricImage is generally considered the most powerful Macintosh 3D animation program on the market and certainly one of the best available on a microcomputer platform. The program retails for about $7,500 and animation professionals say it is worth every penny. The program has been used to create effects for such Hollywood movies as *Terminator II* and *Alien II*.

To create animation, you can have ElectricImage add shapes to your scenes or import models from other programs. As discussed earlier, animation is controlled by a time-line dialog box where cameras, sound, and objects can all be controlled independently. Thus, camera and lighting movements are possible even when objects are moving onscreen. You can also synchronize sound to the movement of objects onscreen. To fine-tune movement, you can click and drag using a variety of different spline controls to adjust the animation path. ElectricImage also provides several features which automatically control objects. Its hierarchy system allows the linking of one object to another. Using hierarchical control, you can have the finger on one hand move independently of the others; yet when the hand moves, all of the fingers move with it. ElectricImage also includes a Look at Object feature. This allows you to have one object move or turn as another object moves or turns. This feature can be handy when trying to make a spotlight follow a moving object.

ElectricImage also provides a number of controls for creating twisting, shearing, and bending effects. It also includes a particle generator for creating sparks and spurts of water. It features extensive lighting and camera movement functions—and as you might imagine at a price of over $7,000, it provides excellent rendering capabilities, allowing Gouraud and Phong shading. Figure 11-18 was modeled in form•Z, then rendered in ElectricImage. The image, which appeared in *Computer Shopper* magazine, accompanied an illustration for an article on graphic computer programs.

## Autodessys form•Z

Autodessys form•Z is considered one of the most powerful modeling programs available on the Macintosh platform. This program is one of the few, and perhaps the only, *solids modelers* available on a microcomputer. A solids modeler treats objects as solids rather than polygons, with skin stretched across their surfaces. A

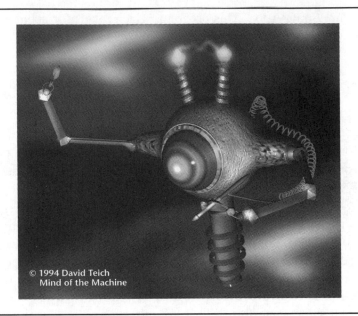

© 1994 David Teich
Mind of the Machine

Image created
by New
Jersey artist
David Teich
rendered in
ElectricImage

**FIGURE 11-18**

solids modeler allows you to slice an image in half. Once the image is sliced, it maintains the properties of the former solid, but you can see a cutaway view within the objects. Autodessys form•Z features almost unlimited undoes. Smooth lines and curves can be generated using NURBS, splines, and Bézier curves. Figure 11-19 shows an image created in form•Z, rendered in ElectricImage, and composited in Adobe Photoshop. The image was created for a commercial illustration for DataRAM of Princeton, New Jersey.

## AutoDesk 3D Studio

AutoDesk 3D Studio is one of the most popular high-end 3D modeling, rendering, and animation packages available on the PC. The program, which is DOS-based, features sophisticated modeling, lighting, and texturing tools. It also features fast, accurate rendering, including Phong rendering. The program is built around several integrated modules—each with a different function. For instance, the 2D shapers create basic 2D shapes. The 3D lofter extrudes the 3D shapes, while the 3D editor allows you to extensively edit the 3D shapes. When you've perfected your 3D shapes, the 3D editor renders them. Once the image is rendered, it can be animated,

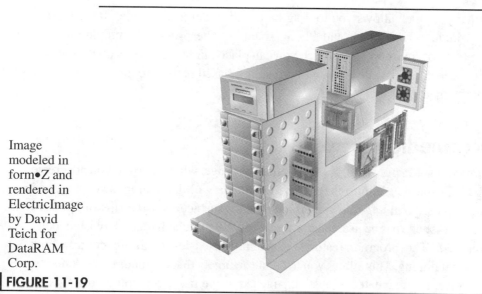

Image modeled in form•Z and rendered in ElectricImage by David Teich for DataRAM Corp.

**FIGURE 11-19**

using the Key Framer. The program provides field rendering when images are output to videotape. Third-party plug-in modules for 3D Studio create a variety of effects, such as page flips, lightning, comet flares, melting, and marbleizing.

## Crystal Topas Professional

Crystal Topas Professional is one of the few PC programs that go head to head with AutoDesk 3D Studio Pro. Although it may not match every feature of 3D Studio, it comes close and is a bit cheaper. It offers spline-based editing, vertex-level editing, and Phong rendering. Unlike 3D Studio, Crystal Topas Professional doesn't support third-party plug-in modules.

## Caligari truespace2

Caligari truespace2 is a rising star in the 3D windows world. Building on its reputation earned on the Amiga platform, Caligari has produced an impressive 3D modeling, rendering, and animation program that won't break your budget. As a modeler, truespace2 allows you to create models from splines, then extrude or lathe them. It allows vertex-level editing, Boolean operations, and an Organic

11

Deformation which allows you to drag on a grid to deform a model. Its rendering features include ray-tracing and Phong shading. The program's animation tools allow a form of rotoscoping in which you can place animated objects on the surface of other objects. It also allows you to use spline-based paths to control the route of animated objects.

## Macromedia MacroModel

Macromedia's MacroModel is a modeling package which allows you to create intricate 2D shapes and turn them into 3D models with its lathing, sweeping, and skinning tools. (*Skinning* allows you to stretch a surface over the ribs of splines.) Once the 3D shape has been created, it can easily be stretched, rotated, twisted, bent, and tapered. The program features excellent vertex-level editing controls and hierarchical linking. This allows you to create an object that responds to movements. For instance, if you created a joystick attached to the base, you could create a link at the joint. When you move the joystick, the base wouldn't move because of the joint at the base. The highest-level rendering provided by the program is Phong rendering. High-level rendering is provided by exporting to Pixar's RenderMan software. Figure 11-20 shows an image modeled in Macromedia MacroModel and rendered in Specular Infini-D by Chuck Carter.

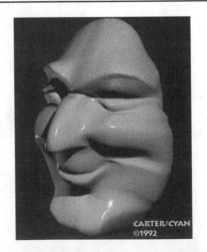

Image modeled in Macromedia MacroModel and rendered in Specular Infini-D by Chuck Carter

**FIGURE 11-20**

# Alias Sketch

Alias Sketch is one of the top modeling and rendering programs available on the Mac. As mentioned earlier, Sketch is one of the few 3D programs that provides NURBS-based editing. NURBS allows advanced curve editing and arc creation. Unlike many 3D programs, Sketch provides powerful 3D text features, allowing you to change Adobe Type 1 PostScript fonts into 3D objects.

Artists who usually work in two dimensions using drawing programs like Adobe Illustrator and Macromedia Freehand will find it easy to get acclimated to the Sketch environment because it's very much like a drawing program, using pencil, pen, and scissors tools. Images created in Illustrator and Freehand can easily be imported into Sketch for transformation into 3D models. Sketch also features fast, accurate ray-tracing rendering capabilities. To view two images created in Alias Sketch, turn to the color insert.

# Sculptor, Sculpt 3D, and Sculpt 4D

Byte by Byte Corporation markets a family of high-end 3D products. All packages are full-featured 3D modules which include vertex, spline, and NURBS-based editing. All packages also feature Boolean functions. Sculpt 3D, which retails for about $3,000, adds fast ray-trace rendering capabilities. Sculpt 4D includes ray-tracing and animation features. An example of an image created and rendered in Sculpt 3D is shown in the color insert.

# Presenter Professional 3.0

VIDI's Presenter Professional has the distinction of being the oldest Macintosh 3D rendering, modeling, and animation software package. At $2,000, the program is a strong competitor in the ranks of high-end products. Presenter Professional features spline-based editing and Boolean functions. The program includes a MacRenderman rendering plug-in and can even create stereograms—3D images that are hidden within shapes and images—which are used in posters and advertisements.

As an animation package, Presenter Professional allows you not only to add sound to your animations but to precisely control the sound by placing microphones at different parts of objects. Thus, the roar of an approaching spaceship could gradually get louder and louder. The program allows you to control the path of animation by editing spline-based paths with added controls for real-world sensations of gravity and wind.

## Newtek Lightwave 3D

Lightwave 3D is one of the few products that is available on the PC, SGI, and Amiga platforms. The PC version of the program, which retails for about $1,000, allows you to create models from freehand shapes or to use spline curves to create organic objects. The program lets you create your own macros and provides Boolean functions. Its animation module is key-frame-based and allows for hierarchical motion controls.

## Fractal Design Poser

Fractal Design Poser is a 3D modeling and rendering program specifically designed to create models of the human body. In many respects Poser allows you to build a digital creation similar to the wooden dummies used to pose human figures on an artist's desktop. Using the program's Figure Type menu, you can choose a variety of basic forms, such as Male Body, Female Body, Mannequin, and Skeleton. A library of figures lets you select from a variety of possibilities. Choices include Ideal Adult, Superhero, and Guy five pounds overweight, ten pounds overweight, and five pounds underweight. You can also change the model's proportions using Poser's Scale tools. You can also bend and rotate the figure. When you drag on a hand or foot, the program is sophisticated enough to know to move the connected body parts.

Models can be saved in PICT format for exporting to Fractal Design Painter or to image-editing programs such as Photoshop. Poser also allows files to be saved in RIB and DXF format for sophisticated rendering in other programs.

## TIPS of the TRADE

### Poser Tip
**by John Derry**

Fractal Design Poser is not capable of creating shadows, but here's an interesting way to "cheat":

# TIPS of the TRADE

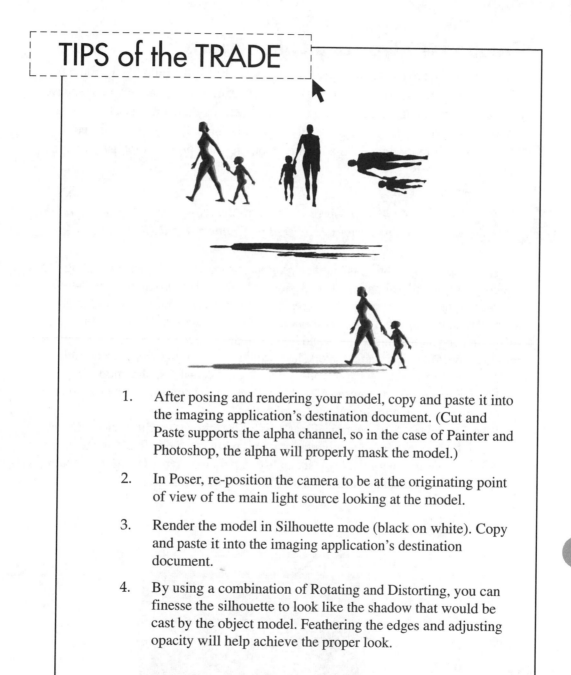

1. After posing and rendering your model, copy and paste it into the imaging application's destination document. (Cut and Paste supports the alpha channel, so in the case of Painter and Photoshop, the alpha will properly mask the model.)

2. In Poser, re-position the camera to be at the originating point of view of the main light source looking at the model.

3. Render the model in Silhouette mode (black on white). Copy and paste it into the imaging application's destination document.

4. By using a combination of Rotating and Distorting, you can finesse the silhouette to look like the shadow that would be cast by the object model. Feathering the edges and adjusting opacity will help achieve the proper look.

*John Derry is VP of Creative Design at Fractal Design.*

11

# Creating 3D Type and Other Effects

If you don't need to create sophisticated 3D scenes but still would like to add a few 3D effects to objects and text, you may be interested in several relatively inexpensive programs. One of the easiest to use is Ray Dream's Add Depth. The program automatically adds depth to type, bevels edges, and includes a Pen tool for editing. The program imports Freehand and Illustrator files and provides realistic lighting and shading effects.

**n**   **OTE:**   *Adobe Dimensions also allows you to create 3D type and other 3D effects. Dimensions is covered in Chapters 4 and 15.*

Specular's LogoMotion is another program primarily designed for adding 3D effects to type and animating it, if desired. Unlike other products, LogoMotion allows you to create cubes and spheres from primitives, then resize and reshape them. In many respects LogoMotion is like a mini-modeling animation program. Images can be lathed, and textures and lights can be applied to objects. The program provides multiple views and a Workshop window where you can extrude objects with the mouse. Once you've made your design decisions, the model can be rendered, then animated. Figure 11-21 shows the Camera window from an animated type sequence created in Specular's LogoMotion.

Like Specular's LogoMotion, Pixar's Typestry allows you to create 3D type effects and animate them. The program provides many beveled effects and textures. One of its more unusual features is its ability to perforate type. Using this feature, you could quickly create effects similar to the well-known IBM logo.

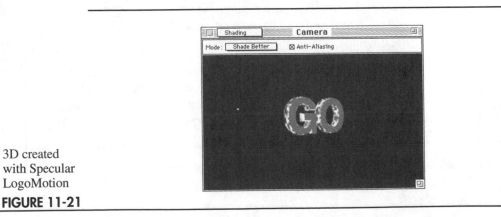

3D created
with Specular
LogoMotion

**FIGURE 11-21**

## High-End Minicomputer 3D Software

If your find that your Mac or PC just can't render fast enough, or if you need more sophisticated 3D software, you may wish to investigate UNIX-based 3D programs such as Alias AnimatorPro, ElectroGig, WaveFront, and Microsoft SoftImage. These are the software packages used to create most of the animated effects seen in TV commercials and Hollywood movies.

Although you may eventually see UNIX-based software running on Macs and PCs, don't expect your Mac or PC to rival a Silicon Graphics workstation quite yet. One of the reasons that SGI workstations are the choice of the entertainment industry is that they feature graphics library routines, called OpenGL, which are built right into the hardware of the computer. These routines speed the creation and updating of polygons, quickly shade 3D models, and increase the overall rendering speed. Figures 11-22, 11-23, and 11-24 were all created on Silicon Graphics workstations.

# Conclusion

Over the past few years, desktop computers have become more and more powerful. At the same time, 3D software has started to blossom with new features and prices

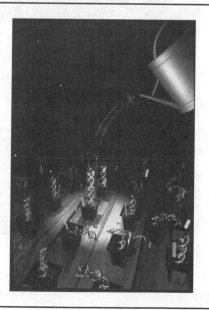

3D image created in Microsoft SoftImage by the design firm of Oko and Mano by Alejandro Arce and Mirko Ilić

**FIGURE 11-22**

11

3D image
created in
ElectroGig by
Ben Leider

**FIGURE 11-23**

have begun to drop. So if you've been considering the purchase of 3D modeling, rendering, or animation software, now is a good time to take the plunge.

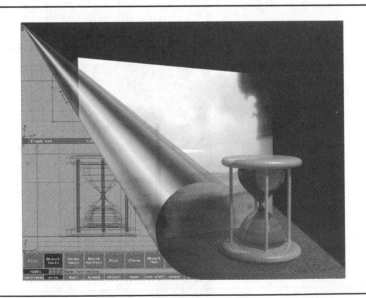

3D image
created in
Alias
PowerAnimator
by David
Chalk

**FIGURE 11-24**

# 12

## Stocking Up on Digital Images

W here do you turn when you're under a tight deadline and need an image to add to a photo montage, a page layout, or a multimedia production? You could send someone off with a digital camera to take a quick shot of the required image. Of course, if you need a picture of a Paris street scene, sending a photographer might not be too practical.

These days, the easiest way to obtain digital images is to load them from a CD-ROM disc. In fact, many of the images you've seen in this book were chosen from CD-ROM discs supplied by stock image suppliers. If you don't have a collection of images on CD-ROMs, you can secure them from online picture services.

This chapter provides an overview of CD-ROM collections, photo suppliers, and online services that provide stock digital images. If you haven't kept abreast of the digital imaging world, you'll be amazed at the number of sources for digital stock photos, textures, backgrounds, clip art, and multimedia digital movies.

# CD-ROM Stock Photo Suppliers

The drop in CD-ROM drive prices, coupled with the booming need for digital images, has spawned a new industry of digital stock suppliers. You can now find CD-ROMs with digitized images of almost any subject—from indigenous peoples to photographs of art from the world's museums. Most photo suppliers save images in either Kodak's Photo CD format or the TIFF file format. This allows Mac, PC, and even UNIX users to work with the images.

One reason why stock image CDs are so attractive is that many companies offer the images royalty-free. For the most part, this means you can freely use the images in ads, brochures, or company presentations without having to worry about negotiating usage fees. Another valuable feature of CD-ROM stock collections is that they are often packaged with mini versions of image cataloging software. Using the software on the CD-ROM, you can quickly click your way through thumbnail images, or search for images by name or keyword.

Prices for royalty-free stock image CDs vary greatly. Some CD-ROM discs, such as those sold by Corel Corporation, sell for under $100, while others cost as much as $300. We've compiled a brief review of stock photo suppliers, and have included some black-and-white samples of a variety of images from CD-ROM discs. As you look through the images, remember that most stock photos on CDs are in color.

Before purchasing a CD-ROM disc, you might want to see samples. Many stock suppliers sell low-priced samplers that can give you a good idea of the subject matter and photographic quality.

**BEACHWARE NATURE PHOTO COLLECTION**   This royalty-free CD-ROM includes 8- and 24-bit TIFF images of nature scenes. The disc includes rivers, streams, mountains, seashores, skies, rocks, and plants. An image from this collection appears in Chapter 15.

**DIGITAL STOCK CORP.**   Digital Stock sells several volumes of stock photography. Most discs include over 40 images in Photo CD format. Digital Stock titles include Active Lifestyles; American Civil War; Animals; Babies & Children; Flowers; Food; Italy Signature Series; Men, Women & Romance; New York City Signature Series; Ocean & Coasts; Space & Space Flight; Transportation; Trees; Undersea Life; Western Scenes; and World War II. Images may be used for print, advertising, brochures, reports, and demonstrations. See Chapters 9, 10, 14, and 15 for images from Digital Stock.

**DANA PUBLISHING'S THE BALTHIS COLLECTION**   This is a diverse collection of digitized photographs taken by nature photographer Frank Balthis, who has photographed images for *National Geographic,* The Sierra Club, Time/Life Books, and *Popular Photography*. Images in the collection may be used as proofs or published in limited numbers (under 100 copies). Images can be displayed on computers in public events such as trade shows. The CD includes a usage request form for those who need other uses beyond those allowed in the licensing agreement.

**COREL PROFESSIONAL PHOTOS**   Corel Corporation sells dozens of stock photography titles, all saved in Kodak's Photo CD format. Think of a subject, and Corel undoubtedly has an image. Corel photos are sold totally royalty-free. For samples, see Chapters 9, 10, 14, and 15.

**D'PIX, A DIVISION OF AMBER PRODUCTIONS, INC.**   D'pix publishes a CD-ROM entitled, "Peeping ROM," filled with 928 full-page images and retailing for less than $200. The disc includes a version of Multi-Ad Search software, which allows you to quickly scan through the images: state parks, sunsets, travel shots, fabrics, marbles, nostalgic scenes, and so on. Images are saved in TIFF format at 72 ppi at sizes from 9 x 12 to 9 x 22 inches. To obtain a high-resolution version of an image, you can contact the company. The first high-res scan is free. Additional high-res images are $175. Images also may be purchased as 4 x 5 transparencies or 35mm slides for $175 each.

**12**

**DíAMAR PORTFOLIOS** DíAMAR provides numerous CD-ROM stock photography titles. All images are saved in Photo CD Format. Titles include Nature and Animals, Cities, Castles, Flowers, Background and Textures, and People and LifeStyles. Images are royalty-free. The company prohibits use of its images in pornography. An image cannot be used if it is the primary vehicle of work (such as postcards and calendars). Each DíAMAR disc includes over 50 images. See Chapters 14 and 15 for other examples of images from DíAMAR Portfolios.

**HSC KPT POWER PHOTOS** HSC has published several sets of CD-ROMs. Subjects include natural backgrounds and textures, sports and recreation, food, sky, water, and landscapes. Sample volumes contain low-res images for placement. Other

volumes contain high-res images for professional publishing. HSC's licensing agreement allows you to use images royalty-free as long as the HSC images are not the primary subject of the work. Images can be used in promotions and advertisements. The sample disc even includes several free filters from HSC's renowned Kai's Power Tools. Some of the images in Power Photos are *masked* (silhouetted) so that the primary image in the photo can easily be copied and pasted into image- editing or page layout software without the picture background. Shown here is an image from HSC's Sports and Recreation Volume 5 CD-ROM. For other examples of images from HSC KPT Power Photos, see Chapters 14 and 15.

**IMAGE CLUB PHOTOGEAR** This company publishes several volumes of stock

images saved in TIFF format at high, medium, and low resolutions. The high-res versions are suitable for full-page reproduction at 150 lpi. Each volume contains a version of Adobe Fetch Browser to facilitate previewing and locating images. Titles in the Photogear collection include sky, landscapes, "snackgrounds," business images, mountainscapes, backgrounds, and textures. Shown here is an image of fortune cookies from Image Club's Photogear number 4, "snackgrounds" CD-ROM. For another example of images from Image Club Photogear, see Chapter 4.

**ADC IMAGEVAULT**   ADC publishes a variety of royalty-free photos packaged in different sets. Its Volume 1 General Interest collection contains four CD-ROMs with over 380 images of people, places, outdoor, and business scenes. Images are saved in Photo CD format. To view sample images from ImageVault's CD collection, see Chapter 9.

**CMCD STOCK**   Clement Mok's design studio (Mok is the former Art Director of Apple Computer) publishes several CDs that focus on everyday objects. The company's Visual Symbols disc includes images of water bottles, dice, and telephones. CMCD's Metaphorically Speaking disc includes a horseshoe, a needle and a haystack, a ladder, a life preserver, a fortune cookie, an eight ball, a white picket fence, and a hare and a tortoise. CMCD's Tools disc features such objects as a saw, a bucket, a bicycle pump, a scrub brush, and a pair of pliers. The company's Hands disc includes photographs of male and female hands using American Sign Language. Hands also are shown holding a variety of tools and objects. Images are royalty-free but cannot be used in pornography or in any way that is defamatory to a person or business. Chapters 9 and 10 show samples from CMCD's CD-ROMs.

**WORK FOR HIRE CLASSICPHOTO**   Work for Hire publishes three stock discs, each containing 100 images stored in Photo CD format. Most of the images are individual shots of everyday objects. For instance, Volume 1 contains pictures of a pocket watch, a magnifying glass, a flashlight, a dart, a globe, and an umbrella. Volume 2 features an assortment of different objects along with images of clouds and sunsets. Shown here is a snowman image from Work for Hire's ClassicPhoto Volume 3 disc. For another example of a Work for Hire's ClassicPhoto, see Chapter 15.

**CLASSIC PHOTOGRAPHIC IMAGE OBJECTS**   N e e d images of clocks, radios, microphones, and memorabilia from the '40s and '50s? Classic PIO Partners may have what you're looking for. PIO sells a sampler disc which includes old typewriters, lamps, cameras, blenders, toasters, and alarm clocks. Images are saved in high- and low-res formats. Shown here is an old-time jukebox from the PIO sampler disc.

**COLORBYTES**   ColorBytes publishes two CD-ROMs in its Designer Series of background textures. Volume One is Paper & Fibers, Volume Two is Stone & Minerals. Their Mini-Sampler, Sampler One, and Sampler Two CD-ROMs include photographic images. The CD-ROM images are stored in PICT, TIFF, JPEG, and BMP file formats. Shown here is an image from ColorBytes's Sampler One disc, photographed by Eric Wunrow. For other examples of images from ColorBytes, see Chapters 4 and 6.

**DIGITAL WISDOM BODYSHOTS** If you don't want to spend time and money shooting a model, you might consider Digital Wisdom BodyShots. This CD-ROM includes over 300 photographs featuring people in a wide variety of poses and dress. Each is a 24-bit, 300-ppi TIFF image. The first BodyShots CD-ROM features business poses, such as the one shown here. Future titles will include Health and Fitness, Children, and Romantic poses. All models are shot against a white background and have signed model releases. The CD-ROM includes an excellent booklet which explains resolution and file format issues. The licensing agreement requires you to register with Digital Wisdom before using the images for commercial purposes. The licensing agreement also allows unrestricted use of the images within your organization.

**DIGITAL WISDOM MOUNTAIN HIGH MAPS, FRONTIERS, AND GLOBESHOTS** This company publishes several volumes of relief maps, including Mountain High Maps, Frontiers, and GlobeShots. The Mountain High collection includes high-quality map projections and global views that can easily be colorized. Oceans are masked so that continents can be colorized and emphasized. Every Mountain High map is saved in three resolutions: 300 ppi TIFF, 100 ppi TIFF, and 72 ppi PICT and BMP. The Frontiers CD has editable vector outline maps with accurate political borders that can be colorized. The Frontier

CD includes files saved in Macromedia Freehand, Adobe Illustrator, and TIFF formats. The GlobeShots CD features 250 colored globes supplied with different backgrounds and special effects. GlobeShot images are saved in TIFF, PICT, and BMP formats. High-resolution images are 13.9MB 300-ppi TIFF files.

**FOTOROM**  WEKA Publishing Inc. offers FotoROM, a multipurpose photo collection on two CD-ROM discs. Images in the collection are shot by professional photographers from around the world. FotoROM is royalty-free for commercial and private use. One CD in the collection contains 72-ppi images saved in TIFF format; the other contains 300-ppi images saved in uncompressed TIFF format. Packaged with the CD-ROM is a three-ring binder that contains full-size color prints of all the images on the CDs. Among the subjects included are sports and recreation, people, business and technology, animals, still life

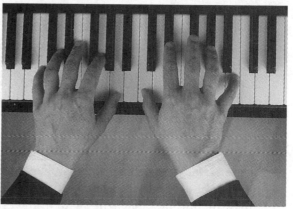

and art, backgrounds and special effects, and nature and science. Shown here is an image shot by S. Holzmann from the FotoROM collection.

**DIGITAL ZONE CD-ROMS**  Digital Zone publishes several volumes of stock images on CD-ROM. Most collections include the work of one photographer on a wide variety of subjects. For instance, the CD-ROM featuring the work of travel photographer Cliff Hollenbeck includes travel scenes, and images of cities, people, and nature. Digital Zone also publishes a CD-ROM entitled *NASA: The New Frontier,* which includes NASA spaceships as well as outer space scenes. Images used from this disc must include a photo credit; Digital Zone requests that those using images from the CD-ROM in books and advertising submit a layout and copy to NASA prior to release.

**PLANET ART**  Planet Art publishes a series of CDs comprised of photographs of art from around the world. All images are saved in Photo CD format. The company sells a sampler disk and offers a catalog of their titles. Chapter 9 shows an image from one of their collections.

**OTHER CD-ROM STOCK SUPPLIERS**  Other CD-ROM stock suppliers include PhotoDisc, Aztech New Media Corp., Gazelle Technologies, Pacific Publishing

Group, PhotoSphere, Softkey, Digital Media Stock Clips, Simon's Alphabet, PhotoLab, Wayzata Technology, and Digital Media Stock Options.

# Traditional Stock Photo Suppliers

Before CD-ROMs jumped into the spotlight, the traditional method of obtaining stock images was to thumb through a catalog from a photo supply house, pick an image, and pay for the reproduction rights. Generally, after you agreed to the licensing terms, the stock agency supplied you with a print or transparency (which had to be returned) to use for your publication. You may well wonder, Why pay for the rights to an image if you can use the ones purchased on CD-ROMs royalty-free?

Traditional suppliers often provide greater variety and higher-quality photos than can be found on CD-ROMs. You also may find that the images you use from a traditional stock house aren't as likely to appear in a competitor's annual report or newsletter. In fact, one advantage of paying for individual photo rights is that the supplier can provide you with a detailed history of an image's usage.

This section includes a short list of traditional photo supply agencies who do not provide royalty-free images. Fees charged by different agencies vary and are generally based on the usage rather than the picture. If you will be reproducing a small picture in a magazine with a low circulation, you will be charged less than if you use the picture at a larger size in an international advertising campaign. Several agencies have published low-res catalogs of their images on CD-ROM.

**ANIMALS ANIMALS/EARTH SCENES**   This photo supplier specializes in animals. Archives include 35mm transparencies and black-and-white prints. The company's earth science division provides images on subjects such as agriculture, flowers, geology, plants, weather, national parks, pollution, and scenics.

**THE BETTMAN ARCHIVE**   This famous archive features "15,000" years' worth of pictures. Bettman owns the rights to everything from images of ancient cave paintings to thousands of news photos. The company's enormous stock library includes black-and-white photos, engravings, movie stills, and photo libraries from the United Press and Reuters. The company has access to over 25 million images.

**COMSTOCK, INC.**   Comstock publishes a seven-volume encyclopedia of images, which are provided free to "qualified art directors." Comstock has over 4 million images on file.

**CULVER PICTURES**    The Culver Pictures library includes over 9 million images. The library is composed mostly of black-and-white engravings, etchings, and prints. Old movie stills, sheet music, and turn-of-the-century cartoons are also available.

**FPG INTERNATIONAL**    This company provides images for a broad range of clients including ad agencies, designers, retailers, and travel agencies. FPG is a resource for over 6 million contemporary and historical images. Each year over 150,000 images from over 200 professional photographers are added to the stock collection.

**THE IMAGE BANK**    The Image Bank maintains a large collection of stock pictures on a wide variety of subjects, including general stock, human interest, celebrities, glamour, agriculture, and food. Professional photographers, illustrators, and cinematographers provide the images. The company has thousands of movie clips that are available for viewing on laser discs.

**THE STOCK MARKET**    The Stock Market maintains a large selection of images on many diverse subjects. The company also publishes a CD-ROM with over 6,000 low-res images.

**TONY STONE IMAGES**    Tony Stone Images represents over 500 photographers from around the world. Subject matter is suitable for advertising, design, corporate, and editorial markets.

*n* **OTE:** *The Picture Agency Council of America in Northfield, Minnesota publishes a booklet listing the names and phone numbers of most of the major stock agency image suppliers in the United States. If you'd like a copy of the book, call 1-800-457-7222.*

# Stock Backgrounds and Textures

Texture and background images can help convey a mood and add style to artwork and multimedia productions. If you use a 3D program with rendering capabilities, you can wrap stock image textures around your 3D objects. Here's a brief review of some of the textures and background available. All of the following images are sold royalty-free.

12

**ARTBEATS** ArtBeats publishes several volumes of textures and backgrounds. The collection includes Marble Paper Textures, Wood, and Paper. Many of the discs include not only textures but also buttons for use in multimedia productions. Images are saved in TIFF format in low, medium, and high resolutions. Included in each CD-ROM are extras such as parchment and metallic backgrounds. Each disc is packaged with an in-depth manual. For example, the Marbled Paper texture manual includes "A Brief History of Marbling." The manual also discusses converting from RGB to CMYK, as well as the difference between output for

print and multimedia. Shown here is a Marble Paper background sample from ArtBeats Marble Paper CD-ROM.

**D'PIX FOLIO** This is a set of five CD-ROMs that feature a variety of different textures. The fabric disc includes white satin, red velvet, striped oxford, and burlap textures. The food disc includes bread crust, lettuce, pickling spices, wild rice, and mushrooms. The masonry disc includes brick walks, stucco, granite, and Gothic. Shown here is a brick walkway from the

D'pix Masonry CD-ROM. Other CDs feature textures of Marble, Metal, and Nature. Images are stored in TIFF format at medium and high resolutions. High-res images are 9 x 12 inches at 266 ppi, medium-resolution images are 7 x 12 inches at 74 ppi. Medium-res images are also stored in PICT format. For another image from a D'pix CD-ROM, see Chapter 15.

**FOTOSETS PHOTOGRAPHIC ORIGINALS** This is a set of 100 backgrounds shot by photographer Robin Ginsberg. Each image is created from a variety of different textures. The backgrounds include water scenes, fabrics, nature, and buildings. Images are stored in Photo CD

format. Shown here is a background image from FotoSets Photographic Originals CD-ROM.

**PIXAR CLASSIC TEXTURES**   Pixar publishes two volumes of textures, One Twenty Eight and Classic Textures, that include images of water, exotic marble, earth tiles, clouds, fur, and leather. Shown here is the Alloy Diamond Plate texture from Pixar's One Twenty Eight CD-ROM. Images are saved in TIFF format at 300 ppi at sizes up to 13.1 x 13.3 inches. The CD includes an Adobe Photoshop-compatible plug-in that allows you to fill images in your image-editing or painting program with textures.

**NEO CANVAS**   Neo's custom-painted environment CDs are produced by a design team that creates background murals, wall coverings, and fabrics for the design community. Shown here is an image from the Neo Canvas Volume 1 disc. Many of the images in the Neo Canvas collection are hand-painted on canvas. Some designs feature metallic and brilliant colors that are virtually impossible to create on the computer. The images are saved in Photo CD format.

**VISUAL SOFTWARE TEXTURE FOR PROFES-SIONALS**   This CD-ROM contains hundreds of textures. Subjects include construction, food, marble, rock, and textiles. Shown here is a rock texture from the collection. The disc contains 360 textures at 640 x 480 pixels and 320 x 240 pixels, and 60 element images (flowers, bushes, trees, and so on) at 1024 x 768 pixels. Images are stored in TGA format for PC users and TIFF format for Macintosh users.

**XAOS TOOLS ARTIST IN RESIDENCE FRESCO**   This collection includes 80 textural images. Many of the images feature unusual textures because they were synthetically created. Shown here is the "Yarrow" background from the Artist in Residence Fresco

**12**

CD-ROM. Images are stored in different formats: 300 ppi images are 9 x 13 inches and stored as JPEG compressed PICT format; 72 ppi images are 9 x 12 inches and saved in PICT format. Images to be shown on a computer screen are 640 x 480 pixels stored as 8-bit (256 colors) PICT files.

**VIVID DETAILS** This company specializes in stunning backgrounds composed of flowers, old paint, rustic wood, granite, slate, marble, leather, clouds, and sunsets. All the images on the CD-ROM are photographed on a Hasselblad camera by award-winning commercial photographer Larry Willet. All images were scanned on a high-end drum scanner and were converted from RGB color to CMYK color, sharpened and saved in TIFF format. Each disc features high- and low-resolution images. High-res images are 9 x 12 inches at 300 ppi (37.1MB). Vivid Details sells a preview disc displaying the entire collection for $39. The preview disc also contains 12 high-res images. Shown here is Vivid Details' Embossed Leather background from the Leather Volume 3 disc. For another example of a Vivid Details image, see Chapter 14.

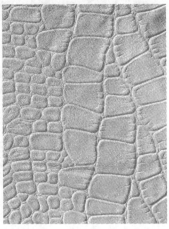

**FRACTAL DESIGN WALLS AND RELIEF, MILES OF TILES** Fractal Design publishes two 2-floppy disk volumes of textures that can be loaded into the Fractal Design Painter's Art Materials: Papers palette. The textures can be used to add backgrounds or textures to brush strokes. See Chapter 15 for an example of Miles of Tiles texture.

**OTHER CD-ROM BACKGROUND TEXTURE SUPPLIERS** Other companies that publish background textures include Form & Function, Just Software's World Arts Foto Media CD, Letraset (Phototone library), and World Art.

# Stock Clip Art

Clip art disk and CD collections contain images created in drawing programs and/or scanned from line art. Clip art is often used in newsletters and business presentations. Most clip art disks retail from approximately $50 to $200. Here are a few providers.

**ARRO INTERNATIONAL**   This company publishes a variety of clip art collections which include from 35 to 75 images on high-density disks. Most of the company's clip art is environmentally oriented. Titles include: Energy, Living Planet, Pollution, Recycling, Accents, Wildlife, and Environment Vol 1. Shown here is a puffin from one of the Arro International clip art disks.

**COREL GALLERY**   C o r e l Gallery includes over 10,000 clip art images from different sources on a wide variety of subjects. The CD-ROM collection is packaged with a 344-page book that shows every image in the collection. The clip art includes portraits of famous people, animals, fruit, maps, ships, landmarks, money, and designs. Shown here is a cartoon image created by Totem Graphics from the Corel Gallery clip art collection. Images for the Mac version are saved in PICT format; the PC version is saved in BMP format.

**IMAGE CLUB ARTROOM**   This extensive CD collective contains thousands of EPS images and hundreds of PICT color and black-and-white images. The CD-ROM disc includes a version of Adobe Fetch Browser for fast retrieval and searches. The collection is sold with a large spiral-bound book showing all the art in the collection, which includes maps, letters, people, design elements, and sports scenes. The collection includes a variety of styles—some are serious and businesslike, others are humorous. Shown here is a cartoon image from the Image Club ArtRoom collection. For another example of an image from this collection, see Chapter 10.

**PERIWINKLE PAST TINTS**   Periwinkle Past Tints is an unusual set of antique images created from the 1880s to the 1920s. Images were scanned at 1,200 ppi and saved in TIFF format. (Duplicate files are also saved at 300 ppi.) Categories include Domestic Animals, People, Sea Life, Whimsy, and Wild Animals. The sampler disk contains images from each volume. See Chapters 6 and 9 for examples of Periwinkle Past Tints.

**NEW VISION TASK FORCE CLIP ART** This package consists of over a thousand clip art images. New Vision thoughtfully includes disks with their CD-ROMs—for those who don't have a CD-ROM. The images are sold with a large manual showing samples of all clip art. The manual also includes a discussion of the difference between PICT, EPS, and other file formats, as well as the difference between vector and raster image formats. Subjects include people, science, high tech, special occasions, cartoons, home, and religion. The company also produces Presentation Task Force, which includes over 3,500 clip art images saved in CBM and Windows metafile formats. Shown here is an example from the New Vision Task Force Clip art collection.

**WAYZATA TECHNOLOGY CLIP ARTS** W a y z a t a Technology publishes various clip art CD-ROMs. There are four volumes in the epsPRO Series: Design Elements, Everyday Images, Cartoon Stock, and Business Images. Shown here is an image from the epsPRO Cartoon Stock CD-ROM. Each epsPRO CD-ROM sells for $59. Wayzata also sells a Quick Art Deluxe Volume with over 3,200 black-and-white illustrations for $349 and a Quick Art Lite Volume with 1,600 black-and-white illustrations for $119.

**T/MAKER COMPANY CLIP ARTS** T/Maker Company sells several clip art collections. The company's Incredible Image Pak 200 features over 2,000 full color images, and 40

fonts. Subject matter includes: Business & Office, Animals & Outdoors, Children & Education, Art & Entertainment, Fitness & Sports, and Travel & Entertainment. One of the company's most unusual collections is Famous Magazine Cartoons, which features over 500 cartoons on one CD-ROM disc. The licensing agreement for the cartoons disc allows you to use the cartoons in personal correspondence, slide shows, charts and diagrams, printed forms, sales brochures, in-house newsletters, direct mail advertising of less than 100,000 pieces, and periodical publications with circulation under 30,000. T/Maker's ClickArt Art Parts collection includes over 300 "wacky yet somehow useful" clip art images. Many of the images in this collection are created in a woodcut-like cartoon style. An example is shown here.

**TECHPOOL SOFTWARE SUPER ANATOMY CD-ROMS**   Techpool publishes several CD-ROMs of human anatomy. The company's Super Anatomy 2 disc includes cellular, cardiac, and external anatomy illustrations as well as hand-related images. The Super Anatomy 3 disc includes musculoskeletal, neuroanatomy, obstetrics, and foot-related images.

**OTHER CD-ROM CLIP ART SUPPLIERS**   Other companies that sell clip art include, Totem Graphics, World Art, One Mile Up, ScanROM, Broderbund, Zedcor, Metro ImageBase, 3G Graphics Inc., Archive Arts, RT Computer Graphics, Casady & Greene, WEKA Publishing, and ProVektor.

# Multimedia Clip Art

The boom in multimedia has spawned a small industry of multimedia clip art. Most multimedia clip art includes QuickTime movie scenes that can be integrated into projects created in such programs as Macromedia Director, Macromedia Authorware, and Macromedia Action, as well as in Adobe Premiere and Adobe After Effects, Strata Media Paint, and Linker Systems' The Animation Stand. Clip art geared specifically for multimedia interactive presentations often includes backgrounds and buttons. Most CD-ROM collections in this area are royalty-free. However, be sure to read all licensing information because some companies do place certain restrictions on usage and distribution.

**BEACHWARE MULTIWARE MULTIMEDIA COLLECTION**   This CD-ROM includes 240 backgrounds, 140 QuickTime movies, over 200 sounds and music clips, and 100 color buttons. The buttons can be used as clickable objects to control navigation in multimedia productions. For instance, the button shown here could be used to allow a user to move to the next screen page.

BeachWare's QuickTime movies include airport scenes, clouds, hot air balloons, sports, weddings, and business scenes. See Chapter 4 for an example of a BeachWare Multiware Multi-Media collection QuickTime clip.

**BEACHWARE PHOTO TEXTURES**   This CD-ROM includes 100 8-bit (256 colors) background textures for multimedia projects. The disc also includes 50 high-res

12

textures for desktop publishing. Textures include underwater scenes, seashore, skies, earth, rock, and plants.

**STAT MEDIA INSTANT BUTTONS AND CONTROLS VERSION 2**   This entertaining CD-ROM includes numerous animated buttons and controls specifically designed

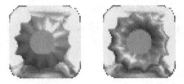

to work in Macromedia Director. The CD-ROM includes levers, and rotary, humorous, artistic, 3D, and futuristic buttons as shown here. It also includes backgrounds, sounds, and QuickTime movies.

**MACROMEDIA CLIPMEDIA 1 BUSINESS AND TECHNOLOGY**   Although the title of the CD is Business and Technology, this CD-ROM is packed with images of all subjects. The CD includes numerous backgrounds, PICS format animations, QuickTime movies, sounds, music, and beveled buttons, as seen here.

Also included are animated sequences featuring adding machines, alarm clocks, cups, coffeemakers, and flags. QuickTime movies show bungee jumping, city scenes, money being counted, and the statue of liberty. The package includes a listing of all items on the CD as well as a color directory displaying frames from the animated sequences and QuickTime movies.

**MACROMEDIA CLIPMEDIA 2 INDUSTRY AT WORK**   Like ClipMedia 1, this CD-ROM includes graphics, animations, QuickTime and PICS movies, sound effects, and music. Animated sequences show backgrounds, as well as computer, educational, financial, medical, telecommunications, and manufacturing scenes. Graphics include buttons, people, and a variety of other subjects.

**WAYZATA TECHNOLOGY**   Wayzata produces a CD of stock film clips called World of Motion, in addition to clip art, stock photography, movies, sounds, fonts, and other CD-ROMs. Wayzata's MusicScapes Professional includes 16 royalty-free professional audio tracks for use in multimedia projects and presentations. The disc includes country, rock, sci-fi, mellow acoustic, and more. Wayzata's Sound Library Pro includes sound effects of animals, household instruments, nature, special effects, and voice. See Chapter 4 for an example of a Wayzata Technology World of Motion QuickTime clip.

**PHOTODEX PICTURE FACTORY**   Photodex's CD-ROM includes 3,300 royalty-free photos, clip art images, and sounds. Subjects include business, fashion, holidays, people, space, food, international, backgrounds, midwestern, and travel scenes. Chapter 15 shows an image from this collection.

**KILLER TRACKS MUSIC LIBRARIES**   Killer Tracks licenses production music and sound effects created by Hollywood and international composers. The company publishes CD-ROMs for several libraries including production music, scoring, classics, and cartoon sound effects. Licensing for most libraries involves paying an initial fee of $575, $500 of which is credited to a year's usage fees. Licensing also can be arranged on an annual basis depending upon music clearances needed.

## Other CD-ROM Multimedia and Sound Suppliers

Other publishers of multimedia clip art and sounds include Cambium Development, Prosonus, Index Stock's Photos To Go, Jasmine Multimedia Publishing's In-Motion & Still CD Series, and MPI Multimedia.

# 3D Clip Art

Three-dimensional images can add sophistication and excitement to print and multimedia presentations. Unfortunately, creating sophisticated 3D art can be quite time consuming and difficult. Several vendors now offer 3D clip media.

**STRATA CLIP 3D**   Strata publishes a CD-ROM filled with 3D shapes and textures. Users can phone Strata for a password to unlock images on the disc. Formats can be read by Strata Vision 3D and Strata StudioPro. The disc includes shapes, cars, whale shapes, anatomy shapes, and dinosaurs. Images from Strata Clip 3d appear in Chapter 10.

**SPECULAR REPLICAS**   Specular publishes a CD-ROM that contains over 600 3D models and surfaces. The images are saved in Specular Infini-D and DXF format. Categories available on the CD-ROM include office furniture, lamps and chairs, starter surfaces, exotic woods, packaging, patterns, transportation 1, marbles, dinosaurs, transportation, star ships, humanoids, and human characters. Images from Specular Replicas appear in Chapter 10.

**12**

**VALIS**   The Valis Group publishes several disc-based products that can be used with Pixar's Showplace and MacRenderMan 3D software packages. Valis Prime RIB contains over 200 building block images to aid in the creation of 3D objects. Shapes include vases, bottles, bowls, a man, and a woman. Valis' Darrel's Microbots disk contains several 3D robotlike objects, along with spacecrafts and aeromobiles. Valis also creates VG Shaders and Vglooks, libraries of 3D surfaces.

**VIEWPOINT**   This company sells over a thousand wire-frame *"data set"* models for 3D programs. Viewpoint's catalog previews wire frames for airplanes, people, animals, imaginary characters, and miscellaneous everyday objects. Data sets cost from $49 (an alarm clock) to over $2,000 (a vertebral column). Files are sold in formats for most major 3D software packages. ReadySets include the Interior Man, Flying Machines, Digital Creatures, and the Virtual Highway. They can be purchased for $99 each. Models can be ordered in numerous media formats including SyQuest and DAT tape. For users of Wavefront, SoftImage, and 3D Studio, Viewpoint offers a CD-ROM which can be unlocked.

**ACURIS**   Acuris sells a CD of wire-frame models. Models include furniture and fully articulated men and women. Images are sold for Mac and PC in DCF format. Formats for Silicon Graphics' platform software are also available. Interiors, geography, human forms, exteriors, and trees are included. Custom models can be purchased. An image from Acuris appears in Chapter 4.

# Online Picture Services

If you need access to thousands of images, but don't wish to wear out the tray loader on your CD-ROM or get blisters from thumbing through stock image catalogs, you might hunt for images online. Online services can provide access to storehouses of stock images over the telephone. Using the software provided by an online service, you can quickly search for images that might otherwise take days to research.

## Kodak Picture Exchange

Kodak Picture Exchange (KPX) offers 24-hour access to over 50,000 images. The images don't belong to Kodak; they're from the libraries of over 20 stock agencies. KPX, which is available on CompuServe, is designed to make searching for images as painless as possible. For example, you can search for an image according to the number, sex, or ages of the people in the image. You also can narrow the search to such topics as indoor and outdoor.

After you execute a search, images that meet the search criteria appear onscreen as tiny thumbnails. You then can preview larger size versions and download them as "design proofs," which are saved at a resolution of 256 x 344 pixels (Kodak's Base /4 Photo CD resolution). Images this size can be used as comps, or design samples. The cost for the design proof is $9, which is only a small part of the fees charged by KPX.

The KPX registration fee for up to five computers is about $400. While working online, you're charged $1.42 per minute, which translates to a little over $85 an hour. The main disadvantage of using KPX is that you still need to negotiate fees with the stock agency that owns the images. Thus, after picking the images you need, you must call the stock house and discuss licensing agreements.

## PNI's Seymour

Picture Network International's Seymour is a 24-hour online picture service that allows users not only to search for images but also to download high-res images.

Seymour allows you to search for images using English phrases, and to view the images that are found in thumbnail versions. Once you find an image you'd like to use, you can specify how you are going to use it. After you tell Seymour the size of the image and the audience that will view it, a price appears on screen. If you agree to the price, you can download the high-res image immediately.

## Press Link

Knight-Ridder created Press Link as an online service primarily for supplying news photos and text to its subscribers. Press Link image providers include Knight-Ridder/Tribune, *The New York Times,* Reuters, Bettman Archive, Los Angeles Times Syndicate, Agence France-Press, and Gannett. Press Link has recently expanded its services and is now offering stock photos. The registration fee for Press Link is $50. Online time is billed at $15.95 an hour, and $5.75 per downloaded kilobyte.

# Conclusion

As you've seen in this chapter, the variety of stock images available is enormous. When shopping for stock images, don't assume images are royalty-free. Be sure to read all licensing agreements that come with CD-ROM stock collections. If you have any questions, call the stock image supplier. A list of stock suppliers and their phone numbers is included in the Appendix.

# 13

## Copyright Issues

**D**o you have the right to scan an image from an old magazine and use it free of charge in a work of art you are creating? To photocopy a picture from a stock photography library and use it in a sample layout you intend to show to a client? To videotape someone sitting in a park and use the image in a multimedia production or publication? To photograph centuries-old artwork in a museum with your digital camera, then incorporate the photos into your artwork without permission from the museum? If you are creating digital images or using existing ones, you should know the answer to these questions.

As artists and publishers expand their use of digital imaging techniques, litigation over image reproduction rights has increased. In the past few years, several well-publicized cases have made painfully clear the importance of understanding copyright law. For instance, recently a Long Island newspaper was sued because one of its artists scanned a portion of an image from a stock photo catalog and used it as part of an article illustration. The newspaper was forced to pay $20,000 to the stock agency, plus a portion of their legal fees, plus $15,500 to the photographer. The 1994 winner of Corel's Design Contest was sued for copying a stock photography image. Even though the artist claims he didn't scan the stock photo, he still was sued because he manually copied a significant portion of the image. (This case was still pending as this book went to press.) In 1990, a Cleveland advertising agency was sued for three copyright infringements. The agency photocopied a picture of Franklin Roosevelt's empty wheelchair to use as a sample ad. The ad agency showed it to their client, who approved the ad, and the agency hired its own photographer to re-create the photo. The original photographer of the wheelchair was awarded $140,000 in damages and legal fees. As you can see from these examples, ignorance of copyright laws can be costly and can take the fun out of working with digital images.

If you create, use, or distribute digital images, a working knowledge of copyright laws is as important as knowing how to scan an image and or how to use the latest features of your digital imaging software. If you're not familiar with how copyright laws apply to digital images, this chapter will introduce you to the basic issues.

# The Right to Copy

The United States copyright law was written to protect an artist's rights of expression. Works created by artists, photographers, and writers are all covered under this law, which specifies who has the right to reproduce a work. In the United States, the Copyright Act of 1976 (which took effect in 1978) designates the rights of copyright owners. It states that copyright law protects all works as soon as they are created, automatically. The law stipulates that the copyright owner has the right to:

► Copy his or her work.

► Create derivative works (new versions based on the original).

► Distribute the work and copies of it.

► Perform the work.

► Exhibit the work or control who exhibits it.

In March 1989, when the United States joined an international copyright treaty, an important portion of the copyright law was changed—after that date, no copyright notice is required. Thus, even if a work created after March 1989 does not display the familiar copyright symbol (©) or is not registered in the United States Copyright Office, it is nevertheless considered copyrighted.

# Copyright Ownership and Terms

If you have created a work of art privately—that is, outside a company you work for—you own the copyright as soon as the work is created. You don't, however, own it forever. The length of time you are entitled to copyright protection depends on when the work was created.

For works created on or after January 1, 1978, copyright belongs to the creator for his or her life—and until 50 years after his or her death. Before 1978, different copyright laws were in effect. From 1909 to 1977, copyright was granted for 28 years after publication. The copyright could be renewed only once—for another 28 years. However, when Congress changed the copyright law in 1976, it added an extra bit of protection which complicated the formula. Works still in their first term of protection were granted another 47 years of protection. Works in their second term of protection were granted 75 years of protection from the date of first

**13**

publication. Unpublished works created before 1978 may be protected until the year 2027. To complicate matters even more, as this book goes to press, legislation is pending to make these terms even longer!

To anyone using digital images, these figures are important. You might assume that the copyright of an image published in 1930 has expired. But mathematically, it could still be protected. The copyright could have been renewed once in 1958, then in 1978 it would have received copyright protection through the year 2005. To be safe, assume that any work created after 1922 is copyrighted.

# Work for Hire

The copyright law makes a distinction between independent contractors who create works of art privately and employees who do so for an employer. If you are employed by an ad agency, publishing company, or design studio, your creations are considered "works for hire"; your employer, who has paid you to create them, owns the copyright. Thus, if while employed by a publisher you create a picture that is published in a book or magazine, you do not have the right to republish it or even create a new work from the image. This is true for every type of work that you create for your employer, regardless of whether you create the work at home or on the job.

Under the law, your employer owns the copyright for 75 years after the work is published or 100 years after the work was created—whichever comes first. The rules are quite different, however, if you are an independent contractor.

# Independent Contractors

Independent contractors are generally considered to be the copyright owners of their own works—as long as they actually create the work. Thus, if you hire an independent artist or photographer to shoot an image for you, he or she owns the copyright—not you. If you are an artist and are hired for a day's work at a design studio or ad agency, you probably own the copyright of works you create, even if others at the company told you what the images you work on should look like. However, if you sign a document that says that you transfer or "assign" the copyright, then you no longer own the copyright of your work.

# Works in the Public Domain

When the copyright of a work expires, it is generally considered to be *in the public domain.* This means that no one owns the copyright, and thus the image or work can be freely copied, used, and distributed.

How do you determine if a work is in the public domain? If it was published before 1922, the copyright has most likely expired. Mathematically, the work cannot still be protected. For instance if a work of art was created in 1921, it could have been renewed once in 1949. Twenty-eight years later, in 1977, the work would have entered the public domain.

If you can't determine the copyright status of a work, you can seek the help of professionals. For a fee, Thomson and Thomson of Washington, DC and BZ/Rights and Permissions of New York will locate copyright owners. Thomson and Thomson will only conduct copyright searches; BZ/Rights and Permissions will negotiate rights on your behalf. Total Clearance of San Francisco will approach rights holders and negotiate clearances for audio/visual material. You may also be able to save yourself money by simply calling the U.S. Copyright Office and inquiring about the copyright status of a specific work. You can conduct limited copyright searches on the Internet by Telnet at "Marvel.loc.gov". Log on as "marvel" and you can search portions of the U.S. Copyright Office database.

*n* OTE: *You might be surprised to know that museums control the right to reproduce the public domain works of art they own by controlling access to the art. Copyright laws in foreign countries are different from those in the United States. Obtaining reproduction rights for artwork in foreign museums may be quite complex.*

# Copyright and the Rights of Privacy

If you decide that you don't want to rely on other people's photographs, and wish to take your own, it's important to realize that you can't necessarily take photos or videos of people in the street and incorporate them into your digital images or QuickTime movies. Although only the federal government can create and change copyright laws, some states—California and New York, in particular—have passed privacy laws. In these states, you are violating a person's right to privacy by photographing him or her and using the photograph without written permission (which can be obtained in the form of a release). Exceptions apply for the news media.

# Registering a Work of Art

Prior to 1978, the only way to ensure copyright protection for published works was to place a copyright notice on it and register it with the United States Copyright Office. As mentioned earlier, copyright is now granted as soon as a work is created. Thus, registering a work to protect copyright is not necessary, but it is required if you ever wish to sue for copyright infringement. Registering a work costs $20 and does not require a lawyer. You simply fill out forms that can be obtained from the U.S. Copyright Office and send in your check with the forms, along with one or two copies of the work.

If you're concerned about copyright infringement, put your copyright notice on your works and register them as soon as they are completed because it normally takes several months to receive your copyright certificate. Note that a copyright notice includes three components:

1. The words "Copyright," "Copr," or the symbol "©"

2. The year of first publication (if the work has been published)

3. The copyright holder's name

To register, contact: The Copyright Office, Information and Publication Section, LM-455, Library of Congress, Washington, DC 20559, or call (202) 707-3000.

# How to Ensure That You Are Not Breaking the Law

The best way to avoid copyright problems is to avoid copying or reproducing any image without the copyright owner's permission. You may copy a small portion of someone else's work with impunity if you've made it totally unrecognizable, and if the work you've created doesn't interfere with the copyright owner's ability to profit from it. However, from a strictly legal standpoint, you should not copy a work in any form without written permission from the copyright holder. When you do get written permission, make sure all rights are specified, including how many times the work can be reproduced. If you obtain rights to use a work, don't assume you can use it for advertisements or in different media. For example, if you obtain the rights to publish a work in a book, it doesn't mean you also can reproduce it on the CD-ROM version.

*n* **OTE:**   *The copyright law also provides for fair use copying of images. In general, this means that portions of works can be copied without permission for journalistic and educational purposes—so long as the market for the original is not affected.*

## Royalty-Free CD-ROMS

Perhaps the easiest way to ensure that you are not breaking copyright law is to use royalty-free images available from many stock image suppliers on CD ROMs. Many vendors such as CMCD and Corel grant free rights without stipulations. Be aware, though, that some "royalty-free" stock suppliers place restrictions on how you can use their images. For instance, the licensing agreement that accompanies DíAMAR Portfolios' CD-ROMs states that their images are royalty-free for "most creative work." You cannot use their images in pornography or in products where the images are the "primary value"—such as postcards and greeting cards. Other companies such as Professional Stock allow you to use their images but may require special permission or dispensation if you plan to include them in products that will be sold—such as multimedia CD-ROMS.

If you are purchasing *clip media* which includes graphics, sound effects, or digital movies, you might find that certain restrictions apply—even though the images are essentially royalty-free. For instance, Macromedia's Business and Technology Clip Media 1 can be used in multimedia productions, but it cannot be the central part of the production, or broadcast on television, or used in any production where admission is charged. Although many commercial image houses do not provide any royalty-free images, they may charge lesser fees for in-house use.

## TIPS of the TRADE

# Copyright Tips
by Frederic M. Wilf

## Tip #1: Three Things to Know About Copyrights

Copyright law has many rules, so it's often hard to keep track of what you can do, and what you can't do, and what you *should* do. Here are three things you should remember about copyright law:

1. **Copyright law does not protect ideas; it only protects *expressions* of ideas.** If you create an image, the underlying ideas and functionality are *not* protected. Copyright law protects only the way by which your idea is expressed, which means that anyone looking at your work can create a new expression of your idea without infringing your copyright.

2. **Copyright law automatically protects original and non-trivial expressions "fixed in a tangible medium of expression."** As soon as pen touches paper, film is exposed (even latent images), or a file is saved to disk, copyright law protects it.

3. **Copyright notice (e.g., "Copyright © 1995, Jane Doe") and copyright registration are both optional, but both are recommended for works that have value and that can be copied**. Call the U.S. Copyright Office at (202) 707-3000 for free copyright application forms and information on how to fill them out. You should register your copyright for all of your works that are worth anything to you, and you can often group many images (dozens!) into a single copyright application, which allows you to protect many images with a single application fee of $20.

# TIPS of the TRADE

## Tip #2: Assume Everything Is Protected

Prior to 1989, you could assume that any image or text published in the U.S. without a copyright notice was not protected under copyright law. That's because the law then required that all published works have a copyright notice on them.

In 1989, that all changed. Copyright notice became optional. Now you have to assume that *all* images, text, and other works are protected by copyright law, regardless of whether there is a copyright notice on the work or not. This may put a crimp in your style; you should not copy anything published since 1922 unless there is a statement that the work is in the public domain. Still, it's better not to copy than it is to make copy and get sued for it later. When in doubt, don't copy anyone else's work.

## Tip #3: Don't Mail It to Yourself

There's an old wives' tale going around that you can protect your work by mailing yourself a copy. It's not true.

If you saw the movie *Quiz Show*, you saw a game show contestant mail himself a copy of the questions. In the 1950s, that helped prove that the contestant received the questions before he was supposed to have heard them on the show. But mailing yourself a copy of your work does not necessarily prove that you created the work prior to the postmark date on the envelope. After all, it's now easier to open—or re-open—a sealed envelope than it was in the 1950s.

If you want to prove that you created your work by a certain date, then file a copyright application for your work. It proves that a federal agency—the Copyright Office—received a copy of your work when it received the application. The $20 application fee is not much more expensive than sending a copy of your work (or many works, as mentioned in the first tip) to yourself by registered or certified mail. And it's *much* more effective should you have to sue a copyright infringer.

**13**

## TIPS of the TRADE

*Frederic M. Wilf is a member of the law firm of Elman, Wilf & Fried, an intellectual property law firm that practices patent, trademark, copyright, and business law. Mr. Wilf writes and speaks extensively on topics involving computers and the law. He prepares and prosecutes copyright and trademark applications, including appeals and proceedings. Mr. Wilf's clients include photographers, writers, and software developers.*

*Frederic M. Wilf, Elman Wilf & Fried, 20 West Third Street, Media, PA 19063, CompuServe: 72300, 2061, Internet: wilf@elman.com*

## For More Information

Although you might have heard artists and politicians claim that the copyright laws don't adequately address the concerns of the digital age, there is some indication that the basic copyright laws will be changed. However, don't expect a loosening of restrictions soon just because it's so hard to police the copyright law in the digital age. If you need more information, here are a few sources:

► *Intellectual Property Rights in an Age of Electronics and Information*, Office of Technology Assessment, U.S. Government Printing Office, Washington, DC. This informational pamphlet outlines basic copyright issues.

► Media Photographers Copyright Agency, Princeton, NJ, (609) 799-8300. This agency, which is part of the American Society of Media Photographers, deals with copyright issues involving digital images.

► "Legal Aspects of Multimedia Productions," by Frederic M. Wilf in *The McGraw-Hill Multimedia Handbook,* edited by Jessica Keyes. McGraw-Hill, 1994. This book covers a broad range of subjects involving multimedia issues and production.

# 14

## Enhancing Images

One of the most fascinating aspects of working with digital imaging software packages is their magical ability to transform flat, poorly colored images into ones that sparkle and seem to jump off the page. Using a computer, you can not only change the colors in an image but also its appearance. You can remove dust and scratches from a digital image, as well as unsightly items such as power lines, telephone poles, and garbage.

Digital correction is an important and often essential part of the production process. When you scan an image or capture an image with a digital camera, correction is often required. Reasons vary. The digitized version may not be as sharp as the original image or scene, or the digitized colors may not accurately reflect the colors in the original. Scanned images, especially old photographs, may need to be retouched to remove scratches, blemishes, or dust particles. Grayscale images may need tonal correction to improve brightness or contrast.

This chapter provides an overview of the digital correction process and how to use digital tools needed for this process. You'll learn how to enhance colors through image correcting and how to remove dust and scratches through retouching. You'll also learn the basics of sharpening images so they don't look blurry or soft. Before you start retouching or color correcting you should have an understanding of how digital *masks* are used in the image-correction process.

# Creating Masks

When you retouch or color-correct an image, you may need to isolate an area so that only that specific area is edited. By creating a "digital fence" around image areas that you work in, you prevent yourself from adversely affecting the rest of the image. This digitally protected area is called a *mask*. In many ways a mask is like a stencil that can be placed over your image. Cutouts in the stencil give you access to areas beneath the stencil while other areas are left protected.

If you're unfamiliar with the concept of a mask, assume you need to paint a window sill. To prevent the paint from spilling over to the walls, you might place masking tape along the edges of the sill. Masks are like digital masking tape with the added advantage that they can be transformed into any shape.

Before you can begin to color-correct or retouch, you should learn how to isolate images with masks so that only the area you wish to change is affected by your editing. In most image-editing and painting programs, masks are created in similar ways. Many programs allow you to create masks using selection tools, a Bézier Pen tool, and masking brushes.

## Using Selection Tools to Create Masks

In many graphics programs, selection tools allow you to isolate image areas so that you can copy or cut portions of images and paste them into different areas. Most painting and image-editing programs let you create oval, rectangular, and simple free-form selections. Usually, these appear onscreen as a series of blinking lines, often known as "marching ants." When you begin color-correcting images, these blinking selection marquees can often be used as masks. For instance, in Adobe Photoshop, you can create a selection with the program's Marquee selection tool. Once the selection is onscreen, you can paint and edit only within the blinking lines of the selection area. Many programs also feature free-form selection tools—often called Lasso tools. In Photoshop, you can click and drag with the Lasso tool to create  a selection around a shape or element. Mac users can press and hold the OPTION (Windows users: ALT) key to constrain selections to straight lines.

Sometimes when creating masks, you need to make selections with soft edges. When you edit and correct images, the soft edge can help seamlessly blend your changes into surrounding image areas. When you create a soft-edge selection, you often use an option called *feathering*. In Photoshop, you can set the feathering amount in a tool's options palette as shown below.

Figure 14-1a shows a selection marquee around two people from Digital Stock Image's People and Places stock image collection. Figure 14-1b shows the effect of creating a selection with a feathered edge and then copying and pasting that selection to a new document.

 Another selection tool, often found in painting and image-editing programs, is the Magic Wand. This digital tool works its magic by selecting pixels according to color similarity. For instance, assume you wish to lighten the water in a blue lake in a mountain scene. Instead of trying to click and drag with a Lasso tool to select the fine edge of the water, you could simply click in the middle of the water with the Magic Wand. The Magic Wand then would select all colors similar to the specific

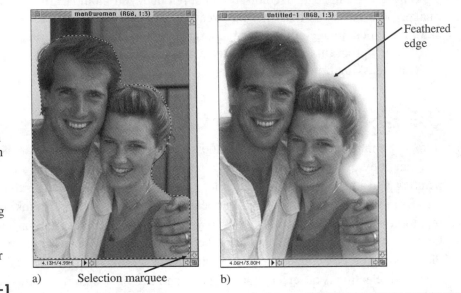

a) Selection created with feathering option set.
b) Image after pasting into new document with feather option

a)                    Selection marquee                    b)

**FIGURE 14-1**

blue color that you clicked on. The number of shades of blue that are selected depends upon the settings you make in the Magic Wand's dialog box or tool palette. For instance, in Fractal Design Painter you increase the color range selected by the wand by clicking and dragging on a slider. In Photoshop, you increase the tolerance range by increasing the value in the Magic Wand palette's Tolerance settings field. An example of the power of the Magic Wand selection tool is shown in Figure 14-2a, b, and c. In Figure 14-2a we needed to isolate the flower from the black background. Since the flower was on a solid background with a different color than the flower, we simply clicked in the black area around the flower with the Magic Wand to select the background. The Magic Wand immediately selected everything but the flower. Once the background was selected, we inverted the selection so that everything but the background would be selected—in other words, just the flower, as shown in Figure 14-2a. Once only the flower was selected, we copied and pasted it into a new background as shown in Figure 14-2b. Both the flower and background are CD-ROM stock images from Vivid Details.

**OTE:**   *In addition to using selection tools to isolate images, you can often use them in conjunction with keyboard commands that allow you to add to or subtract from a selection. For example, in many programs you can press the SHIFT key to add to a selection.*

a) Image
of flower
and black
background
with the
flower
selected.
b) Image of
flower on
a new
background.
Images
courtesy of
Vivid Details

a)

b)

**FIGURE 14-2**

# Working with the Bézier Pen Tool

One of the most powerful masking tools provided by image-editing and painting programs is the Bézier Pen tool. This tool is used because it allows for the most precise editing of masks by creating both smooth curves and straight lines. Bézier Pen tools used to create masks are very similar to Bézier Pen tools used in drawing programs such as Adobe Illustrator, Macromedia Freehand, and CorelDRAW. In these programs, the Bézier Pen tool is used to create sophisticated shapes that are often stroked or filled with color.

Unlike most other selection tools, the Bézier Pen tool creates wire-frame lines and curves onscreen. The combination of lines and curves created with the Bézier Pen tool is usually called a *path*. Creating and editing paths is a skill that doesn't come overnight. It usually takes hours of practice to become proficient.

After you have created a path in an image-editing or painting program, you can often use it as a mask. In many programs, clicking a button or executing a menu command turns the wire-frame path shape onscreen into a blinking selection that functions as a mask. In HSC's Live Picture, the Pen tool's path can be converted directly to a "stencil." The stencil hides the protected areas of the image and reveals the image area that can be edited. Figure 14-3 shows a simple path created using HSC Live Picture's Pen tool. The flower image is from HSC's collection of stock photos, HSC Power Photos.

**14**

Path created
around flower
with HSC
Live Picture's
Pen tool

Path created with Pen tool

**FIGURE 14-3**

 **OTE:**   *Since Pen paths are often difficult to create, many programs allow you to select with a selection tool, then convert the selection to a path. Once the path is onscreen, you can edit it by clicking and dragging on different path points.*

## Using Brushes to Create Masks

Most image-editing and high-end painting programs allow you to create and edit masks by using digital paintbrushes. Creating and editing masks using a masking brush is often easier than creating masks with a Bézier Pen tool. Masking brushes allow you to create masks with soft edges, which can aid in blending edited objects together.

In Painter, Photoshop, Live Picture, and Fauve Xres, you can switch to a brush-masking mode by clicking on a screen button or executing a menu command. As you paint with a brush you can create a mask or edit an existing one. Once the mask is created, retouching and color-correcting only affect the unprotected areas of the mask. For instance, in Painter, you click a screen icon to enter the program's masking mode. Once you've done this, you can paint with one of the masking brushes chosen from the Brushes palette. Painter allows you to choose from a variety of masking brushes that you can easily customize. You can change the masking brush size to work with a large brush in large areas and a small brush in small areas. You can use a soft- or hard-edge brush. Figure 14-4 shows an area being masked in Painter with a red overlay color that defines the protected area of the image. Once the image is masked, only the area not covered by the red overlay can be edited. The flower is a stock CD-ROM image from DíAMAR Portfolios.

In Photoshop, you can also paint with a masking brush. The easiest way to do this is to click on the QuickMask option in the program's Toolbox. Once in QuickMask mode, you can paint to create and edit a mask with Photoshop's Paintbrush, Airbrush, or Pencil tools. You can pick a brush size in Photoshop's Brushes palette, as well as choose whether you wish to use a soft- or hard-edge brush. After you have created your mask and exited the QuickMask mode, Photoshop automatically converts the mask into a selection. Once the selection is onscreen, all editing changes affect only the area within the selection.

## Saving Masks in Alpha Channels

When image editing and retouching, you often need to reuse masks. Most programs provide a means of saving masks. Many programs, including Photoshop, store masks in areas called *alpha channels.* After a mask is stored, you can return it to the screen and use it after loading the selection from the alpha channel. If you use many digital imaging programs you'll see that alpha channels are used to store image silhouettes in digital image and 3D programs as well.

## Working with Scitex Mask Cutter Pro

Scitex Mask Cutter and Mask Cutter Pro are stand-alone masking programs that allow you to create masks and export them as EPS files. Mask Cutter Pro also allows you to export your mask to Scitex workstations—high-end image-editing computers used at prepress houses.

Why buy a mask program if you already have an image-editing program? Both Mask Cutter and Mask Cutter Pro include a Polygon and Smooth Polygon tool that are easier to use than image-editing Pen tools. The programs also feature an AutoMask command that automatically marks the edges of images that have distinct borders. Options in the AutoMask dialog box also allow you to control how smooth the mask is. Figure 14-5 shows an image masked using Scitex Mask Cutter Pro. The image in the Navigator window provides a preview of the image unmasked. Mask Cutter Pro provides a translucent mask so you can see both the masked area and the

Masking Chalk brush icon

Red → overlay

Flower being masked in Painter

**FIGURE 14-4**

areas outside of the mask beneath the overlay. The image is of the Shuttle Atlantis from NASA, courtesy of Digital Stock Corp.

 **OTE:** *The Human Software Company's AutoMask is a Photoshop-compatible plug-in that allows you to sample colors from your image and automatically create masks based upon the colors you select.*

# Preparing for the Correction Process

Once you've mastered the masking capabilities of your painting or editing program, you're ready to start correcting images. Before you begin you might need to ensure that you have the right equipment, and make sure that your monitor is displaying accurate colors. Then you should begin to analyze images and decide whether you will be editing RGB or CMYK images.

# Calibration

Before you begin to correct images, you should realize that colors on monitors are not always accurate. Different brands of monitors and different video boards can display colors in different ways. The lighting in the room you work in also affects how color is displayed. Over time, the colors of a monitor also change. In order to help ensure that your screen displays accurate colors, you should follow all calibration instructions provided by your image-editing software. For instance, Photoshop includes settings for specific monitors and room lighting conditions.

**IP:** *Photoshop also includes a Printing Inks Setup dialog box where you specify the inks and printing system that will be used for the image you are correcting. Choosing an option in the Printing Inks Setup dialog box causes Photoshop to lighten or darken the display to compensate for dot gain on press (dot gain is the spreading of ink on paper which often causes images to darken when printed).*

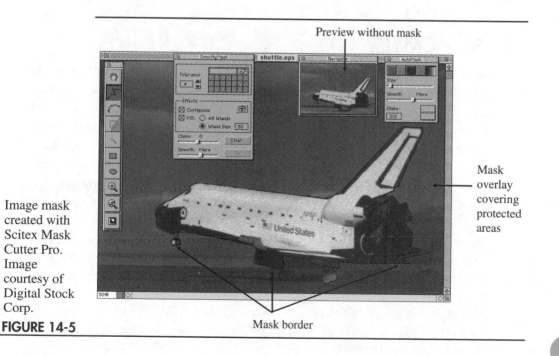

Preview without mask

Mask overlay covering protected areas

Image mask created with Scitex Mask Cutter Pro. Image courtesy of Digital Stock Corp.

**FIGURE 14-5**

Mask border

To help calibrate your system, you may wish to purchase a monitor calibrator. These devices, manufactured by companies such as Radius and X-Rite, attach to the front of your monitor and can adjust the levels of red, green, and blue to help ensure that your monitor provides accurate colors. Several products are also available that allow you to calibrate not only your monitor but also your scanner and printer. For more information about color calibration, see Chapter 17.

## 24-Bit Color Cards

If you are going to be correcting color photographic images that will be output on a printing press, you will need a 24-bit color card. As discussed in Chapter 2, a 24-bit card can display over 16 million colors. If you don't have one, the gradations of colors onscreen will not be smooth, and you will not be able to see the different shades of color that correspond to the countless colors of nature. If you don't have a 24-bit color card in your computer, a digitized image of a color slide or photograph, or an image taken by a digital camera, may look jagged onscreen and the colors may not be properly represented.

## RGB or CMYK?

If you are going to be color-correcting, one of your first decisions will be to decide whether to use an RGB or CMYK image. CMYK images consume more memory because they are composed of four color channels (cyan, magenta, yellow, and black) rather than three (red, green, and blue). If you will be producing a multimedia presentation that will be displayed on a computer monitor or TV screen, you'll want to correct RGB images. As discussed in Chapter 3, monitors create colors using red, green, and blue colors, so this is the most appropriate mode to work in for multimedia. If you will be printing your image on a commercial printing press, at some point you will need to convert your image into a CMYK color file.

Many prepress professionals prefer to edit CMYK images because cyan, magenta, yellow, and black are the actual colors of the inks used to produce the image on a printing press. By color-correcting using CMYK colors, they can do a better job of matching screen colors to printed colors.

Although you might be tempted to color-correct in CMYK mode, you should realize that CMYK files are larger than RGB files. This can make the editing process slower and more cumbersome. You should also be aware that not all image-editing programs allow you to edit CMYK files. Adobe Photoshop, HSC Live Picture, and

Fauve Xres are three that do. Scanning and separation programs such as PixelCraft's Color Access also allow you to correct CMYK images. Most painting programs do not. If you are going to correct in CMYK mode, you should have a good concept of how colors are created using the four process colors, and how the black plate can be used to darken images and add contrast. If your image was scanned on a high-end scanner, it may already be a CMYK color file. If this is the case, you should correct it in CMYK mode.

If you want to convert an RGB color image to CMYK colors, be aware that many programs that do this require specific settings and procedures to ensure the conversion produces accurate colors. You should investigate these procedures before you color-correct an RGB image that will be converted to CMYK. In programs like Photoshop, a variety of settings affiliated with this conversion affect how light or dark an image appears onscreen while you are working in RGB mode. (To learn more about the color separation process, see Chapter 17.) If you don't know the proper steps to convert an image to CMYK, your best bet is to correct in RGB mode. When you've finished correcting your image, you can let your service bureau or prepress house handle the conversion.

## Analyzing Images

Although the process of correcting digital images may seem magical, don't expect miracles. Always try to use the best possible images. If no details exist in the brightest or darkest areas of an image, image-editing programs won't be able to produce them out of thin air. Also remember the expression: "garbage in, garbage out." Don't expect wonderful results from a high-end scan if your original image is in poor condition.

When correcting, you should realize a poor-quality image may not be worth the time to correct. Often your best bet is to obtain a substitute image or investigate whether you can have the image redigitized. If you scanned the image yourself on a low-end flatbed scanner, you may need to pay a prepress house to rescan it on better equipment.

## The Color-Correction Process

Before you begin color-correcting important images, you should practice on sample images. If possible, obtain proofs (sample printouts) of the images and analyze how closely the final versions of the image match the image onscreen. Based upon the output from proofs, you may wish to change software and hardware settings which

**14**

affect how images are dislayed on your screen. Once you become familiar with your software and have taken the steps to ensure that your system is as calibrated as possible, you can start color-correcting seriously. The following sections describe different steps in this process.

## Backing Up Your Work

Before you start any correcting work, the most important step is to back up the images that you will be altering. Even seasoned professionals make mistakes. When they do, they can always return to the original image, if need be. Apart from always keeping a backup of your original images, it's important to keep making copies of your work as you correct images. That way, if you make a mistake, you can return to the last good version of the file, rather than starting over from scratch.

## Viewing a Histogram

A *histogram* provides a graph of an image's tonal values. It can help you quickly analyze which image areas to focus on when you color-correct. Figure 14-6a shows a histogram created in Adobe Photoshop of an image (shown in Figure 14-9a) before colors and tones were adjusted. Figure 14-6b shows the histogram after colors and tones were adjusted. (See Figure 14-9b to view the image after adjustments were made.)

In the histogram, dark pixels are plotted on the left side, bright pixels on the right side of the graph. The histogram also displays the total number of pixels in the image, and the mean, median, and standard deviation of the pixels in the image. The gradient below the graph shows the different levels from black to white plotted by the histogram.

If a histogram bulges on the right, the image is predominantly filled with bright pixels. If the histogram bulges on the left, it is primarily filled with dark pixels. If the histogram image bulges in the middle, it is predominantly filled with midtone pixels. Viewing an image's histogram can help you decide which areas to focus on when you begin your corrections. For instance, just because an image's histogram indicates that it is comprised of predominantly bright pixels doesn't mean you need to darken it. It means that the focus of attention in the image is probably in its brightest areas. Consequently, these are the areas that you should ensure provide adequate details and color. If you are working with an  image that is predominantly

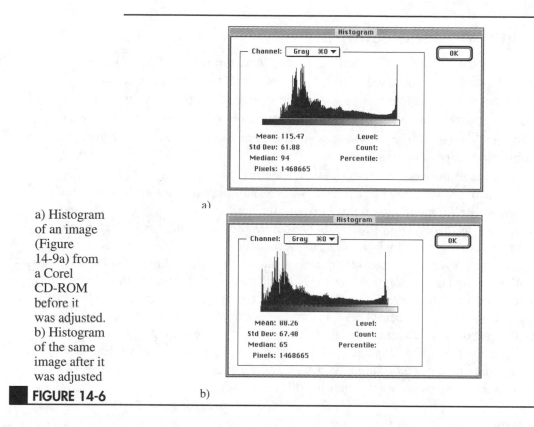

a)

a) Histogram of an image (Figure 14-9a) from a Corel CD-ROM before it was adjusted.
b) Histogram of the same image after it was adjusted

**FIGURE 14-6**                b)

bright, it may mean that you can successfully correct it by darkening it overall. Since nothing of interest appears in the darker areas of the image, you may be able to get away with allowing dark areas to become darker.

Notice the straight line at the far right of the histogram in Figure 14-6a. This indicates that many highlight (or lightest) pixels in the image are at the same brightness level. At the dark end of the histogram there are few dark pixels. Thus, even if the brightness controls of your monitor were set incorrectly, the histogram indicates that this image is predominantly bright. When you begin to analyze histograms, you should realize that there is no perfect histogram. Some images should be predominantly bright or predominantly light. Figure 14-6b shows the histogram of the image after it was enhanced. (Figure 14-9b shows the image after setting the white and black points.) Notice that the pixels are stretched out over a broader tonal range.

14

## Adjusting Tonal Control

Often when an image is digitized, its *tonal range,* the range from its lightest to darkest points, is condensed. Often this condensed tonal range is visible in a histogram that shows few highlight or shadow pixels. If you scan your images on desktop scanners or use digital cameras, you'll often see this shrinkage when viewing a histogram. The shrinkage occurs because these devices can't capture the entire tonal range of an image.

To expand the tonal range of an image, editing and scanning programs often allow you to set white and black points. *White and black points* define the endpoints for the image's tonal range. In most images, the white point should be the lightest color area that displays tone (it shouldn't be pure white), while the black point should be the darkest area in which you wish to view detail.

Programs such as Photoshop and many scanning programs allow you to specify CMYK percentages to set the white and black points. For instance, a common white point used in color printing is cyan 5 to 7 percent, magenta 3 percent, yellow 3 percent, and black 0 percent. These percentages ensure that the white doesn't exhibit a color cast of cyan, magenta, or yellow. If you're going to be setting white and black points using CMYK percentages, it's a good idea to discuss the percentages with your commercial printer or prepress house. The paper and the types of images you are correcting may necessitate choosing different settings.

 **OTE:**  *If you use images scanned on high-end scanners, there's usually no need to set white and black points. This procedure is handled by the prepress house when scanning the image.*

After entering specific CMYK values to set white and black points, your next step in some software packages is to pick specific image areas as the tonal black and white points for your image. For instance, to manually set white and black points in Photoshop, you can open either the Curves or Levels dialog box. Both feature a white and black eyedropper tool. Figure 14-7 shows Photoshop's Levels dialog box with its eyedropper icons. Notice that the Levels dialog box includes a histogram and sliders. The sliders allow you to fine-tune the image by adjusting slider controls for shadow, midtone, and highlight image areas.

Figure 14-8 shows Live Picture's Color Levels dialog box with its eyedropper icons and histogram.

To set the white point visually in either program, you click on the white eyedropper, move to the lightest part of your image that contains detail, and click

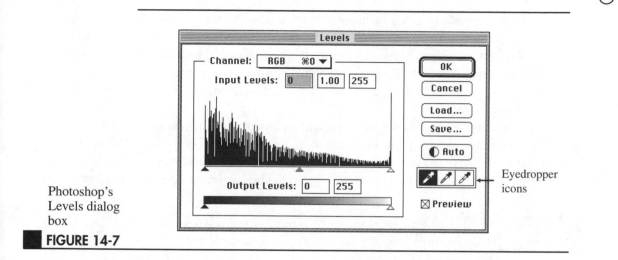

Photoshop's
Levels dialog
box

**FIGURE 14-7**

the mouse. To set the black point visually, you click on the black eyedropper in the
dialog, move to the lightest part of your image that contains detail, and click the
mouse. To help locate the appropriate point for setting the white and black points,
most software programs provide an Info palette which reads out the RGB, HSB, or
CMYK color values of the pixels you move the pointer over.

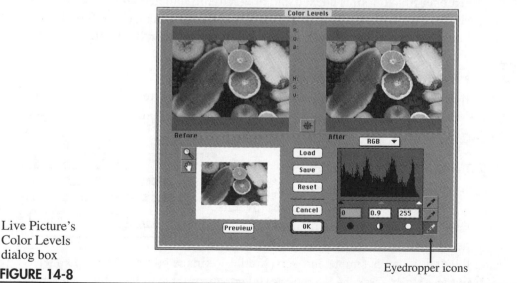

Live Picture's
Color Levels
dialog box

**FIGURE 14-8**

After you click to specify white and black points, the tonal range of your image is adjusted proportionally based upon the image areas you've specified as your white and black points. Often this process results in a more well-balanced image exhibiting better contrast. However, if you set the white point in an area that is too dark, your image will be too light. If you set the black point in an area that is too light, your image will be too dark.

After you've adjusted the tonal range of an image, your next step is to fine-tune different image areas. Figure 14-9a shows an image from a Corel CD-ROM before adjustments. Before we corrected this image, we took readings using Photoshop's Info palette to view the exact color values for the highlight, midtone, and shadows.

> *OTE:* *As you work to color-correct images, always refer to your image editor's Info palette, which displays the numeric values of color components. This way, you don't rely too much on the brightness and color levels of your monitor, which may not perfectly represent the true color and tone in an image.*

Figure 14-9b shows the image after fine-tuning highlight, midtone, and shadow areas and after adding texture to the overexposed areas. We used Photoshop's Rubber Stamp tool to add detail around the bread and cloth. Figure 14-10 shows the Rubber Stamp tool adding tone to an image area by cloning an area with tone over an area without it. In the figure, the crosshair indicates the sampled area used for cloning. As the Rubber Stamp tool is clicked and dragged, the sampled area is cloned over the area beneath the Rubber Stamp. This tool will be discussed later in this chapter. To add tone to the cheese, we added some yellow color using the Airbrush tool.

# Simple Color Corrections

Most image-editing programs provide several methods of correcting color and tone. If you are a beginner or don't wish to delve too deeply into image correction, you might wish to use a few of these commands.

## Brightness and Contrast

Using the Brightness and Contrast command found in many programs, you can change the overall brightness and contrast of an image. Painter's Brightness/Contrast command is shown here.

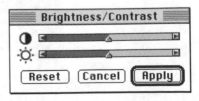

Using the dialog box is simple and very similar to image editing. The top slider is the Brightness slider. Drag the Brightness slider to the right to lighten the image, drag

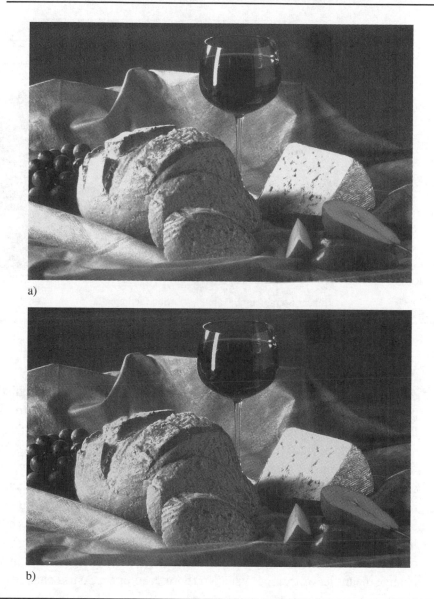

a)

b)

a) Image
before
adjusting it.
b) Final
image after
setting white
and black
points and
retouching

**FIGURE 14-9**

to the left to darken it. The bottom slider controls Contrast. It often can help sharpen an image. Drag the slider to the right to add contrast to your image, to the left to decrease contrast.

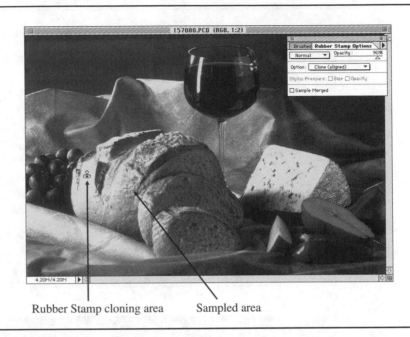

The Rubber
Stamp tool in
action

Rubber Stamp cloning area          Sampled area

**FIGURE 14-10**

## Variations

Although Photoshop's color-correction commands are quite sophisticated, the program provides several options that can ease a beginner into the process. Perhaps the easiest color-correction command is the Variations command, which allows you to correct black-and-white and gray images. Figure 14-11 shows Photoshop's Variations command dialog box. Most users can figure out how to use these commands without reading the manual. For example, if you wish to adjust the midtones (the tonal areas between shadows and highlights), you click on the Midtones button. When you click on the More Red button, more red is added to your image; click on Less Red, and red is subtracted from it. By clicking and dragging on the Fine/Coarse slider, you control the degree of change in the image. A Fine change means less difference when you correct colors, a Coarse change means more.

## Advanced Correction Commands

Each image-editing program has its own specific commands that allow you to fine-tune grayscale and color images. Most programs allow you to correct color and

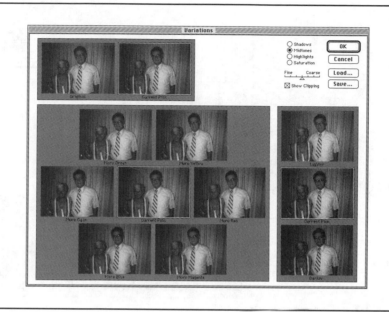

Photoshop's
Variations
dialog box

**FIGURE 14-11**

tone by clicking and dragging on a curve that represents the tonal or color range in
an image. Figure 14-12 shows Photoshop's Curves dialog box. Notice that the curve
starts as a diagonal. Dark image areas are plotted at the bottom, light image areas at
the top of the curve. If you click on the gradation bar below the curve, you can change
the gradation bar so that light image areas are plotted at the bottom of the curve and
dark image areas are plotted at the top of the curve. Image values range from 0 to
255. In Photoshop, you can find where any image area is plotted on the curve by
clicking in your image. After you click, a white circle appears on the curve showing
you where that image area is plotted. You can see this tiny circle at the top of the
curve in Figure 14-13. Also notice that the Info palette in Figure 14-12 (in the
top-right corner) displays the RGB values and CMYK percentages of the area that
is clicked on. If you click on an RGB color that is not in the CMYK color gamut,
an exclamation mark appears after the CMYK percentages in the Info palette. RGB
colors are usually more saturated than CMYK colors. Therefore, if you desaturate
an RGB color, you can often steer it back into the CMYK color gamut. For more
information about color gamuts, see Chapter 3.

   If you wish to make overall adjustments to your image, you can click and drag
on the curve. For instance, if you wish to brighten the image, drag the curve down;
to darken it, drag the curve up (when the gradation bar starts with black and goes to

**14**

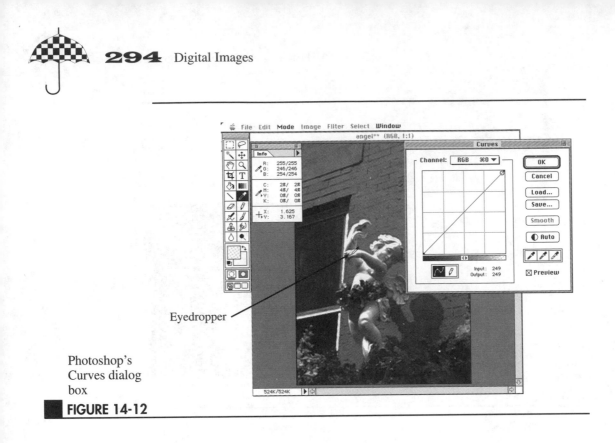

Eyedropper

Photoshop's
Curves dialog
box

**FIGURE 14-12**

Readouts          Eyedropper

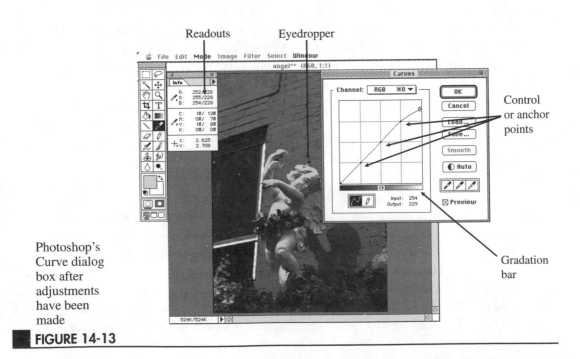

Control
or anchor
points

Gradation
bar

Photoshop's
Curve dialog
box after
adjustments
have been
made

**FIGURE 14-13**

white). By clicking and dragging in the middle of the curve, you primarily affect the midtones of the image. By clicking and dragging at the top of the curve, you primarily affect highlight areas; clicking and dragging on the bottom of the curve primarily affects shadow areas (when the gradation bar starts with black and goes to white).

As you work with the curve, Photoshop and Live Picture provide feedback displaying your adjustments by showing you input and output values. When the gradation bar at the bottom of Photoshop's Curves palette starts with black and goes to white, all input and output values are measured from 0 to 255. When the gradation bar at the bottom of the Curves palette starts with white and goes to black, all input and output values are measured from 0 to 100 percent. Before any changes are made to the curve, input and output values are the same. Once you change the curve, the output value changes to show the amount of change, as illustrated in Figure 14-13.

**IP:** *Since CMYK color values and grayscale values are measured in percentages, when working with a CMYK or grayscale file, it's a good idea to set the gradation bar in Photoshop's Curves dialog box so that you are working in percentages rather than values between 0 and 255.*

As you work with the curve, dragging one portion up or down changes the overall image. If you wish to concentrate on one image area, you can create anchor, or control, points on the curve. If you look closely at Figure 14-13, you'll notice small black dots at the bottom left and the middle of the curve. These were created by simply clicking the mouse at these areas of the curve. Once the control points were established, clicking and dragging at the top right had little or no effect on the image areas between the control points.

In Figure 14-13, the top portion of the curve was dragged down to darken the highlights of the image (since the gradation bar was set to black to white). Notice that Photoshop's Info palette displays two readouts after RGB and CMYK. The first represents the old value, before adjusting the curve number; the second represents the new value, after adjusting the curve number. Figure 14-14a shows the original image before the curve adjustments were made; Figure 14-14b shows it after the curve adjustments. Notice the window from 14-14a is missing from Figure 14-14b. It was removed by simply copying and pasting different areas of the wall to the window area.

You can also create an S-shape curve to enhance an image. An S-shape curve increases contrast in your image by increasing the shadows and reducing the highlights Figure 14-15 shows Live Picture's Color Control dialog with the curve in an S-shape.

a) An image taken with a Dycam digital camera.
b) An image taken with a Dycam digital camera after color-correcting and retouching

a)

b)

**FIGURE 14-14**

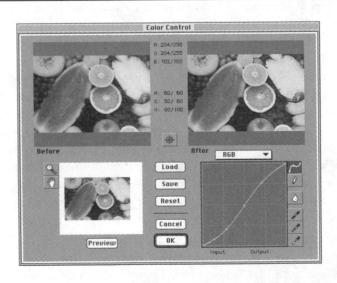

S-shape curve in Live Picture used to increase contrast

**FIGURE 14-15**

Curve-correcting capabilities of most software allow you to provide a curve for each color component of the image. Live Picture, Photoshop, and Xres all allow you to correct images by using the individual curves for specific color components. This can be particularly helpful for removing color casts. For instance, after an image is scanned or digitized by a digital camera, you may see a blue tint in the image. To remove the blue tint, you could pick the curve for the blue channel of the image and drag it up to remove the blue tint.

If you start using curves to correct colors, it's important to remember color theory. When you add a color, you remove its complement. Thus, if you click on the cyan curve of a CMYK image in order to add cyan, you remove red—cyan's complement.

**π IP:** *Save your curves. Most image-editing programs allow you to save the curves you use. This can save you time in the correction process by allowing you to load predefined correction curves. Some prepress houses and printers supply their customers with custom curves to aid them in the production process.*

**n OTE:** *The Human Software Company's Select allows you to correct CMYK colors from within Photoshop or QuarkXPress. Select allows you to make global color corrections or apply correction to each CMYK color component of an image. An onscreen preview instantly shows the effects of your color adjustments.*

## Working with the Dodge and Burn Tools

Programs such as Adobe Photoshop and Fractal Design Painter allow you to adjust the tones in your image using the Dodge and Burn tools. These tools allow you to lighten and darken small, intricate areas of your image. These are traditional darkroom tools used by photographers to change exposure levels in images. The Dodge tool lightens areas and the Burn tool darkens them. In Photoshop, when you select one of these tools, you can choose a brush size and pick either a soft- or hard-edge brush from the Brushes palette. In the Toning Tools Option palette shown here, you can set the exposure and whether you will be lightening or darkening the shadows, midtones, or highlights. If you have a stylus you can control the size and

14

exposure with the amount of pressure you apply to the stylus. See Chapter 2 for more information about using a stylus.

# Retouching Images

In addition to correcting tones and colors, digital artists often need to retouch images as well. Retouching usually involves correcting image flaws such as dust spots and scratches. It can also mean transforming an image so that it looks better than reality. For instance, retouching magic can remove wrinkles from models, whiten their teeth, put a glow in their eyes. Retouching can also reconstruct the composition of an image completely. For instance, an image editor's Cloning tools can copy trees and sky over unsightly power lines or unattractive buildings.

 **OTE:** *Always make a backup of your original image. That way, if you make a mistake when retouching, you can always return to your original.*

Before you begin retouching, your first steps are to familiarize yourself with the digital tools that you'll be using. In order to make your retouching work look as natural as possible, you may need to use more than one tool.

Photoshop and Fauve Xres feature Rubber Stamp tools that can be used for cloning. Fractal Design Painter features Cloning brushes. In most programs, you begin the cloning process by *sampling* the area onscreen that you wish to clone. The sampled region is the area you want to copy, not replace. Often this is accomplished by moving the mouse over the area to be sampled, pressing the OPTION (Mac users) or ALT key (Windows users) on the keyboard, then clicking the mouse. Your next step is to move to the area that you wish to clone the sample over. When you click and drag, the sampled area begins to replace the area that you click and drag over.

To use cloning to remove wrinkles around a person's eyes, you perform a digital skin graft. You sample an area that doesn't have a wrinkle and clone that part of the skin over the wrinkled area, as shown in Figure 14-16a. For a more natural look, you should use a medium size, soft-edge brush with the opacity set to somewhere between 30 and 80 percent. To complete the retouching process of Figure 14-16a, dark circles under the model's eyes were removed using Photoshop's Rubber Stamp and Airbrush tools. The teeth were primarily retouched using the Airbrush tool. Figure 14-16b shows the final image after retouching.

In addition to using a Cloning tool, you may also want to add some soft airbrush strokes to better blend the new and old image areas together. To add a soft effect, you can often blur image areas together using an image editor's Blur and/or Smudge tool.

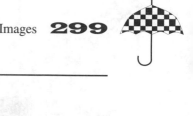

Cloned area
Sampled area

a) Wrinkles cloned away with Photoshop's Rubber Stamp tool. b) Image after removing wrinkles and dark circles under eyes and retouching teeth

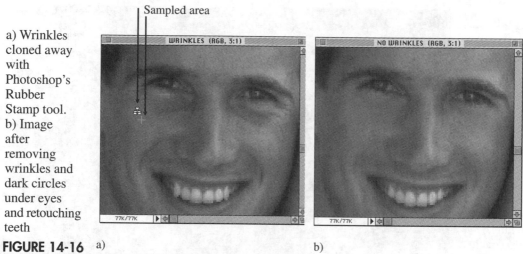

**FIGURE 14-16** a)                                                        b)

# Retouching Old Photographs

Retouching is often necessary to correct old but valuable photographs that have become faded and scratched over the years, as shown in Figure 14-17a. Figure 14-17b shows the image after it was retouched using Photoshop's Dust & Scratches filter, the Rubber Stamp cloning option, and the Airbrush tool.

Photoshop's Dust & Scratches filter provides one of the fastest ways to remove imperfections from images. To use this filter, first select an area that you want to retouch, then choose the Dust & Scratches filter from Photoshop's Filter menu.

In the Dust & Scratches dialog box, shown here, the Threshold and Radius sliders allow you to control the clean-up effect. The Threshold slider tells the filter exactly which pixels in the image should be analyzed. It does this by comparing the difference between pixel values. If you drag the slider to the right, the difference between pixel values must be greater in order for the filter to adjust them. The Radius slider tells Photoshop how far away to hunt for pixels with different values (based upon the Threshold value). By combining different Threshold and Radius values, you can often quickly remove dust and scratches. Those scratches that are not removed by the filter can be eradicated with cloning and painting tools.

**14**

a) Photograph
before
retouching.
b) Photograph
after
retouching

**FIGURE 14-17**

a)                                              b)

**IP:** *After retouching an old grayscale photograph you may be so amazed at the results that you'll want to add color to it. Photoshop allows you to create duotones and sepia images by switching from Grayscale mode to Duotone. In Photoshop's Duotone dialog box, you choose the number of colors you want in your image: one (monotone), two (duotone), three (tritone), or four (quadtone). An image with two colors is a duotone. Many times a sepia image is made up of three colors (tritone). After you pick the number of colors, you can use a curve to add more or less of a particular color. For more Photoshop tips and techniques, see* Fundamental Photoshop: A Complete Introduction, Second Edition *by Adele Droblas Greenberg and Seth Greenberg (Osborne/McGraw-Hill, 1995).*

# Sharpening an Image

Image sharpening is often used during the correction process to make image edges and contours more distinct. If your image is scanned on a high-end drum scanner, sharpening is often applied during the scanning process. When an image is sharpened, the computer searches for image edges and contours, and increases the contrast in these areas.

# Unsharp Masking

One of the most frequently used sharpening techniques is *unsharp masking*. To many new users, the term Unsharp Mask sounds like a contradiction in terms. Why is a sharpening technique called *unsharp mask*? The term is based upon a photographic process in which a copy of a negative is blurred and overlaid on top of the original negative. Thus, by first unsharpening the image, it can later be sharpened.

Many programs that provide image-correcting options feature unsharp masking. Image-editing, scanning, painting, and Photo CD conversion programs often provide unsharp masking capabilities. Some programs simply allow you to enter an unsharp mask percentage in a dialog box. The higher the percentage, the greater the sharpening. Other programs such as Photoshop, PixelCraft Color Access, and HSC's KPT Convolver provide Threshold and Radius settings to fine-tune the sharpening effect. Some unsharp mask commands also smooth non-edge areas to help remove noise or grain in the image. Shown here is Color Access' UnSharp Masking dialog box. When the Threshold is higher, more of the image is sharpened and less of it is smoothed.

Shown here is Photoshop's Unsharp Mask dialog box. The Amount Value controls the intensity of the sharpening—the greater the sharpening, the greater the

contrast between pixels. If you are working with a high-resolution image, Adobe recommends entering an amount between 150 and 200 percent. The Radius value determines how far from contour edges the image will be sharpened. Usually, a radius of 1 to 2 is suitable for high-resolution images. The Threshold slider allows you to control exactly which pixels in the image will be sharpened. When you increase the Threshold value, you specify how different adjacent pixels must be before sharpening occurs. If you enter 0, all pixels in the image are sharpened.

## Other Image-Correction Options

HSC's KPT Convolver is a free-form image-correction and special effects plug-in that can be used by most image-editing and painting programs. The program provides virtually unlimited sharpening, blurring, and colorizing capabilities. It includes unsharp masking and controls for changing the hue, saturation, and brightness. Convolver often allows you to preview changes by showing several versions of the image onscreen, each slightly different than the previous. You can pick the image you want simply by clicking on it.

The KPT Convolver opening screen provides three buttons: Explore, Design, and Tweak. If you click the Design button, you can change the brightness of your image. This mode provides 15 different versions of your image to choose from. After you make your choice, you can make the image still lighter or darker. If you click on the Tweak button, you can fine-tune the image by adjusting sharpening, blurring, and color controls, as shown in Figure 14-18. To make a change, click and drag on one of the round marble icons. To access the Unsharp Mask controls, click on the Tweak button's down arrow. Like Photoshop, KPT Convolver allows for Radius and Threshold controls when executing unsharp masking.

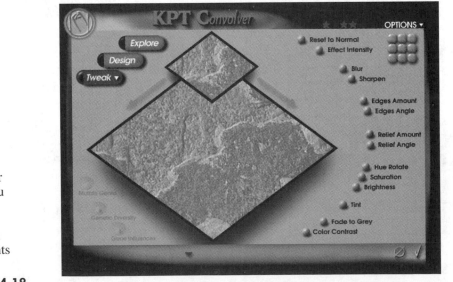

KPT Convolver allows you to apply numerous correction adjustments to images

**FIGURE 14-18**

Monaco Systems MonacoCOLOR software is a Photoshop plug-in designed to correct images during conversion from RGB to CMYK. MonacoCOLOR can automatically balance color, set white and black points, correct brightness, and remove color casts. The program provides unsharp masking capabilities and batch processing, which enables you to process many images without operator intervention.

DPA Software's Intellihance provides another Photoshop plug-in designed to ease and speed the correction of digital images. It automatically corrects under- and overexposed images and color saturation problems, as well as sharpening images and reducing noise and image graininess.

# TIPS of the TRADE

## Convolver Tips
**by Scott Fegette**

When performing a stock correction on a series of images such as scans or Photo CDs, you usually need to plow through several different dialogs, save settings, navigate filters, and then make a macro that runs through all of the steps in sequence for each image, reloading the settings for the dialog boxes, and so on.

With Convolver, however, it is really easy to batch work with the same settings for a number of images. Correct one, and then apply the filter. The rest of the images can have exactly the same correction applied by just opening each image and hitting COMMAND-F to reapply the last filter, and COMMAND-S to save it. No more tedious navigation through numerous dialogs and filters. And with a macro program like Tempo II or QuickKeys, it's easy to automate it as well.

Another very important feature of Convolver in the Explore and Design Modes is scrubbing. Often overlooked, *scrubbing* occurs when you click and drag on any of the 15 smaller kernel previews, and smoothly interpolate between the current kernel in the Preview Diamond and the kernel you have clicked upon. In Design Mode, this is really handy to use for viewing the in-between states for any of the kernels. As opposed to just 15 possibilities, this gives you a huge range of variable control over your Convolver imaging.

## TIPS of the TRADE

A very interesting visual trick for color images with Convolver and Photoshop 3.0 is to select all of your image, hit COMMAND-J (Float), and float the selection. Next, apply a medium Gaussian Blur at a radius of 10 or so depending on your image size (should be enough to blur out the image but not enough to kill all the color). This is followed by a Hue Rotate of around 90 degrees. Apply the filter and then switch the floating selection layer to Difference mode in the Layers Palette and vary the opacity to taste. Bizarre but cool.

*Scott Fegette is an Online Associate at HSC Software.*

# Conclusion

Color correcting and retouching images are often considered difficult tasks. If you're new to digital imaging, don't be afraid to test the waters. Start with practice images to hone your skills. When you work with actual images, don't do anything too drastic, and make sure that you back up your work. You'll gradually find that with practice comes success.

# 15

## Creating Special Effects

**Y**ou've seen *The Mask, The Terminator,* and *Jurassic Park.* Now it's your turn. Although many of Hollywood's special effects are created on high-end Silicon Graphics workstations, some of the digital imaging tricks available to Hollywood now can be performed on desktop computers. All you need is some special software to create special effects.

Special-effects programs allow you to generate unusual, attractive, and amazing digital images. Special-effects software can turn 2D images into 3D objects, bend and twist them as if they were made of rubber, or swirl them into digital soup. They also allow you to transform digital images into bizarre, funny, frightening, and even gruesome creations. On a more serious note, special-effects programs also can add shadows, lighting, and textures to help convey information, impart points of view, or achieve artistic goals.

The special-effects programs discussed in this chapter provide a wide variety of effects, from creating unusual backgrounds to distorting images to add interest, humor, and entertainment. Some of the programs even create animated effects that can be used as digital movies to liven up your multimedia presentations.

This chapter primarily focuses on easy-to-use plug-in programs that can create textured backgrounds and warp and bend images. You'll also learn about morphing programs, which can distort and transform one image into another. For example, you could morph an old person into a teenager, a cat into a dog, or a flower into a tree. You'll also see how different artists create special effects with 3D and image-editing programs to produce fascinating works of digital art.

*n* **OTE:**   *Programs that create 3D and lighting effects often require a math coprocessor (FPU, or floating-point processor). If your computer does not have an FPU, you may be able to purchase one and install it in your computer. Computers with PowerPC CPUs do not need an FPU to run special-effects software.*

# Filters and Plug-Ins

The most widely used special-effects programs are called *plug-in filters* (often simply referred to as plug-ins or filters). They're called plug-ins because they are

15

run from the menus in other programs, primarily painting and image-editing programs. For instance, in Fractal Design Painter, third-party plug-ins can be run directly from Painter's Effects menu. In Adobe Photoshop, the plug-ins are in submenus accessed from Photoshop's Filter menu.

Plug-in filters allow you to quickly create effects that surpass or extend those provided by paint and image-editing programs. For instance, Andromeda's Series 2 filters can take a digital image and wrap it around a cube, sphere, or cylinder. Xaos Tools Terrazzo can transform a digital image into a kaleidoscopic pattern. Xaos Tools Paint Alchemy and Adobe Gallery Effects apply painterly effects to digital images. Both can turn a simple scanned image of a photograph into a colorful, artistic image that looks like a painting. KPT (Kai's Power Tools) can create countless textures, gradients, and shapes. It also can add a "page turn" to an image so that one of its corners is rolled up to show an image area below the page turn. KPT also can be used to wrap textures around digitally created doughnut shapes.

 **OTE:**  *Photoshop can read plug-ins in sub-folders; most other software cannot.*

Most plug-ins cost about $100 and are easily installed. After a plug-in is copied to your hard disk, you usually need to load your painting or image-editing program and specify in which folder or directory the plug-in can be found. This is often accomplished by executing a "preference" command in the program. Next, you need to quit, then restart your image-editing or painting program. After you've installed the plug-in, set preferences, and restarted your software, you can use the plug-in. To access the plug-in, call it up from a menu in your software painting or image-editing software. Photoshop's Filter menu with a variety of third-party plug-ins accessible is shown here.

| Filter |  |
| --- | --- |
| Last Filter | ⌘F |
| Alien Skin | ▶ |
| Andromeda | ▶ |
| Blur | ▶ |
| Distort | ▶ |
| Gallery Effects: Classic Art 1 | ▶ |
| Gallery Effects: Classic Art 2 | ▶ |
| Gallery Effects: Classic Art 3 | ▶ |
| HUMAN SOFTWARE | ▶ |
| KPT 2.1 | ▶ |
| KPT Convolver | ▶ |
| Noise | ▶ |
| Pattern Workshop | ▶ |
| Pixelate | ▶ |
| Render | ▶ |
| Sharpen | ▶ |
| Stylize | ▶ |
| Video | ▶ |
| Virtus | ▶ |
| Xaos Tools | ▶ |
| Other | ▶ |

## How Plug-In Filters Work

Although each plug-in program creates different effects, most work by analyzing every pixel in an image or every pixel selected by the image-editing software's selection tools. The effect that the plug-in applies is usually based upon mathematical formulas that change the color values of the pixels in an image. For instance, a simple filter that creates *noise* might analyze every pixel in an image and change the color values of pixels based upon randomly generated color values. A filter that creates painterly effects might soften image edges by reducing the contrast between neighboring pixels and intensifying colors.

 **OTE:** *If the mathematics of plug-ins interest you, some image-editing programs such as Photoshop include options for creating your own custom filters. If you would like to write your own commercial filters, you can join the Adobe Software Developers Association. Call 415-961-4111 for information.*

# Plug-In Filter Overview

The following sections provide a review of a variety of plug-ins that create special effects. Each is compatible with Photoshop and most can be run in nearly any software package that is compatible with Photoshop plug-ins. Some file conversion programs such as Equilibrium DeBabelizer also allow Photoshop-compatible plug-ins to be applied. Since Photoshop was largely responsible for the growth of the plug-in industry, this overview starts with a look at plug-in filters included in Photoshop.

**OTE:** *Plug-in filters that create special effects are also available for Adobe Illustrator. Plug-in manufacturers include HSC, BeInfinite Inc., and Letraset.*

## Adobe Photoshop's Filters

Adobe Photoshop includes numerous filters that allow you to generate scores of special effects. Photoshop divides its filters into nine different filter categories: Blur, Distort, Noise, Pixelate, Render, Sharpen, Stylize, Video, and Other. Within each category are several filters. Photoshop's Blur filters are Blur, Blur More, Gaussian Blur, Motion Blur, and Radial Blur. You can use these filters to blur a background scene; to blur away an unwanted pattern, such as a moiré pattern, by using the Gaussian Blur filter; or to add motion to an image by using the Motion Blur filter. Photoshop's Noise filters are Add Noise, Despeckle, Dust & Scratches, and Median. These filters can be used to add texture to an image (with the Add Noise filter), to

15

remove noise from an image (with the Despeckle filter, which removes moiré patterns, or the Median filter, which blends by replacing the pixels in an area with the median brightness value of adjacent pixels), or to remove dust and scratches (with the Dust & Scratches filter, as seen in Chapter 14). Photoshop's Sharpen filters are Sharpen, Sharpen Edges, Sharpen More, and Unsharp Mask. These filters are used to sharpen an image. The Unsharp Mask filter is one of the tools most widely used for this purpose. Review Chapter 14 for more information on this filter. Photoshop's Render filters are Texture Fill, Lighting Effects, Clouds, Difference Clouds, and Lens Flare. These filters allow you to create lighting effects with the Lens Flare and Lighting Effects filters. You also can add textures to an image or create some amazing colored backgrounds by using the Texture Fill and Lighting Effects filter.

We started by creating a new RGB color file 4 x 4 inches. Then we set the foreground color to red and the background color to yellow and applied the Render/Clouds filter to create a colored background. Next, we clicked on the New Channel icon in the Channels palette and created an alpha channel named Flower Texture. With the new alpha channel activated, we loaded the Texture Fill filter. Then we located a grayscale image of a flower, shown here, and the filter automatically repeated the flower within the entire alpha channel. Next, we activated the RGB channel and loaded the Lighting Effects filter. Shown here is the Lighting Effects

dialog box where we chose the flower texture option from the Texture pop-up menu at the bottom of the dialog box. See Chapter 11 to see the final flower texture wrapped onto a 3D object in Strata StudioPro.

Photoshop's Pixelate filters include Color Halftone, Crystallize, Facet, Fragment, Mezzotint, Mosaic, and Pontillize. These filters primarily create effects that accentuate the tiny rectangular pixels that compose a digital image. Photoshop's Distort filters are Displace, Pinch, Polar Coordinates, Ripple,

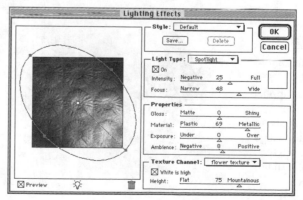

Shear, Spherize, Twirl, Wave, and ZigZag. The Distort filters allow you to create amazing special effects that can bend and twist an image as if it were made of rubber. Using Distort filters, you can create earthquake-like effects, and even warp images to create effects similar to those used in the Academy Award-winning movie *The Mask*. Figure 15-1 shows the effects of applying Photoshop's Shear filter to an image.

Photoshop's Stylize filters are Diffuse, Emboss, Extrude, Find Edges, Trace Contour, Solarize, Tiles, and Wind. The Stylize filters each create a different style effect. For instance, Emboss creates 3D relief effects; Wind makes your image appear as if it is in a windstorm.

Photoshop's video filters, NTSC Colors and Deinterlace, are used to enhance images grabbed from video, not to create special effects. Photoshop's Other filters are Custom, High Pass, Maximum, Minimum, Offset, and Filter Factory. Photoshop's Other group of filters creates a variety of different effects. For instance, Custom and Filter Factory allow you to create your own custom filters based upon numbers or formulas that you enter into dialog boxes.

## Andromeda Software Series 1 and 2 Filters

Andromeda Software Series 1 includes ten filters that allow you to create rainbows, halos, stars, and reflections. It also includes filters that add velocity effects to an

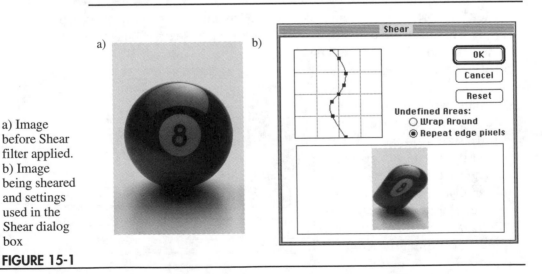

a) Image before Shear filter applied.
b) Image being sheared and settings used in the Shear dialog box

**FIGURE 15-1**

image to simulate motion effects. Andromeda Series 2 allows you to quickly and easily wrap an image around a cube, sphere, or cylinder.

To use a Series 2 filter, you load an image into your image-editing or painting software, then activate the filter. In the dialog box that appears, first choose whether you want to wrap your image around a cylinder, box, or sphere. Next, adjust the 3D shape until you've reached the desired size. Figure 15-2a shows an example of an image wrapped around a cube. Figure 15-2b shows the image, from BeachWare's Nature Photo Collection CD-ROM, before the effect was applied. Figure 15-2c shows the settings used in the dialog box to create the 3D effect.

 **OTE:** *See Chapter 13 for more information on using 3D programs and creating sophisticated 3D effects.*

a)

b)

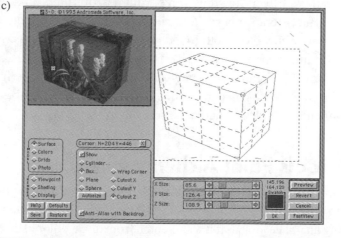

c)

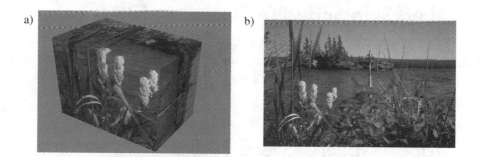

a) Image wrapped around cube using Andromeda Series 2 Filter.
b) Original image before applying 3D effect.
c) Andromeda Filter dialog box settings for 3D effect

**FIGURE 15-2**

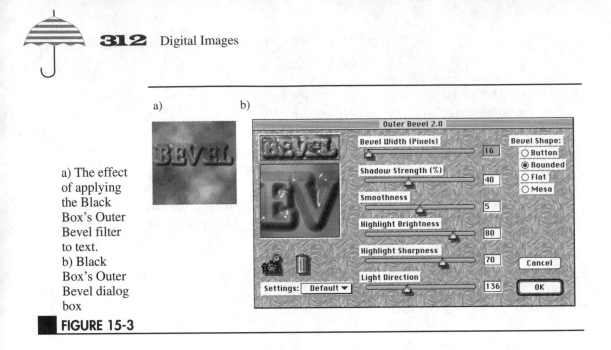

a) The effect of applying the Black Box's Outer Bevel filter to text.
b) Black Box's Outer Bevel dialog box

**FIGURE 15-3**

## Alien Skin Software Black Box Filters

Black Box filters allow you to quickly and easily create special effects. Filters include Drop Shadow, Outer Bevel, Inner Bevel, Carve, Cutout, Glow, Glass, Swirl, HSB Noise, and Motion Trail. Figure 15-3a shows the effect of applying the Outer Bevel filter to some text. Figure 15-3b shows the Outer Bevel dialog box.

## Adobe Gallery Effects Filters

Adobe Gallery Effects features three volumes of filters that allow you to add painterly effects to an image. You can apply traditional effects such as Chalk & Charcoal and Watercolor (both found in Volume 1) and Colored Pencil and Rough Pastels (Volume 2), or more unusual effects such as Stained Glass, Sumi-é, and Neon Glow(Volume 3). Figure 15-4 shows a CD-ROM stock image from BeachWare's Nature Photo Collection and the settings used to convert a digitized photograph into an image with a Chalk & Charcoal effect.

## Xaos Tools Paint Alchemy Filters

Xaos Tools Paint Alchemy, like Adobe Gallery Effects, allows you to add painterly effects to digitized photographs. It also allows you to add other unusual effects, such as making an image look as if it was created from thick, colored threads. Once you've

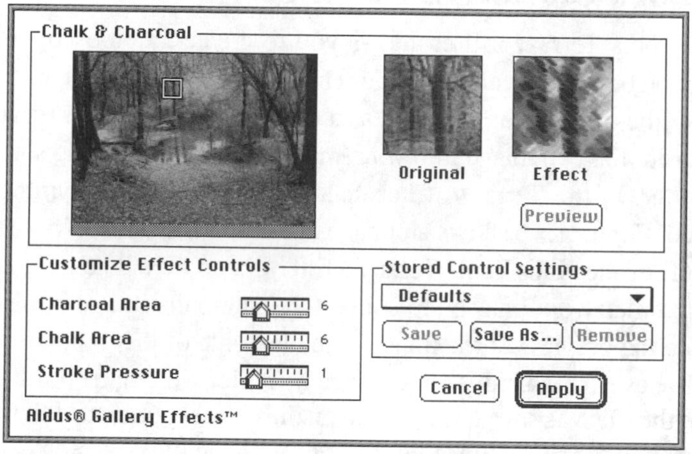

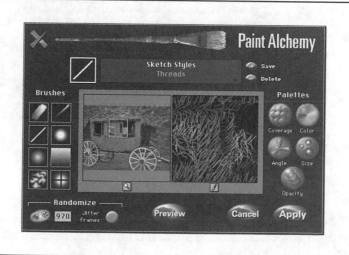

Adobe Gallery Effects Chalk & Charcoal dialog box settings for Chalk & Charcoal filter

**FIGURE 15-4**

created an effect, you can save it as a style so that you can apply it over and over again. Figure 15-5 shows an image from Photodex's Picture Factory CD-ROM and the settings used to convert a digitized photograph into an image that looks as though it was created from threads. Notice the Paint Alchemy dialog box allows you to change the brush, coverage, color, angle, size, and opacity of a style.

Xaos Tools dialog box settings

**FIGURE 15-5**

## Xaos Tools Terrazzo Filter

Xaos Tools Terrazzo filter allows you to create kaleidoscopic images out of any selection or out of an entire image. These kaleidoscopic images can either be applied to the image onscreen or saved as a tile to be used later to create a pattern. To use Terrazzo, load an image into your image-editing or painting software, then activate the filter. In the Terrazzo filter dialog box, choose the Symmetry option of your choice. Figure 15-6 shows an image of gumballs from a D'pix Disc 1 CD-ROM on the left of the Xaos Tools Terrazzo filter dialog box. The image on the right shows the symmetry option used to convert the gumballs image into a kaleidoscopic tile. Notice the preview of the image in the left side of the dialog box.

To save the kaleidoscopic image as a tile, we clicked on the Save Tile button. Once the tile was saved, we clicked on the Cancel button to exit the dialog box. Next, we opened the saved tile in Photoshop. With the tile onscreen, we selected the entire tile, then chose Define Tile from Photoshop's Edit menu. Once the tile was defined, we closed the file and created a new file in which to apply the pattern. To apply the pattern, we chose Fill from the Edit menu. In the Fill dialog box, we chose Pattern as our fill method. After we clicked OK, the pattern was applied.

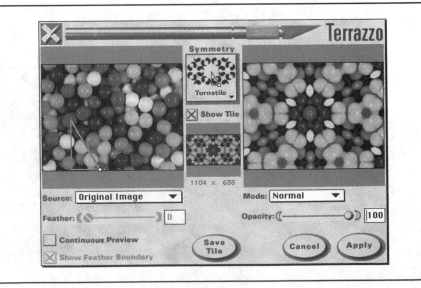

Settings
used to create
Kaleidoscopic
tile

**FIGURE 15-6**

## MicroFrontier's Pattern Workshop Filter

MicroFrontier's Pattern Workshop allows you to capture part of an image and save it as a pattern and then edit the pattern. To create a pattern with Pattern Workshop, load an image into your painting or image-editing program, then select a portion of it. Next, load the Pattern Edit filter. In the Pattern Edit dialog box, select a pattern type, then click on the Grab From Image button. This opens up the Grab Pattern dialog box, shown in Figure 15-7. This dialog box allows you to set a pattern size in pixels and shows the image you are using as a basis for a pattern. (We used Thatched Wood from a D'pix Disc 3 CD-ROM collection.)

## Virtus' Alien Skin TextureShop Filter

Virtus Alien Skin TextureShop allows you to create countless interesting and seamless 2D and 3D textures. All you need to do is open the file that you want to apply the texture to, then load TextureShop from your painting or image-editing program. In the dialog box that appears, shown in Figure 15-8a, choose a texture from a variety of choices. After you choose a texture, you can drag and drop it into the preview box (in the upper-left corner of the screen) and mutate it. The slider on the right of the preview window allows you to mutate an image from the highest

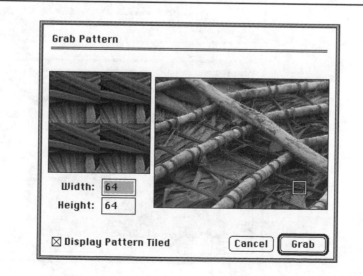

Pattern
Workshop's
Grab Pattern
dialog box

**FIGURE 15-7**

mutation possible, "oodles" to none. The mutated images are on the right. If desired, you can drag and drop an already mutated image over the preview box and mutate it oodles more.

After you've created an effect that you like, you can apply it to your file onscreen. To apply an image, simply drag it to the Apply button at the bottom of the dialog box. Instantly, another dialog box appears. In this dialog box, you can change the size of a tile, texture map, height map, and color map, as shown in Figure 15-8b. Once you've made your adjustments, click on the Apply button to apply the effects.

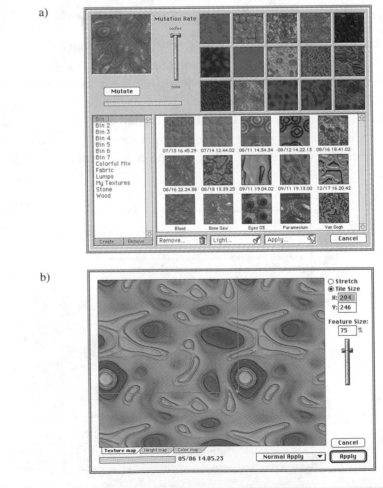

a)

b)

a) Virtus Alien Skin TextureShop dialog box.
b) Alien Skin TextureShop dialog box options allow you to adjust texture, height, and color of your custom pattern

**FIGURE 15-8**

# HSC Software's Kai's Power Tools Filter

KPT, or Kai's Power Tools, includes many filters that allow you to create an unlimited number of shapes, gradients, textures, and other special effects. KPT Fractal Explorer, KPT Gradient Designer, and KPT Texture Explorer, all included in KPT Power Tools, allow you to create unusual backgrounds. Once you activate one of these filters, a dialog box appears allowing you to pick an element as a starting point. After you've picked a starting point, you can then alter it by making more choices. For example, in the Texture Explorer dialog box, as shown in Figure 15-9, you can pick an option from the pop-up menu at the bottom as a starting texture. The pop-up menu includes numerous choices, including fabrics, liquids, marble, metal, nature, wood, and fire. The texture you choose appears in the preview box in the dialog box. If you wish, you can vary the swatches around the texture by clicking on the ball icons on the left side of the dialog box. When you see a texture that you like, simply click on it and the texture in the preview box changes to that texture.

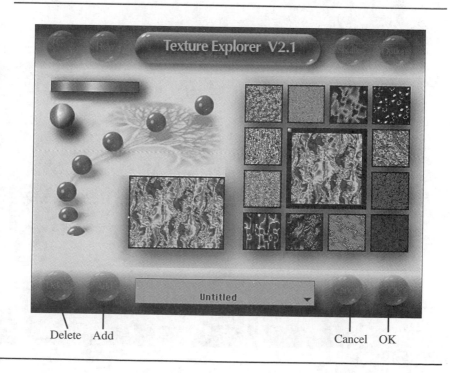

KPT Texture
Explorer
dialog box

Delete  Add                                                      Cancel  OK

**FIGURE 15-9**

You can then continue to alter the new texture or save it before you alter it so that you can return to it at a later time. Once you are happy with the texture, you can apply it to the file onscreen by clicking on the OK button (the sphere at the bottom of the dialog box at the far right). KPT also includes filters to create special effects such as a page curl and fractals. Figure 15-10, shows the Fractal Explorer dialog box.

 **OTE:** *HSC also sells a version of Kai's Power Tools for Autodesk's 3D Studio. This version even provides animated effects.*

## Knoll Software's CyberMesh

CyberMesh converts a grayscale image into a 3D data file in DXF format, which can then be exported into a 3D modeling program. CyberMesh uses the light and dark values in an image to define elevation and depression of the 3D data. When it creates 3D data, CyberMesh converts each pixel to a one-dimensional polygon in the model output file.

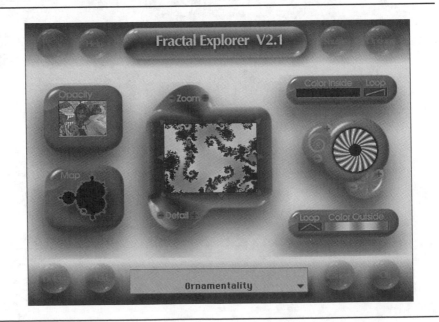

KPT Fractal
Explorer
dialog box

**FIGURE 15-10**

# TIPS of the TRADE

## KPT Filter Tip

**by Phil Clevenger, HSC Software**

While it is easy to create striking "KPT TEXTURES" with KPT, they are often very much identifiable as such. More pleasing, and true to our intent, are subtle uses of KPT.

For instance, use the Texture Explorer to generate a very noisy, high frequency texture of almost any kind or use PixelWind at a maximum setting on an existing image. The idea is to get a very noisy, colorful wash. Then use Convolver or Photoshop to desaturate that color until it is almost completely gone and very mild.

The trick here that almost nobody knows, and that I use all the time, is to return to the Texture Explorer and select the preset "Vertical Soft Cast Shadows." From the Options menu choose the Multiply apply mode. Make sure your tile size is set to either Size Of Image or 512 x 512, then apply.

The result is that your pale textured wash now looks like folded curtains, gently wavy. Very, very nice for deep backgrounds of all kinds. This is one you'll use all the time, once you know it!

Another technique many folks never consider is Fractals and alpha channels. For this example, use a portrait as your starting image, and make sure that the Preferences for the Fractal Explorer are set to "Launch to Previous State."

Open the Fractal Explorer and look for a fractal that you like. Next trick: change the inside or outside color of the fractal to Transparent. This reveals portions of your portrait in the preview area. Then zoom and pan through the fractal to find just the right spot for fractal elements to frame, or enhance your portrait without blocking important features. Next, apply to your image.

Next, create a new alpha channel and return to the Fractal Explorer (since you will return to the previous state, the fractal will be just as you left it). Change the inside color to white and the outside to black; render the fractal into your new alpha channel. You now can use this alpha channel selection of the complex fractal shape any way you like! I suggest the following.

# TIPS of the TRADE

Create a drop shadow. This is pure Photoshop stuff which Kai has documented in his early Tips and Tricks docs, but I will outline it briefly here.

Duplicate your alpha channel. Then use the Photoshop Filter/Other/Offset filter to offset your new alpha channel by some factor, say 5 to 10 pixels vertically and horizontally (be sure "Repeat Edge Pixels" is selected). Next, use the Image/Calculations dialog box to Subtract the new alpha channel from the old, and send the result to a new channel.

You may now use this resulting alpha channel as a fractal shadow selection! Just load it in as a selection, and fill it with 50 to 75 percent black using the Multiply mode.

The result is a portrait that has been augmented with floating fractalesque smears, frames, or other shapes as you determined. This is a very useful technique, and is not as obtuse as it may appear from this description. It is certainly a very underlooked and unexpected way to use fractals for something other than Grateful Dead, psycho-noodlehead, tie-dye, hippie, math stuff.

Enjoy!

Dave Teich used CyberMesh, Autodessys form•Z, and ElectricImage Animation System to create the image shown in Figure 15-11. The image is called Terezin Children, a pro bono poster created for a reading of poetry written by children incarcerated in Nazi concentration camps. The background is a scanned page of a Hebrew prayer converted to a wire-frame mesh.

Dave started by scanning some Hebrew text, then cropping and sampling it down to 60K. Afterwards, he used Photoshop's Levels command to reduce the contrast in the image. Next, the image was blurred and loaded into CyberMesh, as shown in Figure 15-12. After adjusting the 3D effect and saving the file, Dave created the barbed wire clips in form•Z.

To create the final image, David loaded all of the image elements into ElectricImage Animation System in order to render it to apply lighting and texture. Figure 15-13 shows the wire and CyberMesh background in ElectricImage. The screenshot shows the front, top, and side views of the image represented as bounding boxes. The camera view shows the text, shadow, and spotlight effects.

## 15

Image created
by Dave Teich
using Knoll
Software
CyberMesh,
Autodessys
form•Z, and
ElectricImage
Animation
System

**FIGURE 15-11**

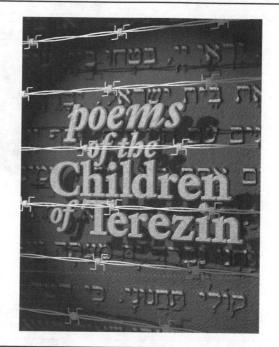

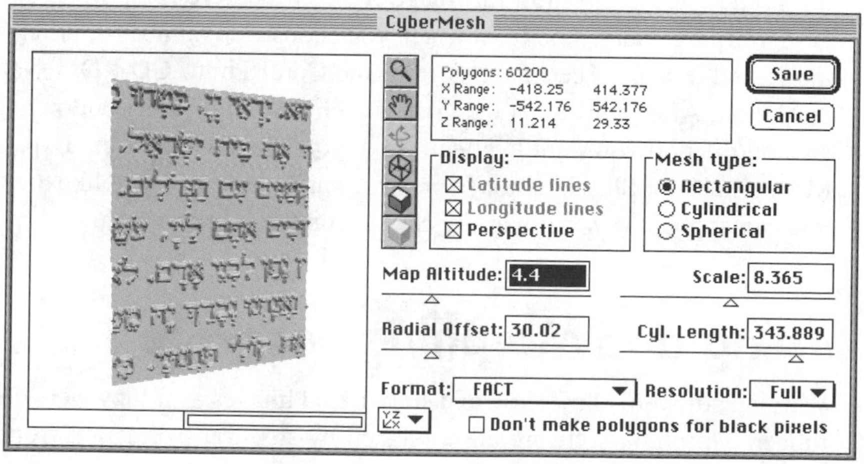

Hebrew text
in Knoll
Software
CyberMesh

**FIGURE 15-12**

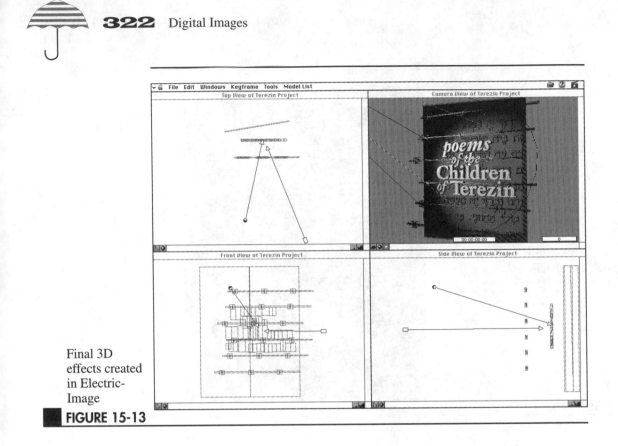

Final 3D
effects created
in Electric-
Image

**FIGURE 15-13**

## Human Software Squizz Filter

Human Software's Squizz filter allows you to warp an image by using either a brush or a grid. Figure 15-14 shows an image of a cactus before being warped and Squizz's Grid Warping dialog box, from which you choose the number of grids you want on the X and Y axes. The image is from the Corel Photo CD-ROM Nature Scenes collection. After you've set the grid, you click on the Select button and select the area on the grid you want to affect. Next, you click on either the Expand, Enlarge, Move, Pinch, or Shrink button to create a warp preview. If you like the warp effect, you can apply it to your image by clicking on the Apply button.

# Warping and Morphing Software

Warping software allows you to distort digital images as if they were created out of rubber. Morphing software allows a step-by-step transformation from one image

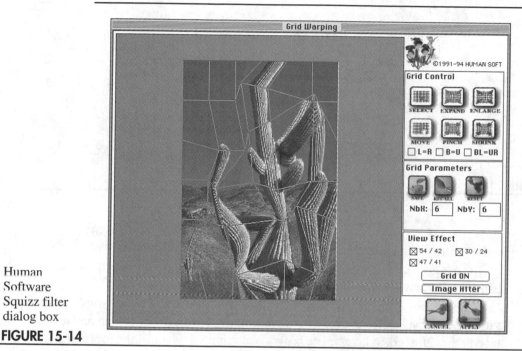

Human
Software
Squizz filter
dialog box

**FIGURE 15-14**

into another. Using a morphing program, you can not only change a man into a woman or a dog into a cat, but you can also make an old person young again or a young person old.

Morphing programs can also be used to create time-sequence effects. For instance, in a multimedia sequence, you could morph a small tree into a large tree to show the effects of time. Most programs that allow you to morph also allow you to warp or bend images to create unusual or even frightening effects. This section reviews several such programs.

## Valis MetaFlo and MovieFlo

Valis MetaFlo's specialty is turning digital images into rubber. By simply clicking and dragging a mouse, you can make subtle or radical distortions that twist, bend, and reshape images. Figure 15-15a shows a clock from Work For Hire's Classic-Photo CD-ROM collection number 3. Figure 15-15b shows the same clock after being warped in MovieFlo. MovieFlo (which includes MetaFlow) also allows you to create morphing effects and save distortions frame-by-frame to create QuickTime

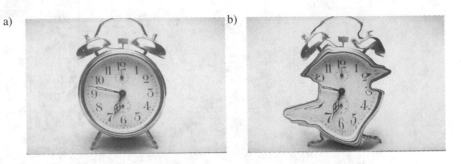

a) Clock
image before
warping.
b) Clock
image after
warping
in Valis
MovieFlo

**FIGURE 15-15**

movies. The program can be used for printing effects, multimedia special effects, and for creating caricatures. Valis suggests that its software can even be used for cosmetic surgery visualization.

Although the program is very easy to use, it has quite a few sophisticated features. For instance, it allows you to place multiple images onscreen and to view and edit these images in layers. The program also includes a masking tool that allows you to hide different areas of different layers. Once an area is hidden, you can combine the nonhidden areas from one image in one layer with the nonhidden areas of another image in another layer.

One of MetaFlo's most intriguing effects is its ability to create a distortion "template" so that you can map an image's distortion into the shape of another image. For instance, we loaded an image of a camel onscreen into one layer, and a clock into another layer. We selected both layers, then executed the Set-Up Template command. Next, we clicked on various image areas on the camel's face to set up a template guide. We chose the Distort to Template command—in a few minutes the watch was distorted into the shape of the camel's face.

For multimedia producers, Valis MovieFlo allows you to create animated morphing effects or frame-by-frame distortions and save them frame by frame into the program's Key framed windows. The program also allows you to control the frame rate using the industry standard, SMPTE (Society of Motion Picture and Television Engineers) time code. If you already have digital movies, you can load them into MovieFlo and apply effects to the movie on a frame-by-frame basis. To get you started, MovieFlo is packaged with several stock images and short tutorials.

# Gryphon Morph

If you're interested in getting started with morphing effects and don't want to invest a lot of money, you should investigate Gryphon Morph. With this program, you can easily create animated morphing sequences and still-frame distortions. To create a morph, you need at least one pair of images, which are opened up into the

storyboard window as shown here. The eagle and lion images are from the DíAMAR Portfolios Nature & Animals CD-ROM collection.

Next, you set the duration of the morph. To specify the image areas that are transformed from one image to another, you use Morph's Keypoints tools. You start by clicking in the image areas that should be transformed in one image. As you click, corresponding points are created in the second image. After you're finished creating the Keypoints, you can adjust and connect them with Morph's Line tool. Before creating a morphing sequence, you can preview individual frames of the morph to fine-tune it.

Once you're satisfied with the morph, you can save your work as a QuickTime movie or save individual frames. Figure 15-16 shows a transitional image of the final morph between the eagle and the lion.

# Elastic Reality

Elastic Reality is one of the most powerful warping and morphing effects programs available on the Mac, Windows, and Silicon Graphics platforms. Elastic Reality has been used in many movies such as *Forrest Gump, The Mask,* and *The Santa Clause.* On TV it has been used in *StarTrek: Deep Space Nine, Northern Exposure,* and *Babylon Five.* The program allows morphing, warping animation, and compositing effects.

Elastic Reality uses a film industry interface in which images to be morphed are imported into either an A or B roll track. An FX roll controls the timing of morphing effects. Elastic Reality's Edit window allows you to precisely control morphing effects between the A and B rolls with a Bézier Pen tool. To create a simple morph effect, outline the shapes you wish to control in one image, and then copy it into the B roll, where it can be edited. Morph effects can be previewed in different modes; one of the fastest is Elastic Reality's Wire frame mode. When previewing, images

Eagle to Lion
morph frame

**FIGURE 15-16**

in A or B rolls can be viewed individually or overlapping, so you can watch how the transformation from one image to another occurs.

Elastic Reality also allows you to create effects in which animated images can be accelerated or decelerated. Additionally, the program allows *mattes* (masks) to be created around images. By creating a matte, you can mask out the background of an image in roll A and replace it with the image in roll B.

Using Elastic Reality to apply unusual warping effects to images is quite easy. By drawing a simple shape such as a circle or a square and joining it to another circle or square with motion lines, you can quickly warp an object. Figure 15-17a shows an image of a llama before warping. The image is from the Digital Stock Animals CD-ROM stock collection. To create the warping effect shown in Figure 15-17b, two circles were joined and then the image was warped after changing the Outer Edge Handling option in Elastic Reality's Preview Options dialog box.

## Creating Special Effects in Other Programs

The following sections review several other stand-alone programs that can be used to create 3D backgrounds and textures. Each program allows digital images to be saved in different file formats so that they can be used in print media and in onscreen presentations.

a)                                          b)

a) Image
before
warping.
b) Image after
warping

**FIGURE 15-17**

# KPT Bryce

If your design work requires natural, supernatural, or extraterrestrial terrains—or if you just want to have a lot of fun creating imaginary landscapes—you might wish to explore KPT Bryce. Created by Eric Wanger, with an interface designed by Kai Krause, Bryce provides the user with an easy-to-use 3D program specifically geared to creating fantastic landscapes. Although Bryce is quite sophisticated, it's easy to get up and running. The program makes creating 3D images almost effortless because all of its commands focus on specific aspects of creating terrain, and atmospheric and lighting effects.

Figure 15-18 shows an example of a terrain created in KPT Bryce by artist Gary Clark. The background of the image was created entirely in Bryce; Gary later added the telescope and more lighting effects using Fractal Design Painter.

To create the background, Gary used Bryce's Create and Edit modes. Figure 15-19 shows Bryce's Edit palette and the wire-frame model Gary used to create his final image. In Bryce's Edit mode, you can edit wire-frame objects by clicking the cubes on the bottom-left of the palette. The cubes on the right side of the palette

Image created
using KPT
Bryce and
Fractal
Design Painter

**FIGURE 15-18**

KPT Bryce's
Edit palette

**FIGURE 15-19**

allow you to rotate the wire frame. By clicking on the middle-left button, you can open the Terrain Editor, which allows you to choose erosion, lightening, and darkening effects.

Once Gary finished editing the terrain, he used Bryce's Sky and Fog palettes to add atmospheric effects and adjust lighting. To add texture to his objects, Gary used Bryce's materials shown here. The palette allows you to choose textures visually by clicking and dragging on different icons.

Ill 15-5

Once he was satisfied with the image, Gary rendered the wire-frame version to create the 3D background and atmospheric effects. Then he saved the image in PICT format and loaded Painter, where he added the telescope image and other lighting controls.

## Specular TextureScape

Specular TextureScape is a stand-alone program that allows you to create an unlimited number of textures for print, video, and multimedia. Using TextureScape, you can create both flat geometric and intricate 3D patterns that resemble wood or marble. The program even allows you to create a sequence of textures and export them as digital movies in QuickTime, PICs, or Numbered PICT format. After you've finished creating your pattern, it can be rendered at different resolutions and output in PICT, TIFF, or EPS format.

TextureScape provides controls for changing the shape, lighting, layering, texture spacing, and softness of a pattern. To create a pattern in TextureScape, you can start with a predefined pattern and edit it, or you can start from scratch. Next, you use the program's Shape palette to create custom shapes by clicking and dragging the mouse. Shapes can control the pattern in a marble texture, or can be combined with the program's bevel controls to add 3D effects. Figure 15-20 shows buttons created from a rectangular-shaped pattern combined with marbled patterns from underlying layers.

To alter the effects of a pattern, you change settings in TextureScape's different palettes. Using the sliders in the Attribute palette, you can control surface textures. Sliders in the palette allow you to control the gloss, bumpiness, softness, and transparency of the texture. The program's composite control icons shown at the bottom of the Attribute palette allow you to control whether shapes blend or overlap. To fine-tune patterns and add a lush effect, TextureScape's Light palette allows you to adjust the angle, direction, and intensity of the lighting. As you work, you can add more effects to your patterns by choosing from predefined shapes, changing colors, reordering pattern layers, or changing the underlying grid beneath each layer's patterns.

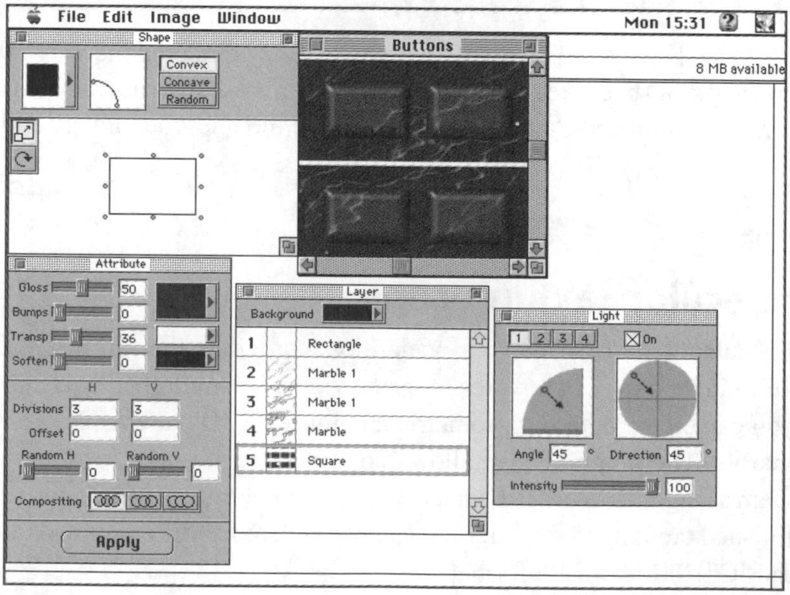

Specular
TextureScape
palettes

**FIGURE 15-20**

# Adobe TextureMaker

Adobe TextureMaker is a stand-alone program that allows you to create countless textures and export them as TIFF or PICT files. Like Specular TextureShop, Texture-Maker also allows you to export a sequence of textures as a QuickTime movie.

Creating and editing textures in TextureMaker is handled from one main "work" window, shown in Figure 15-21. Controls to create or edit predefined textures are easily accessible from the main texture window. By simply clicking on the pop-up menus below the texture preview, you can change lighting and surface textures and edge effects. The Add and Delete buttons allow you to add and delete the texture layers listed above the buttons. By clicking on a layer, you can access the color and pattern attributes of the layer. To enhance the layer effects, TextureMaker allows you to change how one layer blends with another by choosing composite modes and changing layer opacities. The program also allows you to apply Photoshop-compatible filters to the textures and import PICT images to use as shapes within your textures.

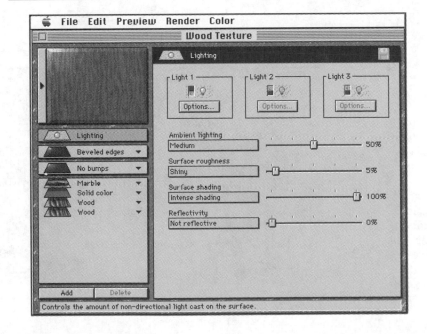

Adobe
TextureMaker
work window

**FIGURE 15-21**

# Using HSC Live Picture to Distort Images

HSC Live Picture allows you to quickly create composite effects with large images. This program also can be used to create numerous special effects. One of the easiest ways to create special effects is to apply the program's Image Distortion command. Figure 15-22a shows an image before it was distorted. Figure 15-22b shows the image after it was distorted in Live Picture.

Before an image can be loaded into Live Picture it must first be converted to IVUE format After the image is converted, you can load it into Live Picture and distort it using a paintbrush. To load the image, choose Image Distortion from the menu. Then locate the file to be distorted and click on the Open button. When the image appears onscreen, activate the Paintbrush and choose a distortion option: Freehand, Radial, or Shimmer. Then start painting on the image. As you paint, the image slowly gets distorted. If you wish to undo any of the distortion, you simply activate the Eraser tool and choose the Undistort option, then click and drag to return the image to its original state. When you finish, you need to execute Live Picture's Build command in order to generate a high-resolution version and/or place it in another program. To learn more about the Build command, see Chapter 6.

a) An HSC KPT Power Photo image before distorting.
b) The same image after distorting it in HSC Live Picture

**FIGURE 15-22**

Text effect
created in
Adobe
Dimensions

**FIGURE 15-23**

## Using Adobe Dimensions to Wrap Text Around a 3D Shape

Adobe Dimensions allows you not only to convert a 2D Adobe Illustrator or Macromedia Freehand shape into a 3D shape, but also to create interesting text effects, as shown in Figure 15-23.

Here are the steps to create the effect in Figure 15-23:

1. First, create a 3D wire-frame cylinder, using the Cylinder tool found in the Toolbox.

2. With the wire-frame cylinder onscreen, select the face of the cylinder with the Direct Selection tool and choose Map Artwork from the Appearance menu.

3. In the Mapped Artwork dialog box, type the letters of the alphabet so that they run horizontally across the dialog box. After adjusting the letters to the desired size, convert the text to outlines so that you can fill half the text with black and half with gray. (We filled the text using the Surface Properties palette which is accessed from the Appearance menu.) In the dialog box, fill the text in the gray area with gray and the text in the white area with black. The gray area represents the rear of the cylinder and the

white area represents the front area of the cylinder. Then duplicate the text twice as seen here in the Mapped Artwork dialog box.

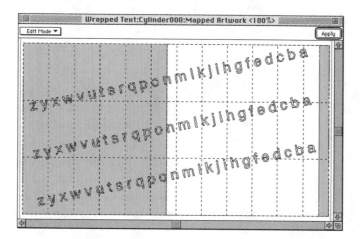

4. To wrap the text around the 3D cylinder, click the Apply button in the Mapped Artwork dialog box. Instantly, the text appears around a wire-frame cylinder, as shown here.

5. If you want the text to wrap around a 3D shape but don't want to see the shape, set the Fill and Stroke of the cylinder to None in the Surface

Properties palette. To see the text wrap around thin air, render the cylinder and the text. The result: text wrapped around an invisible 3D cylinder, as shown in Figure 15-23.

**6.** Dimensions allows you to export files to Illustrator and Photoshop. To do so, choose Export from the Edit menu. In the dialog box that appears, name your file and then choose a Preview and Compatibility option. Next, click on the Export button. Once a Dimensions image is saved in Illustrator format, it can be imported into either Illustrator or Photoshop.

## Using Adobe Photoshop to Create an Embossed Effect

Earlier in this chapter you saw how you could use filters to create special effects. In this section you'll use an alpha channel and layers to create a soft embossed text effect as shown in Figure 15-24.

Here are the steps to create embossed text. You can follow these same steps to create an embossed effect out of anything.

**1.** Start by opening an image that you want to use as a background. If you wish, you can create a background using different filters.

**2.** Next, create some text using the Text tool (or create a shape or object using one of the Selection tools). Keep the text selection onscreen. To see

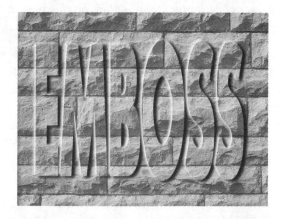

Embossed
type created
in Adobe
Photoshop

**FIGURE 15-24**

the background through the text selection, set the Opacity slider in the Layers palette to 1%. Keep the text selected.

3. With the text selection onscreen, scale the text using the Scale command so the text covers about 75% of the background. Once you've scaled the text, save the text selection to an alpha channel by choosing Save Selection from the Select menu. (Instantly, an alpha channel is created in the Channels palette.) By saving the text selection to an alpha channel, you can reload the selection at any time. Now, deselect the text by choosing None from the Select menu.

4. Next, choose Load Selection from the Select menu. Instantly, the selection is loaded.

5. If the Layers palette is not onscreen, choose Layers from the Window/Palettes submenu. Notice that a Background layer exists. To float the text selection above the background, choose Float from the Select menu. Notice that the words "Floating Selection" appear in the Layers palette. Create a new layer for the floating selection by dragging the words "Floating Selection" over the New Layer icon in the Layers palette. When the Layer Options dialog box appears, name the layer "Text." After closing the Layer Options dialog box, set the Opacity in the Layers palette back to 100%.

6. In order to create the shadow and highlight layer, you need to duplicate the text layer twice. To begin, drag the Text layer over the New Layer icon. This automatically creates a new layer. Double-click on the New Layer icon in the Layers palette, and name it "Shadow." Duplicate the Text layer once more. Double-click on this new layer and name it "Highlight."

7. Next, activate the Shadow layer and fill the layer with black by choosing Fill from the Edit menu. In the Fill dialog box, choose Black and Normal as the mode and set the Opacity to 100%. Be sure to select the Preserve Transparency (this assures that only the text and not the transparent background is filled). Click OK to activate the changes. Next, use the Move tool to move the black text diagonally down and to the right a few pixels.

8. Now activate the Highlight layer. Fill the text in the Highlight layer with white by choosing Fill from the Edit menu. In the Fill dialog box, choose White and Normal as the mode and set the Opacity to 100%. Once again,

select the Preserve Transparency text box. Click OK to activate the changes. Next, use the Move tool to move the white text diagonally up and to the left.

**9.** To create the soft emboss effect, activate the Shadow layer and apply the Gaussian Blur filter. Use a blur with the Amount set from 3 to 15. Next activate the Highlight layer, and apply the Gaussian Blur filter again. To soften the text, you also can apply a small blur from 1 to 3 on the text layer itself.

**10.** Save your work in Photoshop's native format if you want to save the layers. If you want to reduce the size of your file, flatten the layers by choosing Flatten Layers from the Layers palette pop-up menu. Next, save your file in TIFF format using the LZW compression option, if desired. See Chapter 5 for more information on working with different file formats. See Chapter 14 for more information on working with Layers.

## Using Fractal Design Painter to Create Drop Shadows

Creating drop shadows is easy in Fractal Design Painter using the program's Drop Shadow command. You can apply drop shadows to any *floater.* Floaters are selected objects that float in a separate layer above the background pixels. You can make an object a floater by selecting it and then clicking inside the selection with the Floating Selection tool. Here are the steps for creating the drop shadow seen in Figure 15-25.

**1.** Start by creating a new file at least 4 by 4 inches.

**2.** Next, fill the background with a color, gradation, weave, or texture. In Figure 15-25 we applied texture to the canvas by using the Apply Surface Texture command with the Using pop-up menu set to Paper Grain. The Paper Grain that was used is called Alhambra, a paper grain from the Miles of Tiles 1 set sold separately by Fractal Design. To lighten the texture, the primary painting color was set to white, then the Color Overlay command was applied.

**3.** Once the texture was created, text was applied to the canvas using the Text Selection tool. After the Text was onscreen, it was converted into a floater using the Floating Selection tool.

Drop shadow
created in
Fractal
Design Painter

**FIGURE 15-25**

**4.** Next, the Drop Shadow command was applied by choosing Drop Shadow from the Effects/Objects submenu. When the drop shadow is created, Painter creates another layer with the shadow in it. This is helpful because it allows you to alter the shadow independently of the text.

**5.** If desired, you can duplicate the shadow floater, fill it with white, and offset it so that it is diagonally up and to the right of the text to create an embossed effect. Alternatively, you can leave the text filled with the background texture or fill it with a color, gradation, or weave.

**6.** To save your file with its floaters, you must save the file in Painter's native format, RIFF, or Photoshop 3 format.

 **OTE:** *Fractal Design Painter features many other commands that allow you to quickly create special effects such as Image Warp, Blobs, Marbling, Make Fractal Pattern, and more.*

# Conclusion

This chapter should give you an idea of the special effects that can be created from a variety of software packages. As you experiment, you'll find that there is no limit to the number and kinds of effects you can create.

# 16

## Using Multimedia Programs

**M**ultimedia software can turn your computer into an interactive video jukebox where images, animation, and sound combine to create educational and entertaining digital productions. Multimedia computer applications have been used to create games such as Myst, interactive storybooks such as Dazzeloids, and extravaganzas such as David Bowie's Jump, Brian Eno's Head Candy, the Beatles' A Hard Day's Night, and Laurie Anderson's Puppet Motel with Hsin-Chien Huang. Even a few rock videos and TV commercials have been assembled in multimedia programs. As multimedia grows in popularity, more and more digital artists and business people must learn how to use multimedia programs to produce polished multimedia projects. For many in the graphics and design profession, this presents a new challenge: To use multimedia software, you not only need to know how to create digital images, but how to program navigational elements so one image or animated sequence flows into another. Learning how to use a multimedia program may also require a bit of knowledge about video, animation, and sound.

This chapter is designed to teach you the basics of how digital images are used in multimedia programs. You'll learn how multimedia productions are created in three cross-platform multimedia authoring programs: Macromedia Director, Macromedia Authorware, and Apple Media Tool. Each of these programs allows the user to integrate digital images, digital movies, sound, and text to create interactive multimedia productions. This chapter also covers how to create multimedia productions using Adobe Premiere, Adobe After Effects, and Avid VideoShop, which allow you to combine images, sounds, and video clips to create digital movies. Animation programs such as The Animation Stand, Strata MediaPaint, and Strata Instant Replay are also reviewed.

You'll also gain some insights into the creation of one popular multimedia production from an interview with the creators of Myst at the end of this chapter.

 **OTE:** *Some presentation programs such as Adobe Persuasion, Gold Disk Astound, and Macromedia Action include multimedia features.*

# Planning a Multimedia Production

Before you begin to use any multimedia program, you must realize that creating a multimedia production is quite different than creating a digital image project in other programs. One of the most crucial elements in a multimedia production is planning. Since a multimedia project usually involves graphics, sound, and navigation, creating a production is more like producing a Hollywood movie than simply compositing images together in a painting, drawing, or image-editing program. Just as a movie, television show, or commercial follows a script, multimedia productions follow a flow chart and script. For instance, assume you want to create a multimedia travelogue. You plan to create numerous screens showing different locales around the world with digital movie clips of the most exciting places. As the user learns about the different countries, you want authentic music from each country to play. You also want to include interactive buttons. By clicking on one of these buttons, the user can visit different countries and view digital movie clips of the sights.

Before you begin your production, you need to know what images and sounds are required for each step of the production. Most multimedia producers create a flow chart on paper or use a drawing, drafting, or flow charting program to plan each step of the production. The flow chart shows how the production can branch from one screen to different areas. In your multimedia travelogue of the world, you might wish to allow the user to click on live buttons onscreen to explore North America, South America, Europe, Australia, or Asia. Your flow chart should show each path that is possible when a user clicks a button. If you provide printing features so the user can print the screen or allow the user to navigate backwards and forwards, these navigational elements should also be included in the flow chart.

Once you've mapped out the production on paper, you can decide whether you need a multimedia program that provides simple navigation controls or sophisticated interactive elements which require a programming language. The following sections are designed to provide you with an idea of how to integrate digital images and set up navigation in three interactive multimedia programs.

# Using Macromedia Director

Macromedia Director is one of the most popular and powerful multimedia programs available on both Mac and PC platforms. It is used by many multimedia producers to create interactive CD-ROMs and business presentations. In fact, most of the

CD-ROM titles mentioned at the beginning of this chapter were produced in Director. Some companies such as Sony Electronics are also using multimedia programs to simulate the design of new products. Seth Greenberg, one of the authors of this book, helped a team at Sony Electronics program an interactive multimedia project that simulated the features of a new cellular telephone. The designers at the Sony Design Center created a screen model of a prototype telephone. A team consisting of Geoff Anderson, Masa Akahane, Andrew Zidel, and Sophie Klym, with Lingo programming language consulting by Seth Greenberg, assembled the graphics and programmed the buttons on the prototype phone so that the user could simulate turning on the phone and using its internal database to make phone calls. Figure 16-1 shows a screenshot of the cellular phone created in Macromedia Director. If you see the phone again, chances are it will be in the hands of someone using it.

Figure 16-2 shows an example of a multimedia production created in Macromedia Director by DreamLight Inc. for Eastman Kodak. The production leads users through the steps of making a photographic print using a Kodak Creation Station Kiosk. The 3D images were created in Macromedia's MacroModel. DreamLight also created a game in Macromedia Director called Verttice. In this game, the user must race against time to contain a laser light reaction by navigating photons through an ever-changing lattice. The color insert of this book includes a scene from Dazzeloids, an interactive entertainment production produced in Macromedia Director by Rodney Alan Greenblat and published by Voyager.

Director has become the standard authoring environment for many multimedia producers because it is packed with so many features. It allows you to animate sequences on a frame-by-frame basis. You can draw, paint, and create text directly

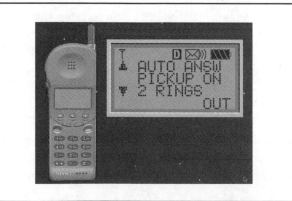

A screenshot of the cellular phone in Macromedia Director

**FIGURE 16-1**

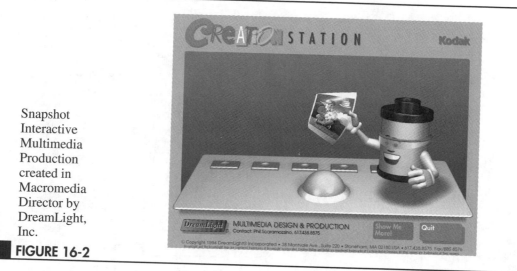

Snapshot
Interactive
Multimedia
Production
created in
Macromedia
Director by
DreamLight,
Inc.

**FIGURE 16-2**

in the program. You can also import images and digital movies created in drawing, painting, and animation programs.

Undoubtedly, one of Director's most important features is its programming language, Lingo, which allows you to write anything from short "go to" navigation statements to sophisticated programs that drive complex multimedia animation sequences.

The following sections show you how to create simple navigation routines to program buttons and play digital movies.

## Creating Images and Animating in Director

Using Director to create simple animation sequences is quite simple. Before you begin, you must first acquaint yourself with the Director interface, which utilizes a movicmaking metaphor. The prime elements of the Director screen are the stage, a score, and cast members. The Stage is where you see your movie running; the cast members are the elements in the movie. The Score is a visual representation of movie frames, set in multiple channels. Each channel is like a separate track or layer that can run simultaneously with other layers. Figure 16-3 shows the Director Score with the Cast Member palette open. In the upper-right corner is the Control Panel. By clicking on Control Panel buttons you can start, stop, or change the speed of the animation.

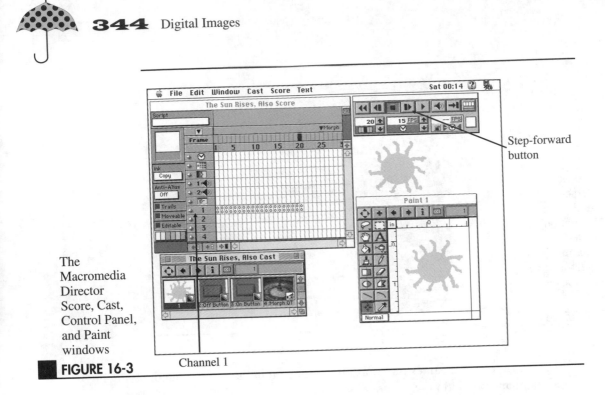

Step-forward button

The Macromedia Director Score, Cast, Control Panel, and Paint windows

**FIGURE 16-3**

Channel 1

To provide an example of how a simple sequence can be created in Director, we decided to animate a rising sun. To create the sun, we opened Director's Paint window. Using the Oval tool and Paintbrush, we created a yellow sun which Director automatically added to its Cast palette. You can see the sun in the Paint window, Cast palette, and on the Director Stage in Figure 16-3. We decided to animate the sun sequence in Channel 1. To produce our animation sequence, we needed to create frames of the sun gradually rising. Director allows you to animate by recording sequences step by step, or you can have the program create an animated sequence automatically by simply picking a starting and ending point. After your endpoints, Director fills the in-between frames with different images.

To animate by *step recording*, you simply need to click on a frame in the Score, then drag an image from the Cast palette to the Stage. Once you drag the object onto the stage, Director turns on its recording light. Then, you move the object and click on the Step-forward button in the Control Panel. Each time you click the Step-forward button, Director records your last movement. To animate the sun rising, we could have dragged the sun vertically, step-by-step and recorded each step; instead, we decided to take the easy way out by having Director automatically animate the sequence. We began by clicking in frame 1 of Channel 1. Then we dragged the sun from the Cast palette to the area onstage where we wanted the animation to start. Next, we clicked on frame 20 of Channel 1, then dragged the sun to where we wanted the sequence to end. Next we selected from frame 1 to frame 20 with the mouse, then chose In Between Linear from Director's Score menu. Director filled in the animation between the starting and the ending positions. When we clicked on the Play button in the Control Panel, the sun gradually rose across the screen.

# Integrating Graphics and Digital Movies into Director

Multimedia productions often need to utilize graphics created in other programs. For instance, Director allows you to import files created in many of the programs discussed in Chapters 10 and 11. To give you an idea of how graphics and digital movies can be integrated into Director, we decided to import buttons that we created in Specular TextureScape and a Morphing movie made in Elastic Reality. Our goal: to program the button so that it sends you to a new screen where our morphing sequence starts.

In order to load our buttons into Director, we saved them in PICT format (PC users should save graphics in BMP format). After we saved, we loaded the buttons into Director using the program's File/Import command. As soon as the command was completed, the buttons were automatically placed into the Cast palette. We loaded our QuickTime movie (the PC version can read Video for Windows movies), using the same File/Import command. Immediately, Director placed the movie into our Cast palette.

To give ourselves room to add additional animation, we placed the QuickTime movie into frame 20 of Channel 1. Next, we needed to tell Director to pause at frame 20, then wait until our movie was over before proceeding with the rest of the production. To set up the pause in the production, we double-clicked in frame 20 of Director's Tempo channel. This opened the Set Tempo dialog box, shown below, where we clicked on the Wait for Digital Movie radio button. To keep ourselves better organized, we created a *marker* so that we could see exactly where our morphing began. A marker is simply a space in the score that can be named. We named our marker Morph. Later we would be able to instruct our navigational button to move to the Morph sequence by simply creating the script line: go to "morph".

```
Set Tempo
○ Tempo:    ◁▭▭▭▭▭▷ fps
○ Wait:     ◁▭▭▭▭▭▷ seconds          OK
○ Wait for Mouse Click or Key
○ Wait for Sound1 To Finish          Cancel
○ Wait for Sound2 To Finish
◉ Wait for Digital Video Movie
   to Finish in Channel: [1]          Help
```

Our next step was to program the button that would go to the morphing sequence.

# Programming a Button in Macromedia Director

Although you can create buttons in a variety of different graphics programs, the simplest way to create a button in Director is to click and drag onscreen using its button creation tool. This creates a "hot" area onscreen that can be used for navigational programming. We wanted to write a more sophisticated button sequence out of the beveled buttons we created in TextureScape, so we needed to write a Lingo script. We wanted to program the script so that the Off button would be replaced by the On button when the user clicked on it. This would give the user feedback that he or she was actually pressing the mouse on a live area onscreen. To add further feedback, we decided to program in a sound sequence that would play when the user clicked on the button. The programming sequences we used should give you an idea how Director's Lingo programming language works. If you've ever used a programming language, you'll find that creating simple animation with Lingo is quite easy. However, as your needs grow more complicated, you'll want to invest a fair amount of time to thoroughly master the more sophisticated features of the language.

To take full advantage of Lingo, Director users must master the concept of creating a *puppet*. A puppet is not a graphic image; it's essentially a programming term. When you create a puppet, control of a Director Channel is handed over to the Lingo programming language. Creating a puppet can save you animation steps by having Lingo commands automatically replace one image onscreen with another, change colors, and play sounds. In order to turn over control of a Channel to Lingo, you execute a command that turns a Score Channel into a puppet.

We started by writing the following Lingo commands into a script in Director's Score Channel. The script tells Director to turn Channel 4 into a puppet when the playback head exits the Score frame. Once Channel 4 becomes a puppet, the images on stage can be controlled from Lingo programming commands in the Channel.

```
On exitFrame
        PuppetSprite 4, TRUE
end
```

Our next step was to drag our button into the Score area of Channel 4, then we wrote a Lingo script in a frame in the Channel's Score that switched button cast members from our "off" button (castmember 2) to our "on" button (castmember 3). You can see the buttons in the Cast palette of Figure 16-3. We also wanted the script

to play a sound when the mouse button was pressed. To create the script, we clicked on the "off" button's frame in the score, then chose New from the Script pop-up menu.
Here is our script:

```
On MouseDown                          When the mouse is clicked
puppetSound "mydownbeep"              Play sound
Set the Castnum of sprite 4 to 3     Replace the button with cast member 3
updatestage                          Redraw the screen
repeat while the mousedown
    nothing                          This keeps the scene from changing
end repeat                           while the mouse is down
end
```

After this routine, we wrote another script which replaced the "on" button with our "off" button, then moved to the QuickTime movie section of our production.

```
On MouseUp
    PuppetSound "myupbeep"            Play a sound
    set the Castnum of sprite 4 to 2 Replace the button with Castmember 2
    go to "Morph"                    Go to the frame with our Morph
puppetSprite 4, False                Turn offf the puppet
end
```

## Learning More about Director

The previous sections should have provided you with a taste of how Director works. How do you learn more? Your best bet is to purchase the program. Director's manuals and tutorial are some of the best you'll find. Also, the Macromedia forums on America Online and CompuServe are quite lively. You might also wish to check out Macromedia's home page on the Internet. If you're interested in getting started with Director, you'll find that it will run adequately even on older '030 Macs. Windows users should have at least a 486 machine.

# Using Macromedia Authorware

If you don't like to program, yet want to concentrate on creating the visual look and navigation of your multimedia productions, you should consider Macromedia Authorware. Authorware retails for about $5,000. An educational version is available for $995. (If you use the educational version, you cannot distribute your Authorware productions commercially.) Why does Authorware cost so much? Because it lets you quickly create sophisticated multimedia productions without the need for programming. Authorware's simplicity has made it a favorite for creating interactive multimedia educational productions. The program is specifically designed to handle many educationally geared tasks, such as storing responses to questions and calculating how many times a user has attempted to answer a question.

To create a multimedia production in Authorware, you drag and drop icons onto a *Flowline*. Figure 16-4 shows the toolbar, where you access the icons to drop on the Flowline. Like Director, Authorware allows you to create interactive buttons, play digital movies, use sound, and import graphics. The program also allows you to create graphic libraries and drag images from your libraries into your Authorware presentations. This can be helpful if you wish to reuse buttons and icons. The program also allows you to load a formatted text file onscreen (text must be in RTF (Rich Text Format), a format available with many word processors). In the next sections, you'll learn how to navigate and create buttons in Authorware.

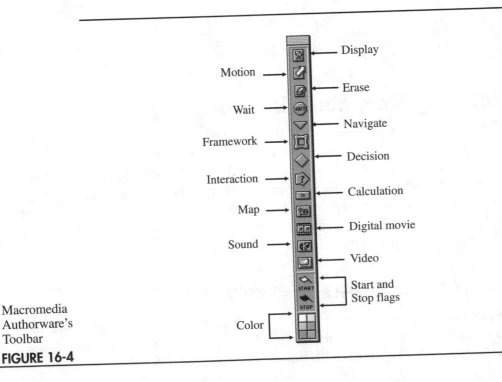

Macromedia
Authorware's
Toolbar

**FIGURE 16-4**

# Importing Graphics and Movies into Authorware

To import graphics into Authorware, you start by clicking on the Display tool and dragging it to the Flowline. After a display icon appears on the Flowline, you double-click on it, then choose Import Graphics from Authorware's File menu. Alternatively, if your graphics are in a library, you can drag an image icon from a

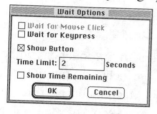

library onto the Flowline. To set timing for graphics onscreen, you can click and drag the Wait icon onto the Flowline. By double-clicking on the Wait icon, you can specify how long you want the previous graphic on the Flowline to appear. Shown here is the Wait Options dialog box. If you use the Wait icon, Authorware can automatically create a Continue button onscreen.

To import a digital movie or a Director movie into Authorware, click on the Digital movie icon and drag it onto the Flowline. This icon opens up a dialog box allowing you to specify how many times you wish the video movie to play and whether you wish the presentation to wait until the movie ends or play concurrently with the movie.

# Creating Animation in Authorware

Although Authorware is known primarily as an interactive multimedia program, you can create animated effects to move objects across the screen. The steps for creating animation are simple. First, drag a display icon onscreen, double-click on it, and load the graphic you wish to animate onscreen. Second, click and drag a Motion icon from the toolbar onto the Flowline. When you double-click on the Motion icon,

you can click and drag the previous graphic that you loaded. To create the animated effect, click and drag the graphic to where you want the animation to end, then set the duration in the Rate field of the dialog box, shown here. When you run the sequence, the graphic moves from its starting point to the end point that you dragged it to.

# Creating Buttons and Using Digital Movies

Creating a button in Authorware is quite different from doing so in Director because you can use preset and custom buttons accessed from a dialog box in Authorware.

To start the process of creating a button, first drag the Interaction icon from the toolbar to the Flowline. Next, drag the Display icon from the toolbox to create the graphic that you want to appear after the user clicks the button. You can also drag the digital movie icon or video icon from the Toolbar to play a video sequence or digital movie after the button is clicked.

## Learning More about Authorware

The previous sections illustrate how you can create interactive productions without programming. To help new users, the Authorware package includes a tutorial which teaches the basics of creating an interactive presentation. Macromedia also provides a separate manual designed to teach you how to use the more sophisticated features of the program: functions and variables.

# Using Apple Media Kit

Apple Media Kit is a multimedia package designed for both programmers and nonprogrammers. The Kit is divided into two components, Apple Media Tool and Apple Media Programming Environment. The price for both modules is $1,100. If you buy the modules separately, Apple Media Tool is $495 and Apple Media Programming Environment is $995. The Apple Media Programming Environment is a very sophisticated, high-end package. Only experienced programmers familiar with Pascal or C will want to work in this high-end multimedia language.

Apple Media Tool is an icon-based authoring program primarily aimed at designers who do not want to program. The Apple Media Programming Environment is a full-fledged programming medium for those who need to create sophisticated interactive features. Using the Apple Media Programming Environment, you can customize applications created with Apple Media Tool or program an entire multimedia production from scratch. The underlying concept behind Apple Media Kit is that multimedia productions are a team effort: Designers can use Apple Media Tool, while programmers can use the Programming Environment.

The following sections review how to use Apple Media Tool and Programming Environment.

# Creating a Multimedia Production with Apple Media Tool

Using Apple Media Tool to create a simple navigational multimedia production is quite straightforward. The best way to start a production is to create a *map*—which provides a chart of your production's navigational flow. Figure 16-5 shows a map we created for an interactive tour of digital imaging. The map was created by clicking on four different locations on the screen with the Creation tool. We named each screen by double-clicking on each icon, then connected the screens by dragging lines from one screen to another.

Our next step was to add a background to the introductory screen. All graphics, movies, and sounds are imported into the program using the Add Media menu command. Once images are loaded, they appear in the Objects palette. To create a background, we loaded a marble background and a button from Macromedia's ClipMedia 1 CD-ROM collection. To add the image onto the screen, we simply clicked on its name in the Objects palette and dragged it into the document window. Next, we clicked on the button filename in the Objects palette and dragged it over our background. Immediately, the actual button appeared over the marbled background.

Our goal was to make the button interactive so that it would cause a jump from our opening screen to our introductory text screen. In Apple Media Tool, navigational scripting is handled by assembling a series of predefined steps that you add to the Action palette. We started by selecting the button in the Objects palette, then used the pop-up menu in the Action palette to specify that we wanted actions to occur when the mouse was pressed. This setup is shown in Figure 16-6.

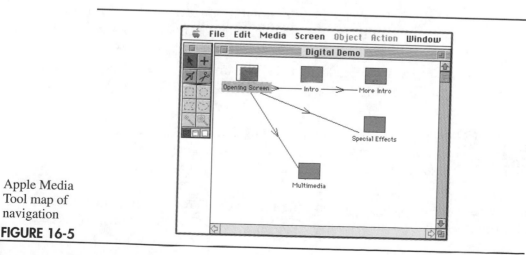

Apple Media
Tool map of
navigation

**FIGURE 16-5**

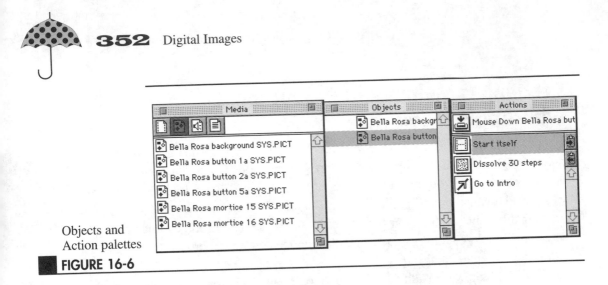

Objects and
Action palettes

We then used the Action menu to insert an effect. From the Effect pop-up menu, we chose Dissolve. After clicking on the button, the opening screen dissolved. Next, we needed to create a link from the opening screen to the Intro Text. To do so, we chose Insert from the program's Action menu. This created a Links pop-up menu in the Action palette. The Links menu automatically adds the names of the images onscreen, so that you can easily move from screen to screen. We chose Go to Intro, as shown here. When the button was clicked in one screen, the navigation jumped to the Intro screen.

# The Media Tool Programming Environment

The Apple Media Programming Environment is designed for experienced programmers who wish to add functionality to productions created in the Apple Media Tool. The programming environment is very much like C or Pascal. In order to program in the Apple Media Program Environment, you should have some knowledge of Apple's MPW (Macintosh Programmers Workshop).

 **OTE:** *To learn about training modules for Apple development, or to join the Apple Multimedia program, call Apple Developer Programs at 1-800-282-2732.*

The easiest way to get started with Apple Media Programming Environment is to enhance an application created with Apple Media Tool. To do this, you need to convert your Apple Media Tool project into text by simply choosing Save As Text from the program's File menu. This creates two files that can be used by the Apple Media Programming Environment. The programming code created should give you an idea of the developmental environment. At this programming level, you can't drag icons on the screen or specify settings in dialog boxes; everything is handled by arduous line-by-line programming. Here is a small sample of some program code that helps define cursors and the display size in the Apple Media Programming Environment.

```
program()
    do
        APPLICATION.MouseInCursor := ARROWCURSOR;
        APPLICATION.MouseOutCursor := DONTCURSOR;
        APPLICATION.MouseSpin := WATCHSPIN;
        APPLICATION.Main(MEDIA, S1_OPENING_SCREEN, 640, 480, 8, void);
    end;
```

**OTE:** *Windows users looking for an entry-level, easy-to-use, icon-based multimedia program should investigate HSC InterActive. This program allows users to combine graphics, video, animation, audio, text, and 3D charts to create multimedia projects.*

# Using Adobe Premiere

Adobe Premiere is a multimedia program that allows you to create and edit digital movies. Unlike Director, Authorware, and Apple Media Tool, Premiere cannot create interactive presentations because buttons and navigational objects cannot be programmed. Premiere is used to assemble graphics, video clips, QuickTime movies, and sounds into a multimedia presentation. Once a production is created in Premiere, it can be saved as a digital movie for use in other programs. Premiere productions can also be exported to videotape. In fact, some video production companies use Premiere to create TV commercials.

## Creating a Digital Movie in Premiere

Although you can create text and title sequences in Premiere, most graphics are imported into the program. Using the program's Import command, Mac users can

import PICT images, PC users, BMP images. Mac users can import QuickTime movies, PC users, Video for Windows movies. Both Mac and Windows versions allow video clips to be imported directly into the program (provided you have the correct hardware—see Chapter 8 for more details). When an image is loaded onscreen, it first appears in Premiere's Project palette. To use the image or movie, you simply drag it from the Project palette to the Video A or B track in Premiere's Construction window. Sounds can be imported into Premiere in much the same way.

 **OTE:** *If you wish to edit sound for multimedia presentations, you can use Macromedia SoundEdit 16. Using SoundEdit 16, you can use your computer to mix narration, sound, and music.*

If you import a digital movie, you can use Premiere's clip window to set *in* and *out* points to specify exactly which section of a clip you wish to use. Figure 16-7 shows the Clip window with the Construction, Project, and Info windows in the background.

## Creating Special Effects in Premiere

To build transitional effects between clips or graphics, Premiere's Transition track is used to transition images from the A track to the B track, or from the B track to

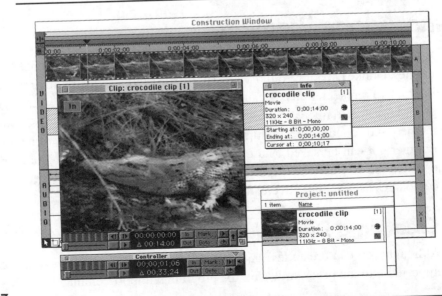

Adobe
Premiere
windows

**FIGURE 16-7**

the A track. Once your images are loaded into the two tracks, you can easily create transitional effects by dragging a transition from the Transitions palette into the Transition video track. For instance, if you choose Wipe, the image in Track A can be wiped away to show the image in Track B (or vice versa) when the sequence is played. The Transitions palette features over 60 transitions. A small portion of the Transitions palette is shown here.

Premiere also allows you to create numerous special effects that can add interest to your digital productions. The easiest way to create special effects is to use Premiere's Filters dialog box, shown in Figure 16-8a. Figure 16-8b shows the dialog box that appears after you choose the Twirl filter. You can use filters to solarize, spherize, or twirl individual frames or sequences. To apply a filter to a sequence, you first must click on the individual frame or sequence in the Construction window, then choose the Filters command from the Clip menu. In the Filters dialog box, you choose a filter name, then click the Add button. If you wish, you can specify the start and end points of the filter by clicking on the Start and End button in the Filters dialog box. Premiere also includes an S1 and S2 video track for creating superimposition effects, called "keying" in television production and "matting" in film production.

# Working with Type in Premiere

Premiere allows you to create rolling credits and animated text. Start by choosing Title from the File/New submenu. In the Title window, shown in Figure 16-9, use

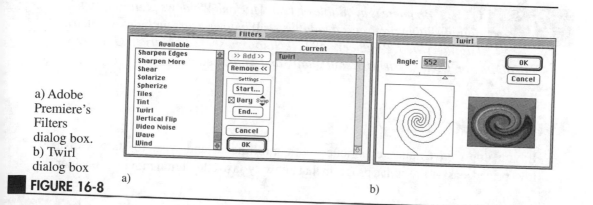

a) Adobe Premiere's Filters dialog box.
b) Twirl dialog box

**FIGURE 16-8**

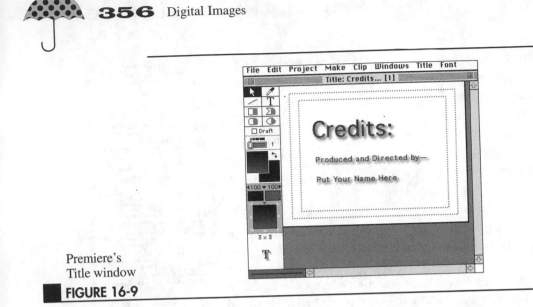

Premiere's
Title window

**FIGURE 16-9**

the Type tool to create some text. To add a drop shadow to your text, simply click

on the "T" at the bottom of the toolbox and drag in the direction you want the shadow to go. To animate the text, simply double-click on it, or choose Text Animation from the Title menu. In the Animation Settings dialog box, shown here, you can set points on the Time line and then stretch or shrink the text. If you want to adjust the width without affecting the height or vice versa, press and hold the SHIFT key and then drag either the v or h slider.

**OTE:** *Premiere is available on both Mac and Windows platforms. Other digital editing programs available for Windows users include: Asymetrix Digital Video Producer, ATI Technologies MediaMerge, Gold Disk VideoDirector, Ulead Systems MediaStudio, and Videomedia Oz.*

# Avid VideoShop

If you don't have much experience with multimedia and wish to start with a low-priced, easy-to-use Mac program that allows you to edit digital movies, consider

Avid VideoShop. Like Adobe Premiere, VideoShop allows you to assemble images, video clips, and QuickTime movies into digital movies. The program allows you to create fade-ins and fade-outs, layer one clip over another, and even create split-screen movies. VideoShop even allows you to create paths that you can use to control animated effects. This means that you can draw a path from an image to a

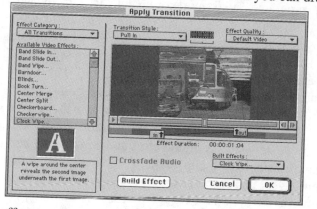

point onscreen, and the image will move along that path when the animation runs. The program includes a full set of filters that allow you to sharpen, blur, and morph one image into another. VideoShop also includes a full set of transitions that allow you to create wipes and mosaic effects as one scene changes to another. VideoShop's Apply Transition dialog box, shown here, can provide a preview of a transitional effect before applying it .

# Adobe After Effects

Adobe After Effects is an extremely powerful digital movie editor and a highly regarded special effects generator for digital movies. One of the program's main features is its ability to composite multiple layers of digital movies and digital images. This allows you to create anything from simple collages to unusual and attractive blends between one video clip and another. The program includes masking tools which allow you to create and edit masks in different video layers so that you can control exactly what parts of an individual video sequence appear in a composited effect.

Like Premiere, After Effects includes special-effects filters. These include Polar Coordinates (which allows you to bend horizontal images), Spherize, Emboss, Blur, Mirror (which splits an image and provides a reflection of it), Brightness and Contrast, Color Balance, and Tint. After Effects also includes a Key filter which allows you to "key out" image areas of a specified color.

One of After Effects' more powerful features is its ability to interpolate between key frames along a path. Using this feature, you can specify key frames and draw a path onscreen between the keyframes; this allows you to animate the image along the path. After Effects' path creation tools are quite sophisticated. You can create not only straight line paths, but also smooth curves using Bézier curve control handles. These allow you to control the size and bump of the curve as you would in a drawing program like Adobe Illustrator, Macromedia Freehand, or CorelDRAW.

To create an After Effects "composition," you start by importing digital movies and/or still images using the program's File/Import command. Once the images and digital movies are imported they appear in the Project palette. The palette in Figure 16-10 shows the filenames of QuickTime movies of a roulette wheel, a bungee jumper, and a hang-glider. These were loaded into After Effects from Macromedia's Clip Media 1 Business and Technology CD-ROM collection. The Olympic Mountain range background was also imported from the clip collection.

After the QuickTime movies and digital images were loaded into the palette, we started the compostion by choosing New from the Composition menu. To start assembling the composition, we dragged the digital clips and still images into the Composition window. As we assembled the clips, After Effects created a timeline showing all of the different layers and their durations. The Time Layout palette displaying the layers is shown at the bottom of Figure 16-10.

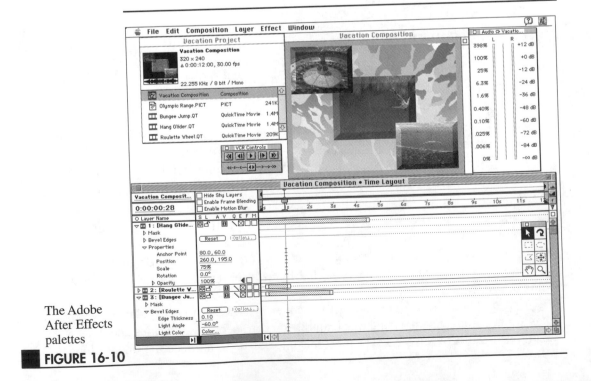

The Adobe
After Effects
palettes

**FIGURE 16-10**

After the images were loaded, the video in- and outpoints were edited in After Effects. The roulette wheel and hang-gliding sequences were scaled down to 75% of their original size and dragged into the corners of the Composition window. When the composition plays, each video clip runs as if it were in its own window. The beveled edges were created using After Effects' Bevel command accessed from its Effect menu. Notice that the Time Layout window for the bungee jumper layer shows the attributes of the Bevel special effect. The effect can be changed by editing the numbers displayed onscreen.

The tiny diamond icon visible at the one-second mark of the timeline indicates that a key frame was created for the image's Opacity. To experiment with compositing effects, we lowered the opacities of both the roulette wheel and the hang-glider at the very beginning of the composition. (The roulette wheel's opacity setting is not visible in the palette.) Using the key frame and After Effects' linear interpolation method, we made the opacity of the roulette wheel and hang-gliding sequence gradually increase to 100% at the one-second mark in the composition. Once the sequence was completed, it was rendered into a QuickTime movie using the Make Movie Command in After Effects' Composition menu.

**n**OTE: *Radius VideoFusion is a digital video program specifically designed to create special effects in QuickTime movies. Using VideoFusion, you can create morphing, warping, and a variety of different compositing effects.*

# Avid Systems Software and Hardware Editing Systems

If you are going to be doing extensive editing of digital movies, and you have a large production budget, you might wish to investigate purchasing a complete digital movie editing system. The most popular digital video editing system in the country is Avid's Media Composer. One of the reasons that Avid has been so successful is that it sells hardware and software editing systems that provide extremely high-quality video output. A typical Avid system includes a computer, hard disks, and software. Avid video systems have been used to create feature films, televison programs, commercials, music videos, documentaries, and industrial videos. One popular system is the Media Composer 1000, which retails for a minimum of $40,000. Figure 16-11 shows a screenshot from the Media Composer editing software. The segment being edited was first created in Adobe After Effects before its inclusion in *Preview Theatre*, a weekly syndicated television program produced by Trillian, Inc. at Edgeworx Productions in New York City. Edgeworx producers Alton Christensen and Dave Tecson often create graphics in Adobe Photoshop, special effects in Adobe After Effects, and assemble the final production on their Avid Media Composer 1000.

**OTE:** *Avid also sells lower-priced editing systems, Avid Media Composer Pro for Macs and Windows, which do not include a computer and hard disks. They are priced at a minimum of about $10,000.*

# Kodak Arrange-It

Kodak Arrange-It is a multimedia program that allows you to create interactive presentations from Photo CD, TIFF, and PICT images and sound files. Once the presentation is finished it is stored in Kodak's Portfolio CD format. Presentations

Title Sequence from *Preview Theatre* being edited using the Avid Media Composer 1000, produced by Trillian, Inc. at Edgeworx Productions

**FIGURE 16-11**

created with Arrange-It must be viewed on Kodak's CD-ROM player. Arrange-It allows you to create navigational paths from one image to another, and control how long each image is displayed onscreen. Interactive options are provided through numbered menus that appear onscreen. The numbers correspond to numbers on remote control devices connected to Kodak's Photo CD player. Users with a standard computer and CD-ROM drive can control the navigation of the presentation by clicking on "hotspots" onscreen. Once you've completed your production, you can take it to a Kodak Photo CD Portfolio service provider. Several days later you can pick up a CD-ROM with your interactive production on it.

*n* **OTE:** *Windows users who wish to create multimedia productions out of Photo CD images should investigate The Multimedia Store's Photo Factory for Windows. This low-cost program ($55) allows you to create slide shows of Photo CD images complete with text and sound.*

# The Animation Stand

The Animation Stand is a high-end, 2D animation program designed for animation professionals. Although the program allows you to import images created in other programs, the Animation Stand includes numerous drawing and painting tools for those who wish to create animations directly in the program.

To control the animation sequences, you use an exposure sheet which is modeled after those used in the animation industry. The exposure sheet provides a description of each frame of the animation. The position and duration of each piece of art in the frame is detailed in the exposure sheet, as shown here. If you update the information in the exposure sheet, the animation sequence is updated accordingly. You can also change the settings in the exposure sheet automatically by clicking and dragging to reposition and change the elements of the images onscreen.

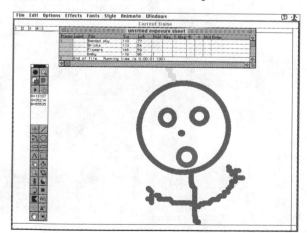

The Animation Stand includes numerous features to take the tedium out of cel-by-cel animation. It provides automatic fade-ins and fade-outs, wipes, and blending effects between layers of graphics in a frame. The program also provides powerful interpolation controls which allow you to create paths that your animations can move along. To edit the paths, you can click and drag on control points as you would in spline-based 3D programs or Bèzier curve-based drawing programs.

# Strata MediaPaint

Strata MediaPaint is an extemely versatile and entertaining digital movie painting program that allows you to paint over digital movies. MediaPaint includes pencil, paintbrush, airbrush tools, as well as blurring, sharpening, and fading controls. Figure 16-12 should provide you with an idea of the numerous tools and palettes that MediaPaint provides when you wish to paint over a digital movie or use its painting tools to create digital movies from scratch. In Figure 16-12, a pattern from MediaPaint is being applied to a QuickTime movie from Macromedia's Clip Collection Volume 1. After creating a selection of the pattern, we used MediaPaint's AutoCopy New function to only copy the new "paint" from one frame into a subsequent frame in the QuickTime movie.

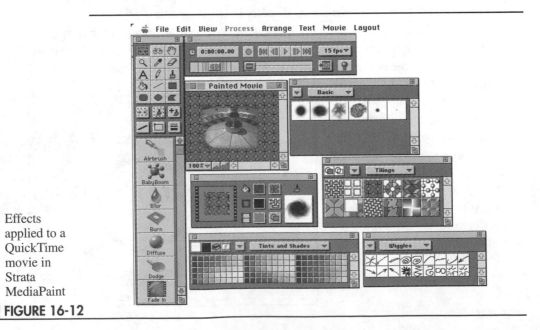

Effects applied to a QuickTime movie in Strata MediaPaint

**FIGURE 16-12**

Apart from a full set of painting tools that allow you to create special effects, MediaPaint features a host of filters that blur, diffuse, fade in, fade out, and sharpen. A mosaic filter turns your image into a mosaic. Most of the filters are *tweenable,* which means you can apply the effects of the filter over a span of movie frames.

Advanced features of the program include a Squiggle generator (for creating wiggling and squirming shapes) and a Stencil Composite Mode, which allows you to layer movies or artwork created in other programs on top of other layers to create sophisticated effects. You can also create *Chroma Key* effects, which allow you to pick a color and control its transparency in one or more movie frames. Also included is a *self-emanating* Particle tool which can create its own particle effects over time.

# Strata Instant Replay

Strata Instant Replay captures screen movements and saves them in QuickTime format. This program is excellent for creating digital movie clips that illustrate how to use computer programs. If you need to narrate the action, you can even record voice or music to accompany the animation (you must have sound input into your computer to do this).

Instant Replay is quite simple to use. All you need to do is press the "hot-keys" on your computer, or you can open the Instant Replay application and click on the Record button. Once you start recording, you perform a series of screen actions. As you move the mouse and click on objects, your actions are recorded. When you press the hot-keys again, the recording stops. Figure 16-13 shows Instant Replay's Recording dialog box, just about to record the mouse movement of opening and using Strata MediaPaint.

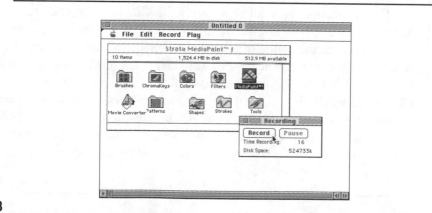

Strata Instant
Replay's
Recording
dialog box

**FIGURE 16-13**

## Behind the Scenes:
## An Interview with the Creators of Myst

Myst is one of the top-selling interactive CD-ROM games in the world. How did its creators, Robyn Miller and Rand Miller, produce the fantastic images that have made the game so popular? Read on ...

*How did you come up with the idea for Myst? How did you plan the entire project before creating it? Did you create sketches? Flow charts?*

We had only been working on children's projects for a long time and decided it was time to do something for adults—something we would enjoy playing. Myst was the natural evolution from the earlier children's projects, which were also "point-and-click" explorations through fantastic worlds. The difference with Myst was that we created much more of a story and gave it a goal.

And, of course, we absolutely had to plan the entire thing out before we started in on the production. Mostly we created maps: We felt that if we were creating a real environment (instead of a virtual one) that we'd do it using maps and sketches. In a nonlinear environment, we find that storyboards are fairly useless.

*What about the sound and animation? How did you get started? What programs did you use, and why?*

The animation was all done on a Macintosh computer using Strata StudioPro (a 3D modeling, rendering, and animation program), unless it was live action (like the acting of Sirrus or Achenar), which we simply filmed in front of a blue screen. The movies were displayed in Myst using QuickTime. Most of the 3D images were created by Robyn Miller; some were created by Chuck Carter. Both created the 3D models in Strata StudioPro. Then they created textures for the models using Adobe Illustrator and Adobe Photoshop. The textures were then imported into Strata StudioPro and applied to the models. Before the models were rendered, lights were added.

## 16

The sound was created by Chris Brandkamp, who recorded various sounds like water, presses, an air gun stapler, an aircompressor, etc. He recorded the sounds with a portable DAT recorder. The sounds were then mixed using DigiDesign Sound Designer and Macromedia Sound Edit.

After the images and sound were created, they were placed into Claris Hypercard, a multimedia authoring program. Most of the programming was done by Rand Miller; with some additional coding by Rich Watson. Since Myst required more sophisticated features than Hypercard allowed, several XCMDs (created in the C programming language) had to be written.

*Why did you create the 3D models and animation in Strata StudioPro? How long did it take you to create some of the models and then render them? How did you learn how to create such amazing 3D models?*

I (Robyn) believe that learning to create models came as a natural extension of my interest in art. In other words, I only learned 3D after I had a fairly strong base in natural media. This happens to be the case with all artists that work at Cyan, perhaps because the art side is so vital to the quality and inventiveness of our 3D work.

While we were using Strata StudioPro, the modeling and rendering took an especially long time, which was probably our only complaint about the software. However, I think they've improved quite a bit in this area since that time. What we liked about it is that we found it to have the best interface of any of the 3D programs (the most conducive to creativity). In addition, its quality of ray-tracing was incredible. Even on the workstations that we now use, we cannot achieve the same level of sophistication in the ray-tracing quality.

*Did you sell your idea to Broderbund before completing it? Or did you decide to create Myst and then decide to find a publisher?*

Myst was funded by Sunsoft, Inc. and ourselves. Broderbund publishes Myst on Mac and PC platforms. Sunsoft now has the game published on several different platforms, including Sega Saturn, Donnelly Play Station, CDI, Atari Jaguar, Sega CD Genesis machine, and Phillips Pioneer laser disc.

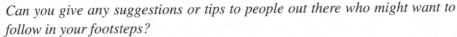 

*Can you give any suggestions or tips to people out there who might want to follow in your footsteps?*

Don't concentrate on flash. Concentrate on story and content. Flash means nothing without a great story.

*What do you have planned for the future?*

Right now we're working on the sequel to Myst, which unfortunately I cannot say much about—though I'm dying to!

# Conclusion

As you've seen from reading this chapter, multimedia software packages are versatile and powerful. However, most multimedia software packages do not include extensive image-editing commands. As you work with multimedia programs, you may wish to review earlier chapters in this book that cover how to digitize images, use file formats, enhance images, and create special effects. If you'll be outputting your multimedia productions to video, be sure to read Chapter 18.

# 17

# Printing and Calibration

Perhaps the most rewarding aspect of creating or participating in the creation of digital images is seeing the final versions printed in a book, magazine, newsletter, or newspaper. Making sure that the final output matches your artistic and/or commercial intent requires a knowledge not only of the software products used for production, but also the digital production process. If you understand how digital images are output, you're more likely to achieve your artistic goals and produce high quality without breaking your budget.

In years past, many aspects of print production were handled by printing professionals who successfully guided images through the treacherous waters of printing preparation. Today, many of the tasks that once were handled by these prepress professionals can be accomplished by individuals on their computers. Despite the power of desktop software to help in this area, many artists still find it more efficient to leave the most technical aspects of print production to service bureaus and prepress houses. In fact, when it comes time to output their images, many artists pack up their files and send them off to prepress houses without ever pausing at the Print or Page Setup dialog boxes. Nonetheless, artists and everyone else working to produce digital images need to understand how images are output in order to communicate with the professionals who output their images.

If you're new to digital imaging, the print production process can seem quite bewildering. Before images can be output, the proper print resolution, screen frequency, and angles must be set. Some images may need to be *trapped*, others may not. To help steer you through the digital production process, this chapter provides you with an overview of the steps involved in print production and some of the concepts you'll need to understand.

# The Digital Production Process

When a color or black-and-white image is printed, the gray tones and color images are actually composed of tiny dots called *halftones*. The size, angle, and color of the dots create the illusion of shades of grays and countless colors. In grayscale images, the different-sized dots determine the shades of gray. When a color photograph is reproduced on a printing press, different-sized cyan, magenta, yellow, and black dots overlaying and adjacent to each other create the illusion of continuous color.

In general, the closer the cyan, magenta, yellow, and black dots, the finer the print job. But quality is also determined by paper and the screen angles at which the dots are created. Why do the dots need to be printed at specific angles? Remember that the printing process requires four printing plates to be created. The ink from one printing plate overlays underlying inks. If all the dots were created exactly the same, each would print directly on the other. If the halftones are not printed at the correct angle, unattractive mottled patterns called *moirès* can occur.

# Understanding Halftones

How do you get from a digital image onscreen to halftone dots on a printing press? To understand the printing journey, you first need to understand how a digital halftone is created.

The size and patterns of the halftone dots are computer-created by an imagesetter, which outputs the dots on one separate piece of film for each process color. The film is not output in color. Each piece of film is a grayscale representation of the image elements broken down into one of the cyan, magenta, yellow, and black components. The commercial printer uses the four pieces of film to create printing plates, one for each process color. On press, cyan ink is applied to the cyan plate, magenta ink to the magenta plate, and so on. As mentioned earlier, overlaying of the four process colors creates the illusion of countless colors in the final image.

One of the most important publishing concepts to grasp is how digital halftones are created from the tiny machine dots output from imagesetters. Once you understand this process, you'll have a better idea of how colors are created and how image quality can be affected by screen frequency settings and *dot gain*—the spreading of ink when an image is printed.

When an imagesetter, and even a common desktop printer, outputs an image, it prints a specific number of dots per inch. Most laser printers print at 300 dots per inch. Imagesetters print from 1,000 to over 2,000 dots per inch—to either paper or film.

When in image is output on an imagesetter, it is *rasterized* into tiny dots, often called "spots" or "pixels." This is handled by a device (sometimes software only) called a RIP (raster image processor). After the image is RIPed, the imagesetter can start outputting the tiny pixels to create the image. When these pixels are output, they're produced in specific patterns that are the basis of halftones. Essentially, the tiny imagesetter pixels create each halftone. Figure 17-1 is a representation of a halftone. The tiny dots that make up the halftone are imagesetter pixels (or spots). The number of halftone dots that are output per inch constitutes the screen frequency of the image. The higher the output screen frequency, the finer the image. At first, you might assume that high-quality images must always output at the highest screen frequency and the greatest number of dots per inch. Unfortunately, dot mathematics produces an inverse relationship between the number of grays that can be output and the screen frequency. Larger halftone dots produce more gray levels than smaller halftone dots (smaller halftones produce more lines per inch on a page).

 **OTE:** *Use the following formula to calculate the number of grays possible in an image: Number of gray levels = Printer (resolution in dpi/screen frequency in lpi)$^2$+1.*

The relationship between the number of grays output and halftone dot size is worth investigating, particularly if you are trying to decide what paper and what type of press should output your images. To understand how halftones affect the number of gray levels in an image, assume you are printing at 600 dpi and your screen frequency is 60. You can calculate the number of imagesetter dots in each halftone by dividing 600 by 60, which equals 10. Thus each halftone dot is comprised of a matrix of 10 x 10 imagesetter dots. This means that you can create 100 shades of gray (10 x 10) plus 1 (for white). In other words, the different combination of dot patterns in a halftone constitute the number of grays that can be produced in an image.

What if you wanted to create more shades of gray? Mathematically, you achieve more gray levels by reducing screen frequency. However, if you reduce the screen frequency, the level of detail in the image is also reduced. If you increase the screen frequency without increasing the laser printer or imagesetter dpi, you'll have fewer gray levels in your image. Essentially, what you have is a tug-of-war between detail and contrast.

 **OTE:** *The optimum number of grays for PostScript printing is 256. The more levels of gray, the better image transitions in digitized photographs and blends.*

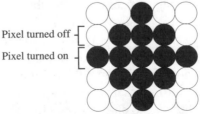

Halftone dot
created from
imagesetter
pixels

**FIGURE 17-1**

If you're using a service bureau to print your work, the obvious solution would seem to be: always print at the highest resolution and the highest screen frequency. Unfortunately, screen frequency is often determined by the paper and inks used in printing. For instance, newsprint is a very porous paper. The screen frequency for newsprint is often between 80 and 90 lpi. If you print at too high a screen frequency on newsprint, your images will not look better, but more likely muddy and smeared. Quality is not based upon printing dpi alone. Dpi and lpi working together are responsible for the quality for your final image.

 **OTE:** *If you know the screen frequency for image output, you can calculate the minimum imagesetter resolution needed to print the image by using this formula: Minimum printer resolution in dots per inch = screen frequency x 16.*

To ensure your images are properly output, work closely with your prepress house and/or printer to determine the best dpi and lpi for your jobs. As discussed in Chapter 4, screen frequency for black-and-white books is often 100 to 133; a common screen frequency for magazines is 133 to 150 lpi. Your prepress house and printer will help you determine the best possible settings to use when your image is output. However, before you begin to print, you should ensure that your system is calibrated.

# Calibration

Before you near the completion of your digital imaging projects and enter the proofing stages, you should attempt to ensure that the colors you see onscreen match those that will be printed. The best way to ensure that colors match is to calibrate your system.

In many respects, the problem of matching screen colors to printed colors is often unavoidable because different printers and monitors produce different ranges of colors. Another factor often at the root of improper color matching is the difference between the RGB and CMYK color gamuts. As discussed in Chapter 3, your computer uses the RGB color model to create colors, while printed images are based on the CMYK color model. Converting from one color space to the other opens up a range of problems that can be helped by properly calibrating your system. When you calibrate your system, you use hardware and software options to ensure the colors you see onscreen match printed output as closely as possible.

 **AUTION:** *If the colors onscreen are beyond the CMYK color gamut, the final printed colors could look very different from the colors on your monitor.*

To start calibrating your system, you should investigate what options are provided by the software and hardware you own. One of the easiest calibration programs to use is Knoll Software's Gamma utility. This utility comes packaged with Adobe Photoshop and several scanners. By clicking on the sliders, you can remove monitor color casts and ensure that the brightness of the monitor is properly adjusted. After you've calibrated your system, you can be better assured that the images you see onscreen closely reflect how they will print. If you are using Photoshop, you can also change calibration settings by specifying your monitor model in the program's Monitor Setup dialog box, shown below.

Another Photoshop calibration aid is its Printing Inks Setup dialog box. In this dialog box's Ink Colors pop-up menu, shown here, you specify the printing system or inks for the job you are creating. You can also choose a printer by name. After you set the printing inks properly, Photoshop lightens or darkens the screen to compensate for dot gain. These settings are extremely important if you will be converting RGB color to CMYK color files. If the values in the Monitor Setup and Printing Inks Setup dialog boxes are not set correctly, the final separated CMYK image may not match the RGB image.

## Monitor Calibrators

Another aid to calibration are *monitor calibrators* sold by companies such as X-Rite, DayStar, and Radius. A monitor calibrator is a device that looks like a suction cup that attaches to your monitor screen. Using the calibration device, you can help ensure that the brightness and contrast controls on your monitor are properly set. Calibrators can also help ensure that the red, green, and blue monitor phosphors are properly calibrated.

Figure 17-2 shows the dialog box that appears when you run the calibration program packaged with SuperMac's Super Match Pro (now Radius) monitor calibration package. The dialog box shows the uncalibrated graph of the red, green, and blue phosphors compared to the corrected graph, after calibration. After running such a calibration routine, you can be better assured that screen colors will match printed colors.

Perhaps one of the best ways to ensure proper monitor calibration is to purchase a monitor specifically designed for color accuracy, such as Radius' PressView 17 SR monitors, available for both PCs and Macs. This monitor, which retails for a little over $2,000, is packaged with a display calibrator and a gray hood that extends over the top and sides of the monitor. The gray hood and the monitor's gray bezel that surrounds the screen ensure that the colors perceived by the viewer are not affected by the frame in which they are viewed. The monitor features a "super resolution" mode of 1,600 x 1,200 pixels, a  25mm aperture grille pitch, and glare-reducing coating— all contributing to highly accurate screen colors and crisp images. At a price of over $5,000, Barco manufactures a color monitor which it advertises as the most precisely calibrated monitor you can buy. The monitor is compatible with Mac, Windows, Silicon Graphics, and Sun computers.

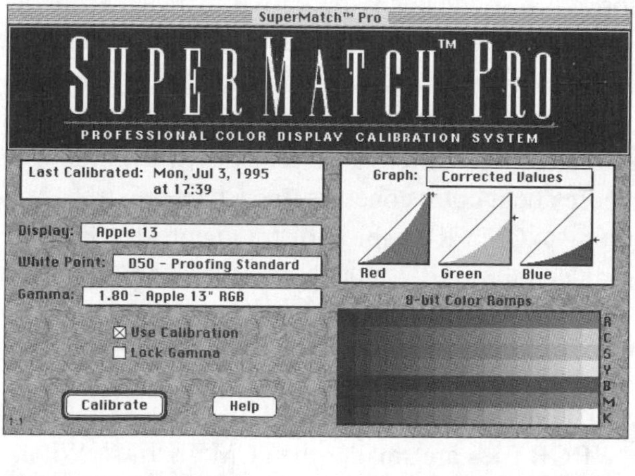

SuperMac
Calibration
dialog box

**FIGURE 17-2**

## Using ColorSync

Recognizing the need for system-wide calibration, several hardware and software companies have created scanner, monitor, and output device calibration systems. Perhaps the most promising entry is Apple's ColorSync 2, support for which is now being built into many graphic software packages. Essentially, ColorSync is a system-level color management system. On the Mac, it is loaded automatically when you install new graphics software or hardware drivers.

ColorSync works by reading color profiles of different devices. The color profiles are a description of how each device produces colors. Using the color profiles, ColorSync transparently translates color information from one device to another to provide color as consistently as possible. When using ColorSync-compatible software or hardware, the user needs to do little more than choose his monitor from a ColorSync pop-up menu. After the monitor setting is chosen, your colors are automatically adjusted depending upon the scanners and printers you are using.

Once your system is calibrated, you can proceed to enter the final stages of outputting your images. One of the final steps for some artists and design studio personnel is to convert from RGB color to CMYK color.

# Converting from RGB Color to CMYK Color

Many artists using painting and image-editing programs create and work with RGB color files. RGB color is used because it is the color space the computer uses to create color. It is also the color space used by many scanners, digital cameras, and 3D programs. In an RGB color file colors are created from the combination of Red, Green, and Blue color components. In order to print these files on a printing press, the RGB color file must be converted to a CMYK color file. In a CMYK color file, colors are created from different percentages of cyan, magenta, yellow, and black. (To learn more about color concepts, see Chapter 3.)

Converting to CMYK can be a frustrating process because the CMYK colors do not always match the RGB colors as closely as desired. That is because the RGB color gamut is not the same as the CMYK color gamut. If you like the way your image looks in RGB, you may want to output your image to slides or chromes to conserve the vibrant colors.

Many artists and design studios prefer to work and fine-tune all their art in RGB because the RGB files are smaller than CMYK files. When the images need to be

**17**

output, they send their work over to a prepress house that handles the RGB to CMYK conversion. Many prepress houses use custom Photoshop tables or high-end Scitex workstations to help ensure that the color conversion process is handled accurately.

If you want to convert your RGB color files to CMYK color, you may want to use an image-editing program such as Adobe Photoshop. Photoshop not only allows you to convert from RGB color to CMYK color, but it also allows you to edit the colors of the CMYK file. Before you convert a file in Photoshop or any other program, make sure that you fully understand all procedures and dialog box options. If you don't, chances are the colors of your CMYK file will not be accurate. Here is an overview of how to convert an RGB color file to a CMYK color file in Photoshop. (Use the same procedures to convert an Indexed color file (256 colors or less) to CMYK color.) Before proceeding, make sure that you create a backup of your file, just in case you need to return to the RGB original after you convert to CMYK.

1. Check to see that the settings in the File/Preferences/Monitor Setup dialog box are accurate. Photoshop uses these settings to help determine how the image will be converted.

2. Next check the settings in the File/Preferences/Printing Inks dialog box. The settings in this dialog box tell Photoshop the printing system and inks you will be using.

3. Choose Preferences/Separation Setup. In the Separation Setup dialog box, shown below, enter the separation settings you wish to use. Many of the settings in the Separation Setup dialog box control the relationship between the black plate and the CMY colors. Consult your commercial printer and/or prepress house before you change any of the settings.

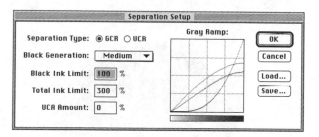

 **OTE:** *The settings in the Printing Inks Setup and Separation Setup dialog boxes can be saved in a Color Separation Table. To do this, choose Preferences/Separation Tables, then click the Save button.*

4. If you wish to preview the CMYK conversion, select Mode/CMYK Preview. To turn off the preview, select CMYK Preview again in the Mode menu.

5. To convert to a CMYK color file, choose CMYK Color in the Mode menu. Photoshop will convert the image to a CMYK color file.

**OTE:** *For an in-depth discussion of converting to CMYK in Photoshop, and more information about using the Monitor Setup, Printing Inks Setup, and Separation Setup dialog boxes, see* Fundamental Photoshop: A Complete Introduction, Second Edition, *by Adele Droblas Greenberg and Seth Greenberg (Osborne/McGraw-Hill, 1995).*

# Trapping

When an image is finally output on a printing press, the imperfections of the process become apparent. *Misregistration,* a slight misalignment between printing plates on-press, can cause gaps where areas from one color adjoin another. The problem often becomes obvious if letters or objects composed of one solid color overprint background images composed of other colors.

To correct this problem, printers developed a technique called *trapping,* in which colors on printing plates can be expanded so that they overlap. The overlapping colors on the printing plate help eliminate the gap, or halo, caused by misregistration. Figure 17-3 gives you an idea of what an untrapped image looks like. Notice the white gap on the edge of the star.

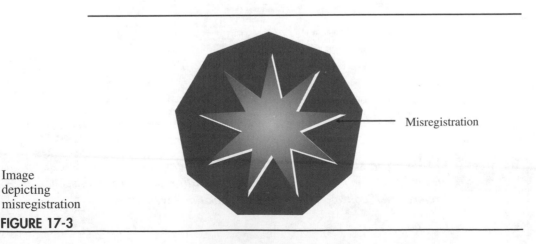

Misregistration

Image depicting misregistration

**FIGURE 17-3**

Fortunately, trapping isn't always necessary. If you are primarily working with continuous-tone digital images such as digitized photographs, trapping often isn't needed because large blocks of solid colors are normally not apparent. Trapping is more of a necessity when you are working with vector-based programs where the difference between one color and another can be more dramatic. However, trapping usually isn't necessary when one color that is over a background color shares at least 10% of the other color's CMYK color components. If an object or text is black, you can often avoid trapping because black usually overprints other colors (overprinting a color other than black can result in a third color). If you don't overprint, most software packages create a *knock out* .When a knock out occurs, the overlying color cuts out the area beneath it, which can necessitate the need for trapping. If a printed object or text is white, you don't need to trap because any gaps will be filled with the white paper background.

Since trapping can be a complicated process, most desktop publishers find it more efficient to allow prepress houses to handle complicated trapping. Since prepress houses have the expertise and the sophisticated software and equipment, many graphic designers prefer to leave such matters to them. If your images are not that complicated, you may wish to investigate the trapping options provided by your software. Trapping commands are available in some page layout, drawing, and image-editing programs. In these programs, trapping is usually accomplished by *spreading* or *choking* an item over its background. If an item is lighter than its background, as shown in Figure 17-4a, you often use a *spread trap* to expand the colored area of the lighter item. If a colored item is darker than its background, as shown in Figure17-4b, you typically use a *choke trap* to enlarge the lighter background color and shrink the darker item. Note that Figures 17-4a and 17-4b are grayscale representations of trapping. In color printing, the light color might be yellow, the dark color might be blue.

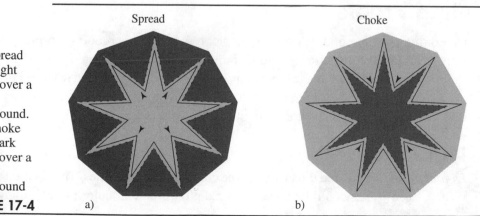

Spread                                      Choke

a) A spread traps light colors over a dark background.
b) A choke traps dark colors over a light background

**FIGURE 17-4**        a)                                      b)

One of the problems of executing traps in page layout software is that you need to perform traps in each separate application you are using. Thus, if you were outputting an image in QuarkXPress that included images created in Photoshop, Illustrator, and Freehand, you would need to execute the traps in each program before you placed the images in QuarkXPress.

Prepress professionals, however, generally use Scitex workstations or expensive trapping software such as Adobe TrapWise and Island Graphics Corp. Island Trapper. Both programs retail for over a $2,000 and can trap images much more effectively than the trapping options provided in most page layout and drawing software. Both programs can accept EPS files for trapping from Freehand, Illustrator, PageMaker, and QuarkXPress, and both can trap embedded EPS files. TrapWise utilizes an edge detection-based system, while Island Trapper uses an object-oriented approach.

Listed below are a few areas that can cause problems, or topics that you may wish to discuss with your prepress house:

▶ How much to trap (Trapping is often measured in 1,000ths of an inch.)

▶ How to trap objects that have both light and dark colors

▶ How to trap small type

▶ How to trap gradations

▶ How to trap photographs over colored backgrounds

How do you know if you have trapped properly? You need to print off-press proofs or press proofs.

# Printing Proofs

One of the most important stages in the prepress process is proofing. A *proof* is a sample printout of your image. Proofs provide a safety net before going to press. Proofs show whether an image is positioned on the page correctly and whether colors need enhancement. They also can predict whether moirés will appear. Proofs can be divided into three main categories: digital, off-press, and press proofs.

## Digital Proofs

*Digital proofs* are created directly from the computer's digital files. Thus, a printout from a laser printer could be considered a digital proof. In color printing, digital proofs are often generated from high-end dye sublimation and high-end inkjet printers such as the Scitex IRIS. Digital proofs are often helpful for evaluating design concepts and obtaining a general idea of how colors will print. Since the images are not printed from the negatives that the commercial printer will use to create printing plates, digital proofs do not accurately reflect the final color of an image, nor can they predict moiré problems. Many service bureaus provide prints on IRIS and dye sublimation printers for under $40 a page. You may be able to save money by properly *prepping* the page for the service bureau. Prepping often means saving the file in the correct file format, such as EPS or TIFF.

**OTE:**   *Several service bureaus in the United States specialize in fine-art IRIS proofs. These service bureaus can output your images on canvas, rice paper, linen, silk, and leather. Here is a short list: Cone Editions Press, 802-439-5751; Digital Pond 415-495-POND; and Nash Editions, 310-545-4352. If you wish to output your images to very large convases, call Noble & Co. at 510-838 5524.*

## Off-Press Proofs

*Off-press proofs* are created from film output from an imagesetter. When a CMYK color file is output, four pieces of film, one for each of the CMYK components, are produced. This is the film that a commercial printer uses to create printing plates. Thus, off-press proofs are considered a highly accurate means of predicting color output as well as problems that may occur on press. The two primary types of off-press proofs are *overlay* and *laminated.* In the overlay system, colored acetate sheets are *overlaid,* combined to create the colored proof. DuPont Cromacheck and 3M Color Key are both widely known systems for creating overlay proofs.

Although overlay proofs are accurate, laminated proofs such as 3M's Matchprint, DuPont Cromalin, and Fuji Color are considered more reliable in predicting colors. The quality of laminated proofs can be so accurate that they are often required by printers before they agree to print a job. In the laminated proofing process, color is created in images from filmed negatives on a pigmented substrate and then bound together. (For the color insert of this book, we obtained laminated proofs as a means of predicting how the color images would print.)

## Press Proofs

*Press proofs* are a highly accurate indication of output quality because the proofs are printed on a printing press, using the same paper that the final images will be printed on. Since press proofs are quite expensive, most professionals use off-press laminated proofs as the basis for approving images before they are finally printed.

# Printing

Before you print or send your files to a service bureau, you will often need to specify settings in your program's Page Setup dialog box. In the Page Setup dialog box, you will find options for setting resolution and screen frequency. Photoshop's Page Setup dialog box also includes options for printing a label, a caption, crop marks, registration marks, and calibration bars. Crop marks are used by printers to trim the page; registration marks are used by the printer to help align the film output from the imagesetter. A calibration bar is normally a grayscale bar and/or color bars of CMYK colors. The color bars can help you and your printer analyze dot gain and color fidelity. When you are ready to print, you choose File/Print. If you are outputting a CMYK color file, selecting the Separations option causes Photoshop to output separations.

Figures 17-5a and 17-5b show Photoshop's Page Setup and Print dialog boxes. Figure 17-6 shows an image printed from Photoshop with crop marks, registration marks, and calibration bars.

Figures 17-7a and 17-7b show QuarkXPress' Page Setup and Print dialog boxes. QuarkXPress' Print dialog box allows you to print separations. In the Print dialog box, you can choose which plate will be output from the Plate pop-up menu. The Pantone plate in the pop-up menu is a separate plate for Spot color printing.

# Working with a Service Bureau

Before you begin the process of outputting your images, discuss all questions with your service bureau, prepress house, and/or printer. Most value your business and will be happy to answer any questions that keep you a satisfied customer. To ensure images are produced properly, many prepress houses require a checklist of fonts and other elements to be submitted when files are sent to them for output. Here is a checklist of items to consider.

1. Resize images in image-editing rather than page-layout programs. This can save you time and money when you output your images, and eliminate printing problems.

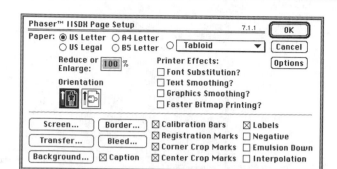

a)

a) Adobe
Photoshop's
Page Setup
dialog box.
b) Adobe
Photoshop's
Print dialog
box

**FIGURE 17-5**

b)

Gradation tint bar    Label    Border    Progressive
color bar

Corner crop
marks

Center crop
marks

Registration
marks

Image Printed
in Adobe
Photoshop

**FIGURE 17-6**

Caption    11-step gray bar

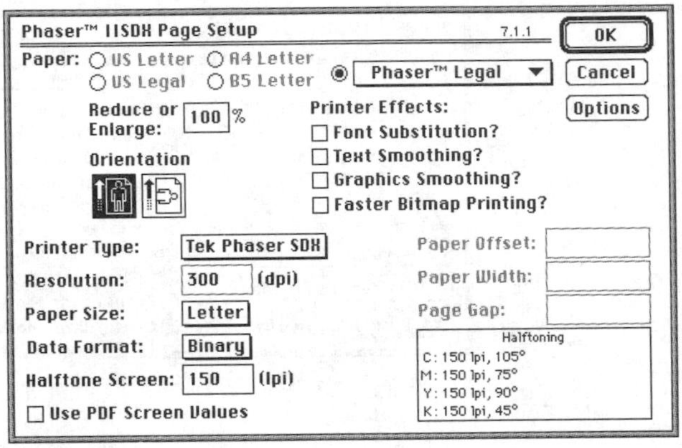

a)

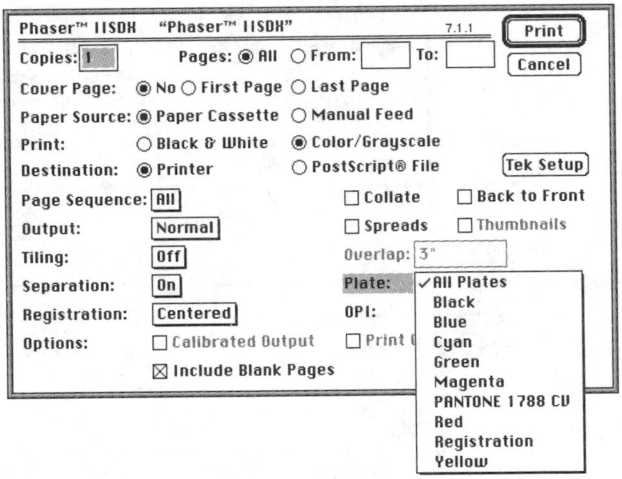

a) QuarkXPress'
Page Setup
dialog box.
b) QuarkXpress'
Print dialog box

b)

**FIGURE 17-7**

2. Provide your prepress house with a list of all fonts used in your projects. You may even wish to give them the fonts themselves, in case your versions differ.

3. Provide black-and-white laser printouts of the entire print job for the prepress house to use as a reference. Use this printout as a proof for yourself to check all elements on every page.

4. Convert files to TIFF and EPS correctly. Read your software manuals to ensure that you save files correctly. Some dialog box settings in image-editing programs will override the settings in page-layout programs if not set correctly.

5. Include all necessary files for graphics in the correct folders. QuarkXPress has a handy utility called Collect for Output that gathers all of the graphics and text needed to print a document together into one file.

# The Future

The printing industry and prepress industries are constantly trying to streamline, speed turnaround time, and improve color reproduction. The past few years have brought new developments that could eventually change how you work with digital imaging files that you wish to output to a printing press. Two of the most recent developments are direct to plate digital printing and stochastic screening.

## Direct to Plate Digital Printing

*Direct to plate printing* is a process in which images are printed directly from digital files. Theoretically, the process is somewhat similar to printing to a standard laser print. No negatives are needed in direct to plate printing. Digital printing is attractive for small print runs because quality color output can be produced quickly and at a low cost.

## Stochastic Screening

In traditional four-color printing, the overlaying of different sized CMYK halftone dots creates the illusion of countless color. *Stochastic screening* (sometimes know as FM or Frequency Modulated Screen) creates colors by producing many dots that are the same size, yet much smaller than halftone dots. Although the dots may appear to be randomly generated, their precise distribution produces the illusion of continuous tone color. In many respects stochastic screening is similar to a process called dithering. Dithering is used by image-editing and multimedia programs as well as inkjet printers to simulate colors. In programs like Photoshop and Macromedia Director, dithering can make an image composed of 256 colors appear to be composed of many more colors.

Many advocates of stochastic screening say that the process shows finer detail and can reproduce some colors better than traditional color printing. Those who have already begun using stochastic screening techniques say that they can scan images at much lower resolutions than they could for traditional color printing.

In general, stochastic screening produces a grainier look in areas with light tones; but as improvements are made in stochastic screening technology, it is predicted that more and more printers will be using the system by the end of the decade.

## Conclusion

To users of digital imaging software, the growth in new printing systems will mean new ways of proofing images, and probably new guidelines for determining the best resolution for creating images in painting and image-editing software. Changes are coming, but don't worry—they'll come gradually.

# 18

## Outputting to the Web, Video, and CD-ROMs

**D**igital images can be output to many devices in a variety of forms. As technology progresses, new and sometimes revolutionary ways are used to output digital images. For instance, companies and individuals around the world are now setting up home pages on the Internet's World Wide Web. These home pages are used to provide information, hawk wares, and even provide entertainment. Animators, artists, and multimedia producers creating QuickTime and AVI movies can output their images to CD-ROM and videotape.

This chapter provides a look at new and unusual ways of outputting digital media. The chapter starts with a look at creating home pages on the Internet, then covers how to output images to video and to CD-ROM.

# Surfing the Internet

The Internet is the largest computer network in the world—and it's just a phone call away via modem. The Internet began as a Defense Department project. The goal was to create a networking system that could handle the transmission of data in the event of a nuclear war. The network technology developed from this Cold War planning is known as *packet switching* and was given the name TCP/IP. In the 1970s, the concept of multiple computers joined together in one interconnected network took shape as the National Science Foundation began promoting the system as a means for scientists around the world to share data. In the late 1980s, the federal government started encouraging Internet connection as a way for universities to share research and information.

In the past few years, interest in the Internet has skyrocketed. Every day more and more companies and individuals are signing on. Why has the Internet become so attractive? One of the answers is simple—graphics. In the early days of the Internet, users accessed it via expensive UNIX workstations. All you saw onscreen was text. Today, using a program called a *browser*, you can *surf* the World Wide Web, a collection of Internet servers that utilizes text-based files to display text and graphical information. By typing in the URL (Universal Resource Locator) of a Web server, you can jump to *home pages* of various companies and individuals.

*n* **OTE:** *Two popular Internet browers are Netscape and Mosaic. Mosaic can be downloaded from the Internet (ftp.ncsa.uiuc.edu).*

## Publishing on the Web

A home page is like the opening screen in a multimedia CD-ROM—very much like a graphical table of contents. Many home pages feature digital images and buttons that you can click on to jump to other pages for more information. One financial institution that actively uses the Web is J.P. Morgan. Figure 18-1 shows that company's home page as it appears when using Netscape, a popular browser for both Macs and PCs. The designers at J.P. Morgan's Corporate Communications department found that earlier versions of the page, which included large graphics, loaded too slowly on computers connected to 2400 and 9600 baud modems; this page has been specifically designed to quickly load onto viewers' screens. Clicking on any one of the opening screen buttons on JP Morgan's home page jumps you to a page with more information, some of which you can download to your own computer. Users can click on text to access background information and corporate news about the company. To view the page on the Internet, set your browser's URL to http://www.jpmorgan.com

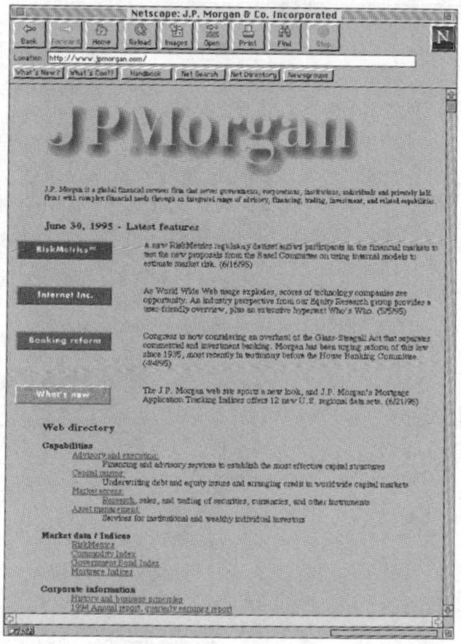

**18**

J.P. Morgan
home page.
Reprinted by
permission of
J.P. Morgan
& Co.
Incorporated

**FIGURE 18-1**

If you're not interested in financial information but would rather see the latest in 3D Internet graphics, you could hop over to the home page of Silicon Graphics (http://www.sgi.com). Today, it's a simple matter to jump from home page to home page. In one Internet session you could go from the home pages of Apple to IBM, from Adobe Systems to Macromedia, from Fractal Design to DayStar Digital. The home pages of most software companies provide product information and software updates. For instance, DayStar Digital's home page (http://www.daystar.com), shown in Figure 18-2, allows you to download software and find out the latest information on the company's accelerator and PowerPC upgrade boards. If you're looking for entertainment, there are home pages for TV shows such as *Seinfeld* and *The X-Files*. The challenge for today's business people and graphic designers is to create attractive and informative Web pages that don't overload a computer with too much graphics and too much information. But before you can start, you have to be connected to the Web.

## Creating a Home Page

In order to set up a home page on the World Wide Web, you need an Internet account, which is available from numerous service providers. If you don't know of a local service provider, call a local users group or computer store for recommendations.

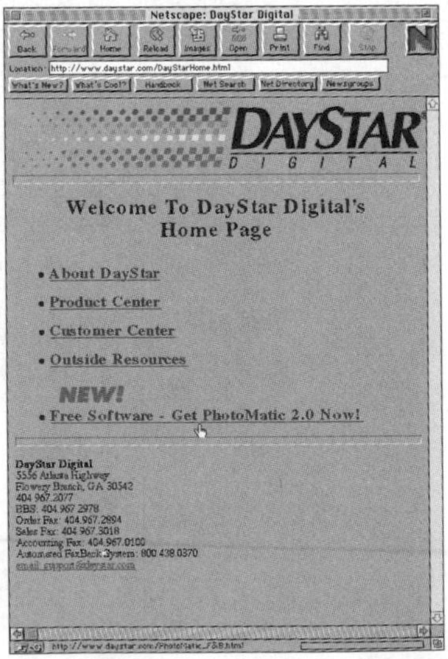

DayStar
Digital home
page

**FIGURE 18-2**

**OTE:** *Internet access is also available through CompuServe and America Online. Instructions for accessing the Web through CompuServe can be found through GO PPP.*

Your service provider will set you up with a SLIP (Serial Line Internet Protocol) or PPP (Point to Point) account. PPP is considered better because it can compress and handle errors better than SLIP. If you are a Mac user, you must install Apple's MacTCP (free with system 7.5). In order to create your own home page, you need to set up a WWW (World Wide Web) server or rent space from your service provider. If you are a small company, the latter is your best bet. Otherwise, you'll have to not only set up a computer as a Web server but also deal with the prospect of thousands of callers phoning in 24 hours a day to view the fantastic designs you've created on your home page.

## Creating a Home Page with HTML

To place a home page on the Web, you can't just create a page in QuarkXPress or Adobe Photoshop and upload into cyberspace. Creating a home page involves learning a simple but annoying programming language called HTML (Hypertext Markup Language). Don't be put off by the word "programming." HTML is less a programming language than a set of codes that resemble style sheets. HTML code can be quite simple. For instance, <H1> is used to designate a heading, and <EM> can be used to emphasize type. But how does all of this translate into a page of graphics? Essentially, the HTML text file is loaded onto the server. Within the text file are tags that describe what files to load and how to get to them.

For example, assume you wish to create a page with text and several navigational buttons. You want users to be able to click a button and see product shots on another page. In order to do this, you need to create separate graphics (GIF or JPEG files) for each page. Next, you create a text file composed of HTML codes that describe the page. One technique for creating buttons is to describe each button as an *ISMAP*. The HTML code that does this might look like this: <IMG SRC="button1.JPG" ISMAP>. To produce ISMAPS, most home page designers use mapping programs that set the buttons' coordinates on the page, then set up a link for the navigational path. In your HTML code, you must specify that a link exists between your main HTML file and the mapping code.

When you use the mapping utility, you select the button on the page, then enter the path name where the file for the image is found on your Web site. If the button sends the users off to another site, you enter the full path name of the URL.

Here is the HTML code that links J.P. Morgan's home page graphics files and produces text on the page. Note that no instructions designate the names of typefaces.

The typeface that the user sees onscreen is chosen by the browsing software that he or she is using. The <HREF> codes determine the buttons on the page. The "SRC=" code tells the browser the name of the GIF format graphic file and the directory it can be found in. Also notice that the <BR> code adds a carriage return which helps determine text and button positions on the page.

```
<HTML>
<TITLE> J.P. Morgan & Co. Incorporated</TITLE>
<BODY>
<BR>

<UL>
<H1><IMG SRC="grafix/JPMLogoShad.gif" ALT="J.P. Morgan"></H1>
<FONT SIZE=2>
J.P. Morgan is a global financial services firm that serves governments,
corporations, institutions, individuals and privately held firms with complex
financial needs through an integrated range of advisory, financing, trading,
investment, and related capabilities.
</FONT>
</UL>

<BR>
<UL>
<H3><!-- startdate -->June 30, 1995<!-- enddate --> - Latest features<BR></H3>
</UL>

<A HREF="MarketDataInd/RiskMetrics/RiskMetrics.html"><IMG
SRC="grafix/RiskMetrics5.gif" align=left BORDER=0 ALT="RiskMetrics(tm)"></a>
<ul>
A new RiskMetrics regulatory dataset allows participants in the financial
markets to test the new proposals from the Basel Committee on using internal
models to estimate market risk. (6/16/95)<P>
</ul>
<BR>
```

## Learning HTML

As you might guess, HTML books and style guides abound. One of the most common methods of learning HTML is to simply download a home page you admire and study the HTML code created. Many resources are also available by downloading from the Internet. Here are a few:

▶ *A Beginners Guide to HTML*:
http://www.NCSA.uiuc.edu/demoweb/html-primer.html

▶ *Composing Good HTML:*
http://www.willamette.edu/html-composition/strict-html.html

▶ *HTML Style Guide:*
http://inof.cern.ch/hypertext/WWW/Provider/Style/Overview.html

Another aid in learning and using HTML is to use HTML editing software. Rick Gates' shareware, HTML Editor for the Mac, helps the process by placing HTML code into a file when you click on pop-up menus and button icons. Some packages, such as SoftQuad's HotMetal Pro for Windows, help place the code in a text file and can show you a preview onscreen of your graphics.

## Graphic Formats for the Internet

If you do create graphic images for the Web, you can save them in GIF, JPEG, or PDF (Acrobat) format. Although GIF has been the standard format for many years, JPEG produces smaller files. GIF utilities also allow you to interlace images on the Web, which makes it seem to appear faster. An interlaced image gradually appears as if it were a mosaic and then gradually sharpens. GIF images can also be made to appear on a transparent background. You can buy utilities to create these files, or you may be able to use the

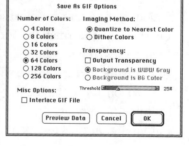

utilities included with your graphics program. Shown here is the Save As GIF Options dialog box featured in Fractal Design Painter, which allows you to create interlaced images and transparent backgrounds on the Web.

**IP:** *To save a Photoshop file in GIF format, first convert it to Indexed Color mode by choosing Mode/Indexed color.*

### Using Adobe Acrobat on the Web

Adobe is developing new software to enable users of Adobe products to easily publish their files on the Internet. Working with Netscape Communications Corp., makers of the Netscape Navigator browser, Adobe is planning to integrate Acrobat's PDF (Portable Document Format) format into the world of Web publishing. Adobe will be releasing Macintosh and Windows versions of Acrobat Weblink, a software plug-in that allows Acrobat documents to link to other documents on the Internet. Together, Adobe and Netscape are working on a new version of Navigator that will allow users to view documents created in Adobe's PDF format.

## Movies on the Web

If you want to dramatically spice up your Web pages, you can add music and sound. QuickTime, AVI, and MPEG files can all be used to add a bit of multimedia to a Web page. Of course, file sizes of digital movies can be quite large, so you should only include short clips and small images. Use a compression format such as Cinepak to save a movie in QuickTime and AVI formats.

# Outputting to Video

Video is one of the most economical and efficient means of presenting and distributing information. Videocassettes are cheap, and most homes and many businesses have videocassette players. Thus, it's not surprising that many multimedia and corporate video producers wish to output effects and animation created on the computer to video. After outputting the digital effects to video, multimedia producers can often integrate them into larger productions. In order to output digital files to video, you must begin to understand the differences between a digital signal and a video signal.

## Computer Output and Video Output

Since computer and video images are both viewed on video monitors, many people assume that the two media are quite similar. In fact, computer and video signals are completely different. Computer images are created from digital signals, while video images use analog signals. In simple terms, this means you can't just connect a video recorder to most computers, press the Record button, and record video. In order to output to video, you need special hardware that translates the computer's digital signal into an analog signal. As discussed in Chapter 8, this usually means purchasing a digitizing board/encoder system that handles the conversion of signals from digital to analog and analog to digital.

 **OTE:** *In some computers, such as several of Apple's PowerMac computers, a digitizing video interface is built in, making extra hardware unnecessary.*

If you will be outputting to video, it's important to understand how a video image is created. A frame of video on American TV is created by two scans of a screen composed of 525 lines. First the odd lines, then the even lines, are scanned. Each scan, which takes 1/30th of a second, is called a field. The two fields (the two screen scans) create one video frame. For optimal quality, video equipment should be able to output 60 fields a second without dropping fields. Less expensive equipment may skip fields and interpolate the missing fields. The result of dropping fields can be blurred images.

**OTE:** *The United States television broadcasting system is based upon the NTSC standard, which utilizes 525 lines at 30 video frames a second. Australia and many European countries chose the PAL system, which draws 625 lines at 25 frames a second. France and Russia use the SECAM system, which also draws a video screen using 625 lines.*

When outputting to video, you also must realize that a few technical issues could mar your hopes of perfectly reproduced computer images. First, since TV resolution is not as fine as that of your monitor, it's important to realize that small type that is easily read on a computer screen will probably look blurry on a television screen.

Colors also can present problems. On a computer, colors are split into separate red, green, and blue components. Consumer and corporate-grade equipment does not reproduce colors in this manner, making the colors less accurate. In addition, the color gamut of video is not as large as that of a computer. Computer colors that overstep video-legal colors often exhibit bleeding when they appear on a TV screen. Fortunately, programs such as Adobe Photoshop, Macromedia Director, and Fractal Design Painter include options to help ensure that the colors you create on your computer fall within the range acceptable for video.

Another factor to consider is that the NTSC standard crops part of the output from a computer screen, particularly the bottom and right sides of the image. Although a standard computer screen can generate 640 x 480 pixels, the actual screen size will be smaller when output to video, or the perimeters of the computer screen will be cut off (depending upon your video digitizing board and software). To avoid such problems, it is generally recommended that you leave a 10 percent blank border around images created on your computer that will be output to video.

# Video Formats

If you need to output your computer work to video, you must possess a basic understanding of video recording formats. It's important to understand the difference between formats because some formats produce higher quality signals than others. Also, once you begin to work with video, you'll find that different recording formats require different cables. Several popular formats are described below.

**COMPOSITE VIDEO**   In composite video, brightness and color information are combined into one channel. This format is used for consumer and semiprofessional video equipment. Most boards that record and output video utilize this format. Computers with built-in video ports, including some models of Apple's PowerMacs, are capable of accepting composite video signals.

**S-VIDEO**   This consumer and semiprofessional format produces better quality than composite video because luminance (brightness) and color are separated into two different signals. This format is often referred to as Y/C video. S-VHS and Hi-8 (8mm camcorders) use this format. Many video digitizing boards accept this format.

**COMPONENT VIDEO (ALSO CALLED YUV)**   In this professional video format, one channel is used for luminance and two for colors. Most commercial broadcasting uses component video. Radius' Telecast is one of the few desktop computer/video systems to utilize this format.

**D-1**   This is the ultimate in video formats at this time. It is a high-end digital format developed by Sony, often used by production houses to create a master version of a videotape. The equipment involved in recording to D-1 is extremely expensive. Most multimedia producers who wish to use D-1 format transfer their productions to Exabyte tape drives using a utility that converts their Mac, PC, or SGI files into Abekas Digital Disk Recorder format. The tape is then delivered to a production facility, where it is recorded in D-1 format by the Abekas DDR.

## The Video Connection

If you wish to output digital images to a videotape directly from your computer, you need a video board installed that can convert the video's analog signal to a digital signal. For best results, choose a system that allows you to capture and record a full frame of video. Many boards sold in the United States provide both NTSC and PAL support. Several provide support for both composite and S-video. The most expensive provide support for component video.

Figure 18-3 shows a typical video system setup utilizing Radius VideoVision that includes a 24-bit video card and an encoder box. The 24-bit video board is installed in the computer. A cable leads from the video board to the video input jack of the encoder. (VideoVision's encoder includes not only video output but also two audio jacks.) For composite video, you connect an RCA video cable from the encoder's video output jack to the video input jack of your VCR or camcorder.

When outputting to video, VideoVision allows you to pick whether to Underscan or Overscan. When you pick Underscan, the entire computer image (including the menu bar) appears on video, though at a smaller size (512 x 385 NTSC, 640 x 480). If you pick Overscan, areas around the perimeter of the desktop will be cut off.

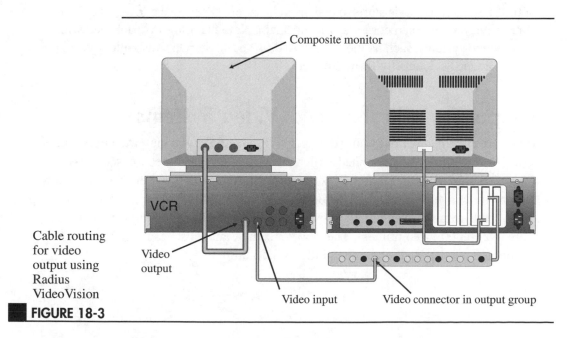

Composite monitor

VCR

Cable routing for video output using Radius VideoVision

Video output

Video input     Video connector in output group

**FIGURE 18-3**

When outputting, VideoVision provides the following options:

> ▶ **Convolution**—This activates VideoVision's advance circuitry to help eliminate flicker.

> ▶ **Genlock**—This provides a means of locking a signal, typically used to overlay titles over the video.

After you've set your outputting options, you simply turn on your video recorder and hit the Record button. On your computer, you start the title or animation sequence you wish to record to video. If you are using Adobe Premiere, that program's Print to Video dialog box, shown in Figure 18-4a, can start the process. If you have third-party plug-ins packaged with video boards, such as those manufactured by RasterOps and Radius, utilize the options provided by these manufacturers directly from Premiere. Figure 18-4b shows the dialog box that appears when you choose RasterOps Print to Video from Premiere; Figure 18-4c shows the dialog box that appears when you choose VideoVision Studio's Print to Video feature. All dialog boxes allow you to blank the screen for a specified amount of time before your movie starts to play from Premiere. They also allow you to loop your movie so you can record it again and again. Note that plug-ins packaged with some video systems, such as those from Radius and RasterOps, also allow you to control a tape deck directly from Premiere.

# Outputting to Professional Video Systems

If you are creating high-end animation or TV commercials, you may want to output to D-1 video format. As mentioned earlier, the most common procedure is to convert your data into Abekas Digital Disk Recorder format. Several vendors provide options for converting to D-1 format using an Exabyte EXB-8500 series 8mm tape drive. Exabyte tape drives can store several gigabytes of data (allowing you to safely store over 5,000 video frames). The newest Exabyte model saves from 7 to 14GB of compressed data and retails for a little over $3,000.

**Print To Video**

Color bars for `5` seconds

Blank screen for `1` seconds

☒ Zoom screen: `Software` ▼

Screen Mode: `Current` ▼

☐ Loop playback

☐ Activate recording deck

[ Cancel ] [ **OK** ]

**VideoVision™ Studio Player** 2.0.1 [ **Play** ]

Video output: ○ Current ⦿ NTSC     [ Cancel ]

○ PAL ○ NTSC 4.43

Movie size: ⦿ Original ○ Maximum (Zoom)

Playback: ○ Play once ⦿ Loop ☒ Play Audio

Blank screen: `2` seconds before, `2` seconds after.

☐ Blank with Color Bars radius

**Export to Video**

┌ Movie Control ─────────────┐  ┌ Movie Display ─────────────┐

Zoom Method: `None` ▼    ☐ Color Bars `0` Seconds

☐ Loop Movie    ☐ Show Time Code

☐ Play Selection    ☐ Clear Screen at End

☐ Start Delay `0` Seconds

☐ End Delay `0` Seconds    ■ Background Color...

[ Play ] [ Cancel ] [ Monitor Setup... ]

a) Premiere's Print to Video dialog box.
b) Video-Vision's Studio Player dialog box.
c) RasterOps' Export to Video dialog box

a)

b)

c)

**FIGURE 18-4**

Conversion utilities include Knoll Software's Missing Link, written by John Knoll, one of the original creators of Photoshop. Elastic Reality, creators of the famous morphing program of the same name, makes drivers for Macs, PCs, Amigas, and Silicon Graphics machines. Elastic Reality's Mac version supports QuickTime PICT files and PICs format. Its Windows program supports JPEG, TGA, BMP, IFF, QRT, SGI, RGB, Alias, SoftImage, and Wavefront formats. One of the few animation programs that include built-in conversion utilities is the ElectricImage animation system. The program's menu that allows you to convert a file from QuickTime to Abekas' format D-1 is shown here.

**Conversions**

Convert PICT to Image...
Convert Targa to Image...
Convert IFF to Image...
Convert Abekas to Image...

Convert Image to PICT...
Convert Image to Targa...
Convert Image to Abekas...

Make Fastload...
Convert Fastload...
Edit Animation...
Append Animations...
Split Into Frames...

Composite Images...
Motion Blur Animation...
Interlace Animation...
Convert To 256 Colors...
Extract Channel...
Match Palettes...
Legalize NTSC Colors...

Make Slide Show...

# Outputting to CD-ROM

If you need to archive and distribute lots of data, your best bet may be to record it on CD-ROM discs. A CD-ROM can store up to 682MB of data on a disc that costs about $25. At this price, the cost per megabyte is four cents—quite a bit cheaper than removable hard drives or optical drives. CD-ROMs are also very cheap to transport. Instead of shipping artwork on fragile removable hard disks, you're safer if the data is burned into a CD-ROM.

Apart from price, another attraction of CD-ROM discs is durability. Unlike hard drive disks and removable cartridges that will wear out in several years, CD-ROMS should last for a few decades. Fortunately, for those seeking to create CD-ROMs, the price of recording hardware has dropped significantly in recent years. If you're willing to invest a few thousand dollars, you can start mastering your own CD-ROM discs.

## Choosing a Recordable CD-ROM Drive

If you are interested in purchasing a recordable CD-ROM drive, one of your first considerations is speed. Older, single-speed models record at about 150KB a second. A quad-speed recorder transfers 600KB a second. FWB, JVC, Pinnacle, and Optima all make quad-speed recorders. Kodak's PCD, which retails for about $3,000, is a hex-speed recorder (900KB a second). It can record an entire CD-ROM in about 10 minutes.

To aid in the data flow from computer to a CD-ROM recorder, most recorders provide a buffer that stores the data in memory so that it can be recorded at a steady rate. Most data buffers store a minimum of 512KB; some can store as much as 32MB. As you might expect, CD-ROM recorders with larger buffers are more expensive than those with smaller ones. In order to ensure that data is transferred at a steady rate, you should also record from a fast computer. Quadras and PowerMacs are recommended for Macs, 486s or better for PCs. If you wish to fill up a CD in one session, you'll probably want to purchase at least a 1GB hard drive—preferably an AV model. As mentioned in Chapter 2, AV drives provide a steady stream of data without pausing for thermal recalibration.

If you're purchasing a CD-ROM recorder, your best bet is to purchase a model that provides *multisessions*—which means that you can record information to the CD and add more data later. This can be a great convenience, although the process does reduce the overall storage space on the CD-ROM.

 **OTE:** *Most CD-ROM recorders are SCSI devices, which means that Mac users can plug the recorder directly into their Mac or integrate it into an existing SCSI chain of peripherals. If you've got a PC, you'll need to purchase a SCSI interface board to connect the CD recorder.*

## CD-ROM Recording Formats

Unfortunately, transferring data to a CD-ROM disc is not as simple as dragging a bunch of icons from your hard disk's icon to a CD-ROM icon on your desktop.

Authoring software is needed to create the files on the CD and specify the CD-ROM authoring formats. Most software provides a choice of recording formats. For instance, the CD-DA format is used for audio files. CD-ROM XA is a standard that allows for audio and video playback.

The standard file format for computer data recorded on CD-ROM is ISO 9660. This is a cross-platform format that allows Macs and PCs to read the same CD-ROMs. However, Mac users will not be able to use the upper/lowercase 32-character filenames they're accustomed to, nor will they be able to view icons. Thus, if you are creating a CD for Mac users only, you may wish to use the Mac HFS file format, which mimics the Mac desktop. One standard that does incorporate Mac icons, and is also compatible with both platforms, is the MAC HFS/ISO 9660. Rockbridge is another cross-platform format that provides support for UNIX workstations.

After deciding on file formats, your next step is to use the premastering software to set up your files. Your best bet is to find premastering software that allows you to create the directories on your computer and a mirror image on your hard drive. To sum things up: before purchasing a CD-ROM recorder, check for speed and data buffer size. Also, make sure that the CD-ROM recorder and software write to the format you wish to use.

## Outputting to Photo CD Format Using Kodak Build-It

If you wish to output images to CD-ROM using Kodak's Photo CD Image Pac format, you may wish to purchase Kodak's Build-It. Using the Build-It software package, you can output any image to CD-ROM in Image Pac format. As discussed in Chapter 9, Kodak's Image Pac Photo CD format allows for images to be compressed and stored at multiple resolutions. A further advantage of the Photo CD format is that the images can be directly loaded into both Mac and PC software.

Using Build-It and a Kodak PCD writer you can create the Image Pacs directly to a CD one at a time, or you can create a premaster file containing many images and then output the master file to CD.

## Outputting Video Movies to CD-ROM

If you are going to be saving a QuickTime or AVI digital movie that will be played back on a CD-ROM, you may wish to output it in Cinepak format, a special compression setting designed for CD-ROM playback. When you choose Cinepak in the QuickTime dialog box, shown here, you can set the CD-ROM playback speed in the Limit data rate to field. (This dialog box appears in most programs that allow you to save QuickTime movies, including Adobe Premiere, Adobe After Effects, Avid VideoShop, ElectricImage Animation System, Strata StudioPro, and Fractal Design Painter.) If you want the data played back on a double-speed CD-ROM, you would enter **200** to set the playback rate to 200,000 bytes per second. If you do use the Cinepak format, be aware that rendering using this setting can be a very time-consuming process.

## Some Final Notes

We hope that you've enjoyed this tour of digital images and have found the numerous examples, industry tips, and technical explanations helpful. We also wish you good luck in your artistic and commercial endeavors in the world of digital imaging. We hope this book has encouraged you to use digital imaging hardware and software as well as to apply your artistic skills, intuition and, of course, imagination to each digital imaging project you undertake.

**Happy Digital Imaging!**

Adele & Seth

Vendor List

The following is a resource list of vendors mentioned in this book. The information is provided so that you can easily get answers to your questions about different products you might be interested in purchasing or using. The companies have been divided into three groups: Hardware; Software; and Stock Images, Footage, and Music.

## Hardware

Acecad, Inc.
2600 Garden Rd., Ste. 121
Monterey, CA 93940
800-676-4223

AGFA Corporation
Division of Bayer
200 Ballardvale Street
Wilmington, MA 01887
508-658-5600 or 800-685-4271

Apple Computer Inc.
One Infinite Loop
Cupertino, CA 95014
408-996-1010 or 800-538-9696

APS Technologies
6131 Deramus Ave.
Kansas City, MO 64120-0087
816-483-1600 or 800-233-7550

ATI Technologies, Inc.
33 Commerce Valley Dr. E.
Thornhill, Ontario
Canada L3T 7N6
905-882-2600

Boxlight Corp.
17771 Fjord Dr. N.E.
Poulsbo, WA 98370
360-779-4479 or 800-762-5757

CalComp
14555 N. 82nd Street
Scottsdale, AZ 85260
602-948-6540 or 800-458-5888

Canon USA, Inc.
1 Canon Plaza
Lake Success, NY 11042
516-488-6700

CIC
275 Shoreline Dr. Ste. 520
Redwood Shores, CA 94065
415-802-7888

Connectix
2655 Campus Dr.
San Mateo, CA 94403
415-571-5100 or 800-950-5880

DayStar Digital, Inc.
5556 Atlanta Highway
Flowery Branch, GA 30542
404-967-2077 or 800-962-2077

DuPont Crosfield
1-800-5DuPont

Eastman Kodak Co.
343 State Street
Rochester, NY 14650-0405
800-242-2424

FWB Inc.
1555 Adams Dr.
Menlo Park, CA 94025
415-325-4392 or 800-581-4392

Hewlett-Packard Co.
16399 W. Bernardo Dr.
San Diego, CA 92127
800-752-0900

Hitachi
408-747-0777 or 800-448-2244

IBM
1133 Westchester Avenue
White Plains, NY 10604
914-642-3000 or 800-426-3333

In Focus Systems, Inc.
27700B SW Parkway Ave.
Wilsonville, OR 97070-9215
800-294-6400

Iomega
800-456-5522 or 800-697-8833

IRIS Graphics
6 Crosby Drive
Bedford, MA 01730
617-275-8777 or 800-947-4712

LaCie
8700 S.W. Creekside Place
Beaverton, OR 97008
800-999-0143

Leaf Systems
250 Turnpike Road
Southborough, MA 01772
800-685-9462

Linotype-Hell Company
425 Oser Avenue
Hauppauge, NY 11788
516-434-2000

3M Company
3M Center 225-3S-05
St. Paul, MN 55144-1000
612-733-4895 or 800-328-9438

Micronet
800-650-DISK

Microtek Labs, Inc.
3715 Doolittle Dr.
Redondo Beach, CA 90278
310-297-5000

Mutoh America
3007 East Chambers Street
Phoeniz, AZ 85040
602-276-5533 or 800-445-8782

NEC Techologies, Inc.
1414 Massachusetts Avenue
Boxborough, MA 01719
508-264-8000 or 800-388-8888

Newer Technology
7803 E. Osie, Ste. 105
Wichita, KS 67207
316-685-4904 or 800-678-3726

Nikon Inc.
1300 Walt Whitman Rd.
Melville, NY 11747-3064
516-547-4200 or 800-645-6635

Océ USA
408-436-1489

Optima Technology Corp.
17062 Murphy Ave.
Irvine, CA 92714
714-476-0515

Optronics
7 Stuart Road
Chelmsford, MA 01824
508-256-4511 or 800-454-5490

Polariod Corp.
575 Technology Square
Cambridge, MA 02139
617-386-6204

Proxima Corp.
9440 Carroll Park Dr.
San Diego, CA 92121-2298
619-457-5500

QMS, Inc.
One Magnum Pass
Mobile, AL 36618
334-633-4300 or 800-523-2696

Radius Inc.
215 Moffett Park Dr.
Sunnyvale, CA 94089-1374
408-541-6100 or 800-227-2795

Scitex America Corp.
Eight Oak Park Drive
Bedford, MA 01730
617-275-5150

Sharp Electronics Corp.
Sharp Plaza Mail Stop One
Mahwah, NJ 07430-2135
800-237-4277

Silicon Graphics Inc.
2011 N. Shoreline Blvd.
Mountain View, CA 94043-1389
415-960-1980

Sony Electronics Inc.
One Sony Dr.
Park Ridge, NJ 07656
201-930-1000

SPIN Peripherals
734 Forest St.
Marlborough, MA 01752
508-787-1200 or 800-466-1200

Storm Software, Inc.
1861 Landings Drive
Mountain View, CA 94043
415-691-6600 or 800-275-5734

Summagraphics Corp.
8500 Cameron Rd.
Austin, TX 78754
512-835-0900 or 800-337-8662

SyQuest Technology Inc.
47071 Bayside Parkway
Fremont, CA 94538-6517
510-226-4000 or 800-249-2440

Tektronix, Inc.
26600 SW Parkway
Wilsonville, OR 97070-1000
503-685-3150 or 800-835-6100

TrueVision Inc.
7340 Shadeland Station
Indianapolis, IN 46256
317-841-0332 or 800-729-2656

TrueVision RasterOps Corp.
2500 Walsh Avenue
Santa Clara, CA 95051
408-562-4200 or 800-729-2656

UMAX Technologies, Inc.
3353 Gateway Boulevard
Fremont, CA 94538
510-651-8883

VideoLabs
10925 Bren Rd. E.
Mtka., MN 55343
612-988-0055

Visioneer
2860 West Bayshore Rd.
Palo Alto, CA 94303
415-812-6400 or 800-787-7007

Wacom Technology, Inc.
501 S.E. Columbia Shores Blvd.,
Suite 300
Vancouver, WA 98661
360-750-8882 or 800-922-6613

X-Rite, Inc.
3100 44th Street S.W.
Grandville, MI 49418
616-534-7663

# Software

Adobe Systems
1585 Charleston Rd.
Mountain View, CA 94039-7900
415-961-4400 or 800-833-6687

Aladdin Systems, Inc.
165 Westridge Drive
Watsonville, CA 95076
408-761-6200

Alias Wavefront
110 Richmond Street E.
Toronto, Ontario M5C 1P1
416-362-9181 or 800-447-2542

Alien Skin Software
2522 Clark Avenue
Raleigh, NC 27607-7214
919-832-4124

Andromeda Software Inc.
699 Hampshire Rd., Ste. 109
Thousand Oaks, CA 91361
800-547-0055

AutoDesk, Inc.
111 McInnis Parkway
San Rafael, CA 94903
415-507-5050 or 800-445-5415

Autodessys Inc.
2011 Riverside Drive
Columbus, OH 43221
614-488-9777

Avid Technology
222 Third Street
Cambridge, MA 02142

Byte by Byte Corp.
3925 West Braker Lane, Ste. 329
Austin, Texas 78759
512-305-0360

Caligari Corp.
1955 Landings Dr.
Mountain View, CA 94043
415-390-9600

Claris Corp.
5201 Patrick Henry Drive
Santa Clara, CA 95052-8168
408-987-7227 or 800-325-2747

Corel Corp.
1600 Carling Avenue
Ottawa, ON Canada K1Z 8R7
613-728-8200 or 800-772-6735

Crystal Graphics, Inc.
3110 Patrick Henry Dr.
Santa Clara, CA 95054
408-496-6175 or 800-394-0700

Eastman Kodak Co.
*See Hardware listing*

Elastic Reality
925 Stewart Street
Madison, WI 53713
608-273-6585

Electric Image Inc.
117 E. Colorado Blvd. Ste. 300
Pasadena, CA 91105
818-577-1627

ElectroGIG Inc.
50 Osgood Place, Ste. 120
San Francisco, CA 94133
415-956-8212

Electronic For Imaging, Inc. (EFI)
2855 Campus Dr.
San Mateo, CA 94403
415-286-8600 or 800-285-4565

Equilibrium
475 Gate Five Road, Ste. 225
Sausalito, CA 94965
415-332-4343

Fauve Software, Inc.
594 Howard St., Ste. 400
San Francisco, CA 94105
800-898-ARTS

Fractal Design Corp.
335 Spreckels Drive
Aptos, CA 95003
408-688-5300 or 800-297-2665

Frame Technology Corp.
333 West San Carlos St.
San Jose, CA 95110
408-975-6000 or 800-U4-FRAME

Graphsoft Inc.
10270 Old Columbia Rd.
Columbia, Maryland 21046
410-290-5114

Gryphon Software, Inc.
7220 Trade St., Ste. 120
San Diego, CA 92121
619-536-8815 or 800-795-0981

HSC Software
6303 Carpinteria Avenue
Carpinteria, CA 93013
805-566-6200

Human Software Co.
14407 Big Basin Way
Saratoga, CA 95070-0280
408-741-5101

Imspace Systems Corp.
2665 Ariane Dr. Ste. 207
San Diego, CA 92117
619-272-2600 or 800-488-5836

Island Graphics Corp.
4000 Civic Center Dr.
San Rafael, CA 94903
415-491-1000

Knoll Software
415-453-2471

Light Source Computer Images, Inc.
17 East Sir Francis Drake Blvd., Ste. 100
Larkspur, CA 94939
415-925-4200 or 800-231-SCAN

Linker Systems
13612 Onkayha Circle
Irvine, CA 92720
714-552-1904

Macromedia
600 Townsend Street
San Francisco, CA 94103
415-252-2000 or 800-326-2128

MicroFrontier
3401 101 St. Ste. E
Des Moines, IA 50322
515-270-8109

Micrografx
1303 East Arapaho Rd.
Richardson, TX 75081
214-234-1769

Microsoft Corp.
One Microsoft Way
Redmond, WA 98052-6399
800-426-9400

Pantone, Inc.
590 Commerce Blvd.
Carlstadt, NJ 07072-3098
201-935-5500

Pixar Animation Studio
1001 West Cutting Blvd.
Richmond, CA 94804
510-236-4000 or 800-888-9856

PixelCraft Inc.
130 Doolittle Drive #19
San Leandro, CA 94577-1028
510-562-2480 or 800-933-0330

Pixel Resources, Inc.
PO Box 921848
Norcross, GA 30092
404-449-4947 or 800-851-1427

Quark, Inc.
1800 Grant Street
Denver, CO 80203
303-894-8888

Ray Dream Inc.
1804 North Shoreline Blvd.
Mountain View, CA 94043
415-960-0768

Specular International
479 West Street
Amherst, MA 01002
413-253-3100 or 800-433-SPEC

Stack Electronics
12636 High Bluff Dr., 4th Floor
San Diego, CA 92130
619-794-4300

Strata, Inc.
2 West St. George Blvd, Ste. 2100
St. George, UT 84770
801-628-5218 or 800-STRATA3D

Symantec
10201 Torre Ave.
Cupertino, CA 95014-2132
408-253-9600

The Valis Group
2270 Paradise Dr.
Tiburon, CA 94920
800-VALIS 04

VIDI (Visual Information Development) Inc.
136 West Olive Avenue
Monrovia, CA 91016
818-358-3936

Visual Software, Inc.
21731 Ventura Blvd. Ste. 310
Woodland Hills, CA 91364
818-593-3500 or 800-699-7318

Virtus Corp.
118 MacKenan Drive, Ste. 250
Cary, NC 27511
919-467-9700

Xaos Tools
600 Townsend Street, Suite 270
San Fransico, CA 94103
415-487-7000 or 800-833-9267

# Stock Images, Footage, and Music

Acuris, Inc.
931 Hamilton Ave.
Menlo Park, CA 94025
415-329-1920

Animals Animals/Earth Scenes
580 Broadway, Ste. 1102
New York, NY 10012
212-925-2110

Arro Clipart
717-296-5490

ArtBeats
P.O Box 709
Myrtle Creek, OR 97457
503-863-4429 or 800-444-9392

BeachWare, Inc.
9419 Mt. Israel Rd.
Escondido, CA 92029
619-735-8945

Bettmann
902 Broadway, 5th Floor
New York, NY 10010
212-777-6200

Classic PIO Partners
87 E. Green Street, Ste. 309
Pasadena, CA 91105
818-564-8106 or 800-370-2746

ColorBytes, Inc.
830 Kipling St., Ste. 200
Lakewood, CO 80215
303-989-9205 or 800-825-2656

Comstock Inc.
30 Irving Place
NY, NY 10003
212-353-8600 or 800-225-2727

Corel Corp.
*See Software Listing*

Culver Pictures Inc.
150 West 22nd Street #300
New York, NY 10011
212-645-1672

DÍAMAR Interactive
600 University Street, Ste. 1701
Seattle, WA 98101
206-340-5975

Digital Impact, Inc.
6506 South Lewis, Ste. 250
Tulsa, OK 74136
918-742-2022

Digital Stock, Inc.
400 South Sierra Ave., Ste. 100
Solana Beach, CA 92075
619-794-4040 or 800-545-4514

Digital Wisdom Inc.
PO Box 2070
Tappahannock, VA 22560-2070
804-758-0670 or 800-800-8560

Digital Zone Inc.
PO Box 5562
Bellevue, WA 98006
206-623-3456

D'pix, Inc.
Division of Amber Productions, Inc.
414 West 4th Avenue
Columbus, OH 43201
614-299-7192

Eastman Kodak
*See Hardware listing*

Fotosets
4104 Twenty-Fourth Street
San Francisco, CA 94114
415-621-2061 or 800-577-1215

FPG International Corp.
32 Union Square East
New York, NY 10003
212-777-4210

The Image Bank, Inc.
5221 North OBlvd. #700
Irving, TX 75039-3798
214-432-3900

Image Club Graphics, Inc.
729 Twenty Fourth Avenue
Southeast Calgary, Alberta
Canada T2G 5K8
403-262-8008 or 800-661-9410

Killer Tracks
6534 Sunset Blvd.
Hollywood, CA 90028
213-957-4455

Letraset USA
40 Eisenhower Drive
Paramus, NJ 07652
201-845-6100 or 800-343-8973

Macromedia
*See Software listing*

Neo Custom Painted Environments
2000 W. Fulton Street
Chicago, IL 60612
312-226-2426

New Vision Technologies Inc.
PO Box 5486
Station F
Nepean, Ontario
Canada K2C-3M1
613-727-8184

Periwinkle Software
7475 Brydon Road
La Verne, CA 91750
909-593-5062 or 800-730-3556

Photodex
1781 Barcelona Street
Livermore, CA 94550
510-449-9079

PhotoDisc Inc.
2013 4th Avenue, Ste. 200
Seattle, WA 98121
206-441-9355 or 800-528-3472

Picture Network International
2000 14th Street North, Ste. 600
Arlington, VA 22201
800-764-7427

Pixar Corp.
*See Software listing*

Planet Art
505 S. Beverly Drive, Ste. 242
Beverly Hills, CA 90212
213-651-3405 or 800-200-3405

PressLink
11800 Sunrise Valley Dr.,
Ste. 1130
Reston, VA 22091
703-758-1740

Specular International
*See Software listing*

Stat Media
7077 East Shorecrest Drive
Anaheim Hills, CA 92807-4506
714-280-0038

The Stock Market
360 Park Avenue South
New York, NY 10010
212-684-7878

Strata, Inc.
*See Software listing*

T/Maker Co.
1390 Villa Street
Mountain View, CA 94041
415-962-0195

Techpool Software
800-382-2256

Tony Stone Images
500 N. Michigan Avenue,
Ste. 1700
Chicago, IL 60611
312-644-7880 or 800-234-7880

The Valis Group
*See Software listing*

Viewpoint DataLabs
625 South State St.
Orem, UT 84058
801-229-3000 or 800-328-2738

Vivid Details
8228 Sulphur Mtn. Road
Ojai, CA 93023-9372
805-646-0217

Wayzata Technology
21 N.E. 4th St.
Grand Rapids, MN 55744
218-326-0597 or 800-735-7321

Weka Publishing Inc.
1077 Bridgeport Avenue
Shelton, CT 06484
800-222-9352

Work For Hire
PO Box 121
Pleasantville, NY 10570

Xaos Tools
*See Software listing*

## A

**INDEX**

## G

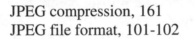

## K

## L

## M

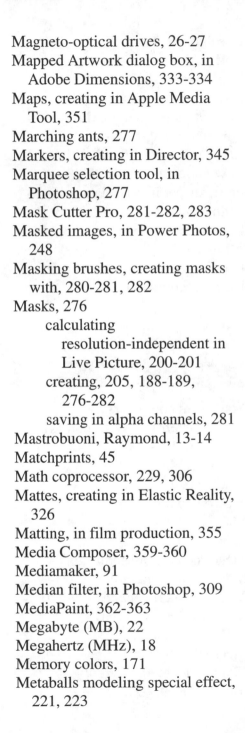

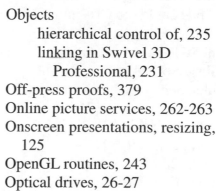

## N

## O

## P

## Q

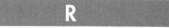

# W

# MY TOUGHEST CRITICS RIDE TRICYCLES, PLAY PATTY-CAKE, AND REFUSE TO EAT THEIR PEAS.

Hi, I'm Eric Brown. As executive editor for *NewMedia* magazine, it's my job to evaluate new multimedia technology.

As a parent, it's my job to help my kids discover the joy of learning.

The critics and their mother

That's why I've selected and reviewed the best 100 fun educational titles on the market in my new book **That's Edutainment!**

**That's Edutainment!** explores the new thinking behind the latest edutainment software and offers tips on building lifelong learning skills. It even includes a CD-ROM packed with try-before-you-buy software and demos.

It's not easy to get applause

from media-savvy kids like Cecilia and Isabela-- not to mention their mom

ISBN: 0-07-882083-9,
400 pages, $29.95, U.S.A.
Includes one CD-ROM.

Cynthia--but **That's Edutainment!** has earned the respect from critics who really count.

**That's Edutainment!** A Parent's Guide to Educational Software is available now at book and computer stores.

Or call toll-free 1-800-822-8158 and use your VISA, American Express, Discover, or MasterCard.

BC640SL

OSBORNE McGraw Hill

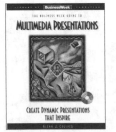

# ORDER BOOKS DIRECTLY FROM OSBORNE/McGRAW-HILL

For a complete catalog of Osborne's books, call 510-549-6600 or write to us at 2600 Tenth Street, Berkeley, CA 94710

**Call Toll-Free: 1-800-822-8158**
24 hours a day, 7 days a week in U.S. and Canada

**Mail this order form to:**
McGraw-Hill, Inc.
Customer Service Dept.
P.O. Box 547
Blacklick, OH 43004

**Fax this order form to:**
1-614-759-3644

**EMAIL**
7007.1531@COMPUSERVE.COM
COMPUSERVE GO MH

**Ship to:**

Name _____

Company _____

Address _____

City / State / Zip _____

Daytime Telephone: _____
(We'll contact you if there's a question about your order.)

| ISBN # | BOOK TITLE | Quantity | Price | Total |
|--------|-----------|----------|-------|-------|
| 0-07-88 | | | | |
| 0-07-88 | | | | |
| 0-07-88 | | | | |
| 0-07-88 | | | | |
| 0-07-88 | | | | |
| 0-07088 | | | | |
| 0-07-88 | | | | |
| 0-07-88 | | | | |
| 0-07-88 | | | | |
| 0-07-88 | | | | |
| 0-07-88 | | | | |
| 0-07-88 | | | | |
| 0-07-88 | | | | |
| 0-07-88 | | | | |

| | | |
|---|---|---|
| *Shipping & Handling Charge from Chart Below* | | |
| *Subtotal* | | |
| *Please Add Applicable State & Local Sales Tax* | | |
| *TOTAL* | | |

## Shipping & Handling Charges

| Order Amount | U.S. | Outside U.S. |
|--------------|------|--------------|
| Less than $15 | $3.50 | $5.50 |
| $15.00 - $24.99 | $4.00 | $6.00 |
| $25.00 - $49.99 | $5.00 | $7.00 |
| $50.00 - $74.99 | $6.00 | $8.00 |
| $75.00 - and up | $7.00 | $9.00 |

*Occasionally we allow other selected companies to use our mailing list. If you would prefer that we not include you in these extra mailings, please check here:* ☐

## METHOD OF PAYMENT

☐ Check or money order enclosed (payable to Osborne/McGraw-Hill)

☐ AMERICAN EXPRESS ☐ DISCOVER ☐ MasterCard ☐ VISA

Account No. [ ][ ][ ][ ][ ][ ][ ][ ][ ][ ][ ][ ][ ][ ][ ][ ]

Expiration Date _____

Signature _____

*In a hurry? Call 1-800-822-8158 anytime, day or night, or visit your local bookstore.*

***Thank you for your order***        Code BC640SL